FEELING FEMINISM

MW01711347

FEELING FEMINISM
Activism, Affect, and Canada's Second Wave

Edited by Lara Campbell, Michael Dawson,
and Catherine Gidney

UBCPress
1971–2021

© UBC Press 2022

All rights reserved. No part of this publication may be reproduced, stored in a retrieval system, or transmitted, in any form or by any means, without prior written permission of the publisher, or, in Canada, in the case of photocopying or other reprographic copying, a licence from Access Copyright, www.accesscopyright.ca.

31 30 29 28 27 26 25 24 23 22   5 4 3 2 1

Printed in Canada on FSC-certified ancient-forest-free paper (100% post-consumer recycled) that is processed chlorine- and acid-free.

Library and Archives Canada Cataloguing in Publication

Title: Feeling feminism : activism, affect, and Canada's second wave / edited by Lara Campbell, Michael Dawson, and Catherine Gidney.
Names: Campbell, Lara, editor. | Dawson, Michael, editor. | Gidney, Catherine, editor.
Description: Includes bibliographical references and index.
Identifiers: Canadiana (print) 20210384069 | Canadiana (ebook) 20210384263 | ISBN 9780774866507 (hardcover) | 9780774866514 (softcover) | ISBN 9780774866521 (PDF) | ISBN 9780774866538 (EPUB)
Subjects: LCSH: Second-wave feminism – Canada. | LCSH: Feminism – Canada – History – 20th century. | LCSH: Affect (Psychology) – Social aspects – Canada. | LCSH: Emotions – Social aspects – Canada.
Classification: LCC HQ1453 .F44 2022 | DDC 305.420971—dc23

Canada

UBC Press gratefully acknowledges the financial support for our publishing program of the Government of Canada (through the Canada Book Fund), the Canada Council for the Arts, and the British Columbia Arts Council.

This book has been published with the help of a grant from the Canadian Federation for the Humanities and Social Sciences, through the Awards to Scholarly Publications Program, using funds provided by the Social Sciences and Humanities Research Council of Canada.

UBC Press
The University of British Columbia
2029 West Mall
Vancouver, BC V6T 1Z2
www.ubcpress.ca

Contents

Acknowledgments

This collection is the result of fruitful conversations over a number of years among the editors and contributors. It brings together the work of scholars in different disciplines and with diverging interests, many of whom had never met one another – and some of whom we have yet to meet. Several authors tested out their ideas by presenting early versions of their chapters at meetings of the Canadian Historical Association in 2016 and 2017, and many of us came together for a collection workshop, held at the University of Toronto in 2017. In developing the open call for the collection, we asked potential contributors to think about their respective research topics in diverse areas of second-wave feminism, a period broadly construed from the perspective of the history of emotions. What, we asked, could insights from the history of emotions and affect theory bring to the history of Canadian second-wave feminism? The collaborative and engaged process of speaking together and learning from each other has strengthened this collection and allowed us all to think in imaginative and interdisciplinary ways about feminist history. The results are an intriguing and diverse set of chapters that challenge the timelines and chronological markers of feminist activism, explore the intimacy, joy, power, and despair of social activism, and ultimately ask us to take seriously the extraordinary political power of collective action, emotion, and feeling. We thank the contributors for undertaking this intellectual and emotional journey with us. We also extend our gratitude to the anonymous peer reviewers for their detailed and thoughtful suggestions.

The workshop was supported by a St. Thomas University Conference Organizer Award and research funding from the Faculty of Arts and Social Sciences, Simon Fraser University. We would also like to thank Elizabeth Smyth, who as Vice Dean (Programs), School of Graduate Studies, University of Toronto, kindly provided us with a comfortable meeting space as well as useful insight. Kristine Alexander kindly joined our workshop and provided valuable feedback. Käthe Roth provided the translation of Chapter 11, which was supported by Simon Fraser University's University Publications Fund and the SFU/SSHRC Small Research Grant. We would like to thank Eric Wredenhagen for his editing assistance. James MacNevin, our editor at UBC Press, has skilfully answered our innumerable questions. Many thanks to James and the UBC Press production staff (particularly Katrina Petrik) for their support and to Robyn So for her astute copyediting.

FEELING FEMINISM

Introduction
Second-Wave Feminism and the History of Emotions

LARA CAMPBELL, MICHAEL DAWSON, AND
CATHERINE GIDNEY

In 1967, Judi Bernstein, Peggy Morton, Linda Seese, and Myrna Wood wrote *Sisters, Brothers, Lovers ... Listen ...*, a position paper denouncing men's treatment of women within the Student Union for Peace Action. They lamented that their comrades' sexism made the organization feel "like a civil rights organization with a leadership of southern racists."[1] In 1970, members of the Vancouver Women's Caucus led a caravan across Canada to protest the criminalization of abortion. They employed powerful props such as coat hangers and coffins to symbolize the danger and death associated with illegal abortion. In local communities along the way, they held public meetings, some of which descended to face slapping as they took on anti-abortionists.[2] As part of the postwar women's peace movement, women knit baby clothes for Vietnamese children devastated by American bombing, campaigned against war toys, and went on hunger strikes. And at the Indochinese Women's Conference, held in Vancouver in spring 1971 in protest of the Vietnam War, media reports and memoirs recorded strong disagreement – generally verbal but sometimes physical – between feminists who passionately argued over the degree to which patriarchy, imperialism, race, and sexuality should be assessed in relation to war.[3]

All of these activities involved emotions. Sometimes women acted out of pain and anger. At other times, they were driven by the hope of liberation and freedom. They experienced excitement, exhilaration, desire, rage, and deep personal connections with other women. Their activism, arising from firmly held political beliefs about women's rights and aspirations for a peaceful future, also drew from emotional reactions to the injustices they experienced and encountered.

This edited collection grew out of a desire to draw from insights provided by the literature on the history of emotions to capture the excitement, passion, and frustration that have flowed through Canadian feminism. Building on the historiography of the second wave, the chapters draw on the interdisciplinary insights of gender and women's studies, affect theory, and the history of emotions – fields of study informed by cultural and literary theory, social psychology, and sociology – to examine how emotions intersected with, and informed, the development of second-wave feminist activism.[4] The collection aims to tell new and different stories about the history of Canadian feminism.

Placing the historiography of second-wave feminism in conversation with interdisciplinary examinations of feeling and emotion highlights a range of questions about the relationship between the personal experience of being in a social movement and the way that a collective movement develops and grows. For example, it allows historians to emphasize the desire for intimacy and points of connection, the disaffection and despair of not being seen or understood, and the sense of power that comes in moments of feeling recognized. Bringing the question of emotion to the history of feminism, as social psychologist Margaret Wetherell notes, requires us "to recognize the way the world moves us."[5] This framework also demands that historians interrogate the intersection of power and emotions. As educational scholar Megan Boler asks, How is it that we come to "feel *power*," or learn the "emotional expressions and silences" that accord with social rules and expectations? And, equally, how do historical subjects come to *feel* power in order to resist their "oppression and subjugation"?[6] As historians of feminist activism, the authors in this collection explore why people feel the desire to change the deep-rooted social inequities of the world but go further to ask how, in turn, emotions, desires, and actions have the power to move, and ultimately, to change, the world.

Second-Wave Historiography in Canada

Despite the transformative impact of second-wave feminist movements in Canada, there is currently no historical academic synthesis of second-wave feminism and very few scholarly edited collections focused on the topic.[7] Much of the historical research on second-wave feminism is incorporated into the histories of other movements in the postwar period. There is rich scholarship, for example, on the postwar women's peace movement and protests against nuclear weapons proliferation and on the interconnection between women's liberation movements and the New Left, antiwar, and student movements.[8] The strength of this historiography is that it reflects the intersections of political activism which coalesced to address subordination and injustice. Yet this focus often subsumes the particularities of gender and sexual oppression within larger chronologies, stories, events, or political movements. And to date, it has given short shrift to the emotional experience of the activists themselves.

Still, scholars have unearthed a diverse range of women's activism during this period. Historians have examined feminist institution-building as activists created feminist bookstores and publishing houses, rape crisis centres and shelters for victims of domestic violence, feminist trade unions, organizations to promote women in the professions, and new fields of academic inquiry such as women's studies.[9] They have explored second-wave feminism through the causes that have driven some of the most vibrant aspects of the movement, including reproductive justice and reproductive rights activism, the history of child care, lesbian feminist organizing, the value of domestic labour, the relationship between the women's movement and socialist and social democratic parties, and the push for workplace rights, unionization, and pay equity.[10]

There is also a rich tradition of feminist scholarship on the complicated relationship between the women's movement and the state, both in Anglophone and Francophone contexts.[11] Scholars have examined how state funding and the development of equity and human rights policies have influenced feminist services and organizations.[12] As the women's movement grew in influence and increasing numbers of mostly white women accessed paid labour and higher education, the federal government was pressured to address a range of women's concerns. The resulting Royal Commission on the Status of Women has received scholarly attention, as have the multiple organizations that emerged to monitor state progress on gender equity, including the National Action Committee on the Status of Women (1971), the Canadian Advisory Council on the Status of Women (1973–95), and Status of Women Canada, which had provincial and municipal committees across the country.[13]

Yet there is much to be done to broaden and deepen this history of feminist activism. Historian Joan Sangster, among others, has questioned the over-simplistic characterization of the second wave as solely middle class and liberal, challenging historians to take seriously the role of socialist feminists in the women's liberation movement. Recent histories examining the intersection of gender and race question a historiography that has posited a once "united" feminist movement later divided by the growth of identity politics. These histories point to the complex and already existing relationship between feminist activism and organizing against racism and settler colonialism, the long-term campaigns waged by Indigenous and racialized women against racism within mainstream women's movements, and the formation by racialized women of their own organizational bodies and collectives.[14]

This collection aims to add to the study of second-wave feminism by examining a wide range of activism, from protests against beauty pageants to firebombings of pornographic video stores. It focuses on the development and evolution of activism, from individual issues to collective struggle, be it in women's search for the experience of natural childbirth, the rise of lesbian community-building and organizing, or the process of naming and confronting sexism in professional life. In doing so, this collection seeks to consciously expand the timeline associated with second-wave feminism in Canada to enhance our understanding of the movement's impact on contemporary Canada and to underscore the contested nature of the movement itself. Finally, while the chapters in this collection engage with the themes explored by historians of feminist movements, they use the lens of the history of emotions to examine different issues: how a sense of connection developed while building collectives and institutions, the process by which activists came to imagine or understand the world differently, or how relationships of care, love, and passion shaped women's commitment to imagining, building, and sustaining a new world.

The "Long Second Wave"

This collection is framed around the concept of a "long second wave," with the height of the movement running from approximately the mid-1960s to the early 1990s but with roots reaching back to the post-suffrage era and a legacy extending to the present day. Numerous scholars and activists have pointed out problems with the metaphor of the wave, noting that it flattens out ideological differences between feminists in a given time period, downplays continuities and assumes little feminist activity between historical periods, and marginalizes intersectional social justice activism within racialized communities that does not fit a narrow model of the women's rights movement.[15]

The metaphor of the wave dates to the suffrage movement but only became common in the later twentieth century, as members of the women's movement sought to understand and categorize the history of feminism.[16] In broad terms, the era of first-wave feminism has been commonly understood as the period between the mid- to late-nineteenth century and approximately 1920, when many white settler women in North America and elsewhere fought for and achieved suffrage, or the right to vote.[17] Second-wave feminism has been generally described as an upsurge of feminist organizing between the mid-1960s and the early 1980s, while third-wave feminism, a term coined in 1992 by American writer Rebecca Walker, is often defined as consisting of the metaphorical daughters of the second wave who opposed mainstream assertions that North America had entered a postfeminist era.[18] Some feminists today argue that we are in a period of fourth-wave feminism, which is differentiated from earlier phases by the use of social media and hashtag activism, both of which have harnessed the power of technology and increased the global reach of marginalized activist communities.[19] Over time, this wave metaphor has hardened into a periodization that assumes that feminist activism can be traced through the peaks and troughs of collective activism.

There have been myriad suggestions for improving the periodization of feminist activism. Some scholars have rejected the idea of waves altogether. Others have tried to rethink how we understand the metaphor itself – redefining a wave as an oceanic tide or a tidal wave, for example, or perhaps a radio wave, which allows "us to think about movements of different lengths and frequencies."[20] Joan Sangster suggests imagining feminism as "flowing in streams, rather than cresting in congealed troughs and waves ... as they ebb and flow over the twentieth century."[21] For want of a better term, some feminist academics still see the metaphor of the wave as a useful way to denote historical periods that have experienced an upsurge of diverse feminist activities while also cautioning us not to take it too literally or to define it too tightly.[22] Indeed, the second-wave metaphor only emerged as an increasingly common reference point in the last quarter of the twentieth century as feminist writers, scholars, historians, and activists attempted to compare, analyze, and categorize the shifts in feminist activism over time and in relation to one another.[23] The title of this collection maintains the wave metaphor to capture the demographic, political, and historical context of feminist activism but simultaneously acknowledges that this is a loose, fluid, and imperfect definition that must include a longer time frame *and* challenge the tendency to centre the largely white-led women's liberation and mainstream women's movements of the late 1960s and the 1970s.

By taking a longer approach to periodization, this collection draws out continuities between feminist waves, points to ways in which ideas central to the second wave fermented and developed during the so-called trough from the 1930s to the 1950s, and demonstrates that feminist activism in this period was not limited to the mainstream women's movement. For example, the maternalist rhetoric and activity of Indigenous women's Homemakers' Clubs highlighted by Sarah Nickel not only harken back to first-wave maternal feminism but also evoke the maternalism of postwar groups like Voice of Women. Through these clubs, Indigenous women politicized their positions as mothers to promote women's leadership as well as Indigenous cultural practices within their communities, and developed spaces from which a particular vision of Indigenous rights could emerge. Similarly, Whitney Wood shows that the roots of a distinct women's health movement, so often associated with the women's liberation movement and cultural feminism of the 1970s, can be partially located in an earlier transnational natural childbirth movement that emerged in the 1940s and 1950s and reflected women's desires for greater control over their bodies. These roots can also be found in the early 1960s, fuelled by the emotions generated by the impact of the thalidomide tragedy on women and children, as seen in the chapter by Cheryl Krasnick Warsh.

There are, of course, differences between second- and third-wave feminism but this divide is not a solid one. Indeed, several of the chapters highlight important connections between the second and third waves. Funké Aladejebi's chapter on Black female teachers, for example, underscores the presence of anti-racist activism during the second wave. Indeed, her contribution suggests that although Black women were often separated from mainstream movements, some Ontario teachers engaged in continuous forms of race- and gender-based activism from the 1970s to the 1990s. Black women not only challenged both organized labour and the women's movement but they also created organizations that prioritized their intersectional experiences. And many of the concerns about sexual violence, which were powerfully articulated in the 1970s and were often at the core of second-wave feminist activism, would be heard in new ways during the 1990s and early 2000s, as Matthew Fesnak demonstrates in his chapter on campus activism and the development of university-based women's centres.

To say that one wave of feminism eclipsed the other would be inaccurate. Indeed, as we enter what some are calling the fourth wave, many issues that were of profound concern to activists in the 1960s, 1970s, and 1980s have today risen to the forefront of public consciousness. Sexual harassment and violence against women have made a resurgence in public headlines in the past few years – from the criminal trial of CBC radio personality Jian Ghomeshi to the Dalhousie University dental school sexism scandal in 2015 to the #MeToo movement – perhaps finally slaying the popular postfeminist notion that women's equality has been fully achieved.[24] New ways of understanding and articulating sexual and gender diversity have also been at the forefront of twenty-first-century politics. As Fesnak's chapter indicates, for example, trans inclusion has shifted the language on sexual diversity and LGBTQ+ rights and has had a major impact on campus politics and university women's studies programs. Issues central to feminist activism remain crucial to this day, but they have been reimagined and rearticulated in the twenty-first century.

History of Emotions

The idea that the "personal is political" was a central component of women's liberation. This insistence that women's experiences of oppression were felt deeply and personally but were also connected to systemic oppression makes the feminist movement especially suitable for a framework which centres the feelings or experiences of emotion. The history of emotions thus offers historians new ways of interrogating women's felt experiences in feminist activism and women's and social movements.

Interest in the history of emotions has gained momentum since the late 1990s. One of the earliest and most influential works in the field belongs to Peter N. Stearns and Carol Zisowitz Stearns. Their 1985 article, "Emotionology," drew on historical research on the emotional bonds of the family and called for explicit attention to emotions and their history, especially the emotional norms of society.[25] Cultural historian and literary scholar Erin Sullivan notes that the Stearnses distinguish between "social attitudes towards emotions, a subject which they argue *can* be fruitfully studied by the historian, and the actual experience of emotion, which they argue cannot." As a result, their focus is on "the way that a culture talks about particular emotions, paying attention to how feelings are valorized, marginalized, scientifically defined, or religiously encoded," and their work has propelled the close study of specific emotions such as anger, jealousy, fear, and pain.[26]

Historians have pushed the history of emotions in new directions, delving into the complex ways that emotional expression can both uphold and transform cultural norms. Eighteenth- and nineteenth-century French historian William Reddy has investigated the role of emotions in political culture.[27] He developed the concept of "emotional regimes," denoting the dominant emotional norms reinforced within existing power structures, as well as "emotional refuges" where individuals seek "emotional release and freedom from such regimes."[28] Through affective speech, utterances, expressions, gestures – what Reddy terms "emotives" – individuals translate inner feelings into outward expression. That process can be put to use to reinforce emotional and cultural norms. Yet the inability to translate these feelings into acceptable cultural norms can result in emotional uncertainty.[29] As historian Rob Boddice explains, Reddy argues that "this tension ... drives historical change, for where the members of an emotional 'refuge' find the numbers, the momentum, or the precise political conditions, this community can break out and assume a dominant position, supplant the previous 'regime' and install its own conventions as both 'natural' and hegemonic."[30] Medievalist Barbara Rosenwein, however, has argued for attention to the multiple "emotional communities" that individuals pass through in a single day – from home to workplace, from tavern to church, for example – and to which they adapt their affective styles. She notes that "not only does every society call forth, shape, constrain and express emotions differently, but even *within the same society* contradictory values and models, not to mention deviant individuals, find their place."[31]

This early work on the history of emotions asks historians to pay attention to the powerful role emotions play in the creation and reinforcement of, or challenge to, dominant cultural codes, as well as to identify the historically specific nature and expression of emotions. As the field develops, historians have borrowed widely from scholars in sociology, anthropology, cultural and literary studies, queer theory, feminist theory, and psychology. The resulting interdisciplinarity has provided useful insights and advanced new historical approaches, particularly to how power operates in relation to gender and sexuality. For example, Arlie Russell Hochschild's sociological study of the work performed by female flight attendants illuminates the significant role of emotional labour in the service industry, as women worked to control or suppress certain bodily expressions of emotion – and to project others – in order to create a particular atmosphere of comfort for customers.[32] Sociologists have provided important insights into the role of affective relations in collective consciousness-making and organizing, looking to ways that emotions play a role in the development and shape of social movements and social protest, while political theorists have explored the role of emotion in political organizing and state formation.[33] Literary scholar Rosemary Hennessy's recent work on labour organizing in Mexican maquiladoras draws on Marxist feminist theory, ethnography, affect theory, and sexuality studies to examine what she calls "affect-culture," or the ways that emotions and feelings create and propel activist cultures. Hennessy argues that "bonds of loyalty, camaraderie, and friendship, of competition, jealousy, and betrayal are seething presences that act on and meddle with the processes whereby the collective bonds are formed that enable people to take action." Equally, she notes, affective relations often play a central role in the unravelling of social movements.[34]

Scholars in cultural studies, queer studies, and feminist theory have taken an interdisciplinary approach, drawing on history, literary theory, psychology, and physiology to explore how emotions are both physiologically expressed – and culturally interpreted – in individual and collective bodies.[35] Many scholars in these fields have been influenced by affect theory, an approach that Hennessy notes has a "slippery vocabulary" and is notoriously difficult to define.[36] Affect is rooted in the work of psychologist Silvan Tomkins, whose research, mainly in the 1950s and 1960s, attempted to define and trace how a range of emotions (such as anger, shame, and contempt, among others) was expressed in and through bodies.[37] Cultural theorists have taken up this idea, along with the psychoanalytic emphasis on the unconscious, to explore how affect, or the "visceral forces beneath, alongside or generally *other than* conscious knowing ... can serve to drive us toward movement, toward thought and extension."[38] Some scholars continue to adopt the word "affect," while others use the concepts of "feeling" or "emotion." All tend to emphasize how forces operate in ways that are not always a consciously deliberate or rational response to living in, and responding to, the world around us.

Scholars working in this disciplinary style are perhaps most well known for their attentiveness to theorizing how power operates at levels beyond the consciously rational. In such cases, theorists of affect seek to understand "how power circulates through feeling and how politically salient ways of being and knowing are produced through affective relations and discourses."[39] This interpretive lens allows scholars to ask a range of questions about when and why humans feel disgust or contempt for themselves or others, how shame functions in social movements, how political power operates, how individuals come to identify with larger communities or nation states, and why people become profoundly "attached" to particular dreams, ways of being, or "good-life fantasies" even when the cost of attempting to achieve them is so high.[40] The concept of "affective economies," developed by feminist scholar Sara Ahmed, emphasizes how feelings and emotions produce meaning in their circulation and especially in the meeting points between people and power structures or institutions. In her influential *The Cultural Politics of Emotion*, Ahmed is clear that she is less interested in what emotions *are* than the work emotions *do*.[41] As an example of the work that emotions do, Ahmed writes about the figure of the "feminist killjoy," the person whose experience and articulation of oppression gets in the way of others' desire for comfort and happiness. The figure of the killjoy appears throughout this collection, especially in the anti–beauty pageant protests explored by Patrizia Gentile and in the campus protests against sexist orientation activities and panty raids examined by Matthew Fesnak. Ahmed tells us that the killjoy can "acquire" both "vitality or energy from a scene of difficulty" and argues that "there can be joy in finding killjoys; there can be joy in killing joy." When feminists recognize each other in that scene or moment of difficulty, something larger and more fundamental can emerge: from these moments can come "movement," Ahmed writes, and together, these moments "can build a movement."[42]

The range of approaches to defining, researching, and analyzing emotions across the social sciences and humanities means that both affect theory and the history of emotions can be usefully employed to help analyze the role emotions play in the development of social and political movements – including second-wave feminism. Emotions that may be experienced individually or personally can be expressed collectively and can lead to political expression.[43] Indeed, feelings can be transferred or "caught"; they can be contagious, leaping "from one body to another."[44] Ahmed focuses on "how emotions circulate," attach themselves or "stick" to certain surfaces, and move relationally between bodies and objects.[45] In the process, she notes that emotions like pain and anger can help "move subjects into a different relation to the world."[46] For example, she argues that feminist activism can transform the emotional pain and anger of injustice into a new emotional condition of hopefulness, if hopefulness is understood as imagining a different world and acting to transform it.[47] This builds on the earlier call by feminist writer Audre Lorde for women, especially women of colour, to acknowledge the deepest of feelings as a "reserve of creativity and power" and a place from which "true knowledge, and therefore, lasting action comes."[48] The chapters in this collection document the myriad ways that activists experienced pain, attempted to dismantle the structures of power that caused suffering for themselves and others, imagined and desired feminist alternatives, and acted to bring those alternate visions into being.

Many of the contributions reflect historian Piroska Nagy's assertion that emotions "are a powerful tool of social change."[49] But all emotions and responses to suffering remain embedded in multiple sites of hierarchies and relations of power. Control over emotional expression involves inclusion in, and exclusion from, emotional communities.[50] Cultural studies scholar Elspeth Probyn cautions us to remember that social movements can shame those who "fall short" of the movement's ideals. "Feminism," writes Probyn, is "underwritten by a plethora of rules and unstated knowledges. It's easy to trip over one's principles and easier still to trip over someone else's."[51] This warning to trace the powerful mechanisms of exclusion reflects important critiques of affect theory as a field that has written out the feminist and critical race theory produced by racialized scholars.[52] The influential work of cultural theorists Audre Lorde, bell hooks, Gloria Anzaldúa, and Patricia Hill Collins, for example, links the power of emotions and deep feeling of "connectedness as a primary way of knowing" with feminist and anti-racist activism.[53] Their work rejects the emphasis on rational "objectivity" and locates emotions as powerful tools for women of colour to challenge racism and patriarchy, to imagine alternatives to oppression, to build alternate knowledge production based on shared experiences, and to find power in relationships of intense connection. Lorde's influential writing imagined women's feelings as a source of power and potential freedom, as well as an important "spawning ground" for making change. Gloria Anzaldúa called the deep "sense feeling" of racially marginalized women "*la facultad*" and named this embodied and sensory awareness as women's powerful ability to see under the surface structures of life in order to name, recognize, and survive oppression.[54]

Because emotions can incite or propel action, they can, as Ute Frevert argues, help to *make* history.[55] As a result, insights drawn from the history of emotions and affect theory are essential for examining the histories of feminist movements. Despite the extensive literature exploring the role of emotion in social movements and the influence of affect theory on feminist theory, there has been little explicit research on the intersection of the histories of emotions and second-wave feminism. This collection sets out to address this shortcoming.

The Chapters

Most theorists and historians of emotion argue that emotions are productive; in other words, as emotions are felt, recognized, and expressed they propel individuals to seek connections with others and to develop community and political ties based on a sense of shared feelings and experiences.

Emotions can politicize individuals and communities, create collective bonds, and incite political action.[56] The joy and excitement some women felt as they discovered like-minded feminists led them to create women-centred gathering places, bookstores, dances, university courses, conferences, women's shelters, and daycares. For others, the warmth that arose from a sense of belonging fuelled the energy involved in sustaining the work and many activities of the women's movement. Still others, like the women quoted by Liz Millward on lesbian community-building in Chapter 7, felt an intense pride having taken part "in the world-changing potential of politicised lesbianism." Women were driven by hope for a better future for themselves and perhaps their children; the possibility and joy of personal and sexual liberation; or a desire for greater personal freedom.

Yet feminists also acted out of pain or anger, guilt or shame, grief or sadness. Such complex feelings can be seen in Chapter 5, where Patrizia Gentile illuminates how feminist protests against beauty pageants were motivated by anger and, in return, incited angry responses. Equally, Eryk Martin's discussion, in Chapter 8, on the Wimmin's Fire Brigade and their firebombing of pornographic video outlets shows that women's powerful emotional response to watching pornography mobilized direct action. In the "National Day of Mourning," organized in 1973 by the National Action Committee on the Status of Women to protest Indigenous women's unequal treatment under the Indian Act, women strategically employed grief rather than anger. This "emotional refusal," as Sarah Nickel calls it in Chapter 3, aimed to elicit empathy and to avoid provoking a defensiveness that might lead to the dismissal of their cause. Chapters 1 and 2, by Whitney Wood and Cheryl Krasnick Warsh, respectively, explore pride, shame, and fear associated with pregnancy, birth, and women's and children's bodies. Wood examines how the desire for natural childbirth could encourage women to exert control over a fear-based birthing process but could also lead to a sense of shame and failure if it was not achieved. Krasnick Warsh traces the responses to the thalidomide crisis in the 1960s, as pregnant women in North America grappled with emotions of fear, panic, and helplessness in the face of medical authorities and modern technology.

Intense feelings about sexism and inequality shaped a great deal of feminist collective activism. It is now a historical trope that women felt growing anger at the sexism of the New Left, especially the refusal of men to seriously acknowledge gender oppression and their treatment of women's bodies as "goods" to be distributed among male radicals. Kevin Brushett shows in Chapter 4 that female volunteers in the Company of Young Canadians took issue with being assigned to clerical and fundraising tasks while men were deployed as leading political strategists, speakers, and decision-makers. The sexism of progressive allies seemed to hurt much more – and feel more personal – than the insults and actions of the broader patriarchal society. It led individual women to break from existing male-led groups to form new collectives, an action pursued not only by white feminists as they came up against sexism on the left, but also by Black and Indigenous women as they repeatedly faced racism within the mainstream women's movement. Individual experiences fuelled a collective sense of anger, outrage, and hurt, motivating collective action more broadly.

Women's feelings of pride, liberation, joyfulness, and passion often created a deep sense of connection to each other, to the larger movement, or to communities built on shared beliefs, values, or identities. But those communities were neither all-inclusive nor permanent. Patrizia Gentile shows that radical feminists' opposition to the Miss Canada pageant in 1976 included a distancing from, and critique of, an increasingly dominant mainstream feminist expression and what they saw as the co-optation of the more radical roots of International Women's Day by the Canadian government. Both Chapter 6, by Lynne Marks, Margaret Little, Marin Beck, Emma Paszat, and Taylor Antoniazzi, and the contribution by Liz Millward demonstrate that as feminists forged new emotional communities that supported their aims and values and created a sense of belonging, they both intentionally and unintentionally established their own forms of conformity and sets of exclusion, be it an unspoken acceptance of secularism in the former case or the desire to reflect an "authentic" lesbianism in the latter.

Members of feminist communities also came into conflict with each other. The language of emotion surrounding debates about difference within feminism created a complex articulation of how gender intersected with race, ethnicity, sexuality, and religion, and how women should attempt to relate to one another across those differences. While some in the mainstream women's movement tried to build bridges with Indigenous women in response to the sexism encoded in the Indian Act, Sarah Nickel argues that there was little space within mainstream second-wave feminism for Indigenous feminist politics focused on fighting colonialism. Marks, Little, Beck, Paszat, and Antoniazzi note that while the secular outlook of many white feminist activists created a powerful common viewpoint, it contributed to their separation from immigrant women's movements. While Eryk Martin shows that anger and rage could motivate feminist activism around issues of prostitution and pornography, in Chapter 9, Emma McKenna reveals that a fear-based politics of solidarity against sex work could foreclose the possibility of expansive feminist alliances by excluding sex workers from the collective "we" understood to be the victims of sexist violence. And Funké Aladejebi illuminates, in Chapter 10, the racial tensions among teachers, with some Black educators feeling let down by the unwillingness of their unions to take up a clear anti-racist stance. If the sexism of allies in the New Left and other progressive movements hit women hard, both the underlying and overt racism within their unions left many Black teachers feeling isolated. All of these chapters bring into sharp relief the many ways in which feminism could be a source of exclusion, rejection, and pain.

At the same time, Aladejebi's chapter complicates our understanding of consciousness-raising. The creation of feminist awareness through consciousness-raising is usually portrayed as productive work that helped ignite and sustain second-wave feminism. This process is clearly illustrated in Chapter 11, on the 1981 women journalists' conference in Quebec, in which Josette Brun, Laurie Laplanche, and Sophie Doucet document both journalists' efforts to transform individual injustices into collective consciousness as well as the fundamental courage it took for them to speak of the sexism they faced at the workplace. Still, Aladejebi shows that consciousness-raising could serve "as a form of oppression," with Black women's inclusion in unions marked by a "constant reliving and retelling of issues of racism" (Chap. 10). Inclusion, in this sense, often ended at the level of personal dialogue rather than structural and organizational change, something that Matthew Fesnak also points to in his chapter, which explores the phenomenon of universities co-opting women's centres for their own political purposes.

Many of the chapters show that as much as emotions could incite action, they could also dampen hope or lead to exhaustion. Indeed, a number of the contributions clearly demonstrate the emotional toll of feminist activism: organizing work was rewarding but also isolating, painful, exhausting, and sometimes depressing. Pain could motivate action but could also immobilize, leading women to withdraw from collective action.[57] Using a history of emotions framework gives feminist historians an opportunity to investigate moments of tension and conflict within second-wave feminism and to examine how women have broken down older emotional frameworks and created new ones. It also raises new questions about the connections that activists seek, build, and attempt to maintain with others in the process of organizing. Placing those connections at the centre of the story and naming them as prime motivating factors in activism helps to explain the sense of shame, hurt, and anger when those connections were not fully realized, when they were broken or betrayed, or when they acted to exclude or ignore.

Emotional Women versus Rational Women with Emotions

Although these discussions about gender, feminism, and emotions are productive, any attempt to bring together the history of emotion with the history of feminism is bound to raise concerns about re-inscribing the stereotype of the irrational or overly emotional woman. In the tradition of Western philosophy, reason has long been associated with ostensibly masculine characteristics, in particular, the ability and power to keep one's subjective emotions "under control." The charge of a lack of emotional control has historically been used to undermine the credibility of various groups. In Chapter 4, for example, Kevin Brushett notes that critics used "the emotional nature of sixties social activism" to discredit the goals of the various movements of the time, characterizing them as "immature or neurotic" and thus not fully developed or rational.

Women have long felt the brunt of such assumptions. Indeed, Cheryl Krasnick Warsh reminds us in Chapter 2 that the term "hysteria" comes from the Latin *hystericus*, meaning, literally, "of the womb." Women's emotional nature was linked to their reproductive organs which, in turn, were classified as inferior to men's. Femininity was associated with the natural world, emotional volatility, subjectivity, and private life, while masculinity was equated with the public sphere, reason, control, and objectivity. These divisions have shaped women's experiences and created structural inequalities in politics, the family, and the workplace. Hence, feminist theorists have produced a significant body of literature critiquing simplistic and gendered conceptions of emotions and highlighting the ways in which emotions are socially constructed.[58] And yet dominant and unreflexive conceptions of emotions continue to inform understandings of the world around us. For example, Brun, Laplanche, and Doucet note that contemporary journalism continues to treat emotional or empathetic writing as a kind of "soft news," thus devaluing the work of female journalists who are often ghettoized into producing human interest stories aimed at women (Chap. 11).

Women – especially those agitating for political and social equality – have had to fight such stereotypes depicting them as angry, irrational, or out of control. The result is that they have often gone to great lengths to present their case in the commonly accepted language of rationality, defined along Western philosophical traditions. For example, Brushett argues that despite the search for greater authenticity and personal expression that characterized the student movement and the New Left, the Company of Young Canadians still "placed a premium on highly gendered forms of intellectualism" (Chap. 4). Nickel notes a similar pattern among male Indigenous leadership in the mid-1970s. Equally, despite the powerful and emotion-evoking language used in *Sisters, Brothers, Lovers ... Listen ...*, as noted in our opening paragraph, its textual presentation is akin to a philosophical treatise, laying out "the human condition in New Left terms" and women's role as it exists within that framework.[59] Yet Audre Lorde's work on the erotic as a "nonrational" place of power, and especially on anger as a transformative response to racism, reminds us that Black feminist thought has long rejected these dichotomies and imagined a feminist approach to emotion, which could be liberating and a "powerful source of energy serving progress and change."[60]

While emotion is often code for lack of control, many of the chapters in this collection show how women used emotion *for* control. Moreover, as Brun, Laplanche, and Doucet argue, emotion was often the engine powering individual realizations of injustice, collective consciousness, and women's activism. Women drew on their feelings and experiences to build and develop organizations and to effect lasting and systemic change.

***

This collection is not about "emotional" women but, rather, about the ways in which feminist activists drew on emotion for a variety of purposes. With other feminist scholars before us, we reject the assumption that emotion is subjective and coded female while "reason" is objective and coded masculine. That the feminist activists in these chapters were driven by feelings of connection, desire, and emotion did not make them irrational or out of control. Indeed, if we take a page from new research in neuroscience, no one, even if they are seemingly driven by rationality, is in actuality any less devoid of emotion. That science suggests not only that affect is "necessary for wisdom; it's also irrevocably woven into the fabric of every decision" one takes.[61] Thus, our aim in this collection is to highlight and give historical weight to the emotions and feelings underlying and animating feminist activism.

That focus on activism challenges the notion of emotion as solely an individual experience. While emotions may be situated in an individual body, the meanings attached to them are created within particular social and cultural contexts. Emotions are both private and public, individual and collective. They are both expressions of physiology and the product and expression of lived experience. They emerge from our individual bodies yet are "collaboratively constructed terrain."[62] A study of emotions offers insight not only into individual women's emotional reactions to their particular situations but also into collective experiences of subjugation and liberation.

Emotions are a powerful but often unexamined force in historical change. The chapters in this collection engage with the history of emotions and affect theory to capture, describe, and convey the deep passion, the sense of possibility and transformation, and the energizing political commitment that characterized feminism in Canada. Indeed, the various chapters are suggestive of the fruitful ways in which the literature on emotions might enrich studies of the second wave – and feminism more broadly. We hope this collection will encourage further research in this area.

Notes

Our thanks to Stephanie Olsen for providing useful feedback on an earlier version of this chapter.

1 Judi Bernstein, Peggy Morton, Linda Seese, and Myrna Wood, *Sisters, Brothers, Lovers ... Listen ...* (Boston: New England Free Press, 1967), 6.

2 Christabelle Sethna and Steve Hewitt, "Clandestine Operations: The Vancouver Women's Caucus, the Abortion Caravan, and the RCMP," *Canadian Historical Review* 90, 3 (2009): 463–96.

3 See Frances Early, "Re-imaging War: The Voice of Women, the Canadian Aid for Vietnam Civilians, and the Knitting Project for Vietnamese Children, 1966–1976," *Peace and Change* 34, 2 (2009): 148–63; Braden Hutchinson, "Fighting the War at Home: Voice of Women and War Toy Activism in Postwar Canada," in *Worth Fighting For: Canada's Tradition of War Resistance from 1812 to the War on Terror,* ed. Lara Campbell, Michael Dawson, and Catherine Gidney (Toronto: Between the Lines, 2015), 147–58; Judy Tzu-Chun Wu, *Radicals on the Road: Internationalism, Orientalism, and Feminism* (Ithaca, NY: Cornell University Press, 2013); and Candice Klein, "Sisterhood Is Powerful but Not Easy: Conflict and the Vancouver Indochinese Women's Conference of 1971" (master's thesis, Simon Fraser University, 2018).

4 The chapters in this collection do not examine the history of singular emotions but draw on the history of emotions to gain new insights into second-wave feminism. For a useful introduction to the historiography on the history of emotions, see Rob Boddice, *The History of Emotions* (Manchester, UK: Manchester University Press, 2018).

5 Margaret Wetherell, cited in David Beer, "The Future of Affect Theory: An Interview with Margaret Wetherell," *Theory, Culture and Society,* October 15, 2014: para. 4, https://www.theoryculturesociety.org/the-future-of-affect-theory-an-interview-with-margaret-wetherell/.

6 Megan Boler, *Feeling Power: Emotions and Education* (New York: Routledge, 1999), xvii, 4 (emphasis in original).

7 For overviews of the movement, see Amanda Ricci, "There's No Place like Home: Feminist Communities, Social Citizenship and (Un)Belonging in Montreal's Long

Women's Movement, 1952–1992" (PhD diss., McGill University, 2015); Vijay Agnew, *Resisting Discrimination: Women from Asia, Africa, and the Caribbean and the Women's Movement in Canada* (Toronto: University of Toronto Press, 1996); Nancy Adamson, Linda Briskin, and Margaret McPhail, *Feminists Organizing for Change: The Contemporary Women's Movement in Canada* (Toronto: Oxford University Press, 1988); Naomi Black, "The Canadian Women's Movement: The Second Wave," in *Changing Patterns: Women in Canada*, ed. Sandra Burt, Lorraine Code, and Lindsay Dorney (Toronto: McClelland and Stewart, 1993), 151–76; and Denise Lemieux, "Mouvements sociaux et culture: Le mouvement féministe au Québec," *Journal of Canadian Studies/Revue d'études canadiennes* 30, 1 (1995): 75–89. Edited collections include Constance Backhouse and David Flaherty, eds., *Challenging Times: The Women's Movement in Canada and the United States* (Montreal/Kingston: McGill-Queen's University Press, 1992); and Micheline Dumont and Louise Toupin, eds., *La pensée féministe au Québec: Anthologie (1900–1985)* (Montreal: Remue-ménage, 2003).

8 For example, see Doug Owram, *Born at the Right Time: A History of the Baby Boom Generation* (Toronto: University of Toronto Press, 1996); Frances Early, "Canadian Women and the International Arena in the Sixties: The Voice of Women/La voix des femmes and the Opposition to the Vietnam War," in *The Sixties: Passion, Politics, and Style*, ed. Dimitry Anastakis (Montreal/Kingston: McGill-Queen's University Press, 2008), 25–41; Ian McKay, "Margaret Ells Russell, Women Strike for Peace, and the Global Politics of 'Intelligent Compassion,' 1961–1965," in *Worth Fighting For: Canada's Tradition of War Resistance from 1812 to the War on Terror*, ed. Lara Campbell, Michael Dawson, and Catherine Gidney (Toronto: Between the Lines, 2015), 119–32; Marie Hammond-Callaghan, "Bridging and Breaching Cold War Divides: Transnational Peace Building, State Surveillance, and the Voice of Women," in *Worth Fighting For*, 135–45; and Tarah Brookfield, *Cold War Comforts: Canadian Women, Child Safety, and Global Insecurity* (Waterloo, ON: Wilfrid Laurier University Press, 2012).

On the relationship between the New Left and women's liberation, see Nancy Adamson, "Feminists, Libbers, Lefties, and Radicals: The Emergence of the Women's Liberation Movement," in *A Diversity of Women: Ontario, 1945–1980*, ed. Joy Parr (Toronto: University of Toronto Press, 1995), 252–80; Shannon Stettner, "'We Are Forced to Declare War': Linkages between Women's Anti-war Protests and the 1970 Abortion Caravan," *Social History/Histoire sociale* 46, 92 (2013): 159–78; Bryan Palmer, *Canada's 1960s: The Ironies of Identity in a Rebellious Era* (Toronto: University of Toronto Press, 2009); Ian Milligan, *Rebel Youth: 1960s Labour Unrest, Young Workers, and New Leftists in English Canada* (Vancouver: UBC Press, 2014); Roberta Lexier, "How Did the Canadian Women's Liberation Movement Emerge from the Sixties Student Movements? The Case of Simon Fraser University," in *Women and Social Movements in the United States* 13, 2 (2009); Lara Campbell, "Women United against the War: Gender Politics, Feminism, and the Vietnam Draft Resistance in Canada," in *New World Coming: The Sixties and the Shaping of Global Consciousness*, ed. Karen Dubinsky, Catherine Krull, Susan Lord, Sean Mills, and Scott Rutherford (Toronto: Between the Lines, 2009), 339–46; Sean Mills, *The Empire Within: Postcolonial Thought and Political Activism in Sixties Montreal* (Montreal/Kingston: McGill-Queen's University Press,

2010); and Christabelle Sethna and Steve Hewitt, *Just Watch Us: RCMP Surveillance of the Women's Liberation Movement in Cold War Canada* (Montreal/Kingston: McGill-Queen's University Press, 2018).

9 See Nancy Janovicek, *No Place to Go: Local Histories of the Battered Women's Shelter Movement* (Vancouver: UBC Press, 2007); Wendy Robbins, Meg Luxton, Margrit Eichler, and Francine Descarries, eds., *Minds of Our Own: Inventing Feminist Scholarship and Women's Studies in Canada and Québec, 1966–76* (Waterloo, ON: Wilfrid Laurier University Press, 2008); Julia Smith, "An 'Entirely Different' Kind of Union: The Service, Office, and Retail Workers' Union of Canada (SORWOC), 1972–1986," *Labour/Le Travail* 73 (2014): 23–65; Meg Luxton, "Feminism as a Class Act: Working-Class Feminism and the Women's Movement in Canada," *Labour/Le Travail* 48 (2001): 63–88; Tessa Jordan, *Feminist Acts:* Branching Out *Magazine and the Making of Canadian Feminism* (Edmonton: University of Alberta Press, 2019); Sean Mills, "*Québécoises deboutte!* Nationalism and Feminism in Quebec, 1969–1975," in *Rethinking Canada: The Promise of Women's History*, 7th ed., ed. Lara Campbell, Tamara Myers, and Adele Perry (Don Mills, ON: Oxford University Press, 2016), 353–65.

10 See Shannon Stettner, Kristin Burnett, and Travis Hay, *Abortion: History, Politics, and Reproductive Justice after Morgentaler* (Vancouver: UBC Press, 2017); Karin Wells, *The Abortion Caravan* (Toronto: Second Story Press, 2020); Beth Palmer, "Lonely, Tragic, but Legally Necessary Pilgrimages: Transnational Abortion Travel in the 1970s," *Canadian Historical Review* 92, 4 (2011): 637–64; Sarah Marie Wiebe and Erin Marie Konsmo, "Indigenous Body as Contaminated Site? Examining Struggles for Reproductive Justice in Aamjiwnaang," in *Fertile Ground: Exploring Reproduction in Canada*, ed. Stephanie Paterson, Francesca Scala, and Marlene Sokolon (Montreal/Kingston: McGill-Queen's University Press, 2014), 325–58; Christabelle Sethna, "The Evolution of the *Birth Control Handbook:* From Student Peer-Education Manual to Feminist Self-Empowerment Text, 1968–1975," *Canadian Bulletin of Medical History* 23, 1 (2006): 89–117; Jessica Haynes, "Insulated from the Law: Married Women, the Pill, and the 'Public Good,'" in *No Place for the State: The Origins and Legacies of the 1969 Omnibus Bill*, ed. Christopher Dummitt and Christabelle Sethna (Vancouver: UBC Press, 2020), 175–99; Karen Pearlston, "'Something More': The State's Place in the Bedrooms of Lesbian Nation," in *No Place for the State*, 200–22; Becki Ross, *The House That Jill Built: A Lesbian Nation in Formation* (Toronto: University of Toronto Press, 1995); Patrizia Gentile, Gary Kinsman, and L. Pauline Rankin, eds., *We Still Demand! Redefining Resistance in Sex and Gender Struggles* (Vancouver: UBC Press, 2017); Elise Chenier, ed., An Army of Lovers: Lesbian, Bisexual, Two Spirit, and Queer Women in the 1970s and 80s (website), https://alotarchives.org/army (n.d.); Lisa Pasolli, *Working Mothers and the Child Care Dilemma: A History of British Columbia's Social Policy* (Vancouver: UBC Press, 2015); Julia Smith and Lisa Pasolli, "The Labor Relations of Love: Workers, Child Care, and the State in 1970s Vancouver, British Columbia," *Labor: Studies in Working-Class History* 14, 4 (2017): 39–60; Joan Sangster, "Radical Ruptures: Feminism, Labor, and the Left in the Long Sixties in Canada," *American Review of Canadian Studies* 40, 1 (2010): 1–21; Andrée Lévesque, *Madeleine Parent: Activist* (Toronto: Sumach Press, 2005); Varda Burstyn, "The Waffle and the Women's Movement,"

Studies in Political Economy 22 (1990): 175–84; Jocelyne Parud, "La second vague féministe et la féminisation du Parti socialiste français de PQ," *Politique et Sociétés* 17, 1–2 (1998): 71–90.

11 Historians of Quebec have explored the complex interactions between feminist organizing and movements for national sovereignty. See Micheline Dumont, "The Origins of the Women's Movement in Quebec," in *Challenging Times*, 72–89; Diane Lamoureux, *L'amère patrie. Féminisme et nationalisme dans le Québec contemporain* (Montreal: Remue-ménage, 2010); Micheline de Sève, "Féminisme et nationalisme au Québec, une alliance inattendue," *International Journal of Canadian Studies* 17 (1998): 157–76; Diane Lamoureux, "The Paradoxes of Quebec Feminism," in *Quebec Questions: Quebec Studies for the Twenty-First Century*, ed. Stéphan Gervais, Christopher Kirkey, and Jarrett Rudy (Toronto: Oxford University Press, 2011), 307–23; and Chantal Maillé, "French and Quebec Feminism: Influences and Reciprocities," in *Transatlantic Passages: Literary and Cultural Relations between Quebec and Francophone Europe*, ed. Paula Ruth Gilvert and Melena Santoro (Montreal/Kingston: McGill-Queen's University Press, 2010), 50–59.

12 See Dominique Clément, *Equality Deferred: Sex Discrimination and British Columbia's Human Rights State, 1953–84* (Vancouver: UBC Press, 2014); Dominique Clément, "State Funding for Human Rights Activism: Channeling Protest?" *American Behavioral Scientist* 61, 3 (2017): 1703–28; Shirley Tillotson, "Human Rights Law as Prism: Women's Organizations, Unions, and Ontario's Female Employees Fair Remuneration Act (1951)," *Canadian Historical Review* 72, 4 (1991): 532–57; Ruth Frager and Carmela Patrias, "Human Rights Activists and the Question of Sex Discrimination in Postwar Ontario," *Canadian Historical Review* 93, 4 (2012): 583–610; Janine Brodie, "The Great Undoing: State Formation, Gender Politics, and Social Policy in Canada," in *Western Welfare in Decline: Globalization and Women's Poverty*, ed. Catherine Kingfisher (Philadelphia: University of Pennsylvania Press, 2002), 90–110; Judy Fudge, "The Paradoxes of Pay Equity: Reflections on the Law and the Market in Bell Canada and the Public Service Alliance of Canada," *Canadian Journal of Women and the Law* 12 (2000): 313–44; Leslie Pal, *Interests of State: The Politics of Language, Multiculturalism, and Feminism in Canada* (Montreal/Kingston: McGill-Queen's University Press, 1993).

13 See Joan Sangster, "Words of Experience/Experiencing Words: Reading Working Women's Letters to Canada's Royal Commission on the Status of Women," in *Through Feminist Eyes: Essays on Canadian Women's History*, ed. Joan Sangster (Edmonton: Athabasca University Press, 2011), 359–90; Gail G. Campbell, "'Are We Going to Do the Most Important Things?' Senator Muriel McQueen Fergusson, Feminist Identities, and the Royal Commission on the Status of Women," *Acadiensis* 38, 2 (2009): 52–77; Barbara M. Freeman, *The Satellite Sex: The Media and Women's Issues in English Canada, 1966–1971* (Waterloo, ON: Wilfrid Laurier University Press, 2001); Annis May Timpson, "Royal Commissions as Sites of Resistance: Women's Challenges on Child Care in the Royal Commission on the Status of Women," *International Journal of Canadian Studies* 20 (1999): 123–48; Cerise Morris, "Determination and Thoroughness: The Movement for a Royal Commission on the Status of Women in Canada," *Atlantis* 5, 2 (1980): 1–21; Jill Vickers, Pauline Rankin, and Christine Appelle, *Politics as if Women Mattered: A Political Analysis of the National Action*

Committee on the Status of Women (Toronto: University of Toronto Press, 1993); Mary Jo Nadeau, "The Making and Unmaking of a Parliament of Women: Nation, Race, and the Politics of the National Action Committee on the Status of Women (1972–1992)" (PhD diss., York University, 2005).

14 See Joan Sangster, "Creating Popular Histories: Re-interpreting 'Second Wave' Canadian Feminism," *Dialectical Anthropology* 39, 4 (2015): 381–404; Joan Sangster, "*Never Done*: Feminists Reinterpret Their Own History," in *Reading Canadian Women's and Gender History*, ed. Nancy Janovicek and Carmen Neilson (Toronto: University of Toronto Press, 2019), 203–24; Sarah Nickel, "'I Am Not a Women's Libber, although Sometimes I Sound Like One': Indigenous Feminism and Politicized Motherhood," *American Indian Quarterly* 41, 4 (2017): 299–335; Joyce Green, ed., *Making Space for Indigenous Feminism* (Halifax: Fernwood, 2007); Audra Simpson, *Mohawk Interruptus: Political Life across the Borders of Settler States* (Durham, NC: Durham University Press, 2014); Jo-Anne Fiske, "The Womb Is to the Nation as the Heart to the Body: Ethnopolitical Discourses of the Canadian Indigenous Women's Movement," *Studies in Political Economy* 51 (1996): 65–95; Kathleen Jamieson, "Multiple Jeopardy: The Evolution of a Native Women's Movement," *Atlantis: A Women's Studies Journal* 4, 2 (1979): 157–78; Amanda Ricci, "Contesting the Nation(s): Haitian and Mohawk Women's Activism in Montreal," in *Women's Activism and 'Second Wave' Feminism: Transnational Histories*, ed. Barbara Molony and Jennifer Nelson (New York: Bloomsbury, 2017), 273–94; Agnes Calliste and George J. Sefa Dei, eds., *Anti-racist Feminism: Critical Race and Gender Studies* (Halifax: Fernwood, 2000); Sherene Razack, Malinda Smith, and Sunera Thobani, eds., *States of Race: Critical Race Feminism for the 21st Century* (Toronto: Between the Lines, 2010); Njoki Nthani Wane, Katherine Deliovsky, and Erica Lawson, eds., *Back to the Drawing Board: African Canadian Feminism* (Toronto: Sumach Press, 2002); Jennifer Mills, "Conferencing as a Site for the Mobilization of Black Feminist Identities in the Congress of Black Women of Canada," *Journal of Black Studies* (2015): 1–17; Amanda Ricci, "Bâtir une communauté citoyenne: Le militantisme chez les femmes autochtones pendant les années soixante et soixante-dix," *Recherches amérindiennes au Québec*, 46, 1 (2016): 75–85; and Amanda Ricci, "Un féminisme inclusif? La Fédération des femmes du Québec et les femmes immigrantes ou racialisées, 1966–1992," *Bulletin d'histoire politique*, 25, 3 (2017): 102–23.

15 See Barbara Molony and Jennifer Nelson, eds., *Women's Activism and "Second Wave" Feminism: Transnational Histories* (London: Bloomsbury, 2017); Becky Thompson, "Multiracial Feminism: Recasting the Chronology of Second Wave Feminism," *Feminist Studies* 28, 2 (2002): 344; Sangster, "Creating Popular Histories," 383; Lisa Marie Hogeland, "Against Generational Thinking, Or, Some Things That 'Third Wave' Feminism Isn't," *Women's Studies in Communication* 24, 1 (2001): 107–21; Astrid Henry, *Not My Mother's Sister: Generational Conflicts and Third Wave Feminism* (Bloomington: Indiana University Press, 2004); and Melody Berger, *We Don't Need Another Wave: Dispatches from the Next Generation of Feminists* (Berkeley, CA: Seal Press, 2006). See also Natasha Pinterics, "Riding the Feminist Waves: In with the Third?," *Canadian Woman Studies/Les cahiers de la femme* 20/21, 4/1 (2001): 15–21; and Rebecca Ellis, "Second Thoughts about a Third Wave," *Canadian*

Woman Studies/les cahiers de la femme 20/21, 4/1 (2001): 24–26. On the problems of periodization in Canadian history more generally, see Michael Dawson and Catherine Gidney, "Persistence and Inheritance: Rethinking Periodisation and English Canada's 'Twentieth Century,'" in *Contesting Clio's Craft: New Directions and Debates in Canadian History*, ed. Christopher Dummitt and Michael Dawson (London: Institute for the Study of the Americas, 2009), 47–74.

16 In Canada, suffragists used the term "wave" to refer to a tidal or revolutionary wave of suffrage activism. See Lara Campbell, *A Great Revolutionary Wave: Women and the Vote in British Columbia* (Vancouver: UBC Press, 2020). Astrid Henry argued that Martha Weinman Lear popularized the term "second wave" in her 1968 article in the *New York Times*, titled "The Second Feminist Wave," in which Lear attempted to delineate the difference between first- and second-wave feminism and explain the seeming "disappearance" of feminism between these two periods. See Henry, "Waves," in *Rethinking Gender and Women's Studies*, ed. Catherine M. Orr, Ann Braithwaite, and Diane Lichtenstein (New York: Routledge, 2012), 103–4.

17 See Joan Sangster, *One Hundred Years of Struggle: The History of Women and the Vote in Canada* (Vancouver: UBC Press, 2018); Patricia Grimshaw, "Settler Anxieties, Indigenous Peoples and Women's Suffrage in the Colonies of Australia, New Zealand, and Hawai'i, 1888–1902," *Pacific Historical Review* 69/4 (2000): 553–72; Ian Christopher Fletcher, Philippa Levine, and Laura E. Nym, eds., *Women's Suffrage in the British Empire: Citizenship, Nation, and Race* (London: Routledge, 2000); Marilyn Lake, *Progressive New World: How Settler Colonialism and Transpacific Exchange Shaped American Reform* (Cambridge, MA: Harvard University Press, 2019); Marilyn Lake, "Between Old World 'Barbarism' and 'Stone Age' Primitivism: The Double Difference of the White Australian Feminist," in *Australian Women: Contemporary Feminist Thought*, ed. Norma Grieve and Ailsa Burns (Melbourne: Oxford University Press, 1994), 80–91.

18 The phrase "third-wave" feminism places the centre of feminist political shifts in the American context. It was coined in 1992 by Rebecca Walker in response to Anita Hill's claim of sexual harassment before the confirmation hearings of Clarence Thomas. See Rebecca Walker, "Becoming the Third Wave," *Ms. Magazine*, 12 (1992): 39–41. See also Sarah Grimble, ed., *The Routledge Companion to Feminism and Postfeminism* (London: Routledge, 1998).

19 See Jennifer Baumgardner, *F'em!: Goo Goo, Gaga, and Some Thoughts on Balls* (Berkeley, CA: Seal Press, 2011); Eleanor Courtemanche, "The Fourth and Fifth Waves," *Arcade: Literature, Humanities, and the World*, August 1, 2019, https://arcade.stanford.edu/blogs/fourth-and-fifth-waves; Ealasaid Munro, "Feminism: A Fourth Wave?" *Political Insight* 4, 2 (2013): 22–25.

20 Nancy A. Hewitt, "Introduction," in *No Permanent Waves: Recasting Histories of U.S. Feminism*, ed. Nancy A. Hewitt (New Brunswick, NJ: Rutgers University Press, 2010), 8. See also Ednie Kaeh Garrison, "Are We on a Wavelength Yet? On Feminist Oceanography, Radios, and Third Wave Feminism," in *Different Wavelengths: Studies of the Contemporary Women's Movement*, ed. Jo Reger (New York: Routledge, 2005), 237–56; Kim Sawchuk, "Feminism in Waves: Re-Imagining a Watery Metaphor," in *Open Boundaries: A Canadian Women's Studies Reader*, 3rd ed. (Toronto: Pearson, 2009), 58–64; Emily Hoeflinger, "Talking Waves: Structures of Feminist

Moments and the Potential of a Wave Economy," *thirdspace: a journal of feminist theory and culture* 8, 1 (2008): https://journals.sfu.ca/thirdspace/index.php/journal/article/view/hoeflinger/218.

21 Sangster, "*Never Done*," 218.

22 Leila J. Rupp and Verta Taylor, "Foreword," in *Different Wavelengths*, xi.

23 See Google Books Ngram Viewer to trace the usage of the term in published English sources.

24 In 2015, Dalhousie University suspended thirteen male dentistry students pending an investigation into misogynistic comments posted in a Facebook group about female dentistry students and women in general. On social media and #MeToo, see Kaitlynn Mendes, Jessica Ringrose, and Jessalynn Keller, "#MeToo and the Promise and Pitfalls of Challenging Rape Culture though Digital Feminist Activism," *European Journal of Women's Studies* 25, 2 (2018): 236–46.

25 Peter N. Stearns, with Carol Z. Stearns, "Emotionology: Clarifying the History of Emotions and Emotional Standards," *American Historical Review* 90, 4 (1985): 813–36. For overviews of the development of the history of emotions, see Susan J. Matt, "Current Emotion Research in History: Or, Doing History from the Inside Out," *Emotion Review* 3, 1 (2011): 117–24; Susan J. Matt and Peter N. Stearns, "Introduction," in *Doing Emotions History*, ed. Susan J. Matt and Peter N. Stearns (Urbana: University of Illinois Press, 2014), 4; Boddice, *History of Emotions*; and Jan Plamper, *The History of Emotions: An Introduction*, trans. Keith Tribe (Oxford: Oxford University Press, 2017). For the Canadian context, see, for example, Eric H. Reiter, *Wounded Feelings: Litigating Emotions in Quebec, 1870–1950* (Toronto: University of Toronto Press, 2019); Sophie Doucet, "Sur le chemin du paradis: les joies d'aimer, de croire et de s'accomplir de Marie-Louise Globensky (1849–1919)," *Revue d'histoire de d'Amérique française* 70, 3 (2017): 5–29; and Whitney Wood, "'When I Think of What Is before Me, I Feel Afraid': Narratives of Fear, Pain, and Childbirth in Late-Victorian Canada," in *Pain and Emotion in Modern History*, ed. Rob Boddice (Basingstoke, UK: Palgrave Macmillan, 2014), 187–203. It is impossible to list the many publications in the history of emotions. Information on recent research can be found by accessing global research institutes. For a few examples, see the Max Planck Institute for Human Development, History of Emotions Research Centre (https://www.mpib-berlin.mpg.de/research/research-centers/history-of-emotions); Australian Research Council, Centre of Excellence for the History of Emotions (http://www.historyofemotions.org.au/about-the-centre.aspx); and The Queen Mary Centre for the History of Emotions (https://projects.history.qmul.ac.uk/emotions/).

26 Erin Sullivan, "The History of the Emotions: Past, Present, Future," *Cultural Studies* 2, 1 (2013): 95 (emphasis in original). For literature on specific emotions, see Carol Zisowitz Stearns and Peter N. Stearns, *Anger: The Struggle for Emotional Control in America's History* (Chicago: University of Chicago Press, 1986); Peter N. Stearns, *Jealousy: The Evolution of an Emotion in American History* (New York: New York University Press, 1989); Peter N. Stearns, *American Fear: The Causes and Consequences of High Anxiety* (New York: Routledge, 2006); Joanna Bourke, *Fear: A Cultural History* (Emeryville, CA: Shoemaker and Hoard, 2006); Joanna Bourke, *The Story of Pain: From Prayer to Painkillers* (Oxford: Oxford University Press, 2014); Michael Laffan and Max Weiss, eds., *Facing Fear: The History of an Emotion in Global Perspective*

(Princeton, NJ: Princeton University Press, 2012); Ute Frevert, *The Politics of Humiliation: A Modern History* (Oxford: Oxford University Press, 2020); Ute Frevert, "*Hans in Luck* or the Moral Economy of Happiness in the Modern Age," *History of European Ideas* 45, 3 (2019): 363–76; and Fay Bound Alberti, *A Biography of Loneliness: The History of an Emotion* (Oxford: Oxford University Press, 2019). For the Stearnses' impact on the field, see Stephanie Olsen and Rob Boddice, "Styling Emotions History," *Journal of Social History* 51, 3 (2018): 476–87.

27 William Reddy, *The Navigation of Feeling: A Framework for the History of Emotions* (Cambridge: Cambridge University Press, 2001).

28 Matt and Stearns, "Introduction," in *Doing Emotions History*, 8.

29 Rob Boddice, "The Affective Turn: Historicizing the Emotions," in *Psychology and History: Interdisciplinary Explorations*, ed. Cristian Tileagă and Jovan Byford (Cambridge University Press, 2014), 147–65.

30 Boddice, "Affective Turn," 156. Historians are still working out the concepts and terms that most usefully explain the cultural and historic role played by emotions. See Boddice, "Affective Turn," 148, 165.

31 Barbara H. Rosenwein, "Worrying about Emotions in History," *American Historical Review* 107, 3 (2002): 842–43 (emphasis in original).

32 Arlie Russell Hochschild, *The Managed Heart: Commercialization of Human Feeling* (Berkeley: University of California Press, 1983). Kristine Alexander points to this line of inquiry as fruitful for advancing the history of childhood; see Alexander, "Agency and Emotion Work," *Jeunesse: Young People, Texts, Culture* 7, 2 (2015): 123. See also Karen Vallgårda, Kristine Alexander, and Stephanie Olsen, "Emotions and the Global Politics of Childhood," in *Childhood, Youth and Emotions in Modern History*, ed. Stephanie Olsen (Basingstoke, UK: Palgrave, 2015): 12–34.

33 See Jeff Goodwin, James M. Jasper, and Francesca Polletta, eds., *Passionate Politics: Emotions and Social Movements* (Chicago: University of Chicago Press, 2001); Deborah B. Gould, *Moving Politics: Emotion and ACT UP's Fight against AIDS* (Chicago: University of Chicago Press, 2009); Carrie Hamilton, "Moving Feelings: Nationalism, Feminism and the Emotions of Politics," *Oral History* 38, 2 (2010): 85–94; James M. Jasper, "Emotions and Social Movements: Twenty Years of Theory and Research," *Annual Review of Sociology* 37 (2011): 285–303; Paul Hoggett and Simon Thompson, eds., *Politics and the Emotions: The Affective Turn in Contemporary Political Studies* (New York: Continuum, 2012); Marcos Engelken-Jorge, Pedro Ibarra Güell, and Carmelo Moreno, eds., *Politics and Emotions: The Obama Phenomenon* (Wiesbaden, Germany: VS Verlag, 2011); and Lauren Berlant and Lisa Duggan, eds., *Our Monica, Ourselves: The Clinton Affair and the National Interest* (New York: New York University Press, 2001).

34 Rosemary Hennessy, *Fires on the Border: The Passionate Politics of Organizing on the Mexican Frontera* (Minneapolis: University of Minnesota Press, 2014), xii; and Rosemary Hennessy, "Open Secrets: The Affective Cultures of Organizing on Mexico's Northern Border," *Feminist Theory* 10, 3 (2009): 310.

35 Elspeth Probyn, *Blush: Faces of Shame* (Minneapolis: University of Minnesota Press, 2005), xv; Sara Ahmed, *The Cultural Politics of Emotion* (New York: Routledge, 2004); Lauren Berlant, "Thinking about Feeling Historical," *Emotion, Space, and Society* 1, 1 (2008): 4–9; Ann Cvetkovich, *An Archive of Feelings: Trauma, Sexuality,*

and Lesbian Public Cultures (Durham, NC: Duke University Press, 2003); Ann Cvetkovich, "Writing with *The Alphabet of Feeling Bad,*" in *Walking Beside: Challenging the Role of Emotions in Normalization*, ed. Eva Söderberg and Sara Nyhlén (Sundsvall: Mid Sweden University, 2014), 37–51; Ann Cvetkovich, "Affect," in *Keywords for American Cultural Studies,* 2nd ed., ed. Bruce Burgett and Glenn Hendler (New York: New York University Press, 2014), 13–15.

36 Hennessy, *Fires on the Border*, xxiii.

37 Eve Kosofsky Sedgwick and Adam Frank, ed., *Shame and Its Sisters: A Silvan Tomkins Reader* (Durham, NC: Duke University Press, 1995); Silvan Tomkins, *Affect, Imagery, Consciousness: The Complete Edition, Vol. I and II* (New York: Springer Publishing, 2008).

38 Melissa Gregg and Gregory J. Seigworth, "An Inventory of Shimmers," in *The Affect Theory Reader*, ed. Melissa Gregg and Gregory J. Seigworth (Durham, NC: Duke University Press, 2010), 1 (emphasis in original).

39 Carolyn Pedwell and Anne Whitehead, "Affecting Feminism: Questions of Feeling in Feminist Theory," *Feminist Theory* 13, 2 (2012): 116. See also Kristyn Gorton, "Theorizing Emotion and Affect: Feminist Engagements," *Feminist Theory* 8, 3 (2007): 333–34. On "felt experiences" or "emotional knowledge" see Dian Million, "Felt Theory: An Indigenous Feminist Approach to Affect and History," *Wicazo Sa Review* 24, 2 (2009): 53–76.

40 Lauren Berlant, *Cruel Optimism* (Durham, NC: Duke University Press, 2011), 2. See also Eve Kosofsky Sedgwick, *Touching Feeling: Affect, Pedagogy, Performativity* (Durham, NC: Duke University Press, 2003); and Lauren Berlant, ed., *Compassion: The Cutural Politics of an Emotion* (New York: Routledge, 2004).

41 Ahmed, *Cultural Politics of Emotion*, 4.

42 Sara Ahmed, *Living a Feminist Life* (Durham, NC: Duke University Press, 2017), 268. See also Ahmed, "Killing Joy: Feminism and the History of Happiness," *Signs: Journal of Women in Culture and Society* 35, 3 (2010): 571–94.

43 Probyn, *Blush*, x, xvi.

44 Anna Gibbs, "Contagious Feelings: Pauline Hanson and the Epidemiology of Affect," *Australian Humanities Review* (2001), cited in Gorton, "Theorizing Emotion and Affect," 337. Equally important are the limits of affective movement. Margaret Wetherwell asks, "Why does affect not leap across some barriers? ... Why does it stop travelling?" See "Trends in the Turn to Affect: A Social Psychological Critique," *Body and Society* 21, 2 (2015): 154.

45 Ahmed, *Cultural Politics of Emotion*, 4.

46 Ahmed, *Cultural Politics of Emotion*, 201.

47 Ahmed, *Cultural Politics of Emotion*, 171–77.

48 Audre Lorde, "Poetry Is Not a Luxury," in *Sister Outsider: Essays and Speeches by Audre Lorde* (Berkeley, CA: Crossing Press, 2007), 37.

49 Piroska Nagy, "Historians and Emotions: New Theories, New Questions" (presentation, Cultural History of Emotions in Premodernity International Colloquium, Umeå University, Umeå, Sweden, October 23–26, 2008), para. 32, http://emma.hypotheses.org/147. For new ways to think about affect and decolonization, see Helen Moewaka Barnes et al., "Feeling and Spirit: Developing an Indigenous Wairua Approach to Research," *Qualitative Research* 17, 3 (2017): 313–25.

50 Boddice, "Affective Turn," 155.
51 Probyn, *Blush*, 76.
52 Claudia Garcia-Rojas, "(Un)Disciplined Futures: Women of Color Feminism as a Disruptive to White Affect Studies," *Journal of Lesbian Studies* 21, 3 (2017): 254–71; Aimee Carillo Rowe and Francesca T. Royster, "Loving Transgressions: Queer of Color Bodies, Affective Ties, Transformative Community," *Journal of Lesbian Studies* 21, 3 (2017): 243–53. On the politics of citation practices in academic scholarship, see Ahmed, *Living a Feminist Life*, 15–17.
53 Patricia Hill Collins, "The Social Construction of Black Feminist Thought," *Signs: Journal of Women in Culture and Society* 14, 4 (1989): 763.
54 See Lorde, "Poetry Is Not a Luxury," in *Sister Outsider*, 38. See also Lorde, "The Transformation of Silence into Language and Action," in *Sister Outsider*, 40–44; Gloria Anzaldúa, *Borderlands/La Frontera: The New Mestiza* (San Francisco, CA: Aunt Lute Books, 2012), 60–61; Gloria Anzaldúa and Cherríe Morgan, eds., *This Bridge Called My Back: Writings by Radical Women of Color* (New York: Kitchen Table, Women of Color Press, 1983); Patricia Hill Collins, *Black Feminist Thought: Knowledge, Consciousness and the Politics of Empowerment* (London, UK: Unwin Hyman, 1990).
55 Ute Frevert, *Emotions in History – Lost and Found* (Budapest: Central European University Press, 2011), 219, cited in Boddice, "Affective Turn," 148.
56 Probyn, *Blush*, 38; Ahmed, "Feminist Attachments," in *Cultural Politics of Emotion*, 168–90; bell hooks, *All About Love: New Visions* (New York: William Morrow, 2000).
57 Gloria Anzaldúa points to powerful feelings of immobilization, inadequacy, defensiveness, internalized rage, and contempt. See Anzaldúa, *Borderlands/La Frontera*, 67.
58 For a useful summary of this literature, see Boler, *Feeling Power*, 11–14.
59 Bernstein et al., *Sisters, Brothers, Lovers ... Listen ...*, 1.
60 Lorde, "The Use of the Erotic as Power," 53; and Lorde, "The Uses of Anger," in *Sister Outsider*, 127. Patricia Hill Collins argues that Black feminist epistemology rejects the positivist framework of knowledge production that insists on the elimination of feeling and emotion from all "objects" of study. Collins, "Social Construction of Black Feminist Thought," 753–54.
61 Lisa Feldman Barrett, *How Emotions Are Made: The Secret Life of the Brain* (Boston, MA: Houghton Mifflin Harcourt, 2017), 80. Note also that Patricia Hill Collins discusses the difference between knowledge and wisdom and sees wisdom as "essential to the survival of the subordinate." Collins, "Social Construction of Black Feminist Thought," 759.
62 Boler, *Feeling Power*, 5. See also p. xviii.

1

Pride, Shame, and Anger
Women's Struggles to Achieve Natural Childbirth in Postwar Canada

WHITNEY WOOD

The 1944 publication of British obstetrician Grantly Dick-Read's *Childbirth without Fear* in North America introduced a new and captive audience of Canadian parents to the principles of "natural childbirth" – an ideology that represented some of the first significant and organized opposition to the medicalization of birth that had been ongoing since the mid-nineteenth century.[1] Over the coming decades, a distinct natural childbirth movement emerged in Canada. At the same time, a growing number of Canadians increasingly sought to position the female body at the centre of women's liberation, and choices in childbirth were a key part of this effort. Demands for reproductive choice – including decisions about where and how (and not just whether or not) to give birth – would be central to the emergence and growth of second-wave feminist movements.

Dick-Read was born in Suffolk in 1890, received medical training at the London Hospital in Whitechapel, qualified as a physician in 1914, and served with the Royal Army Medical Corps during the First World War. By the close of the war, Dick-Read had observed what he considered to be striking and memorable examples of "natural" childbirth – the relatively pain-free deliveries of a Whitechapel mother and a Belgian "peasant woman" he saw deliver a child in a field.[2] *Childbirth without Fear* was first published in the United Kingdom in 1933 to significant popular reception. Its 1944 republication garnered significant attention in North America, with Dick-Read's theories and methods enjoying enhanced popularity throughout the 1940s and 1950s. In Canada, natural childbirth enjoyed increasing coverage in the popular press, the subject of a growing number of articles in women's magazines such as *Chatelaine* and the *Canadian Home Journal*.[3] The CBC dedicated a May 1956 broadcast to Dick-Read's vision,[4] and national, regional, and local newspapers commented at length on Dick-Read's teachings and his visit to Canada at the close of the decade.[5] As a result, Canadian audiences regularly received the message that Dick-Read's *Childbirth without Fear* principles represented "the newest and best" way to give birth.[6]

Dick-Read drew attention in particular to the psychological and emotional aspects of the birth experience, arguing that the prevalence of fear within the birthing room and during the birthing process caused tension, contributing to heightened contractility and painful spasms in the cervix. He asserted that prenatal education and training in relaxation were key to overcoming pain in childbirth, and he envisioned the ideal birth as one involving a conscious, confident, and active participant, rather than the accepted practice of a drugged and unconscious patient.[7] And yet, Dick-Read's "new" approach to childbirth was markedly conservative. He drew heavily on nineteenth-century medical folklore that emphasized the relatively pain-free birth experiences of so-called primitive women – a group that included both those who represented racial "others" and, as noted above, members of the working and "peasant" classes. These types of attitudes led women's health scholar Margarete Sandelowski to posit that in the immediate postwar decades, natural childbirth "was distinctively nonfeminist, if not antifeminist."[8] Indeed, in describing the ideal mother as conscious, composed, and silent, Dick-Read imposed a new set of expectations on women as mothers both in the hospital and in the private sphere. In emphasizing the desirability of the passive female patient, he, like many of his British, Canadian, and American contemporaries, articulated above all else the authority of the physician rather than the labouring mother.[9] Fundamentally, Dick-Read's *Childbirth without Fear* teachings upheld maternity as women's highest purpose and the foundation of the family, while reinforcing the image of the ideal postwar woman as the middle-class stay-at-home mother. Still, while natural childbirth was not framed as a feminist childbirth experience, as expectant mothers encountered these ideas many began to articulate new expectations for their childbirth experiences and for the right to choose how they gave birth.

Many women wrote to Dick-Read demanding more information regarding natural childbirth, asking for referrals to physicians amenable to natural childbirth techniques, and expressing their appreciation to this British doctor. This chapter examines over sixty letters he received between 1946 and his death, in 1959, from women from all regions of Canada. Remarkable for the frank discussions of individual birth experiences they contain, these letters offer a valuable window into women's emotional responses to childbirth in the postwar decades. Individual expressions of emotions on the page – through the use of quotation and exclamation marks, underlining, and capitalization – are preserved here in the text wherever possible.

In particular, the letters to Dick-Read illuminate women's feelings of pride, shame, and, increasingly, anger. The natural childbirth movement played a key role in rearticulating the experience of birthing from one based on fear to one that should constitute pride, or the triumph over pain. Yet individual engagements with the burgeoning natural childbirth movement involved a complex interplay of emotions. For those unable to obtain the birth they desired, the resulting feeling was often shame. Thus, while this movement brought more positive attitudes about childbirth, it also placed significant pressure on women to have a particular kind of birth that not all could obtain. In addition to these dominant emotional responses in their letters to Grantly Dick-Read, as well as in other personal narratives, women made increasing note of the difficulties they encountered in "achieving" natural birth in postwar Canadian hospitals. By the late 1950s, a growing number of Canadian women were vocalizing the belief that they and their infants had been cheated out of a natural birth; these individual and collective expressions of anger would lay the groundwork for a sharper criticism of medical control in the decades that followed. An examination of women's emotional responses to natural childbirth in the late 1940s and 1950s – and, on a broader level, to the status quo of postwar obstetric practice – is thus central to understanding the emergence of a distinct women's health movement in the 1960s and 1970s.

Fear in the Birthing Room

When Grantly Dick-Read wrote *Childbirth without Fear*, he was writing in opposition to several generations of medical practice and tradition. The second half of the nineteenth century was a key period in terms of both the medicalization of childbirth and the professionalization of obstetrics in Britain and North America. Following the first clinical uses of inhalation anaesthetics (namely, ether and chloroform) in the late 1840s, anaesthesia became an integral part of the physician's tool kit and was increasingly framed as a valuable medical intervention that distinguished the "modern" and scientifically trained obstetrician from the antiquated and "unskilled" midwife. Alongside a growing body of medical rhetoric that emphasized the unprecedented levels of pain that many women were thought to experience when giving birth, by the turn of the twentieth century the vast majority of physicians embraced the use of obstetric anaesthesia.[10] By the interwar period, anaesthetized birth – at the very least, the provision of some analgesic pain relief during delivery for the majority of urban-dwelling, white, well-to-do women – was commonplace in Canadian obstetric practice, as elsewhere.

The use of anaesthetics was in some sense a means for physicians to contain the emotions in the birthing room. Nineteenth-century physicians, including those who sought to establish themselves as experts in this emerging specialty, argued that the emotional atmosphere of the birthing room played a significant role in determining the progress of labour. Physicians wrote at length on the perceived emotional instability of the parturient patient, about to give birth, and cautioned the young practitioner to conduct himself carefully when attending expectant mothers. William Heath Byford, professor of obstetrics and diseases of women and children at the Chicago Medical College, noted in a popular 1870 text that because parturient women were generally "more or less excited, and some of them impatient and petulant," any "misbehavior" on the part of the patient "should be met by the utmost kindness and indulgence."[11] Medical textbooks readily acknowledged the role that the physician's words could play in shaping the trajectory of births. Byford cautioned students that labour pains could be significantly "enfeebled ... by the announcement that [instrumental or surgical] interference will probably be necessary," and he recounted a case in which the unexpected death of a father-to-be in the birthing room rendered the pains of "a young lady sick in her first labor ... so feeble and inefficient as to require artificial [forceps] delivery."[12] In sum, practitioners learned that "discouragement" of all types often had adverse physiological effects.

Expectant mothers brought their own emotions to the birthing room. During the mid to late Victorian years, the trope of the delicate middle- or upper-class white woman – highly "evolved" and therefore increasingly sensitive to pain – became commonplace in both medical and public discourses. Medicalized descriptions of the heightened pain experienced by this group of women both reflected and reinforced middle-class Anglo-Canadian women's fears of the pain of giving birth and markedly shaped individual recollections of birth experiences.[13] Historian Joanna Bourke has argued, of all the emotions, fear is fundamentally about and rooted in the "fleshy" and "precarious" body. As nineteenth-century fears of live burial, dissection, and untimely and unrespectable death transformed into twentieth-century anxieties surrounding the bodily pains and discomforts of disease, cancer, and old age, the body has remained a central focus point for human fears.[14] Persistent anxieties surrounding pain and parturition fit into this framework. Historian of emotions Barbara Rosenwein has suggested that emotional responses "are about things judged important to us" and "are the result of our values and assessments."[15] Women's fears during pregnancy and anxieties surrounding an upcoming birth can be interpreted as a sign of the enduring significance of maternal identities.

In the late-nineteenth and early-twentieth centuries, women's fears about the pain and suffering associated with giving birth were often accompanied by fears of invalidism following delivery and fears that they or their newborn infants would die in the birthing room. For many Anglo-Canadian women, the uncertainties associated with the birth experience – all the more pronounced as traditional cultures of female-dominated childbirth continued to decline over the course of the nineteenth century – were a major cause of anxiety. Women, including Canadian author Lucy Maud Montgomery, who declared during the final weeks of her first pregnancy in 1912, "I really suffer a martyrdom of misery, partly physical, partly anxious," readily blurred the lines between emotional and physical sufferings during these life stages.[16]

Fear of the birthing room would continue well into the postwar period. Recalling her first birth experience in 1946, Muriel Abbott, of St. Lambert, Quebec, for example, commented that in her experience, childbirth represented "a complete mystery," and she noted, "I was terrified and afraid that I would die."[17] Writing in 1951, Darlene Bell, of Vancouver, reported that her pregnancy was "a time when I was frightened and unhappy."[18] These types of emotions seemed to be widespread. Writing in 1955, Canadian physician Marion Hilliard, head of the Department of Obstetrics and Gynecology at Women's College Hospital in Toronto, recognized fear as "the most distressing force in pregnancy" and noted that "the greatest of all the fears a woman can know is the fear of the unknown. This fear is never so acute and awful as with a first pregnancy."[19]

Still, the first half of the twentieth century brought changing attitudes among medical practitioners and their patients to the practice of childbirth. Some practitioners began to critique what they saw as the overuse of anaesthesia in the birthing room. A 1934 piece in the *Canadian Public Health Journal*, for example, suggested that "the insistent demand for a lessening of the pain and discomfort of childbearing" contributed to high rates of both unnecessary surgical interference during childbirth and maternal mortality.[20] Patients reassessed the experience of childbirth. High rates of infant and maternal mortality persisted throughout the interwar period, spiking with the onset of the Great Depression.[21] As rates began to decline at the end of the 1930s, growing numbers of Canadian women came to expect that they and their infants would survive the experience of birth. In this changing atmosphere, as historian Jacqueline Wolf has argued in her examination of the American context, postwar mothers "judged the quality of care by the compassion and kindness shown to them by doctors and nurses in the hospital."[22] They also increasingly desired a happy and fulfilling birth experience and sought to remain conscious and aware throughout the process.

Criticism over the nature of the birth experience as well as the safety of existing practices provided fuel for the emerging natural childbirth movement. Many who sought to assuage their fears and uncertainties surrounding the events that awaited them in the birthing room found solace in the information presented in Dick-Read's work. Writing to the author, women noted their ongoing fears and asked for information and referrals to physicians amenable to natural childbirth techniques in the hopes of overcoming their negative feelings. For many, like Darlene Bell in Vancouver, reading Dick-Read's *Childbirth without Fear* "was like reaching a port in a storm."[23]

Triumph over Pain

Throughout the 1940s and 1950s, Dick-Read's theories played a major role in shaping both popular and medical understandings of what exactly constituted a natural birth experience. In a 1958 piece in *Chatelaine,* where he answered popular questions on natural childbirth for an explicitly Canadian audience, Dick-Read asserted that he had "never taught that labor was painless." He argued that childbirth required physical effort and emphasized the "mild discomfort" experienced by the majority of women in giving birth. He noted that anaesthesia could and should be used to allay pain in select cases when women experienced unbearable levels of discomfort. Nevertheless, Dick-Read told a captive audience of Canadian women that "93–96 percent" of those who followed his teachings "had their babies naturally with no anaesthesia."[24] In this statement, then, Dick-Read firmly implied that the great majority of "normal" women were able to achieve a successful natural childbirth – one that was defined as completion without recourse to anaesthetic pain relief.

Medical professionals including Dick-Read suggested that unanaesthetized, conscious birth was a noble achievement for the new Canadian mother. In a 1951 response to Edmonton's Ruth McAdam, Dick-Read described the triumph of childbirth as "the most beautiful and engrossing achievement that any woman can have."[25] Canadian physicians echoed his assessment. Writing in *Chatelaine* in 1957, Hilliard commented: "I heartily approve of a woman's being conscious throughout the birth because it is the highest fulfillment she will ever know and she shouldn't miss it."[26]

As women sought to exercise control over the events taking place in the birthing room, they responded to and echoed growing suggestions that the ability to overcome the pain of childbirth was representative of their broader value as mothers. They saw drug-free and conscious births as a considerable accomplishment and described their experiences with a sense of pride and success. Karen Birch, of rural Alberta, an early and enthusiastic devotee to *Childbirth without Fear* methods, described a feeling of "heavenly ecstasy" after the delivery of her fourth child according to Dick-Read's teachings in the late 1940s.[27] One anonymous mother, reporting to the *Canadian Home Journal* in 1952, described "triumphantly" informing a new nurse that there would be "no anaesthetic" used during her delivery.[28] Many mothers were more restrained in their descriptions. Carol Parkham, of St. John's, Newfoundland, reported to Dick-Read in a 1955 letter that she "felt satisfied I did my best" after her self-described – and physician-confirmed – "successful" natural birth in 1955.[29] Muriel Abbott recalled feeling "stimulated" and "elated" after the delivery of her third child in 1957. She described the "cherished moments" of her conscious birth as "the supreme moment of motherhood, which no one can take away from me."[30] Writing in 1958 following her own birth experience, Daphne Harper described "the tremendous satisfaction achieved through natural birth" and asserted: "For the first time in my life I feel fulfilled – as a woman."[31] In the same year, Toronto mother Fay Grabowski suggested to Dick-Read that "there is no-one on earth more egotistical than a woman who has just produced a 10 lb 2 1/2 oz. boy by Natural Childbirth."[32]

This sense of pride extended beyond new mothers to include new fathers, many of whom were increasingly involved with pregnancy and the birth experience – though largely confined to the waiting room, seldom permitted in the labour ward, and overwhelmingly restricted from the delivery room – in the postwar years.[33] In 1953, Saul Kaufman of Winnipeg reported, for example, that both he and his wife cherished the birth of their first child, a son, and he described his wife's natural birth experience as "a great achievement and an extreme peak in our graph of everyday happiness."[34] For his part, Dick-Read enthusiastically congratulated new mothers and fathers alike on the successful outcomes of their natural deliveries.[35]

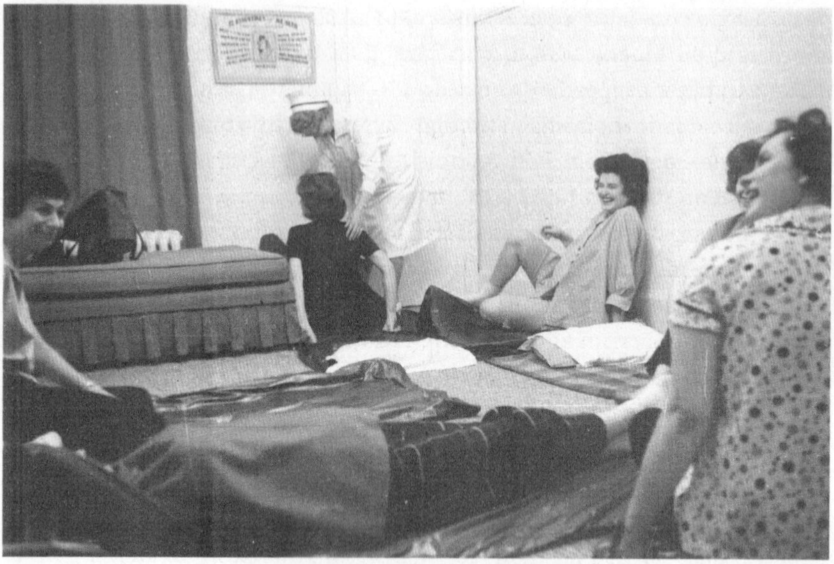

Nursing [sic] Instructing Women during Childbirth Classes, ca. 1954–1963. (Library and Archives Canada, Rosemary Gilliat Eaton fonds, e010974734.)

In *The Story of Pain* (2014), Joanna Bourke suggests that pain represented a source of pride, a "not uncommon emotion for many women during and after childbirth."[36] The argument that the ability to endure the pain of childbirth demonstrated women's innate strength and power was largely characteristic of the late 1960s and 1970s, although some Canadians writing in the 1950s did portray such pain in a positive light. Echoing her husband, Saul's, description of the "great achievement" of her first natural birth, Moira Kaufman recalled that during the "perfect" natural delivery of her second child, in 1958, she "worked like fury, grunting, groaning, and using each contraction for all it was worth."[37] Adopting a medical perspective and writing for an audience of Canadian mothers-to-be, Hilliard argued that the ability to endure the ordeals of childbirth was a legitimate source of pride for many women regardless of the outcome. In a January 1958 piece published in *Chatelaine*, Hilliard asserted that:

> The act of childbirth can light up a woman's life and it is immaterial to that experience whether or not the mother has her baby afterward. This is what I try to tell my unmarried mothers who must give up their infants for adoption and it is a truth that holds even when a first baby doesn't survive. The

> drama of birth, the torment wrapped up with exultation beyond self, is the truest and finest moment a woman can know. It is the trial by fire that gives a soldier inner dignity to sustain him all his life. It grants a woman a piercing, dazzling pride in herself that may become dim but never dingy.[38]

Such views were by no means the norm in the immediate postwar decades, but Hilliard's comments demonstrate the historical roots of attitudes that sacrifice and pain are necessary requirements in the transition to "legitimate motherhood."[39]

While some Canadian women took pride in the physical work and effort they had put into delivering their children without anaesthetic or instrumental interference, the majority of new mothers consistently attributed the responsibility for "successful" deliveries to the doctors who had advised or attended them. They routinely expressed their gratitude to their physicians and, oftentimes, to Dick-Read himself. Writing in the late 1940s, Karen Birch made note of "several grateful young mothers" who had read Dick-Read's *Childbirth without Fear*.[40] Describing the "painless" birth of "a relative of a friend" in 1950, Lorraine Blair commented that though the nurses in the labour ward had congratulated the new mother, she thought that "the compliments should go to the Doctor who has worked and is still working to make childbirth the natural and inspiring thing that it is," and she expressed her gratitude to Dick-Read.[41] Writing in 1951, Mrs. John Strong, of Prince Rupert, British Columbia, credited her "wonderful experience" to Dick-Read's "wonderful book," which she believed "helped me to have my first baby naturally."[42] For some Canadians, expressions of gratitude took a more public form. Kathleen Williams, of Naramata, British Columbia, included "thanks to Dr. Grantly Dick-Read" in the announcement of the birth of her son published in the Penticton newspaper, in 1949.[43] Karen Birch went as far as to name her fourth child "Patrick Read" in honour of the doctor and wrote, "I can never thank you enough for writing that wonderfully inspiring volume."[44] Expressions of gratitude, both public and private, increased throughout the following decade.[45]

Women who experienced difficulties in their attempts to deliver according to Dick-Read's teachings also expressed their thankfulness to the doctor. Such expressions – and willingness to give credit to both Dick-Read and the method – demonstrate how some women found definitions of natural childbirth to be malleable, allowing for considerable medical interventions. Writing in 1955, Laurel Rice, of Toronto, described encountering numerous medical interventions despite her explicitly stated desire for a so-called natural birth. Nevertheless, when she wrote to Dick-Read following the birth of her child, she reported that she was "very happy that the delivery was so easy" and told the doctor, "It is to you I give all the credit. Your words, your teachings, your complete understanding of labour (physically and emotionally) helped me accomplish what amazes even me."[46]

As might be expected, given the traditional doctor-patient relationship, women writers in particular tended to be quite deferential to Dick-Read. In addition to giving him (sometimes sole) credit for their achievements, women regularly apologized for taking up his time with their letters.[47] This deference is emblematic of the broader power dynamics at play in postwar Canadian obstetric wards, a dynamic which, in many ways, explains the ongoing disjuncture between women's articulated desires for a less medicalized birth experience and the events taking place in the birthing room. For some Canadian women, routine hospital birth included the use of physical restraint and forcible anaesthetization against the explicitly stated wishes of the expectant mother in question.[48]

These harmful obstetric practices were rooted in a postwar culture of medical practice that extended beyond the birthing room and emphasized, above all else, the authority of the often male physician over the body of the female patient. Women's individual and collective efforts to challenge medical authority and re-exert control over one's own body – encapsulated, for example, in the 1973 volume *Our Bodies, Ourselves* – were central to the growth of second-wave feminism, and throughout the postwar decades the majority of practitioners, including those supportive of "new" techniques including natural childbirth practices, continued to firmly resent lay incursions into medical decision-making practices.[49] Hilliard, for example, noted at length her approval of women's desires to remain conscious during birth. But she also stated that when it came to determining exactly "how natural" childbirth should be, the decision was one "only an obstetrician can make, not the overeager patient and her friends."[50] Those physicians who were opposed to Dick-Read's ideas – and, on a broader level, the "modern-day cult of childbirth" that developed around such methods[51] – were all the more vocal in their opposition. In a piece published in *Chatelaine* the following decade, Dr. Geraldine Maloney, who in the mid-1960s occupied the chair of the Department of Obstetrics and Gynecology at Women's College Hospital previously occupied by Dr. Hilliard, asserted that she found it "grossly insulting that nineteen-year-old-girls are advising mature, highly trained specialists how they want their babies delivered." As Maloney argued, and as the majority of practitioners agreed, "the choice should be the doctor's."[52]

Throughout the postwar period, then, physicians made clear their belief in their own expertise and thus authority in the birthing room. Still, some, such as Dick-Read and Hilliard, reassessed existing practices and facilitated more natural childbirth experiences. During these decades, as women sought to exercise increasing control over events taking place in the birthing room, feelings of intense fear surrounding childbirth were gradually replaced by feelings of pride in individual triumphs over pain, echoing some of the predominant natural childbirth rhetoric of the period. At the same, women's expressions of pride in enduring the pain of giving birth had their limits, with many quick to attribute the responsibility for a "successful" natural delivery to the attending physician. With increasing challenges to medical authority in the decades that followed, individual and collective expressions of pride in the birthing room took on new meaning alongside the growth of women's health activism.

Failure and Shame

As the movement to achieve a natural birth gained momentum, however, it had a markedly negative impact on how some Canadian women experienced childbirth. Cheryl Krasnick Warsh has suggested that because of Dick-Read's cult-like following, "when women who faithfully followed the methods experienced intense labour pains and required anaesthetics or caesarean sections, they sometimes felt like personal failures."[53] Indeed, the personal narratives of postwar Canadian mothers demonstrate that many women had strong emotional responses – including experiences of disappointment, guilt, and shame – as a result of what they identified as failed natural births. These emotions can be positioned as part of broader anxieties – and potential anguish – surrounding maternity and motherhood in the immediate postwar decades, addressed in the following chapters.[54]

Writing for a Canadian audience in 1958, Dick-Read touched on the potential negative effects of natural childbirth discourses. He noted, quite astutely, that "critics have said that it is bad for a woman psychologically if she fails to achieve a natural birth when she has trained for it." Nevertheless, in the following sentence, he asserted (again) that his method had "a 96 percent chance of success," that "96 percent" of adherents "having anesthetic apparatus and pain relief by their side ... see their babies born naturally without interference or anaesthetics." Though Dick-Read suggested that this figure – and, ostensibly, the fact that the method would not work for 4 percent of mothers – covered the possibilities of both "disappointment and success so that neither of these normal emotions become exaggerated," it is easy to see how the many women who fell outside the alleged 96 percent of "successful" natural deliveries could be easily disappointed.[55] Throughout the immediate postwar decades, furthermore, the responsibility or "blame" for such failures consistently rested with the expectant mother, rather than with the medical practitioners in question. Though a small but growing number of Canadian parents and physicians over the course of the 1950s made note of structural factors in the modern hospital that represented barriers to "successful" natural birth, most Canadian women took such "failures" very personally.

In both his correspondence with Canadians and his published work, Dick-Read suggested that patience, self-control, and hard work would enable expectant mothers to achieve success in the birthing room. The 1944 edition of *Childbirth without Fear* characterized women's requests for anaesthesia or pain relief during labour as "an escape demand," rather than a legitimate desire or need. Dick-Read suggested that when it came to the ability to attain relaxation (and relief) in labour, "some [women] are better than others." Indeed, he positioned labour as the true test of a woman's strength: "In labor a woman shows her true colors – the patient and impatient; the courageous and 'gutless'; the 'I-can-and-I-will' women and the 'Oh-please-I-can't-and-what's-more-I-won't' women are all met with and require different handling, but with one accord they seek encouragement and comfort in the support and strength of their guide and protector in labor."[56]

In individual letters, Dick-Read told the mother-to-be that if she successfully achieved "a state of complete relaxation" during her contractions, she would "patiently await the change to the second stage of labour and then only push your baby into the world when you are unable to avoid doing so." He concluded, "If your mind will allow your body to produce your baby, there is nothing to prevent you very quietly and safely receiving it."[57] Though he told expectant mothers that labour was "not an easy job," he also asserted that it represented "the final test for a woman to prove that she has intelligent understanding and confidence" and an occasion demanding "those three great virtues of Patience, Self-Control, and Hard Work." Labour represented, in other words, "the great test of a woman's character."[58]

In the face of these messages, many women reported feelings of personal responsibility for what they saw as the failure to achieve what they defined as natural birth. Writing to Dick-Read in the mid-1950s, Darlene Bell described her efforts to prepare for a natural childbirth ahead of the birth of her first child. Though Bell attempted to relax and "had hoped [to] thus avoid any great pain," she later recalled that "the pain got worse till I begged for help and even before I got to the pushing stage, the anaesthetic was increased and I faded into oblivion – thank God!" While thankful for the relief from pain, she ultimately described the pain she experienced as "my great disappointment."[59] Eleanor Greenwood, of Nelson, British Columbia, reported her own disappointment, noting that her experiences of discomfort and pain during childbirth occurred "mainly because I panicked."[60]

Women also described "feeling cheated" out of their desired birth experiences. Despite her expressions of gratitude to Dick-Read, Laurel Rice noted that, as she was anaesthetized against her will, "the final triumph in actually delivering my baby (without ether), which I so anticipated, were denied." She expressed profound disappointment in this denial. Noting "also denied were the sympathy and praise I craved for my 'achievement,'" Rice highlighted the emotional impacts of this particular (and unwanted) medical intervention.[61] Though her anaesthetist was a friend and colleague of her husband, and she had pleaded for an unanaesthetized birth, Elizabeth Walker, of Winnipeg, Manitoba, remembered the interventions she encountered during her birth experience in the mid-1940s:

> In the end they told me the baby was arriving too fast and the doctor hadn't arrived and they just put the mask over my face and that was that ... I had missed hearing his first cry, I could not ask the minute he was born what sex he was. I felt dopey, heavy, and dull and apart from being thankful it was all over I couldn't get very excited ... In fact looking back I feel I was cheated out of the most wonderful few hours of a woman's life.[62]

Though rates of both infant and maternal mortality had recently declined, postwar mothers may have felt enduring anxieties surrounding the possibilities of death during childbirth. In this atmosphere, some women may have been wary of expressing "selfish" disappointment in their childbirth experiences. Some mothers instead framed their disappointments in terms of the impact on the health and well-being of their new infants, expressing the belief that the women had cheated their children out of something valuable and important by "failing" to have a natural birth. Describing both her own feelings and those of her sister in a 1949 letter to Dick-Read, Karen Birch wrote of the "one deep regret" the two shared "in the midst of our joy in our natural babies": "We both feel that we have cheated our other children cruelly. Yet unfortunately, they cannot be 'born again,' so we just try and make up with extra sympathy and understanding, both of us realizing a lot of the moodiness and unmanageability is due to the frigid welcome they received."[63]

Over the course of the 1950s and 1960s, Canadian medical professionals increasingly pathologized these particular emotions, chastising women for their feelings of disappointment and guilt. Speaking out against "the current cult of maternity worship" in a May 1964 issue of *Chatelaine*, Maloney described what she saw as a perplexing encounter with a "grief-stricken mother" at Toronto's Women's College Hospital:

> She was in her early twenties, but she shuffled along red-eyed and stooped like a newly bereaved woman of eighty. "Was her baby dead?" I asked sympathetically when she was out of earshot. A nurse shook her head negatively. "Deformed then? Retarded? Blind?" The nurse kept shaking her head. "You'll never guess," she interrupted me. "That woman has a fine healthy baby, nothing wrong with him at all. But she's been crying for three days because she can't breast-feed him."[64]

Lamenting the fact that modern maternity wards were "being turned into testing grounds by mothers who view it as a catastrophe that they had analgesia during their delivery,"[65] Maloney suggested that women's feelings of disappointment represented an abnormal and problematic emotional response to childbirth and the delivery of a healthy child. To this end, Maloney articulated what sociologist Arlie Hochschild has referred to as a "feeling rule," an explicit or implicit value judgment that delineates between acceptable and unacceptable emotions.[66] Women's experiences of shame, "a quintessentially social emotion," during and after childbirth also speak to the boundaries that existed between women as patients and their health care providers.[67] Sara Ahmed posits that experiences of shame are always linked to the failure to meet expectations – as she puts it, "to be witnessed in one's failure is to be ashamed: to have one's shame witnessed is all the more shaming."[68]

Many Canadian women described strong feelings of shame in recalling their encounters with physicians. Karen Birch told Dick-Read that she felt ashamed after hearing doctors describe the birth experiences of other women in the obstetric ward. In response to her own doctor's comment on the "easy" delivery of her neighbour in the hospital, Karen Birch commented, "I felt properly squashed!"[69] Given the unequal power relationships between physicians and their expectant patients, the words and conduct of the doctor could have a particularly pronounced impact. One article, "No Anaesthetic for Me, Thanks!" published in the *Canadian Home Journal*, in November 1952, captured the experiences of an anonymous Canadian mother who described the gruff demeanour of her physician, Dr. O. Despite previously agreeing to allow the mother-to-be to attempt a natural delivery, Dr. O later seemed to resent having made such a concession. Following the unanaesthetized delivery, this anonymous mother remembered the doctor's remark – "you tore yourself" – and described feeling that "the words were an accusation."[70]

Women often took their perceived failures in the birthing room very personally. Though she was proud of the achievement of producing a healthy and large baby boy on her third attempt at natural birth, Fay Grabowski noted two previous failures in attempting Dick-Read's method. Following the delivery of her first daughter in early 1952 – an episode she described as "the failure of my first attempt" – she "felt bruised, literally and metaphorically." Grabowski later told Dick-Read that "my faith in you, and particularly in myself, was at its lowest ebb ... I had to reluctantly admit to myself ... that I was a coward."[71] The anonymous mother and author of "No Anaesthetic for Me, Thanks!" profiled in the *Canadian Home Journal* was hurt by Dr. O's "accusation" that she had conducted herself in a less than ideal manner during childbirth, but nevertheless summarized her experience: "I was a Success."[72] Days after the birth, however, these feelings would be called into question when the new mother discovered that Dr. O had "held the baby's head to prevent her from slipping back after each contraction." Though she "seethed with indignation" and felt anger towards the physician for his action, the new mother was simultaneously "disturbed by a nagging, guilty thought, that it hadn't been natural childbirth at all; that my muscles hadn't done their own work of easing the baby through the canal."[73] As Peter Stearns has argued, feelings of shame and guilt were often intertwined; though the relative power of both emotions shifted over time depending on broader historical context, the twentieth century saw new societal pressures to shame tied to the enforcement of sexual (and gender) conformity and "respectability," especially for women.[74]

Of course, women were by no means the powerless victims of an oppressive medical system. They exercised agency throughout their birth experiences in varying ways, including by vocally expressing their pain to demand the attention of physicians and nurses, and, at times, the provision of anaesthetic pain relief. Laurel Rice, for example, told Dick-Read that she advised women to "YELL LIKE HELL!" in order to ensure that they received the medical treatment they desired, particularly in cases where the expectant mother – labouring quietly according to natural childbirth teachings – suspected that delivery was imminent and the doctor had yet to be called.[75] Additionally, expectant mothers used the term "natural" in a variety of complicated ways, and they often described deliveries that had involved considerable medical interventions, including the use of anaesthesia, as "successful." Fay Grabowski's success, for example, included the administration of Demerol – a pain relieving opioid – during the transition stage, an intervention she described as a "tremendous" help.[76] Individual narratives complicate our historical and present understandings of the concept of the "natural," a term that was and continues to be used to describe a range of birth experiences.[77]

Nevertheless, it is evident that strict definitions of natural childbirth fostered feelings of disappointment and shame for many Canadian women. Writing in 1958, Fay Grabowski told Dick-Read that it was clear to her that "the woman with no previous experience of childbirth can be bitterly disillusioned and feel a great sense of failure if she enters labour with the pre-conception that it will always be painless in normal cases."[78] Growing numbers of women also commented on the structural barriers to the "achievement" of natural birth that existed in the modern Canadian hospital. Darlene Bell noted, for example, that in her hospital in Vancouver, "women who are awaiting labour, those who have started, and those with babies are put in the same ward." Bell appeared to recognize this set-up as presenting a major obstacle to natural birth, commenting, "What chance of relaxation!"[79]

Conclusion: Anger and Activism

Gender and cultural studies scholar Elspeth Probyn suggests that emotions such as shame have the potential to pass from individual bodies to the body politic, effectively becoming politicized as they begin to be collectively experienced.[80] The transformation of individual pains and injustices into a call for broader action, Sara Ahmed argues, "also requires anger; an interpretation that pain is wrong, that it is an outrage, and that something must be done about it."[81] This anger, both individual and collective, was beginning to be felt by an increasing number of Canadian women by the close of the 1950s.

Over the course of the immediate postwar decades, growing numbers of Canadians began to speak out on the questionable procedures in postwar obstetric wards. Practices including the routine use of restraints and anaesthetization without consent represented major barriers to the "achievement" of a successful natural birth, but in the eyes of a growing number of

Canadians, they were also emblematic of a broader culture of harm operating in many Canadian hospitals. Canadian mothers and mothers-to-be had long existed as a distinct "emotional community" motivated by shared interests and values and regularly sharing their experiences of disappointments and triumphs during childbirth with friends and relatives.[82] That informal community was key to "spreading the natural childbirth gospel."[83] By the late 1950s, criticisms of modern obstetric practice – particularly from those women with an interest in natural childbirth theories and methods – became more pronounced, as did growing coverage in both the American and Canadian popular press of "the tortures that go on in modern delivery rooms."[84]

As these criticisms mounted, Canadian women were increasingly willing to challenge the power and authority of their physicians. Laurel Rice, for example, expressed her displeasure to her doctor, whose administration "of anaesthetic at a moment when it was neither needed nor wanted" ended, she wrote, "my hopes for enjoying to the fullest an experience which I had every right to expect – conscious cooperation in the birth of my child."[85] On a more general level, Canadian women increasingly emphasized the value of choice in medical care, drawing attention to the structural and systemic obstacles they encountered in postwar hospitals.

Though some have suggested that natural childbirth was throughout the postwar years distinctively nonfeminist or even antifeminist, a closer historical examination suggests a more nuanced picture. Natural childbirth, despite its limitations, reveals that the women's health movement of the 1960s and 1970s had its roots in the changing attitudes in the immediate postwar years; in advocating for natural childbirth in the 1940s and 1950s and contributing to the spread of this nascent movement, women helped lay the groundwork for growing feminist activism in subsequent decades.[86] Still, the natural childbirth movement has a mixed history. In supporting this form of childbirth, physicians still laid claim to their authority in the birthing room. Moreover, they used the term "natural" in a variety of complicated ways to refer to births that often included considerable medical intervention.

A historical examination of natural childbirth in the immediate postwar decades also reveals shifting emotions surrounding childbirth. In responding and contributing to natural childbirth rhetoric, many Canadian women rearticulated their feelings from expressions of fear to a growing sense of pride – and, for an increasing number, anger with the status quo of postwar obstetric practice – surrounding the birthing experience. Medical and cultural emphases on strict definitions of natural childbirth and the "achievement" of this idealized birth experience also led to experiences of disappointment and shame for many women. While women increasingly highlighted the difficulties they encountered in controlling their birth experiences, and some new mothers reported that they felt "cheated" out of a natural birth, many others felt that they had "failed" in their efforts. Though mothers expressed gratitude and gave the credit for "successful" natural births to their attending physicians – and often to Dick-Read himself – the responsibility or blame for "failures" was overwhelmingly shouldered by the new mother in question.

The interplay of feelings of fear, pride, shame, and anger in women's birthing experiences in the 1940s and 1950s illuminates the complicated history of the natural childbirth movement, offering a potent example of how emotions have been inseparable from the history of Canadian feminism within and beyond the traditionally defined second wave. The idea of natural birth would become an increasingly powerful one with the emergence of a distinct women's health movement, used to denote feminist strength and power. Yet a historical examination of women's emotional engagements with natural childbirth in the immediate postwar decades demonstrates that natural childbirth discourses, and the emphasis on drug-free births, ultimately had the potential to both empower and discipline the women in question. This complicated history suggests the need to take seriously and further study women's stories of, and emotional responses to, the range of "natural" and medicalized birth experiences, as well as broader encounters with twentieth- and twenty-first-century health care systems.

Notes

Thank you to participants at the Second-Wave Feminism and the History of Emotions book workshop for their feedback on an earlier version of this chapter, to the anonymous reviewers for their helpful comments, and to the editors for their guidance in bringing this volume together.

1 Grantly Dick-Read, *Childbirth without Fear: The Principles and Practice of Natural Childbirth* (New York: Harper and Brothers, 1944). This was first published as Grantly Dick-Read, *Natural Childbirth* (London: William Heinemann, 1933).

2 Grantly Dick-Read, "Autobiography: Instalment Two" (unpublished manuscript, 22–24); "Autobiography: Instalment Three" (unpublished manuscript, 7), Wellcome Library, PP/GDR/A.92.

3 Examples include "No Anesthetic for Me, Thanks," *Canadian Home Journal*, November 1952, 20, 68–69, 72–74; Evelyn Hamilton, "Dr. Grantly Dick Read Answers Your Questions on Natural Childbirth," *Chatelaine*, January 1958, 17.

4 Letter writer Helen Scoles recounted listening to the broadcast in her correspondence with Dick-Read; "Helen Scoles to Grantly Dick-Read," May 28, 1956, Wellcome Library, PP/GDR/D.93.
5 The *Globe and Mail,* in particular, covered natural childbirth in a favourable light throughout the decade. See, for examples, "More Mothers Get Prenatal Instruction," *Globe and Mail,* February 18, 1953, 10; "Mothercraft Works for Family Life," *Globe and Mail,* March 7, 1956, 13; Florence Schill, "Group Is Enthusiastic about Natural Birth," *Globe and Mail,* March 8, 1956, 15; and "Readers' Comment: A Mystery What All the Fuss Is About," *Globe and Mail,* January 31, 1957, 18.
6 "No Anaesthetic for Me, Thanks!," 68.
7 Dick-Read, "Pains of Labour" (lecture, Norwich, UK, October 17, 1933), Wellcome Library, PP/GDR/C.71.
8 Margarete Sandelowski, *Pain, Pleasure, and American Childbirth from the Twilight Sleep to the Read Method* (Westport, CT: Greenwood Press, 1984), 136.
9 Mary Thomas, ed., *Post-war Mothers: Childbirth Letters to Grantly Dick-Read, 1946–1956* (Rochester, NY: University of Rochester Press, 1997), 16–17.
10 For more on the shifts that fuelled the growing use of anaesthesia in Canadian obstetric practice, see Whitney Wood, "Shifting Understandings of Labour Pain in Canadian Medical History," *Medical Humanities* 44 (2018): 82–88.
11 William Heath Byford, *A Treatise on the Theory and Practice of Obstetrics* (New York: William Wood, 1870), 220–21.
12 Byford, *Treatise on the Theory and Practice of Obstetrics,* 280–81.
13 For more on fear of the pain of giving birth, see Whitney Wood, "'When I Think of What Is before Me, I Feel Afraid': Narratives of Fear, Pain, and Childbirth in Late-Victorian Canada," in *Pain and Emotion in Modern History,* ed. Rob Boddice (Basingstoke, UK: Palgrave Macmillan, 2014), 187–203.
14 Joanna Bourke, *Fear: A Cultural History* (London: Virago Press, 2005), 8, 118.
15 Rosenwein, in Jan Plamper, "The History of Emotions: An Interview with William Reddy, Barbara Rosenwein, and Peter Stearns," *History and Theory* 49, 2 (2010): 251.
16 Lucy Maud Montgomery, cited in *The Selected Journals of L.M. Montgomery, Volume II: 1910–1920,* ed. Mary Rubio and Elizabeth Waterson (Toronto: Oxford University Press, 1987), 96.
17 In accordance with archival restrictions, all letter writer names are pseudonyms. Muriel Abbott to Grantly Dick-Read, November 26, 1957, Wellcome Library, PP/GDR/D.95.
18 Darlene Bell to Grantly Dick-Read, November 16, 1951, Wellcome Library, PP/GDR/D.90.
19 Like her counterparts a century earlier, Hilliard also noted the impact of emotions in the birthing room: "A buried fear can actually cause a severe inertia during labor and will certainly prolong the process unmercifully." Marion Hilliard, "Your First Baby," *Chatelaine,* January 1957, 47.
20 J.T. Phair, "Why Maternal Deaths?" *Canadian Public Health Journal* 25, 3 (1934): 142.
21 Statistics Canada, *Section B: Vital Statistics and Health,* Table B51-B58: Stillbirths and Rate, Infant Deaths and Rate by Sex, Neonatal Death Rate and Maternal Mortality Rate, Canada, 1921 to 1974, https://www.statcan.gc.ca/pub/11-516-x/sectionb/

4147437-eng.htm. Maternal mortality rates hovered around 5.5 maternal deaths per 1,000 live births throughout the first decades of the twentieth century, peaking at 5.8 deaths per 1,000 live births in 1930. By 1945, the maternal death rate had declined to 2.3 per 1,000 live births. Infant mortality rates experienced a similar decline, from 91 infant deaths per 1,000 live births in 1930, to 52 per 1,000 in 1945.

22 Jacqueline Wolf, *Deliver Me from Pain: Anesthesia and Birth in America* (Baltimore: Johns Hopkins University Press, 2009), 266.

23 Bell to Dick-Read, November 16, 1951.

24 Hamilton, "Dr. Grantly Dick Read Answers Your Questions on Natural Childbirth," 17, 27.

25 Grantly Dick-Read to Ruth McAdam, July 2, 1951, Wellcome Library, PP/GDR/D.92.

26 Hilliard, "Your First Baby," 46.

27 Karen Birch to Grantly Dick-Read, August 30, 1949, Wellcome Library, PP/GDR/D.90.

28 "No Anaesthetic for Me, Thanks!," 72.

29 Carol Parkham to Grantly Dick-Read, November 1, 1955, Wellcome Library, PP/GDR/D.92.

30 Abbott to Dick-Read, November 26, 1957.

31 Daphne Harper to Grantly Dick-Read, October 25, 1958, Wellcome Library, PP/GDR/D.95.

32 Fay Grabowski to Grantly Dick-Read, August 24, 1958, Wellcome Library, PP/GDR/D.95. From the eighteenth century onward, physicians made a variety of arguments about the head (and brain) size of male infants compared with their female counterparts, arguing that expectant mothers experienced the most pain while giving birth to boys rather than girls. See Londa Scheibinger, "Skeletons in the Closet: The First Illustrations of the Female Skeleton in Eighteenth-Century Anatomy," in *The Making of the Modern Body: Sexuality and Society in the Nineteenth-Century,* ed. Catherine Gallagher and Thomas Laqueur (Berkeley: University of California Press, 1987), 42–82. For a Canadian example of this rhetoric, see A. Lapthorn Smith, "What Civilization Is Doing for the Human Female," *Canada Medical Record* 18, 2 (1889): 28–29.

33 For more on the inclusion of fathers in the delivery room, see Judith Walzer Leavitt, *Make Room for Daddy: The Journey from the Waiting Room to the Birthing Room* (Chapel Hill: University of North Carolina Press, 2009).

34 Saul Kaufman to Grantly Dick-Read, March 22, 1954, Wellcome Library, PP/GDR/D.92.

35 See, for example, Grantly Dick-Read to Joy Rames, July 31, 1951, Wellcome Library, PP/GDR/D.92.

36 Joanna Bourke, *The Story of Pain: From Prayer to Painkillers* (Oxford: Oxford University Press, 2014), 16.

37 Moira Kaufman to Grantly Dick-Read, February 1, 1958, Wellcome Library, PP/GDR/D.96.

38 Hilliard, "Your First Baby," 48.

39 Claudia Malacrida and Tiffany Boulton, "Women's Perceptions of Childbirth 'Choices': Competing Discourses of Motherhood, Sexuality, and Selflessness," *Gender and Society* 26, 5 (2012): 758.

40 Karen Birch to Grantly Dick-Read, October 12, 1948, Wellcome Library, PP/GDR/D.90.
41 Lorraine Blair to Grantly Dick-Read, November 28, 1950, Wellcome Library, PP/GDR/D.90.
42 Mrs. John Strong to Grantly Dick-Read, October 25, 1951, Wellcome Library, PP/GDR/D.93.
43 Kathleen Williams to Grantly Dick-Read, September 3, 1949, Wellcome Library, PP/GDR/D.93.
44 Karen Birch to Grantly Dick-Read, May 24, 1949, Wellcome Library, PP/GDR/D.90.
45 Harper to Dick-Read, October 25, 1958.
46 Laurel Rice to Grantly Dick-Read, May 24, 1955, Wellcome Library, PP/GDR/D.92.
47 Hattie Jones, for example, closed a letter by commenting, "I know you are very busy, so please don't take the time to answer this." Hattie Jones to Grantly Dick-Read, January 12, 1951, Wellcome Library, PP/GDR/D.190.
48 For more on these harmful practices, see Whitney Wood, "'Put Right Under': Obstetric Violence in Post-war Canada," *Social History of Medicine* 31, 4 (2018): 796–817.
49 The Boston Women's Health Book Collective, *Our Bodies, Ourselves* (New York: Simon and Schuster, 1973). See also Wendy Kline, "'Please Include This in Your Book': Readers Respond to *Our Bodies, Ourselves*," *Bulletin for the History of Medicine* 79 (2005): 81–110.
50 Hilliard, "Your First Baby," 46.
51 June Callwood, "The Modern Day Cult of Childbirth," *Chatelaine*, March 1964, 21, 42, 46, 48.
52 Quoted in Callwood, "The Modern Day Cult of Childbirth."
53 Cheryl Krasnick Warsh, *Prescribed Norms: Women and Health in Canada and the United States since 1800* (Toronto: University of Toronto Press, 2010), 148.
54 As Cheryl Krasnick Warsh shows in this volume (Chap. 2), these anxieties took on new meaning in the face of shifting environmental and nuclear threats, including, in the early 1960s, the thalidomide crisis. Indigenous women also emphasized the risks of ignoring maternal anguish in the broader struggles for Indigenous sovereignty; see Sarah Nickel in this volume (Chap. 3).
55 Hamilton, "Dr. Grantly Dick Read Answers Your Questions on Natural Childbirth," 27.
56 Dick-Read, *Childbirth without Fear*, 90.
57 Grantly Dick-Read to Karen Birch, November 9, 1948, Wellcome Library, PP/GDR/D.90.
58 Grantly Dick-Read to Eleanor Greenwood, October 5, 1947, Wellcome Library, PP/GDR/D.91.
59 Darlene Bell to Grantly Dick-Read, March 26, 1956, Wellcome Library, PP/GDR/D.90. This disappointment with her childbirth experience was made all the more acute by the birth of a stillborn daughter, and Bell wrote to Dick-Read, "I know this was not a normal case." (Emphasis in original.)
60 Eleanor Greenwood to Grantly Dick-Read, July 2, 1955, Wellcome Library, PP/GDR/D.91.
61 Rice to Dick-Read, May 24, 1955.
62 Elizabeth Walker to Grantly Dick-Read, December 19, 1946, Wellcome Library, PP/GDR/D.93.

63 Birch to Dick-Read, August 30, 1949 (emphasis in original).
64 Maloney, "The Modern-Day Cult of Childbirth," 21.
65 Maloney, "The Modern-Day Cult of Childbirth," 42.
66 Arlie Hochschild, *The Managed Heart: Commercialization of Human Feeling* (Berkeley: University of California Press, 1983), 56–57.
67 Peter N. Stearns, "Shame, and a Challenge for Emotions History," *Emotion Review* 8, 3 (2016): 198.
68 Sara Ahmed, *The Cultural Politics of Emotion*, 2nd ed. (New York: Routledge, 2015), 102–3.
69 Karen Birch to Grantly Dick-Read, October 12, 1948, Wellcome Library, PP/GDR/D.90.
70 "No Anaesthetic for Me, Thanks!," 74.
71 Grabowski to Dick-Read, August 24, 1958.
72 "No Anaesthetic for Me, Thanks!," 74 (capitalization in the original).
73 "No Anaesthetic for Me, Thanks!," 74.
74 Stearns, "Shame, and a Challenge for Emotions History," 203.
75 Rice to Dick-Read, May 24, 1955.
76 Grabowski to Dick-Read, August 24, 1958.
77 With the resurgence of midwifery in Canada, many have called for "a flexible rather than fixed construction of natural birth." See Margaret Macdonald, "Gender Expectations: Natural Bodies and Natural Births in the New Midwifery in Canada," *Medical Anthropology Quarterly* 20, 2 (2006): 235–56.
78 Grabowski to Dick-Read, August 24, 1958.
79 Bell to Dick-Read, March 26, 1956.
80 Elspeth Probyn, *Blush: Faces of Shame* (Minneapolis: University of Minnesota Press, 2005), xvi.
81 Ahmed, *Cultural Politics of Emotion*, 174.
82 Barbara H. Rosenwein, "Worrying about Emotions in History," *American Historical Review* 107, 3 (2002): 842.
83 See Birch to Dick-Read, October 12, 1948.
84 In November 1957, *Ladies' Home Journal*, a popular American women's magazine with wide Canadian readership, published a letter written by a registered nurse in Chicago detailing, at length, the "tortures" that women faced in hospital birth. In response, the magazine received hundreds of similar complaints from other women. Gladys Denny Shultz, "*Journal* Mothers Report on Cruelty in Maternity Wards," *Ladies' Home Journal*, May 1958, 44.
85 Laurel Rice to O.M., June 9, 1955, Wellcome Library, PP/GDR/D.92.
86 Sandelowski, *Pain, Pleasure, and American Childbirth*, 136.

2

The Good Mother of Science
Emotional Letters to Frances Oldham Kelsey during the Thalidomide Crisis

CHERYL KRASNICK WARSH

In the late 1960s and 1970s, as other authors in this collection have shown, the impetus for much feminist public activism included political crises such as the Vietnam War and personalized injustices such as the lack of reproductive rights – specifically access to safe abortions and pain-free childbirth. In Chapter 1, Whitney Wood recounts the efforts of Canadian women, fearful of the pain of childbirth, to access natural childbirth alternatives in the heyday of obstetric medicalization. Deeply personal imperatives also informed the creation of Indigenous women's organizations, like those described by Sarah Nickel in Chapter 3. Nickel notes the expression of pain, despair, and outrage of Indigenous women as they strove to protect their children from starvation and forced adoption in non-Indigenous homes during the notorious Sixties Scoop. The political and personal circumstances led to emotional responses, which many women catalyzed into organized activism, such as the Voice of Women's invocation of first-wave feminism's maternalist discourse conflating the suffering of Vietnamese children under fire with the suffering of all children, including their own. The campaign for access to safe abortions was, by the summer-long protest of the Abortion Caravan in 1970, framed by the emotional desire of young women to retain control of their reproductive choices. Yet what should not be lost to collective memory is the fact that abortion rights, and the maternalist thread in second-wave feminism, were haunted by the ghost of thalidomide.

That expectant mothers in the first years of the 1960s, wanting no more than to protect and nurture their unborn children, should be prescribed tablets that could have – literally – "monstrous" consequences,[1] produced a groundswell of fear, revulsion, and indignation, emotions that have a direct link to the landmark *Roe v Wade* decision in the United States and the liberalization of abortion laws in Canada.[2] This emotional groundswell was apparent in many of the thousands of heartfelt, outraged, and grateful letters received by Dr. Frances Oldham Kelsey, a Canadian-born pharmacologist, physician, and head of the New Drug Investigation Branch of the American Food and Drug Administration (FDA), who became internationally famous in the 1960s for her efforts to keep thalidomide out of the United States and to keep mothers' unborn babies safe throughout the world.

Thalidomide epitomized Bad Science in 1962. Along with the ongoing existential threat of nuclear proliferation, radioactive fallout from atomic bomb tests, and the publication of excerpts of Rachel Carson's *Silent Spring* in the *New Yorker* describing the toxicity of chemical pesticides in drinking water, the little pink tranquilizer from a West German pharmaceutical company confirmed, for many Americans, that unchecked, unregulated science was a menace to their families, as well as to the planet itself.[3] The nuclear threat was not overcome, nor was global environmental poisoning eradicated. Yet the fight against thalidomide had a heroine, whom her employer (FDA), the American government, and an international public were quick to identify as an exemplar of Good Science.

Thalidomide was developed by pharmaceutical company Chemie Grünenthal in 1953 and introduced to the West German market in 1957 as a sleeping pill, becoming very popular for both adults and children. It apparently was so innocuous, it was sold without a prescription. Thalidomide also prevented nausea in pregnancy, so many women with severe morning sickness took the drug. On September 12, 1960, thalidomide's American distributor, William S. Merrell Company, applied to the FDA to approve the drug (called Kevadon) for the US market. Because Merrell included glowing reports about Kevadon's use in Europe, it was considered to be a routine New Drug Application, and the FDA assigned the file to its newest medical officer, Dr. Frances Oldham Kelsey.

Frances Oldham Kelsey

Frances Oldham, born on July 24, 1914, in Cobble Hill, a village in the picturesque Cowichan Valley, on Vancouver Island, was from a privileged background. Her father, like many other gentleman-farmers in the vicinity, was a pensioned British Naval officer, and her mother's family were wealthy, well-educated Scottish gentry. Frances, or "Frankie,"[4] enrolled at age fifteen in the science program at Victoria College (now University of Victoria), then a feeder school for McGill University, before moving on to the Montreal campus, where she majored in human biology. McGill was not a particularly hospitable environment for coeds, especially in the sciences, in the 1930s. It had been only in 1922 that the first five women graduated from its Faculty of Medicine.[5]

Frances followed the very fortuitous advice of a fellow student and enrolled in pharmacology as "an afterthought."[6] Her pharmacological research on the pancreas was part of a significant specialty at McGill. In 1928, James Bertram Collip, a member of the team, with Frederick Banting and Charles Best, that had isolated insulin, was appointed as the chair of biochemistry. He would build a dynamic department focusing on endocrinology, and he established the undergraduate program in biochemistry in which Frances would enroll.[7]

When Frances graduated with a bachelor's degree in biochemistry, she already was a member of a very small group of Canadian women. From 1927 to 1941, female graduates with Bachelor of Science degrees from Canadian universities averaged 13.5 percent of total graduates. Between 1931 and 1936 (Frances completed her degree in 1934), she joined 204 other women, or 13.3 percent of total graduates.[8] Armed with her diploma, Frances hoped for employment in a laboratory, but it was the depth of the Great Depression, and what few jobs were available were filled by men. Frances understood the "general explanation was that men would be the supporters of the family" and she did not think "there was particular grievance at that time that women were overlooked," but she realized it was "graduate studies or the bread line." Dr. Kelsey recalled, somewhat ruefully, that she had not considered graduate school a possibility because "I was a little awed. I thought you had to be really bright and brainy to be a graduate student." After graduating in one year with a master's degree studying the posterior pituitary gland of frogs, Frances found "the same, no work."[9] Now she was part of an even smaller minority – being one of only twenty-three Canadian female graduates between 1931 and 1936 with a Master of Science degree.[10]

Frances kept working in the university laboratory and applied to a number of doctoral programs, her first choice being Dalhousie University. Eventually she was accepted into the doctoral program in the new pharmacology department at the University of Chicago. Her acceptance letter was addressed to Mr. Frances Oldham, and she asked her adviser if she should correct the mistaken assumption that she was a man. Her adviser said she should do so – after she accepted the seat in the program. At the University of Chicago's Department of Pharmacology, she met two men who would shape her life. The first was her thesis adviser and mentor, Dr. E.M.K. Geiling. He had not wanted to work with a female student since a previous candidate had left to get married. Such occurrences fed the common view that marriage and motherhood "could not be meshed with demanding scientific careers." Throughout most of the twentieth century, among scientists and family members alike, "the notion that women could simultaneously be traditional wives, traditional mothers, and productive scientists seemed patently absurd."[11] Geiling soon developed a healthy respect for Frances's work ethic and expertise, and the two would be collaborators and close friends until his death in 1971.

Frances was awarded her doctorate in 1938, but the glass ceiling remained strong in the United States and Canada. In letters to Geiling and friends, she revealed her frustration and despondency when she found herself passed over for permanent appointments while her male colleagues found positions. Frances remained a research fellow in Geiling's lab through the Second World War, but in her private life there was cause for happiness and joy. A wartime addition to the lab was pharmacologist Fremont Ellis Kelsey, whom she married in 1943. In this stage of her life, Frances again "violated prevailing family norms" by continuing to work after marrying and starting a family, a scenario that was "nearly invisible in American science."[12] This was evident in the 1940s, when they were informed that the University of Chicago would not employ a married couple. Frances and Ellis flipped a coin, and as she recalled, "I lost." She entered the medical school, from which she graduated in 1950.

At this point, Ellis's career eclipsed his wife's. Women in science, even to the present day, can find themselves sliding easily, albeit reluctantly, into subordinate status should they collaborate with their husbands.[13] Ellis took up a position at the University of South Dakota, in Vermillion, and Frances worked as an editorial assistant for the *Journal of the American Medical Association*, vetting submissions and developing a deep knowledge of new medical literature. However, she was anything but a stereotypical 1950s faculty wife, as some neighbours commented. She travelled the rural state as a locum practitioner and commuted to Chicago to be certified as a specialist in nuclear medicine, often being away from home for days or weeks at a time. She taught pharmacology as a sessional lecturer at the university and jointly raised daughters Susan and Christine with Ellis, who took up much of the slack at home. In later years, Dr. Kelsey would express feelings of guilt at her extended absences from her young children, an emotion common to most working mothers. By 1960, Ellis had had enough of administrative interference with the science department's academic freedom and, with several of his colleagues, quit the University of South Dakota. The Kelseys turned to their mentor and collaborator, Dr. Geiling, for help in obtaining new positions. Frances was approached at a conference by an associate who worked at the FDA, but she worried about being the sole breadwinner. Shortly thereafter, to the relief of all, Ellis was hired in Washington at the National Institutes of Health, and Frances was offered a position at that agency as well.

Frances spent the summer holiday of 1960 at the family home in Cobble Hill with her two young daughters, pondering her next move. Eventually she decided to take up the FDA offer. Dr. Kelsey was part of the new wave of highly educated, specialized government employees, and her team at the FDA included other chemists and pharmacologists. One of her first files was a New Drug Application from Merrell concerning a drug that was so widespread in Europe, it was considered a straightforward acceptance.

The Menace of Thalidomide and Government Reaction

Dr. Kelsey's team meticulously vetted Merrell's New Drug Application and found serious deficiencies in the data. She asked for more testing, and representatives of Merrell, which had five tons of Kevadon in American warehouses ready to sell, were anxious to have the drug passed. While delaying the approval, Dr. Kelsey undertook a literature review and learned of serious side effects experienced by European thalidomide users, and she further delayed a decision. She related some symptoms, such as peripheral nerve damage, to earlier research she had undertaken at the University of Chicago, where quinine was found to be toxic to fetuses. Merrell underplayed or dismissed Dr. Kelsey's concerns, and during the spring and summer of 1961, company representatives "came to Washington, it seemed, in droves." Dr. Kelsey recalled, "They wrote letters and they telephoned – as often as three times a week. They telephoned my superiors and they came to see them too ... Most of the things they called me, you wouldn't print."[14]

In November 1961, Merrell informed Dr. Kelsey that thalidomide was being withdrawn from the German market because of reports of serious congenital abnormalities in children of users; the abnormalities ranged from brain damage to heart problems. The most horrific consequences were children born without arms and legs, with their hands and feet growing directly from their torsos. Many more were stillborn. An estimated eight thousand to eighty thousand "thalidomide babies" were born in Europe, the discrepancy in numbers due to internal defects which could not be traced to ingestion of the drug for purposes of legal liability.

Dr. Helen Taussig, one of America's leading pediatric cardiologists and developer of the "blue baby" operation that repaired congenital heart defects, visited Europe shortly after the first thalidomide cases were reported and shared her findings with Dr. Kelsey at the FDA, confirming what the latter was discovering in international medical reports. Frances Kelsey had great admiration for Helen Taussig and other luminaries of a small but growing network of female surgeons and practitioners, and this likely facilitated her reception of Dr. Taussig's warnings.[15] Dr. Taussig returned the favour the following year, when she delivered speeches warning about the drug and explained how a similar tragedy had been averted in the United States owing to Dr. Kelsey's actions.

Although some reporters understood the magnitude of her findings, there was little national press coverage. At the same time, Tennessee senator Estes Kefauver was trying to revive his bill on drug safety regulations, which would strengthen the powers of the FDA, that was languishing in Congress for lack of interest on the part of both houses and the Kennedy administration. When one of Kefauver's aides read Taussig's speech, he leaked the story to the *Washington Post,* where the editor, recognizing its potential significance, gave it to a scrappy sports reporter, Morton Mintz, to write. Mintz's front-page story, hailing Dr. Kelsey as the stubborn scientist who saved the American public, was instantly picked up by all of the major newspapers and news services. The Kefauver-Harris bill was unanimously passed by both Houses of Congress, and Kennedy jumped on the bandwagon by hastily including Dr. Kelsey in the upcoming ceremony for a President's Award for Distinguished Federal Civilian Service. The snapshot of Dr. Kelsey receiving the medal from President Kennedy also received national, as well as international, coverage and cemented her position as one of the most famous women of 1962. When the Kefauver-Harris amendments to the Food, Drug, and Cosmetic Act were signed later that year, Dr. Kelsey was invited to the signing in appreciation to her actions on the thalidomide file.

The Canadian government's response to this nation's thalidomide crisis was far less heroic. When the thalidomide story broke, and Canadian cases were highlighted, health minister J. Waldo Monteith denied any responsibility for the tragedy and for the babies damaged by the drug, stating that their care would be part of the province's standard health and welfare jurisdiction.

President John F. Kennedy hands a pen to Dr. Frances Kelsey after the signing of the Kefauver-Harris amendments to the Food, Drug, and Cosmetic Act, 1962. (Food and Drug Administration, President Kennedy and Frances O. Kelsey, FDA 172.)

However, as the Toronto *Globe and Mail* asserted in a number of articles and editorials, the approval of new drugs in the Dominion was part of the mandate of the Food and Drug Directorate of the National Department of Health and Welfare. Thalidomide was rubber-stamped on the basis of information provided by its manufacturers, and the federal government's inaction, even after reports emerged of the drug's dangers, directly led to fetal defects. Subsequently an estimated 4 million tablets were sold in Canada.[16] Thalidomide was approved for sale in Canada on April 1, 1961; "Canadian-Born" Dr. Kelsey had rejected the drug in September 1960. According to the *Globe and Mail*, "Her refusal must have been known in Ottawa, and should have sounded a warning note to the Directorate."[17] On December 1, 1961, medical representatives from companies selling thalidomide went to Ottawa to personally warn C.A. Morrell, director of the Food and Drug Directorate, of the danger to pregnant women of the drug. Yet the directorate did not order the drug withdrawn from the market until March 2, 1962. Therefore, the *Globe* concluded, "it is difficult to understand how Mr. Monteith can deny the responsibility which the reading of this record lays upon his department."[18]

Covering their tracks after a blistering attack by New Democratic Party Member of Parliament Stanley Knowles, who argued that the federal government bore full responsibility for babies crippled by the drug thalidomide, spokesmen for the Health Department maintained that "everything was done to protect the public once the danger was realized," and added that Canada was made to look "remiss by the example of the United States, where ... Dr. Frances Kelsey kept thalidomide from the market. 'However,' he said, 'Dr. Kelsey was concerned because of other suspected effects of the drugs, not because of the effect it might have on unborn children.'" This was a misstatement, since the first warning flag for Dr. Kelsey was the symptom of numbness of the extremities, which she related to other drugs she had studied that crossed the placenta and affected the fetus. And, of course, the *Globe and Mail* wondered why Department of Health officials had not recognized the "other suspected effects of the drugs" in the first instance?[19]

The Heroine of Science and Monsters in the Nuclear Age

When the American newspaper stories broke about Dr. Kelsey's actions and she received the Award for Distinguished Civilian Service, she was similarly lauded in Canadian newspapers, all of which emphasized her Canadian heritage and her family's residency in British Columbia.[20] However, in keeping with the customary downgrading of women scientists' credentials, Dr. Kelsey was characterized in the press as a Canadian pharmacist and reviewer for the FDA, rather than as a doctor in pharmacology, a physician, and chief of the FDA's New Drug Investigation Branch.[21]

The scenario in the American press depicting Dr. Kelsey as the mother-protector against a phalanx of male pharmaceutical executives and wagon-circling politicians was even more evident in the Canadian coverage, as government officials scrambled to reduce their liabilities. The photograph of Dr. Kelsey, with her white gloves and large handbag and wearing a "blue dress, blue pumps, and blue beret-type hat" as recorded for the news wire agencies, receiving her medal from President Kennedy[22] contrasts sharply with the photograph of six Canadian male health ministers posing with papers to look dutifully intelligent and knowledgeable for the National Conference on Thalidomide Babies, which was hastily organized for August 17, 1962.[23]

Frances Kelsey's limelight has been described as "perhaps the most intensive and positive experienced by any female federal official in the history of the United States ... To the mass public, Kelsey appeared as a cerebral and maternal protector of sorts – quiet, unassuming, brilliant but circumspect."[24]

By December 1962, the Gallup Poll named her one of the ten "Most Admired Women of the World," behind "Jacqueline Kennedy and Queen Elizabeth II but ahead of Patricia Nixon, Princess Grace of Monaco, Lady Bird Johnson, Helen Hayes and Bette Davis."[25] Daniel Carpenter has speculated whether the public reception would have been the same if another scientist, that is, a male one, had been profiled as the gatekeeper against thalidomide in America. I would argue that it would not have been as intense or as lasting, and that this was due to Cold War fears and realities. After the two atomic bomb blasts in Japan that ended the Second World War, peacetime did not long herald the end of global hostilities. The Soviet Union, which continued to occupy East Germany and those countries in Eastern Europe that it had liberated from the Nazis, soon obtained nuclear secrets and exploded their own test bombs. This ushered in the Cold War and, in the 1950s in particular, a period of paranoia and existential fear in North America and other parts of the world. Furthermore, as reports of horrific birth defects in children of survivors of the Hiroshima and Nagasaki atomic bombings in Japan emerged, the dangers of nuclear radiation became common currency in the world press. According to polls conducted in several Western nations since the 1950s, fear of the dangers from nuclear energy is far greater among women than men "in every country, at every time." This was connected with a tendency "when any technology was mentioned, for women to think in terms of safety and their children."[26] And this was certainly an emotional response. In post-9/11 monographs published in 2006, historians Peter Stearns and Joanna Bourke both "contend that fear is a dominant, if not the predominant emotion of modern days."[27]

Unlike incendiary bombs, tanks, and missiles, nuclear fallout had the power to mutate fetuses and produce serious or fatal birth defects. Unlike radium poisoning, which from the 1920s also was identified as potentially deadly to fetuses through unsafe X-ray practices, radiation poisoning from nuclear fallout could not be avoided.[28] After the 1954 BRAVO American fusion test, scientists warned that the "fine radioactive dust" could cause birth defects in infants born even thousands of miles away.[29] Public consciousness of nuclear radiation was so great that it directly impeded the flow of early information about thalidomide, resulting in potentially hundreds, if not thousands, of preventable victims. Dr. Widukind Lenz, who first identified the association of thalidomide with Germany's epidemic in birth defects, recounted in 1963 that

> there was a widespread feeling among doctors that the lay public should on no account learn about the outbreak of these malfunctions. I witnessed one

> meeting in which the moderator did not open the discussion before being satisfied that nobody from the press was present. This attitude of hushing up was based upon the fear to arouse panic and upon the fatalistic belief that the malformations were due to fall-out from atomic bombs, about which people felt they could not possibly do anything.[30]

German physicians were so fearful of the possibility that birth defects in their country could be a consequence of nuclear fallout that they kept the extent of the epidemic from the public, the government, and their fellow physicians for many months and so hampered the proper investigation of the maladies.

This fear of inciting public panic and also fear for the doctors' own reputations and livelihoods were compounded by popular revulsion towards physical deformities. There was a growing intolerance towards disabled people as fewer of these individuals were present on urban streets. Pre-industrial cities had been crowded with orphans, beggars, the aged, persons living with mental illness, and people who were disabled. The early nineteenth-century reform movements cleared the streets of the uneconomically productive. Orphans were sent to orphanages or reformatories, the aged and mentally ill (then known as the "insane") to nursing home and asylums, beggars to jails or workhouses. Special institutions or schools were built for persons with disabilities, and the scientific revolution in medicine corrected many deformities and prevented others. Yet absence led to intolerance and the emergence of negative eugenics at the turn of the twentieth century, which culminated in Nazi atrocities against those with mental and physical disabilities, and involuntary sterilization legislation in the United States, Canada, and other jurisdictions. Much of this legislation was still in place in the 1960s.[31]

As Laurie Block concluded in her evocative analysis of popular reactions to the disabled as delineated in didactic and fictional literature, parents could expect their children challenged by disabilities to be confronted by pity, fear, and revulsion.[32] The disabled body has been characterized as an "alien condition" in our "present collective cultural consciousness."[33] Even the medical subspecialty dealing with congenital abnormalities is termed teratology, or the study of monsters. Therefore, the revelation of a chemical production of "monsters" evoked intense emotions, particularly from women, across nations.

The thalidomide story was published in national and local newspapers across North America and elsewhere in the world. National magazine coverage in the *National Enquirer* and *Life* in 1962 brought home the physical and emotional costs of bearing and raising infants with serious deformities.[34] *Life* also profiled Sherri Chessen, an all-American Arizona mother of four who appeared on Phoenix television as Miss Sherri on *Romper Room*, a children's TV series, and whose husband had brought back tranquilizers for her from England. Chessen was refused an abortion in Arizona, and she eventually went to Sweden to end her pregnancy (the fetus was, indeed, grossly deformed and would not have survived).[35] To further emphasize the tragic circumstances, *Life* photographed Sherri Chessen in an anguished pose.[36]

Letters to the Good Mother of Science

In the days, weeks, and months following the breaking of the thalidomide story by the American press, letters flooded into Dr. Kelsey's home and office at the FDA. Sixty to seventy letters per week, more in the first few weeks, arrived, often addressed simply "Dr. Kelsey, Washington, D.C." Like letters to Santa Claus, mail to Dr. Kelsey required no further elaboration for the US Postal Service. Clearly, Dr. Kelsey's actions struck a chord with American mothers, grandmothers, and potential mothers, who wanted to share their emotions with the Good Mother of Science.[37]

Letter writing, whether fan mail or complaints, has been a traditional vehicle for, or at least an attempt at, interactivity. Whether directed to favourite authors; political, religious, or social leaders; or mass media personalities, fan mail constituted "intense, emotional experiences which reveal an honesty of emotional interaction rarely found in printed documents."[38] Letter writing, for the most part a private activity, provides a fertile venue for expressing emotions which may be, in any particular society or time, deemed inappropriate to express publically. William Reddy coined the term "'emotives' to describe the speech act of expressing feelings, [which] are themselves instruments for directly changing, building, hiding, intensifying emotions, instruments that may be more or less successful." Letters also could be seen as "emotional refuges" and as sites for historians to try to get at "the actual feelings of past generations."[39] For those sending fan mail, beyond establishing a connection with an important person, the letter writer also was "impelled by the notion that his action [was] serving some useful or important end."[40]

The most consistent emotions compelling women to write fan mail to Dr. Kelsey were gratitude (overwhelmingly religiously expressed), fear that pregnancies could result in children with disabilities, and outrage at the prospect of corporate greed endangering infant health. That religion remained a strong force in early 1960s America was reflected in the generous use of religious imagery, prayers, and citations in the letters.[41] Mrs. Donald P.'s letter provides a representative example:

> Dear Doctor: As a young wife and mother I would like to say "Thanks." Thank you for remaining steadfast against pressure to approve Thalidomide. You have saved us much heartache. We cannot repay you, except in our prayers. In this day and age there is a pill for every ache and pain, where many are beneficial, a few may be harmful. We depend on people like you, and you sure came through. God put us all on earth for a reason, you have a head start in fulfilling yours, may He bless all your endeavors. You must have a warm feeling when you are off to bed at night knowing you've helped so many. God bless you.[42]

Mrs. P.F. A. was similarly appreciative: "I thank God for creating you Dr Kelsey. If there were only more like you. May you always be healthy and live long to carry on your life's work."[43] Whether urban or rural, professional or homemaker, Catholic, Protestant, or Jewish, American women blessed Dr. Kelsey for her actions. Such sentiments speak not to a particularly religious time period, but to the very core of religiosity itself, a need to control the uncontrollable and know the unknowable: birth and death.

Childbirth is the most natural of processes, how we survive as a species. Yet childbirth remains, even in the most technologically advanced society, unpredictable and mostly uncontrollable. Modern obstetrics can manage risks; it cannot guarantee a totally risk-free experience. As Whitney Wood examines in Chapter 1 of this book, by the postwar years childbirth had become an experience many women expected to control through natural, drug-free deliveries, and when they could not achieve this, they felt cheated and disappointed and that they had failed in their fundamentally womanly act. Yet it was only during the 1940s, just two decades before the thalidomide tragedy, that American women could feel somewhat assured that they would survive childbirth, and infant mortality rates were falling into a more comfortable zone. But losses of mothers, losses of babies, and babies born with defects, all of these tragedies were uncomfortably well known to this generation.

And that was in relatively normal circumstances. Poverty, warfare, heredity – all were recognized as threats to childbirth, but accustomed, localized, knowable threats. But then add nuclear fallout and pharmaceutical poisoning; these were not threats, these were abominations, global in nature, unforeseeable, unavoidable to mothers who wanted nothing more than to protect and nurture their unborn children. For these mothers and fathers and grandparents, only religious blessings adequately expressed their gratitude to Dr. Kelsey.

Mrs. Pat A. remembered Dr. Kelsey and her family in her prayers, as she had "four children, one girl and three boys. My youngest was born a year ago. I had trouble the first three months while carrying him. I feel sure I might have taken this drug if it had been on the market. He is a lovely baby. Everyone thinks he looks like the Gerber baby."[44] Mrs. Miriam D. wrote that she had

> been trying to decide for some time exactly what to say when I write you. After all your honours, "thank you" doesn't seem like much. We have a little boy, eight months old, who's almost the fattest, healthiest baby you could possibly imagine. I took no sleeping pills – no Thalidomide – but who can say a sample of this drug might not have been given to me. What I'm trying to tell you is that we constantly thank God our baby was born normal. Now we want to thank you too![45]

Mrs. Oscar H. F. offered a "note of thanks to you from me, the mother of six healthy children. Though these six are all I personally will have, it is good to know there is someone safeguarding the future births of babies to my children and others."[46]

Other mothers had more than a hypothetical risk, Mrs. Raymond H., for example,

> an expectant mother whose child is due in two weeks. May I express sincere thanks that you prevented the sale of Thalidomide. It so happens that the only time during my pregnancy that I took sleeping pills was the first two months of pregnancy, and thank heaven Thalidomide was not available. It is wonderful to know that we have people such as you working for the FDA.[47]

Mrs. Lou Ellen D. found it

> difficult to express the deep and very personal sense of gratitude I feel towards you. I'm pregnant – and tried many different kinds of pills for severe nausea during the early months. Since Thalidomide was supposed to help nausea, I can't help but wonder whether I would have taken some if it

> had been available to the American market. To all of the international recognition which you have received for your integrity and courage, please add the overwhelming appreciation of one rather insignificant mother-to-be.[48]

Mrs. Ronald P. considered it

> almost an Act of God since I understand that you have only recently held your office. [It is a note] of personal thanks ... because we have a lovely seven and a half month old daughter, she's kind of special because we had three sons first, but adding her present age to the nine months prior to that, while I was pregnant, ... I could very well have been one of those poor mothers and she one of the victims, of the drug Thalidomide. I can't help but think, "There but for the Grace of God, go I."[49]

Other writers in this Cold War era saw more worldly protagonists in the thalidomide drama. Grandmother Mrs. Anna W. and family were "so worried" during her daughter's sixth pregnancy, during the time that

> terrible drug was in circulation ... We tried to assure her that her doctor knows what he was doing, but there were times we didn't know. It was born May 26th. A Baby girl. You can imagine had that baby been born without limbs. 5 boys perfect and a girl with deformed limbs ... It looks like some enemy is out to disable the future generation[.] What would the future generation be without limbs?[50]

Many letter writers identified Dr. Kelsey as the woman's champion, a figure of nobility, and they displayed feminist feelings which percolated under the apparent domestic harmony of the Cold War era. Cultural historian Clarence Karr has argued that letter writers to early twentieth-century Canadian novelists (including Ralph Connor, Lucy Maud Montgomery, and Nellie McClung) lived in a "transitional age [in which] the noble, elevated sentiments of the neo-classical age continued to inform their minds, their emotions, and their spirits. They cherished the values of sacrifice, devotion, order, truth and beauty. Their intense feelings reflected that nobility."[51] Karr did not believe this sensibility, as reflected in fan letters, lasted beyond the 1940s, but these values are evident in letters to Dr. Kelsey, where she is lionized and invested with a variety of heroic qualities.

One such quality was Dr. Kelsey's ethical fortitude, which was portrayed as a "credit for dispassion, neutrality, and objectivity in the pursuit of 'duty.'"[52]

This was a reversal, or perhaps rehabilitation, of the negative stereotype of the unfeeling, male, mad scientist who had wrought nuclear and pharmaceutical destruction. Rose Maria A. called her "a GREAT SAMARITAN – the GOOD SAMARITAN of the twentieth century in OUR MEDICAL profession. You did not take the line of least resistance – wink-turn your head and sign. A 'Lady Doctor'"![53] Mrs. Adeline H. added,

> As one of the million and more of our sex, may I voice my opinion as a woman, mother, and wife, who would certainly like to see some sort of "citation of honour" bestowed upon a Dr Frances Oldham Kelsey, whom I've read of in our newspapers today. "A Woman" who not only stood strong in her convictions towards a deadly drug, but with it prevented millions of more women, especially in these "United States" the "heartbreak and anguish" of perhaps bringing a baby so hopelessly deformed into their home and family. We owe her more than "public thanks" I'm sure you can agree. May God bless Dr Kelsey, and her family from deep in the heart of all womanhood.[54]

Mrs. A. Duncan K. thought Dr. Kelsey should "start off with a ticket [*sic*] tape parade up Broadway and finish by becoming our first lady President."[55] Mrs. Betty D. believed that "what this country of ours needs so badly in these trying times is more women like you in government positions – women of strong character who can oppose these money mad, power mad dictatorial men!"[56]

Mrs. Edith C. wrote to

> thank and compliment you as a person who stands by her beliefs, knowledge, and convictions. We are so very fortunate to have a doctor of your integrity and stability in our administration. Just think of the heartaches and money you have saved the people in this country ... Again, I congratulate you on your holding your own in the business and professional world; for I, who have worked as a widow for eight years, realize the competition and jealousy and resentment one has to contend with and the difficulties one encounters in presenting his [*sic*] beliefs and knowledge to superiors. It is mighty frustrating at times.[57]

Betty Jane P., president of her local Quota Club, joined "with women everywhere to express grateful thanks for a trust well fulfilled. Just as we learned in school days of yesterday's heroines, so will generations to come hear of one woman's unwavering steadfastness to her own principles, and to the trust imposed upon her by profession and government ... You make us proud we are all women!"[58]

Canadians' Emotional Responses to Thalidomide

And what emotions were evoked in Canada concerning thalidomide? While there are no extant letters in the Kelsey Collection from Canadian writers, there were letters sent to health minister Monteith, most of which were from women, and most of which confirmed the "principle of social solidarity" that the nation should support thalidomide families. The emotions evident were intense sympathy and empathy: "Paying taxes for this sort of thing is a privilege" and "Each child is a Canadian child as I am," were two examples. The negative letters, fewer in number, were largely from men: "But I, the taxpayer, did not ask his wife to take the drug (I use no sleeping pills) nor do I, the taxpayer, ask him to sire a child."[59]

There were numerous reports in the *Globe and Mail* that vacillated between criticism of the government's response and conservative support for the patriarchal status quo. The *Globe and Mail* interviewed Bill Morley, of London, Ontario, whose wife, Gail, a registered nurse, had given birth to a healthy son after taking thalidomide for four months during the early stages of pregnancy. Morley commented that his wife was

> near hysteria after another nurse told her the drug could cause deformities. [We] spent sleepless nights. "Our first reaction was fear, and then contempt for those who distribute the drug," Mr. Morley said. "We no longer look at it this way. The drug was given by our doctor in good faith. He has two other patients who have taken the drug thalidomide and both have had healthy babies. In the last few weeks before our baby was born, we began to accept the fact that if the baby was deformed, there was no one we could blame."[60]

This is an interesting contrast to the Chessen case, where abortion was the option taken. In the Morley case, it is traditionally framed as an act of God rather than medical or government negligence. It is, of course, the musings of a father after the crisis had passed and his child was born healthy, and the mother, Gail Morley, was not interviewed.

Along with hysteria, emotions exhibited in Canadian articles on thalidomide included panic, helplessness, and dependency on authority figures. Daniel Case, a twenty-three-year-old father of an infant born armless, legless, with a double hernia, and "mentally deficient," was interviewed in the *Globe and Mail* in July 1962.[61] The nineteen-year-old mother of the infant is nameless, although a picture accompanying the article shows Daniel holding his wife's hand, with the caption "Daniel Case Consoles Wife after Visit to Doctor." They stand face to face, he solemn and she tearful, the strong male rock consoling the inconsolable young mother. He exudes male authority, which he does not possess in this instance outside of his home. In the interview, he described a consultation with William K. Lindsay, a Toronto plastic surgeon, who gave him "more hope than when I went into [the doctor's] office." Case, however, did not elaborate since Lindsay had "criticized him for giving interviews to the press and instructed him not to say any more to reporters." By muzzling the helpless, desperate father of an infant with tragically severe deformities, the physician who held the power of possible (albeit partial) improvement of the child's life was joining politicians, bureaucrats, and other physicians in circling the wagons around any other authority figures who could be held liable for the distribution and prescription of thalidomide in Canada.[62]

Conclusion

This trade in the helplessness of others by figures of authority to maintain the status quo was a situation with which Canadian women in the 1960s were all too familiar. As reactive emotions such as grief and fear evolved into proactive emotions such as anger and resolve, Canadian women, like their sisters in the United States, Britain, and elsewhere in the Western world, worked to take control of their reproductive health. The thalidomide tragedy was a hard lesson that physicians were not infallible, governments were not irreproachable, and pharmaceuticals were not always beneficial. This lesson of the early 1960s helped to spur on women's health reform activities in the later 1960s and 1970s. In 1973, the Boston Women's Health Book Collective published *Our Bodies, Ourselves*, a self-help manual whose many editions were bestsellers in Canada as well as in the United States.[63] Second-wave feminists' sense of outrage and injustice, and their adherents' demands for more self-empowerment in their personal and family health, echoed the maternalist rhetoric of first-wave feminists. That the health of Canadians was indeed a motherhood issue was recognized by prime minister Lester Pearson's appointment of Judy LaMarsh as minister of Health and Welfare in 1963, only the second woman to hold a federal cabinet position, although she was not committed to activist feminism per se. When the peace group Voice of Women linked radioactive fallout to congenital deformities with the symbolic collection of baby teeth, LaMarsh dismissed it as a publicity stunt.[64] Nevertheless, the optics of the all-male conference table determining the fate of thalidomide babies did not play well with the Canadian female voter.

Mere months earlier, however, the gendered descriptions of emotions continued in the Canadian press. Dr. Louis Lasagna, associate professor of pharmacology at Johns Hopkins Medical School, well known to the FDA team, described the public response to the thalidomide tragedy as "frenzied," and he stated that drug regulations needed to be modified "after appropriate deliberations and discussion with clinical investigators and pharmaceutical firms and not as a quick-change act performed in the purple spotlight of hysteric and sensational news headlines."[65] He then engaged in his own sensationalism, opining that if actress Marilyn Monroe, who had committed suicide three weeks earlier, had taken Kevadon tablets instead of barbiturates, she would still be alive. Frenzy and, in particular, hysteria (derived from the Latin *hystericus*, or uterus), were female-gendered emotional descriptors. When these uncontrolled, uncontrollable emotional reactions are facilitated by the greasy wheels of the press (sensationalism), they can interfere, through hasty, "quick-change" political action, with the smooth, unemotional, capitalist-friendly relations between male scientific, professional, bureaucratic, and corporate elites.

Second-wave feminism was based not only in the peace movement, campus culture, and among Betty Friedan's dissatisfied homemakers. Whether from stirrings of sisterhood, personal parturient experiences, or distrust of the impersonal qualities of a bureaucratic corporate North America, the emotions generated by the thalidomide tragedy helped to fuel the nascent women's health and reproductive rights movements and the environmental movement. Dr. Frances Oldham Kelsey, the stubborn, careful scientist, was rewarded with a promotion in 1963 to Chief of the New Investigational Drug Branch of FDA's Division of New Drugs. The consummate bureaucrat, she successfully negotiated herself and her department through a series of Democratic and Republican administrations and FDA restructurings until her retirement in 2005, after forty-five years, at the age of ninety. In those years, as evidenced in the letters, accolades, and public invitations she received, she remained the Good Mother of Science.

Notes

Grateful acknowledgments to John Swann, historian at the Food and Drug Administration; the staff at the Library of Congress; Susan Kelsey Duffield, Christine Kelsey, the late Monica Oldham, Jeremy Oldham, and especially the late Dr. Frances Oldham Kelsey. This research was supported by a SSHRC Connection Grant, an Associated Medical Services research grant, and various grants and other support from Vancouver Island University. Thanks to the following research assistants at Vancouver Island University and in Washington, who have helped sort and manage the thousands of documents from the Kelsey Collection: Angel Cortez, Barb Demers, Michael Hanes, Amy Langford, Ben McTaggart, Diana Pearson, Emily Rowbotham, Persephone Seale, and Jason Weixelbaum.

This chapter is dedicated to the memory of my esteemed colleague, Clarence Karr, who shaped and shepherded the Vancouver Island University Department of History for many years.

1 Teratology, the subspecialty of pharmacology that studies birth defects, is derived from the Greek and translates to the "study of monsters."

2 For more on the politics of the thalidomide tragedy in Canada, see Denyse Baillargeon and Susanne Commend, "A 'Monstrous' Medicine: Public Debates and Media Coverage of the Thalidomide Tragedy in Canada, 1961–1963 [published in French]," *Canadian Bulletin of Medical History/Bulletin canadien d'histoire de la medicine,* 33, 1 (2016): 131–53; Christine Chisholm, "The Curious Case of Thalidomide and the Absent Eugenic Clause in Canada's Amended Abortion Law of 1969," *Canadian Bulletin of Medical History,* 33, 2 (2016): 493–516; Barbara Clow, "An Illness of Nine Months' Duration: Pregnancy and Thalidomide Use in Canada and the United States," in *Women, Health and Nation: Canada and the United States since 1945,* ed. Georgina Feldberg, Molly Ladd-Taylor, Alison Li, and Kathryn McPherson (Montreal/Kingston: McGill-Queen's University Press, 2003), 45–66.

3 Linda Lear, *Rachel Carson: Witness for Nature* (Boston: Houghton Mifflin Harcourt, 2009), 411–12. Thanks to Linda Lear for the reference.

4 A note about names: Frances Oldham Kelsey was Frances Oldham through her doctorate until her marriage, in 1943. While literary convention (read patriarchal literary traditions) is to consistently use one name, to refer to her as "Kelsey" throughout the paper has the effect of erasing her pre-marriage identity. I therefore refer to her as Frances in her earlier years and in personal moments, and Dr. Kelsey for her later years at the FDA. I also refer to her as "Dr. Kelsey" rather than "Kelsey," because it was the name she preferred to use, and it emphasizes the professional accomplishments of a woman in the mid-twentieth century.

5 Joseph Hanaway, *McGill Medicine* (Montreal/Kingston: McGill-Queen's University Press, 1996), 109.

6 Dr. Frances Kelsey, interview with author, Chevy Chase, MD, March 2016.

7 Hanaway, *McGill Medicine*, 145.

8 Paul Axelrod, *Making a Middle Class: Student Life in English Canada during the Thirties* (Montreal/Kingston: McGill-Queen's University Press, 1990), 152.

9 Dr. Frances Kelsey, "Founders Day Speech to St Margaret's School," Victoria, BC, 1987, Susan Kelsey Duffield Private Collection, 10 pp.

10 Axelrod, *Making a Middle Class,* 153. Female graduates with an MSc degree made up 5.9 percent of total MSc graduates.

11 Jonathan Cole and Harriet Zuckerman, "Marriage, Motherhood and Research Performance in Science," in Harriet Zuckerman, Jonathan Cole, and John Bruer, eds., *The Outer Circle: Women in the Scientific Community* (New York: W.W. Norton, 1991), 161.

12 Cole and Zuckerman, "Marriage, Motherhood and Research Performance in Science," 161.

13 Joan Pinner Scott, "Disadvantagement of Women by the Ordinary Processes of Science: The Case of Informal Collaborations," in *Despite the Odds: Essays on Canadian Women and Science,* ed. Marianne G. Ainley (Montreal: Véhicule Press, 1990), 325.

14 J. Mulliken, "A Woman Doctor Who Would Not Be Hurried," *Life,* 53, 1962, 28–9.

15 Frances Kelsey, "An Assembly Talk at the National Cathedral School," January 31, 1967, Susan Kelsey Duffield Private Papers.

16 Chisholm, "Curious Case of Thalidomide," 499.

17 "Credit Canadian-Born MD with Blocking Drug in U.S.," *Globe and Mail,* July 16, 1962, 15.

18 "A Government Responsibility," *Globe and Mail,* July 31, 1962, 6, ProQuest Historical Newspapers. Unless otherwise noted, all newspaper clippings were found in Correspondence files, the Kelsey Collection, Library of Congress, Washington, DC (hereafter, "Kelsey Collection"). Chisolm notes that even after the act was passed, it remained on some pharmacy shelves until May 1962. Chisholm, "Curious Case of Thalidomide," 498–99.

19 Stanley Westall, "Knowles Charges Negligence, Calls Government Responsible," *Globe and Mail,* July 31, 1962, 1.

20 "In the News: Cautious Heroine," *Globe and Mail,* August 2, 1962, 7; "U.S. Gives Medal to Woman MD," *Globe and Mail,* August 8, 1962, 10. The reporting of the medal ceremony included the note that while Dr. Kelsey's two brothers, Stuart Oldham, of Victoria, and John Oldham, of Vancouver, were present at the ceremony, "a sister, Monica, remained at home in Victoria." "U.S. Gives Medal to Woman MD," *Globe and Mail,* 10.

21 See Chisholm, "Curious Case of Thalidomide," 498.

22 "U.S. Gives Medal to Woman MD," 10.

23 "National Conference on Thalidomide Babies," *Globe and Mail,* August 18, 1962, 9.

24 Daniel Carpenter, *Reputation and Power: Organizational Image and Pharmaceutical Regulation at the FDA* (Princeton, NJ: Princeton University Press, 2010), 247.

25 Carpenter, *Reputation and Power,* 248.

26 Spencer R. Weart, *The Rise of Nuclear Fear* (Cambridge, MA: Harvard University Press, 2012), 223.

27 Peter N. Stearns, "Fear and Contemporary History: A Review Essay," *Journal of Social History,* 40, 2 (2006): 477, http://www.jstor.com/stable/4491904. See Peter N. Stearns, *American Fear: The Causes and Consequences of High Anxiety* (New York: Routledge, 2006); Joanna Bourke, *Fear: A Cultural History* (Emeryville, CA: Shoemaker and Hoard, 2006).

28 Weart, *Rise of Nuclear Fear,* 31.

29 Weart, *Rise of Nuclear Fear*, 97.
30 Dr. Widukind Lenz, "Thalidomide Embryopathy in Germany 1960–1961" (paper, 91st annual meeting of the American Public Health Association, Kansas City, Missouri, November 1963), 5–6. Stanley S., of Forest Hills, New York, a viewer of the *Direct Line* TV program, asked Dr. Kelsey, a guest on the show, about the possibility that the malformations were due to "radio-activity." "Comments from the Audience: *Direct Line*," Typescript, Kelsey Collection.
31 Prior to the Second World War, the group of social and scientific initiatives collectively known as the eugenics movement included two streams: positive and negative eugenics. Positive eugenics would be equivalent to our current social safety net, i.e., family allowances, public education, hospital and medicare care, and family planning initiatives to reduce the numbers of indigent, ill, and other non-productive members of society. Negative eugenics, which identified poverty, mental illness, criminality, and addictions with racialized groups, recent immigrants, and the most impoverished members of society, used repressive measures such as sterilization, incarceration, and expulsion from the host nation to lower the numbers of the "undeserving" and "unwanted" classes. For an excellent overview of eugenics in Canada, see Angus McLaren, *Our Own Master Race: Eugenics in Canada, 1885–1945* (Toronto: University of Toronto Press, 2014).
32 Laurie Block, "Cure and the Contempt of Goodwill: Reason and Feeling in Disability Narratives, 1850–1950," in *Healing the World's Children: Interdisciplinary Perspectives on Child Health in the Twentieth Century,* ed. Cynthia Comacchio, Janet Golden, and George Weisz (Montreal/Kingston: McGill-Queen's University Press, 2008): 125–60.
33 Sharon Snyder, Brenda Jo Brueggemann, and Rosemarie Garland, eds., *Disability Studies: Enabling the Humanities* (New York: Modern Language Association of America, 2002), 2.
34 See "Mother Kills Her Tranquilizer Baby!" *National Enquirer*, 36, 49, August 19, 1962, 7; and J. Mulliken, "A Woman Doctor Who Would Not Be Hurried," *Life*, 53, 1962, 28–29.
35 The Finkbine tragedy was referenced in the *Roe v Wade* decision.
36 *Life*, 53, 1962, included a multipage feature on thalidomide.
37 In this study, I examined a sample of 282 letters written by women, most of which arrived from July to September 1962, immediately following the breaking of the story. They came from cities (mostly suburban areas), towns, and villages across thirty-four states, and from the Philippines and the Panama Canal Zone. They were mostly from homemakers of all ages but included a smattering of professional women and club women and crossed religious lines. The letters are housed in the Kelsey Collection at the Library of Congress. Some were written in 1963 and 1964.
38 Clarence Karr, *Authors and Audiences: Popular Canadian Fiction in the Early 20th Century* (Montreal/Kingston: McGill-Queen's University Press, 2000), 154.
39 William Reddy, *The Navigation of Feeling: A Framework for the History of Emotions* (Cambridge: Cambridge University Press, 2001), 105, 128–29.
40 Charlene Simmons, "Dear Radio Broadcaster: Fan Mail as a Form of Perceived Interactivity," *Journal of Broadcasting and Electronic Media*, 53, 3 (2009): 449.

41 This is similar to what Clarence Karr argued in *Authors and Audiences*, where he concluded that citing religious imagery in letters was a nineteenth-century convention; see Chapter 10.
42 Mrs. Donald P., Neptune, NJ, to Dr. Kelsey, August 24, 1962, Kelsey Collection.
43 Mrs. P.F. A., n.p., to Dr. Kelsey, n.d., Kelsey Collection.
44 Mrs. Pat A., n.p., to Dr. Kelsey, August 28, 1962, Kelsey Collection.
45 Mrs. Miriam D., n.p., to Dr. Kelsey, August 13, 1962, Kelsey Collection.
46 Mrs. Oscar H. F., Lawrenceburg, TN, to Dr. Kelsey, July 16, 1962, Kelsey Collection.
47 Mrs. Raymond H., n.p., to Dr. Kelsey, July 15, 1962, Kelsey Collection.
48 Mrs. Lou Ellen D., New York, NY, to Dr. Kelsey, August 3, 1962, Kelsey Collection.
49 Mrs. Ronald P., Mt. Clemens, MI, to Dr. Kelsey, July 20, 1962, Kelsey Collection.
50 Mrs. Anna W., Chicago, IL, to Dr. Kelsey, August 7, 1962.
51 Karr, *Authors and Audiences*, 168.
52 Carpenter, *Reputation and Power*, 249.
53 Rose Maria A., Baltimore, MD, to Dr. Kelsey, October 20, 1962, Kelsey Collection (capitalization in original).
54 Mrs. Adeline H., n.p., to Dr. Kelsey, July 16, 1962, Kelsey Collection.
55 Mrs. A. Duncan K., Montclair, NJ, to Dr. Kelsey, August 5, 1962, Kelsey Collection.
56 Mrs. Betty D., Clermont, FL, to Dr. Kelsey, July 18, 1962, Kelsey Collection.
57 Mrs. Edith C., n.p., to Dr. Kelsey, July 16, 1962, Kelsey Collection (emphasis in original).
58 Betty Jane P., Charlotte, NC, to Dr. Kelsey, August 11, 1962, Kelsey Collection.
59 Cited in Baillargeon and Commend, "A 'Monstrous' Medicine," 138.
60 "Abortion Bid Hinted, despite U.S. Ruling," *Globe and Mail*, July 31, 1962, 4.
61 "Plastic Surgeon Consulted: Parents' Hopes Rise for Child," *Globe and Mail*, July 28, 1962, 5.
62 A week later, Case lost his typewriter servicing job due to, his employer insisted, complaints about his work. "Chatham Job Lost by Father of Drug Baby," *Globe and Mail*, August 2, 1962, 10.
63 Boston Women's Health Book Collective, *Our Bodies, Ourselves* (New York: Simon and Schuster, 1973). The collective continues to be a clearinghouse for global women's health through its website: http://www.ourbodiesourselves.org/default.asp. See Cheryl Krasnick Warsh, *Prescribed Norms: Women and Health in Canada and the United States since 1800* (Toronto: University of Toronto Press, 2010), xiii, for more on the women's health initiatives.
64 Tara Brookfield, *Cold War Comforts: Canadian Women, Child Safety, and Global Insecurity* (Waterloo, ON: Wilfrid Laurier University Press, 2012), 71–72.
65 "Tighter Controls for New Drugs," *Globe and Mail*, September 14, 1962, 7.

3 Therapeutic Political Spaces
Collective Resistance among Indigenous Women in British Columbia

SARAH A. NICKEL

Between the 1960s and 1980s in what is now known as British Columbia, Indigenous women, frustrated with their socioeconomic, legal, and cultural marginalization and determined to improve circumstances for their families and communities, united to form social and political clubs. These formal and informal associations provided safe spaces for women to gather and publicly share their lives with one another, and through this, to develop an awareness that their challenges were not individual but directly linked to their positions as Indigenous women. Over time, these consciousness-raising efforts enabled women to create their own robust Indigenous women's rights movement.[1] Like the consciousness-raising of their peers in the women's movement, which education scholar Megan Boler asserts "provided a language of emotions," Indigenous women's sociopolitical work within their associations had an emotional element to it as women shared their feelings and experiences with colonialism and sexism.[2] Women were then able to mobilize their feelings to build a shared resistance based on what American Indian studies scholar Dian Million labels "felt knowledge" and its "emotional content."[3]

This chapter explores how emotion and affect shaped Indigenous women's political activism in ways that historians of social movements and Indigenous politics have not well acknowledged.[4] While historian Carrie Hamilton's work on the radical Basque nationalist movement from the 1960s to 1980s brings together the history of emotion, feminism, and activist politics, it is one of few studies that does so.[5] Similarly, Indigenous feminist scholars, including those who challenge the prevalence of Indigenous women's domestic narratives and romanticized ideals of gender equality through analyses of labour, activism, and land-based practice, often include references to the emotional aspect of political work but do not analyze these in a sustained or targeted way.[6] Taking cues from feminist scholars and those concerned with the history of emotion, I use Indigenous women's political papers and correspondence in British Columbia to reveal how women used a range of emotion, including love, empathy, grief, and frustration, as a way to share their experiences with each other, improve their lives, drive their political activism, and effect policy changes.[7] These emotions were often used strategically within their organizations, in public legal debates, and across racial, gender, and ideological boundaries, though this was not without personal cost, reminding us that political work is emotional in nature, just as emotions are, in fact, labour. Looking at the role of emotions in Indigenous women's political responses is vital for expanding our understanding of the Indigenous women's movement, as well as the male-dominated Indigenous rights movement, which did not attend to women's political concerns and resisted their political participation.

Early Political Developments

Indigenous women's political activities took place in a number of different arenas. Early associations, like the Indian Homemakers' Clubs, were state-initiated and directed as part of a Canada-wide Department of Indian Affairs' program designed to correct perceived deficiencies in Indigenous homemaking. Originally introduced as an assimilative strategy in Saskatchewan, in 1937, the Indian Homemakers' Clubs (modelled after and initially overseen by settler women's institutes) rapidly expanded across British Columbia and the rest of Canada by the 1950s, necessitating the creation of a national network, the Indian Homemakers' Clubs of Canada.[8] Under the motto, "For Home and Country," which clearly linked nationalism and domesticity as First Nation women's "duties," members took part in sewing, handicraft, and cooking lessons and prenatal information sessions, and they learned about nutrition, disease management, and general health and well-being.[9] In many communities, women also organized community cleanups and landscaping competitions to fill service gaps and instill community pride.[10] While part of a national network, these early clubs were principally concerned with local issues and operated through fundraising and volunteerism.

Outside the Homemakers' network, Indigenous women were equally active. In 1949, Tk'emlúps te Secwépemc member Mildred Gottfriedson, concerned about living conditions for children, the elderly, and people with disabilities in her community of Kamloops, formed the Paul Creek Women's Club to teach "sewing, cooking and other household tasks, First Aid, child care, and [elder care]." Gottfriedson identified needs within her community that a women's group could meet and believed such a club could also "improve the leadership potential for women."[11] Beyond these domestic clubs, women also joined specialty organizations including church auxiliaries, Elders' groups, and associations for arts, culture, and education. Women were often involved in multiple organizations concurrently, demonstrating their diverse interests and strong organizational capacity. Gottfriedson, for example, spearheaded the Paul Creek Women's Club and was a founding member of the British Columbia Native Women's Society. She also created the Paul Creek Tribal Dancers (a dance troupe that performed internationally), and took part in the Interior Cultural Society.[12] Through each of these channels, Gottfriedson promoted Indigenous women's rights, Secwépemc and Interior Salish cultural practices, and Indigenous rights. By the mid-1950s, few communities were untouched by Indigenous women's broad organizational interests, and throughout the 1960s and 1970s, women's networks expanded to include provincial organizations focused on education, employment, health, and legal issues.

Provincial Organizations and Building the Movement

The Indigenous women's movement in British Columbia was held together by shared histories and challenges, many of which validated the dissatisfaction women felt in private and enabled women to support each other. In Dawson Creek, a small but growing Indigenous women's group operated out of the Nawican Friendship Centre that "provide[d] these women with a place to socialize" and discuss their concerns about "providing for their families and getting through the day."[13] In these informal gatherings, women could articulate their hopes and dreams and their emotional harm and trauma. These havens gave them a sense of protection from the constant barrage of overt racism and sexism, as well as indifference, violence, and apathy. Like many of their peers, Indigenous women in British Columbia began to see their struggles not as individual and isolated experiences, but as part of a wider pattern, and they began to explicitly politicize themselves and their clubs in the late 1960s.

Until 1968, the movement in British Columbia was divided across numerous organizations representing the diverse identities and geopolitical spaces across the region. This changed with the nearly simultaneous creation of the provincial British Columbia Indian Homemakers' Association (BCIHA) and the BC Native Women's Society (BCNWS). Designed to unite disparate local clubs to grow the movement, the BCIHA amalgamated existing reserve-based Homemakers' Clubs but reflected a distinctive shift away from Department of Indian Affairs' oversight. In the mid-1960s, many of the local clubs became more politically involved as women saw the futility in their homemaking efforts without accompanying changes to government policy to address structural inequities. In the Fraser Valley, Stó:lō Chehalis club president Rose Charlie explained that the "women started passing resolutions…: we need better education, we need better homes, *we need homes period,* we need sanitation privileges, water system, better education and health services."[14] This was beyond the scope of Indian Affairs' vision for domestic progress, which imagined women's household training and "elbow grease" as sufficient to improve conditions, and the agency withdrew its support, claiming the women were "being too much of a pressure group."[15] Undeterred, the women continued their lobbying by creating an independent, province-wide First Nation women's organization – the BCIHA – which enabled them to pursue policy changes, greater resources for their reserves, and, eventually, limited political influence within the Indigenous rights movement.[16]

The BCNWS, for its part, brought together existing Indigenous women's clubs outside the homemakers' network and interested individuals as a provincial Native women's council.[17] These included the Squamish Women's Club (North Vancouver), Makwalla Native Women's Association (Vancouver), Paul Creek Women's Club (Kamloops), and women's clubs in Chase, Campbell River, Courtenay, Comox, Penticton, Prince George, Fort St. James, Burns Lake, and Terrace.[18] Coordinated by eight Indigenous women from areas surrounding Kamloops and Vancouver, the BCNWS served as a voice for Status and Non-Status women, as well as Métis, urban, and out-of-province Indigenous women not represented by the BCIHA (which was limited to Status, on-reserve women). Its main focus was challenging sexist membership rules within the Indian Act and resisting mass Indigenous child apprehensions taking place, what would become known as the Sixties Scoop.[19] The BCNWS also presented annual merit awards to outstanding Indigenous persons, sponsored the BC Indian Princess Pageant, and established daycare centres, senior citizens' homes, and group homes for students.[20] By the mid-1970s, the BCNWS was a "resource centre providing information, training, and leadership to some seven hundred registered members throughout the province of British Columbia."[21]

As their clubs proliferated, Indigenous women became unofficial community spokespeople. Indigenous women, though capable and willing to act as formal leaders within the principal Indigenous rights organizations, were often excluded. This gendered marginalization was common across women's broad activist experiences, including Black women engaged in Black power movements and white female activists in the New Left.[22] Consciousness-raising activities – whether formal or informal – as well as the creation of new organizations dedicated to women's experiences, provided useful responses to the widespread sexism women faced. Race, then, added another layer challenging women's perceived political capacities and prompted some to practice what Black feminist author Kimberly Springer has termed "interstitial politics" or "politics 'in the cracks.'"[23]

Interstitial politics had to grow within the limited gendered and racialized spaces available and push slowly outward. Indigenous women's voluntary activities were integrated into their busy lives, where they organized meetings, workshops, and conferences while maintaining paid employment outside of the home and/or raising families. Member of Parliament Len Marchand, speaking to Mildred Gottfriedson's political involvement, marvelled at how she "has found time to use her immense organizing ability outside the home [considering her] very heavy domestic load," which included raising twelve biological children and eleven foster children.[24] Of course, Gottfriedson was not alone in managing multiple forms of underappreciated and unpaid labour, which feminist scholars have well documented. Sara Ahmed explains that feminism is "homework" – that it includes work in and around the home – and Indigenous women's feminist work certainly follows this trend.[25] Indigenous women used this homework – this active, emotionally laden, and unpaid labour – to build and maintain organizations that suited their needs, political identities, and capacities. The in-between spaces these women occupied provided powerful support systems for grassroots members, which often translated into strengthening the constituencies of the formal associations, bringing greater awareness for causes like loss of legal status, and providing opportunities for coalition-building outside the Indigenous women's movement – where women used emotions to pursue their political goals.[26]

The Battle for Legal Status

The creation of independent provincial organizations facilitated engagement with non-Indigenous feminists and Indigenous women across Canada, particularly amid the *Lavell* decision (1974). This legal challenge saw Jeannette Lavell and Yvonne Bédard confront Indigenous women's loss of Indian Act status through marriage by appealing to guarantees of gender equality under Canada's Bill of Rights. They noted that while Indigenous men could pass their status on through marriage to their non-Indigenous wives, Indigenous women lost their status upon "marrying out."[27] Strategically working within a settler colonial legal framework that had historically marginalized them, Lavell, Bédard, and their supporters intervened in important, albeit unsuccessful, ways.[28] After a series of hopeful decisions acknowledging that Indigenous women who married non-Indigenous men were treated differently from Indigenous men who married non-Indigenous women, the Supreme Court of Canada ultimately ruled that the Bill of Rights could not override Indian Act legislation. Despite this devastating defeat, the lengthy court process had broadly united Indigenous and non-Indigenous women in common cause.

In response to the Supreme Court decision, the National Action Committee on the Status of Women organized a "National Day of Mourning for the death of the Canadian Bill of Rights" on October 22, 1973.[29] Mobilizing around the concept of grief was a powerful public performance of loss, anguish, and exhaustion. Grief captured the personal and political cost of this decision for Indigenous women in formidable and effective ways, and this was not the first time emotion was intentionally activated to communicate political messages. Indigenous law and literature scholar Cheryl Suzack reveals that Indigenous women during the 1970s used public displays of emotion in arenas (like the courts) where women had little political capital. These emotional demonstrations, she argues, gave a semblance of political control and created awareness for the movement. She gives the example of Nlaka'pamux women Yvelaine Moses and Sharon McIvor strategically and publicly emphasizing their vulnerability and pain after losing their Indian status to work within a system that fundamentally disadvantaged them. Through public presentations of their emotional lived experience, women could use the law as a "critical site of intervention" and facilitate important consciousness-raising efforts.[30] The national day of mourning, in 1973, accomplished similar tasks, bringing collective awareness to Indigenous women experiencing parallel loss and registering opposition to legal processes.

Protests against the Supreme Court's decision in the Jeannette Lavell case. (University of Ottawa Library, Canadian Women Movement Archives Collection, photograph, 10-001-S3-I1368.)

Women were certainly angry and frustrated at the Supreme Court's decision to override universal protections against sexual discrimination in favour of racist and sexist Indian policy, but their calculated use of grief rather than overt anger etched out the boundaries of emotion in ways that legitimized their politics. They were able to perform a type of deliberate and "organized anger" through grief and therefore blurred the lines between emotions that often prompt different responses.[31] The women participated in demonstrations – typically associated with radicalism, which critics often reject as violent and irrational – but by labelling the action a "day of mourning," the women could elicit empathy rather than defensiveness from observers and policy-makers.[32] Further, in using grief to express disappointment and exasperation with the Canadian judicial system, women were also refusing to perform other emotions. This emotional refusal (or withholding certain emotions from outsiders) enabled women to maintain some of the privacy they lost through public battles for status and instead focus on using emotion to build the movement from within. Through the performance of their felt experiences with gender and racial oppression, Indigenous women's emotions fuelled their political work.[33] This confirms women's and gender studies scholar Rosemary Hennessy's assertion that emotional expressions and relationships are critical to collective power and follows historian Joanne McEwan's belief that it is only by paying attention to emotion that we can extend our understandings of women's political manoeuvres and diplomatic strategies.[34] To eliminate emotion from women's political goals would undermine the urgency and meaning of their work.

This is not to say that politicized emotion is always strategic or overt, however. Legal scholar Rachel Flowers reminds us that emotional responses and emotive politics can also be unintentional, and there were certainly instances where Indigenous women in British Columbia simply expressed emotion without considering the political impact it might have.[35] Regardless of purpose and meaning, however, emotions work to drive change and serve as "a technique of self-recognition and resistance," though this is not always linear or predictable.[36]

"Working alongside One Another"

Just as the *Lavell* decision brought Indigenous and non-Indigenous women together, it also prompted conversations within the British Columbia Indigenous women's movement about provincial unity across the two principal women's organizations. In 1973, the BCNWS and BCIHA temporarily joined with the British Columbia Association of Non-Status Indians (BCANSI) in an "Ad Hoc Committee," holding four meetings to discuss the mandate of the committee as well as the feasibility and desirability of uniting under a new association.[37] The women agreed, in principle, with the concept of unity and "working alongside one another," as BCIHA president Rose Charlie put it, but struggled to navigate the touchy subject of inclusivity in terms of legal status.[38] Historical divisions between the BCIHA and BCNWS and within each organization around membership gestured towards irreconcilable differences, with BCNWS and Paul Creek Women's Club president Gottfriedson suggesting that all women influenced by the Indian Act should be included within the committee, and BCNWS member Kitty Maracle insisting that all white women (who had received Indian status through marriage) be excluded.[39] As delegates navigated this difficult terrain, the felt nature of gender and colonial politics was apparent. Issues of status and Indigenous women's struggles were not theoretical problems to be solved, but were based on practical experiences with real-life consequences. The resulting debates mirrored these personal attachments as well as divergences in political ideals.

After attending an executive meeting of the Ad Hoc Committee in early 1974, Makwalla Club president[40] Hattie Ferguson wrote to Kitty Maracle with strong concerns about unity, which Ferguson expressed by weaponizing emotional responses within the movement. She explained,

> I know that [unity] is what you and several other younger women think is a solution to the bickering and cat fighting that goes on among Native women; and I would like to point out to you that it was tried among the male [*sic*] dominated organizations in the B.C. Confederation but it died an ignoble death.[41]

Ferguson and others had watched as the provincial chiefs' organization faltered in its attempts to unite the almost two hundred First Nations in British Columbia, having to decentralize operations by the mid-1970s. She specifically targeted the BCIHA's plan to expand its mandate beyond "little local affairs" as falsely indicative of provincial unity, insisting, "If the Homemakers want to [be] die hard, let them; but I resent them giving the impression that THEY ARE totally representative of the British Columbia Native [*sic*] women."[42]

Disputing the privilege accorded to the BCIHA compared to the other Indigenous women's organizations, while also insisting that uniting as one provincial organization would not address fundamental divisiveness, Ferguson employed stereotypically gendered language to register her disapproval. Referring to debates between the women's organizations as bickering reveals the extent to which "patriarchal reasoning" is deeply internalized by many Indigenous women.[43] Ferguson evaluated personal and political disagreement as evidence of weakness rather than critical debate and negotiation among genuine political stakeholders, and the terms "bickering" and "cat fighting" explicitly gender this assumption.

Coding women's disagreement as bickering implies that women are too emotionally charged and unstable to put forward calm, level-headed discussion. This follows a general pattern of viewing emotions and politics as incompatible – a stance that has long been used to undermine emotionally driven movements including civil rights, radical feminism, and nationalist movements.[44] And the idea that Indigenous women needed to get along and be united undermined the broad intersectionalities across the province. Indigenous women were not a homogenous or harmonious group, but conflict did not undermine their political capabilities. Still, this does not mean Ferguson was antifeminist, but, rather, her Indigenous feminist consciousness produced multiple and conflicting political identities. It also reveals her own political strategizing as she attempted to disrupt the BCIHA's self-imposed privilege using anger, frustration, and resentment to gain more political authority and autonomy for the other organizations she was involved in. Ultimately, a new provincial organization would never materialize, and instead the Ad Hoc Committee coordinated efforts during the *Lavell* case – after which the three participant organizations continued on as previously. But through this, Indigenous women had been brought into political conversation in ways that had previously not been possible, and the growing Indigenous women's movement was met with demands for formal political skills development and training.

Capacity-Building

To meet this need in early 1975, the BCNWS offered three three-day leadership workshops in Prince George, Kamloops, and Campbell River for Indigenous women across the province.[45] Here participants learned about government structure and parliamentary processes, how to chair meetings and engage in public speaking, and how to organize and run a local chapter.[46] One proposed agenda item, "How to effectively inform the leaders (Men) on Band councils and Non-Status locals of needs pertaining to women in that community," was indicative of the state of the Indigenous rights movement at the time, in that the majority of leaders were men, and organizers insisted these men needed to be reminded of women's concerns.[47] The BCNWS noted a general reluctance of male leaders to "take women seriously," and to include them in the macro-political work of the mainstream organizations, explaining this was due to men's "fear of the unknown."[48] That the interests and political involvement of half their membership would be "unknown" to male Indigenous leaders speaks volumes about the political environment Indigenous women were operating within, which grew out of decades of women's legal and political dispossession at the hands of settler agents operating under Euro-Canadian gender norms of separate spheres.[49] Over time, Indigenous women internalized and even reproduced these expectations. In fact, the BCNWS acknowledged some women's reluctance to involve themselves in community and women's issues, noting that "we do not want to push."[50] The BCNWS did, however, want to provide the tools for hesitant women to take up political causes if it suited them, and these leadership workshops represented a significant political turning point in the history of the organization.

Participants – many of who were not yet formally involved in the women's movement – lauded the workshops for highlighting the unique struggles of Indigenous women and providing the tools, confidence, and voice for women to resist. Several participants were surprised by their ability to learn about topics they assumed were too advanced for them.[51] And the ability to express oneself and communicate political opinions was both a common source of pride for conference participants and a concrete political skill. Shirley Barlow noted it would help her in her role as secretary of the Williams Lake Friendship Centre, while Wilma Pattison, from Chase, explained, "[The training] helped me to express who I am, what I am, and who I will be." And Pattison, like many others, viewed this training as key to her political awakening, insisting that "our future will be decided by our action."[52]

For the most part, the workshops challenged gender stereotypes that coded men as political actors and women as politically uninterested, but, at times, they also affirmed conventional gender roles. For example, rather than drawing on the expertise of Indigenous women to teach participants about leadership, workshop organizer and BCNWS president Kitty Maracle enlisted the help of two well-established male political actors to give lectures and workshops – her son Brian Maracle, activist and host of the Canadian Broadcasting Corporation's radio program *Our Native Land* during the 1970s, and Bill Wilson of the United Native Nations.[53] It was not uncommon for some women to internalize and perpetuate beliefs that they had no specialized knowledge and that men held the necessary professional expertise and authority.[54]

Indeed, Maracle struggled to overcome established gender roles or patriarchal reasoning. In addition to leadership training provided by Brian Maracle and Wilson, Kitty Maracle led a session on "good grooming," emphasizing the need for women to dress nicely and maintain their appearances in their capacities as future leaders.[55] This is somewhat surprising considering Kitty Maracle's heavy involvement in the Indigenous women's movement.

Her broad political capacity as an organizer and movement-builder was whittled down to one session on appearance. This inconsistent messaging about women's leadership roles also threaded through delegate feedback. Several participants used maternal language about Kitty Maracle's caring and organizational work in the leadership workshops, describing her as a "nice hostess"[56] who "made sure we all [had] a place to stay for the nights,"[57] while the two men were labelled "instructors" who were "knowledgeable," "intelligent," and "experienced."[58]

It may be that this work can be understood as Indigenous women's "invisible leadership" built on women's supposed traditional support roles as maternal figures who valued care work.[59] Thus, Maracle would simply be acting within her gender appropriate capacity, and training women to equate a nice appearance with political competence supported her emotional labour of caring for and catering to male authority figures. I assert that rather than contradicting Maracle and others' clearly feminist political agenda – visible through their work combatting women's political, social, and economic marginalization – this represents the inherently messy and sometimes politically inconsistent responses to women's complex realities. Maracle could champion women's political leadership, insisting on their broad capacities, *and* simultaneously support (inadvertently or not) patriarchal gender norms, without invalidating her feminism.

Still, while some women's evaluations of the workshops praised the political capabilities of the men and thanked them "for their time in teaching us how to be leaders" and "doing this work for us," others noted the problematic and counterproductive nature of men's leadership at a women's organization.[60] Workshop participant Molly Bonneau, from Vernon, argued, "It seems strange that a women's group should hire *two men* as lecturers. Surely there are a number of capable women who would have done as well."[61] One evaluation even cited Wilson's own conviction that "this is a women's organization and there should be women instructors."[62] The very existence of the workshops confirms that participants recognized the need to develop their own capacity and to take part in training suitable to their experiences as Indigenous women. The male-dominated Indigenous rights movement had consistently proven incompatible with women's needs, as members frequently rebuffed women's efforts to participate in political discussions about land claims, Indigenous rights, and Indigenous sovereignty. These workshop delegates supported drawing on the internal expertise of a number of Indigenous women who were deeply involved in women's political issues and also experienced within Indigenous rights organizations. In this instance it made sense to Maracle, at the very least, to learn from rather than to challenge male authority, but two months later, Maracle and others took a different tactic entirely.

Speaking Out

In May 1975, Mildred Gottfriedson, Kitty Maracle, Rose Charlie, and others publicly challenged a decision made by the provincial chiefs' organization to reject approximately $50 million in federal and provincial funds (including band funding, social assistance, and funding for Indigenous organizations) as an expression of sovereignty.[63] Resisting what they perceived as a masculinist, sovereignty-driven strategy that harmed Indigenous women and children, women's organizations lobbied for continued community access to resources, refused to relinquish their funding, and eventually convinced dozens of reserve communities to do the same.[64]

These women used emotive language – particularly pain and frustration – to appeal the decision and even leveraged government agents against their own leaders. In June 1975, Charlie wrote to minister of Indian Affairs Judd Buchanan, condemning his decision to accept the chiefs' mandate.[65] Charlie "made *desperate pleas* to the Department of Indian Affairs asking that they not be as irresponsible as the Indian leadership," noting that "the Department has a responsibility to keep women and children from starving during the present turmoil."[66] West Coast BCIHA delegate Agnes Dick likewise "urgently request[ed] funding for the less fortunate foster children on our reservation who have been denied proper diets as a result of the recent land claim issue." Dick explained to Buchanan that her Ts'ishaa7ath Chief, Adam Sewish, and band manager, George Watts, denied much-needed foster parent funding and refused to sign food vouchers for the children. Reflecting on this, Dick lamented, "I am very depressed when I see what is happening to our children."[67] In part, women framed their resistance according to the emotional or "felt" impact of lost funding. They positioned themselves and their children as recipients of harm, rather than as autonomous political actors with divergent opinions. They viewed themselves as conscientious sovereign citizens, looking out for the best interests of the community, which helped them strategically sidestep potential accusations that they were trying to overtake men's political roles. Women stressed the practical implications of "stomping on little children and ignoring the anguish of mothers" as a method to achieve Indigenous sovereignty, highlighting the inequalities in the chiefs' vision of sovereignty (which ignored women's exclusion as citizens).[68]

Indigenous women's pain for themselves and others close to them – often felt privately – became a collective experience that women then mobilized as a political tool.[69] Publicly naming pain drew others to experience it, and Indigenous women needed those in charge of politics and policy to understand what this hardship felt like.[70] Robin May Schott suggests the collective articulation of pain in a public forum can be effective in spurring action and, therefore, can be an important political emotion.[71] Here, Indigenous women activated emotion to communicate their experiences (publicizing the emotional impact of political decisions on women's and children's lives) and to appeal to officials' compassion and rationality to incite a response. And the women found some success: they could (and did) evoke empathy from Indian Affairs officials, who ordered investigations into reports of families going hungry and suffering unduly under the chiefs' mandate.[72]

Like the women in Wood's and Warsh's pieces in this collection (Chapters 1 and 2, respectively), the physical and emotional suffering that Indigenous women and children experienced was palpable. Women were reacting not only to the emotional frustration and disappointment of being cast aside in larger structural considerations that failed to account for their needs and recognize their lived expertise, but also to the physical harm that would come to their families and themselves as a result. And of course, for some, this response was ultimately fuelled by the love women had for their families and communities and their need to protect those at all costs.[73] Love and rage were not contradictory emotions here but deeply intertwined.

Women also used emotional language when confronting male leadership about the disastrous funding decision, albeit to a disappointing end. When a small group of women approached West Coast representatives of the chiefs' organization to explain the undue hardship that the lack of funding placed on marginalized community members, the men reacted angrily and told the women to go "scrub floors."[74] Not only were these women denied positions in the Indigenous political realm as stakeholders and interested parties, but they were also reminded – through hostile and reactions – that their rightful place was in the home.[75] Indigenous men's anger also reveals an important double standard within Indigenous politics. Although male Indigenous leaders in British Columbia spoke frequently about the inappropriateness of emotion in politics, reminding their male peers not to "get emotional" in their decision-making, emotions in this context referred to female-coded reactions such as love, pain, and grief, not to male-coded feelings such as anger.[76] In this case, men's emotive responses were seen as acceptable and even useful, while women's were perceived as threatening to the rationality, order, and patriarchy on which the Indigenous rights movement was based.

Indeed, anthropologist Catherine Lutz and historian Danelle van Zyl-Hermann agree that emotions are often associated with privacy and the female-gendered subject and when expressed publicly are seen as irrational, chaotic, subjective, and even threatening.[77] And Megan Boler adds that "emotional rules function to uphold gendered divisions and roles."[78] Indigenous men certainly proved this in their responses to women's political stance. Women were seen as too emotional to be politically effective, since emotion is cast as a lack of critical thought and the inability to remain calm in the face of challenge.[79] This is not unlike the Basque nationalists that Hamilton analyzes, where the political expectations of women were tied to ideals of motherhood. She explains, "Mothers who questioned the political decisions of radical nationalist leaders, or supported children who were considered to be 'traitors,' could themselves become objects of harsh criticism or ostracism."[80] Indigenous women also felt torn between their battle for Indigenous sovereignty and nationalism, and their campaign against gendered oppression, and they experienced a range of oft-contradictory emotions as they navigated this uneven political terrain.[81]

In June 1975, men's criticism of the women intensified and the BCIHA formally requested police presence at its annual general assembly after women reported being afraid to return home over threats of physical violence.[82] Charlie insisted that women were harassed because they represented a risk to the patriarchal empire that male Indigenous leaders had built.[83] But the women refused to back down. At a meeting of the West Coast District Homemakers' Foster Parents group in July, Agnes Dick reported being bullied by younger political men in her community for her public opposition to the provincial chiefs' organization.[84] Rallying around Dick and the other women, members of the BCNWS and BCIHA encouraged them to "speak out their feelings" and use their emotions and roles as Elders to resist criticism.[85] Indigenous women, then, demonstrated how control was essential to their political work and a key part of their emotional code – and this is a keen political strategy and form of resistance. Emotional work is therefore not the antithesis of effective and meaningful political work but the basis of it.

Still, emotionally laden work came at significant personal cost. As Gottfriedson explained, "You neglect your family to help our communities,

[and] it is a thankless job."[86] This is evident in the sacrifices women made to simply participate in a system indifferent at best to their presence but also potentially violent. This holistic political approach, then, was strategic, labour-intensive, emotional, and costly, as well as meaningful and effective.

Conclusion: Demanding Recognition

Systemic barriers to meaningful political participation did not hamper women's determination. In important moments, Indigenous women used emotion as a less threatening source of political power to demand a say in the policies that would affect their lives. Cautiously, women also sought to redefine the parameters of what politics looked like. By the early 1980s, Indigenous women's organizations in BC were ever present in front-line activist work and intervened in decision-making processes. They exposed racism in health services (which caused deaths in remote communities), in racially fuelled child apprehension practices where children were placed in non-Indigenous homes without the consent or involvement of Indigenous communities, in racist curriculum, and in the lack of social assistance and housing for women leaving prison. In each case, Indigenous women in BC offered solutions, including inquests for deaths, Indigenous control over child welfare practices, an education committee to review curriculum, and transition housing for previously incarcerated women.[87]

Further, in addition to holding regular meetings and attending those of other provincial and national women's and male-dominated organizations, representatives from Indigenous women's organizations in BC served on advisory committees and task forces for child welfare, social assistance regulations, family support services, and Indigenous women's rights in the Indian Act and Canadian Constitution. They developed committees on alcohol and drug rehabilitation and outreach for women, and they held workshops on legal issues, employment training for youth and women, and access to education. They also published monthly newsletters and attended a host of training sessions and meetings on sensitivity and self-awareness, understanding service delivery programs, and women's leadership.[88] Indigenous women's organizations were ubiquitous, albeit still marginalized, political forces, pursuing Indigenous women's rights in a wide range of forums. In their multiple and sometimes overlapping capacities as feminists, mothers, and citizens, women used the therapeutic spaces of their organizations to recognize shared experiences and develop collective action.

Notes

Special thanks to Catherine, Lara, and Michael for bringing this collection into being and for their thoughtful comments on my contribution. I am grateful for the workshop many of us participated in at Congress in 2017 and found my own thinking deepened as a result of those and other conversations. The anonymous reviewers provided thoughtful feedback, which greatly strengthened this piece. I am grateful to UBC's editorial team for their sharp eyes and to Eryk Martin for countless conversations about this work. I would like to acknowledge the support of the Social Sciences and Humanities Research Council for its financial support.

1 Consciousness-raising, according to Megan Boler, allowed women to publicly share and examine their emotions, bringing women's experiences out of the private and individualized spheres of their experience to outline systemic gendered oppressions. Megan Boler, *Feeling Power: Emotions and Education* (New York: Routledge, 1999), 114–15.

2 Boler, *Feeling Power*, 114–15.

3 Dian Million, "There Is a River in Me: Theory from Life," in *Theorizing Native Studies*, ed. Audra Simpson and Andrea Smith (Durham, NC: Duke University Press, 2014), 32; Dian Million, "Felt Theory: An Indigenous Feminist Approach to Affect and History," *Wicazo Sa Review* 24, 2 (2009): 58.

4 Rosemary Hennessy, "Open Secrets: The Affective Cultures of Organizing on Mexico's Northern Border," *Feminist Theory* 10, 3 (2009): 309–22. Much of the literature on social movements and emotions tends to come from the field of sociology. See, for example, Jeff Goodwin, James M. Jasper, and Francesca Polletta, eds., *Passionate Politics: Emotions and Social Movements* (Chicago: University of Chicago Press, 2001); Jeff Goodwin and James M. Jasper, *Rethinking Social Movements: Structure, Meaning, and Emotion* (Lanham, MD: Rowman and Littlefield, 2004); and Sarita Srivastava, "Tears, Fears and Careers: Anti-racism and Emotion in Social Movement Organizations," *Canadian Journal of Sociology* 31, 1 (2006): 55–90.

5 Carrie Hamilton, "Moving Feelings: Nationalism, Feminism and the Emotions of Politics," *Oral History* 38, 2 (2010): 85–94.

6 Nathalie Kermoal and Isabel Altamirano-Jimenez, eds., *Living on the Land: Indigenous Women's Understanding of Place* (Edmonton, AB: Athabasca Press, 2016); Mary Jane Logan McCallum, *Indigenous Women, Work, and History, 1940–1980* (Winnipeg: University of Manitoba Press, 2014); Val Napoleon, "Aboriginal Self-Determination: Individual Self and Collective Selves," *Atlantis* 29, 2 (2005): 31–46; Emily Snyder, Val Napoleon, and John Borrows, "Gender and Violence: Drawing on Indigenous Legal Resources," *University of British Columbia Law Review* 48, 2 (2015): 624–54; Carol Williams, ed., *Indigenous Women and Work: From Labor to Activism* (Urbana: University of Illinois Press, 2012).

7 Boler, *Feeling Power*; Hennessy, "Open Secrets: Affective Cultures of Organizing on Mexico's Northern Border"; Robin May Schott, "Pain, Abjection, and Political Emotion," *Passions in Context: International Journal for the History and Theory of Emotions* 2, 1 (2011): 7–34, https://www.passionsincontext.de/uploads/media/02_Schott.pdf; Susan J. Matt and Peter N. Stearns, eds., *Doing Emotions History* (Urbana: University of Illinois Press, 2014); Susan J. Matt, "Current Emotion Research in History:

Or, Doing History from the Inside Out," *Emotion Review* 3, 1 (2011): 117–24; Jan Plamper, "The History of Emotions: An Interview with William Reddy, Barbara Rosenwein, and Peter Stearns," *History and Theory* 49, 2 (2010): 237–65; Barbara H. Rosenwein, "Worrying about Emotions in History," *American Historical Review* 107, 3 (2002): 821–45.

8 Jennifer Milne, "Cultivating Domesticity: The Homemakers' Clubs of Saskatchewan, 1911 to 1961" (master's thesis, University of Saskatchewan, 2004); Sarah Nickel, "Sewing the Threads of Resilience: Twentieth-Century Indian Homemakers' Clubs in Western Canada," in *From Suffragette to Homesteader: Exploring British and Canadian Colonial Histories and Women's Politics through Memoir*, ed. Emily van der Meulen (Halifax: Fernwood, 2018), 157–74.

9 Constitution and Regulations for Indian Homemakers' Clubs, Indian Affairs Branch, Department of Citizenship and Immigration, Ottawa, 1951, Library and Archives Canada (LAC), RG 10, box 1, file 987/24-5, Homemakers' Club – Gen., 1973–1981; Homemakers' Club Bulletin, October 1, 1955, LAC, RG 10, vol. 11481, box 1, file 971/24-5, Homemakers' Club.

10 Resolutions to the Federal Government, 1970, LAC, RG 10, vol. 13462, file 901-24-5-1, Homemakers' Club – Conventions 1969/04-1970/09; John Munro to Kitty Bell Sparrow (IHABC), LAC, RG 10, vol. 4, box 16, file E6417-2254, Homemakers' Association of BC, 1983.

11 Len Marchand, in Application for the Order of Canada Completed by Len Marchand for Mildred Gottfriedson, July 9, 1976, LAC, RG 10-C-IV-7, box 1, file 901-24-1-10 (part 1), BC Native Women's Society, 1971–76.

12 Application for the Order of Canada Completed by Len Marchand for Mildred Gottfriedson, July 9, 1976, LAC; Ad Hoc Committee Meeting, October 16–17, 1974, p. 20–21, University of British Columbia Rare Books and Special Collections (RBSC), Leonard and Kitty Maracle fonds, box 4, file 4-19, Indian Rights for Indian Women – Reports, 1974.

13 Jolene Nickolchuk to Kitty Maracle, December 27, 1975, RBSC, Leonard and Kitty Maracle fonds, box 5, file 5-1, Letters – Incoming to BC Native Women's Society and Native Women's Association of Canada.

14 Rose Charlie, interview with Koni Benson, Chehalis First Nation, Agassiz, BC, June 3, 1998 (emphasis added), Stó:lō Research and Resource Management Centre, Oral History Collection.

15 Charlie, interview with Benson.

16 Sarah Nickel, "'I Am Not a Women's Libber, although Sometimes I Sound Like One': Indigenous Feminism and Politicized Motherhood," *American Indian Quarterly* 41, 4 (2017): 299–334. In part, the formation of the British Columbia Indian Homemakers' Association mirrored efforts within the broader Indigenous community towards political resistance in the 1960s, which saw the rise of provincial and national Indigenous rights organizations, such as the Union of BC Indian Chiefs and the National Indian Brotherhood, and the growth of Red Power ideology and direct action. See Scott Rutherford, "Canada's Other Red Scare: The Anicinabe Park Occupation and Indigenous Decolonization," in *The Hidden 1970s: Histories of Radicalism*, ed. Dan Berger (New Brunswick, NJ: Rutgers University Press, 2010), 77–96; and Bryan Palmer, "'Indians of All Tribes': The Birth of Red Power," in *Debating*

Dissent: Canada and the Sixties, ed. Lara Campbell, Dominique Clément, and Gregory S. Kealey (Toronto: University of Toronto Press, 2012), 193–210. See also: Sarah Nickel, *Assembling Unity: Indigenous Politics, Gender, and the Union of BC Indian Chiefs* (Vancouver: UBC Press, 2019).

17 Under this structure, much like the BCIHA, local clubs continued to act autonomously but also participated in the wider provincial organization.

18 RBSC, Leonard and Kitty Maracle fonds, box 4, file 4-12, BC Native Women's Society – Reports, Memos, 1975.

19 The Sixties Scoop or, as Raven Sinclair terms it, the "Indigenous Child Removal System (ICRS)" refers to the widespread practice by provincial child service workers of removing Indigenous children from their homes and placing them into non-Indigenous homes during the era of residential school decline. Sinclair and others have critiqued the limitations of the term "Sixties Scoop" for failing to address the breadth and longevity of Indigenous child apprehension practices. Raven Sinclair, "Identity Lost and Found: Lessons from the Sixties Scoop," *First Peoples Child and Family Review* 3, 1 (2007): 65–82.

20 Report to the First Citizen's Fund Advisory Committee Presented by the BCNWS, West Vancouver, April 21, 1975, RBSC, Leonard and Kitty Maracle fonds, box 4, file 4-12, BC Native Women's Society – Reports, Memos, 1975; History from the Years 1968 to 1979, LAC, RG 10, box 16, file part 1, E-6417-2255, BC Native Women's Society, 1980/08-1981/02.

21 Report to the First Citizen's Fund Advisory Committee Presented by the BCNWS, West Vancouver, April 21, 1975, RBSC.

22 Jacqueline A. Rouse, "'We Seek to Know ... in Order to Speak the Truth': Nurturing the Seeds of Discontent – Septima P. Clark and Participatory Leadership," in *Sisters in the Struggle: African American Women in the Civil Rights-Black Power Movement*, ed. Bettye Collier-Thomas and V.P. Franklin (New York: New York University Press, 2001), 96–97; Judi Bernstein, Peggy Morton, Linda Seese, and Myrna Wood, *Sisters, Brothers, Lovers ... Listen ...* (Boston: New England Free Press, 1967).

23 As Kimberly Springer argues in her oral history work with Black feminists active between the 1960s and 1980s: Politics in the cracks, or ... 'interstitial politics,' conveyed two meanings for Black feminists and their organizations. First, as activist Linda Burnham noted, Black feminists, not unlike activists in other social movements, fit their activism into their schedules whenever possible, serving as full-time unpaid staff for their organizations. Second, Black feminists developed a collective identity and basis for organizing that reflected the intersecting characteristics that make up black womanhood. Springer, "The Interstitial Politics of Black Feminist Organizations," *Meridians: Feminism, Race, Transnationalism*, 1, 2 (2001): 155–56.

24 Letter from Kitty Maracle to Len Marchand, M.P., December 6, 1973, RBSC, Leonard and Kitty Maracle fonds, box 5, file 5-3, General Correspondence.

25 Sara Ahmed, *Living a Feminist Life* (Durham, NC: Duke University Press, 2017), 7.

26 Ahmed, *Living a Feminist Life*.

27 Kathleen Jamieson, *Indian Women and the Law in Canada: Citizens Minus* (Ottawa: Minister of Supply and Services, 1978), 30.

28 It is important to recognize that Indigenous women were not united in their support for changes to section 12.1.b of the Indian Act, which removed legal status and band

membership upon marriage to non-Indigenous men. Treaty women in Alberta, in particular, voiced concerns about women's status being reinstated, and others across BC and Canada agreed. Advisory Council on the Status of Women, RBSC, Leonard and Kitty Maracle fonds, box 4, file 4-8. Further, while Lavell and Bédard were unsuccessful in this legal challenge, they paved the way for future amendments to the Indian Act, which have incrementally, though not totally, addressed the status issue. For more information on the *Lavell* case, see Kathleen Jamieson, "Sex Discrimination and the Indian Act," in *Arduous Journey: Canadian Indians and Decolonization*, ed. J. Rick Pointing (Toronto: McClelland and Stewart, 1986), 112–36.

29 Indian Homemakers' Association Progress Report, November 1, 1973, LAC, RG 10, box 1, file 987/24-5, Homemakers' Club – Gen, 1973–1981; Minutes of the Meeting of Nat. Indian Rights for Indian Women, held on September 22, 1973, RBSC, Leonard and Kitty Maracle fonds, box 4, file 4-18, Indian Rights for Indian Women – Minutes.

30 Cheryl Suzack, "Emotions before the Law," in *Indigenous Women and Feminism: Politics, Activism, Culture*, ed. Cheryl Suzack, Shari M. Huhndorf, Jeanne Perreault, and Jean Barman (Vancouver: UBC Press, 2010), 128–41.

31 Megan Boler traces the politicization of anger through the civil rights movement and Black Pride into second-wave consciousness-raising and movements combatting violence against women. We can see similarities here in how Indigenous women and their allies used specific emotional expressions. Boler, *Feeling Power*, 113–14.

32 Hamilton, "Moving Feelings: Nationalism, Feminism and the Emotions of Politics."

33 Rachel Flowers, "Refusal to Forgive: Indigenous Women's Love and Rage," *Decolonization, Indigeneity, Education and Society* 4, 2 (2015): 40.

34 Hennessy, "Open Secrets: Affective Cultures of Organizing on Mexico's Northern Border"; Joanne McEwan, "International Women's Day: The History of Emotions and Women's History," Histories of Emotion from Medieval Europe to Contemporary Australia, March 8, 2016, https://historiesofemotion.com/2016/03/08/international-womens-day-the-history-of-emotions-and-womens-history/.

35 Flowers, "Refusal to Forgive: Indigenous Women's Love and Rage," 40.

36 Flowers, "Refusal to Forgive: Indigenous Women's Love and Rage," 40.

37 Second Meeting of Representatives of the BCNWS, BCIHA, and BCANSI – held at the Kent Hotel, Agassiz, June 13–14, 1973, RBSC, Leonard and Kitty Maracle fonds, box 4, file 4-11, BC Native Women's Society – Minutes, 1973–1974.

38 Second Meeting of Representatives of the BCNWS, BCIHA, and BCANSI, 2.

39 Second Meeting of Representatives of the BCNWS, BCIHA, and BCANSI.

40 The Makwalla Club was one of the autonomous local clubs united under the larger BCNWS structure.

41 Hattie Ferguson to Kitty Maracle, February 12, 1974, RBSC, Leonard and Kitty Maracle fonds, box 5, file 5-1, Letters – Incoming to BC Native Women's Society and Native Women's Association of Canada.

42 Ferguson to Maracle, February 12, 1974, RBSC (capitalization in original).

43 Ahmed, *Living a Feminist Life*, 4.

44 Hamilton, "Moving Feelings: Nationalism, Feminism and the Emotions of Politics."

45 Report to the First Citizen's Fund Advisory Committee Presented by the BCNWS, West Vancouver, April 21, 1975, RBSC, Leonard and Kitty Maracle fonds, box 4, file 4-12, BC Native Women's Society – Reports, Memos, 1975.

46 BC Native Women's Society – Leadership Training Program – Notebooks, References, RBSC, Leonard and Kitty Maracle fonds, box 4, file 4-14; BC Native Women's Society Draft Circular, January 10, 1975, RBSC, box 5, file 5-1, Letters – Incoming to BC Native Women's Society and Native Women's Association of Canada.
47 Proposed Agenda, RBSC, Leonard and Kitty Maracle fonds, box 5, file 5-1, Letters – Incoming to BC Native Women's Society and Native Women's Association of Canada.
48 Proposed Agenda, RBSC.
49 State law including the 1876 Act to Amend and Consolidate the Laws Respecting Indians (more commonly referred to as the Indian Act) and its subsequent amendments barred women from running for band leadership positions and imposed increasingly restrictive regulations on Indian Status that considered Indigenous women only in relation to their fathers or husbands, resulting in many losing Status in their own communities or altogether. Canada, An Act for the Gradual Enfranchisement of Indians, the Better Management of Indian Affairs, and to Extend the Provisions of the Act, 1869, 31st Victoria, Chapter 42; Canada, An Act to Amend and Consolidate the Laws Respecting Indians, SC, 1876, c. 18.
50 Proposed Agenda, RBSC.
51 Sally Erickson feedback, March 7–9, 1975, and anonymous feedback, March 9, 1975, RBSC, Leonard and Kitty Maracle fonds, box 4, file 4-13, BC Native Women's Society – Leadership Training Program – Comments, Criticisms, 1975.
52 Wilma Pattison feedback and Shirley Barlow feedback, RBSC, Leonard and Kitty Maracle fonds, box 4, file 4-13, BC Native Women's Society – Leadership Training Program – Comments, Criticisms, 1975.
53 Brian Maracle (Six Nations) worked for several Indigenous organizations in Vancouver during the 1970s. He is the son of Leonard and Kitty Maracle, who were both heavily involved in Indigenous politics in BC. Leonard was the executive director of the BC Association of Non-Status Indians and the public relations director for the Union of BC Indian Chiefs, and he worked for the Native Courtworker program. Bill Wilson is a Kwakwa̱ka̱'wakw lawyer who was instrumental in the Union of BC Indian Chiefs and later worked for the United Native Nations.
54 Whitney Wood, Chapter 1, this volume.
55 Proposed Agenda, RBSC.
56 Cheryl Brooks feedback, RBSC, Leonard and Kitty Maracle fonds, box 4, file 4-13, BC Native Women's Society – Leadership Training Program – Comments, Criticisms, 1975.
57 Delia Shuter feedback, RBSC, Leonard and Kitty Maracle fonds, box 4, file 4-13, BC Native Women's Society – Leadership Training Program – Comments, Criticisms, 1975.
58 Anonymous feedback, Sally Erickson feedback, and Cheryl Brooks feedback, RBSC, Leonard and Kitty Maracle fonds, box 4, file 4-13, BC Native Women's Society – Leadership Training Program – Comments, Criticisms, 1975.
59 Anne Terry Straus and Debra Valentino, "Gender and Community Organization Leadership in the Chicago Indian Community," in *Keeping the Campfires Going: Native Women's Activism in Urban Communities,* ed. Susan Applegate Krouse and Heather Howard (Lincoln: University of Nebraska Press, 2009), 22–33.
60 Anonymous feedback and Jane Manuel, feedback, RBSC.

61 Report from Molly Bonneau, RBSC, Leonard and Kitty Maracle fonds, box 4, file 4-12, BC Native Women's Society – Reports, Memos, 1975 (emphasis in original).
62 M.C. feedback, RBSC, box 4, file 4-13, BC Native Women's Society – Leadership Training Program – Comments, Criticisms, 1975.
63 Release: Bulletin # 3, May 5, 1975, LAC, RG 10, V1994-95/412, box 1, file 987/24-2-12, Union of British Columbia Indian Chiefs, 1972–1981.
64 "Innocent Caught in Cross Fire," *Indian Voice*, June 1975, 13.
65 Rose Charlie, president of the Indian Homemakers' Association, to Judd Buchanan, minister of Indian Affairs, telex, June 30, 1975, LAC, RG 10, box 1, file 901/1-1-1-1, part 1, Office Phaseouts, 5/1975–9/1975; "Tension Mounts in B.C.," *Indian News* 17, 4 (September 1975): 1, 11.
66 "Tension Mounts in B.C.," 11; Rose Charlie to Larry Wight, July 31, 1975 (emphasis added), LAC, RG 10, box 1, file 901/1-1-1-1, part 1, Office Phaseouts, 5/1975–9/1975.
67 Agnes Dick to Judd Buchanan, June 1975, LAC, RG 10, box 1, file 901/1-1-1-1, part 1, Office Phaseouts, 5/1975–9/1975.
68 Agnes Dick to Judd Buchanan, June 1975, LAC, RG 10, box 1, file 901/1-1-1-1, part 1, Office Phaseouts, 5/1975–9/1975. See also Joanne Barker, "Gender, Sovereignty, Rights: Native Women's Activism against Social Inequality and Violence in Canada," *American Quarterly* 60, 2 (2008): 127–61.
69 Schott, "Pain, Abjection, and Political Emotion," 19. See also Sara Ahmed, *The Cultural Politics of Emotion* (Edinburgh: Edinburgh University Press, 2004).
70 Veena Das, cited in Schott, "Pain, Abjection, and Political Emotion," 16.
71 Schott, "Pain, Abjection, and Political Emotion," 16–18.
72 Charlie to Wight, July 31, 1975, LAC; Judd Buchanan to Rose Charlie, telex, July 28, 1975, LAC, RG 10, box 1, file 901/1-1-1-1, part 1, Office Phaseouts, 5/1975–9/1975.
73 Dory Nason, "We Hold Our Hands Up," *Decolonization: Indigeneity, Education, and Society*, February 12, 2013, https://decolonization.wordpress.com/2013/02/12/we-hold-our-hands-up-on-indigenous-womens-love-and-resistance/.
74 "Phillip Given Hell by Homemakers," *Indian Voice*, June 1975, 1, 19; "Phillip Paul: You Can't Undue [*sic*] Life Time of Paternalism in Short Time," *Indian Voice*, June 1975, 1.
75 Dory Nason, "We Hold Our Hands Up"; Flowers, "Refusal to Forgive: Indigenous Women's Love and Rage."
76 Union of BC Indian Chiefs Resource Centre, Minutes of the Union of BC Indian Chiefs General Assembly, Evergreen Hall, Chilliwack, BC, April 25, 1975.
77 Catherine Lutz, cited in Suzack, "Emotions Before the Law," 137; Danelle van Zyl-Hermann, "The Emotional Historian?," Research, University of Cambridge, February 28, 2012, http://www.cam.ac.uk/research/discussion/the-emotional-historian.
78 Boler, *Feeling Power*, xix.
79 Boler, *Feeling Power*, 109.
80 Hamilton, "Moving Feelings: Nationalism, Feminism and the Emotions of Politics," 88.
81 Hamilton, "Moving Feelings: Nationalism, Feminism and the Emotions of Politics," 88.
82 Ron Rose, "Leader of Indian Conference Asks Protection for Delegates," *Vancouver Sun*, June 19, 1975, 1–2; "From the Editor's Chair," *Indian Voice*, June 1975, 4.

83 "Homemaker President Urges Union of All Chiefs," *Indian Voice,* June 1977, 2–3.

84 Rose, "Leader of Indian Conference Asks Protection for Delegates"; Minutes of the Homemakers' Foster Parents Meeting, West Coast District, July 21, 1975, LAC, RG 10, box 1, file 901/1-1-1-1, part 1, Office Phaseouts, 5/1975–9/1975.

85 Minutes of the Homemakers' Foster Parents Meeting, July 21, 1975, LAC.

86 Second Meeting of Representatives of the BCNWS, BCIHA, and BCANSI.

87 Resolutions Passed at the 19th Annual Conference, June 20–24, 1983, LAC, RG 10, box 16, file E6417-2254, Indian Homemakers' Association of B.C., 1983.

88 BC Native Women's Society Proposal for Core Funding for the Fiscal Year 1981–1982, Operations, Kamloops, BC., LAC, RG 10, box 16, file part 1, E-6417-2255, 1994-95/595 GAD, Native Women's Society, 1980/08–1981/02.

4 "Feeling My Way"
Women's Community Activism in the Company of Young Canadians

KEVIN BRUSHETT

In early 1968, *Toronto Telegram* reporter Peter Ward had been following a group of Company of Young Canadians (CYC; Company) volunteers working with residents in the city's Cabbagetown neighbourhood who were facing all kinds of uncertainty due to the city's plans for urban renewal. There he encountered Alice MacNeil, a twenty-year-old native of Truro, Nova Scotia, who had become a CYC volunteer after her mother had shown her an ad in the local paper. Launched in 1965 as part of the Pearson government's War on Poverty, the Company of Young Canadians was widely hailed as Canada's answer to John F. Kennedy's Peace Corps. Like its American counterpart, the CYC intended to put the idealism of young Canadians to work helping communities solve the stubborn social, political, and economic problems that plagued them through the techniques of *animation sociale* and community development.[1] For Alice, as for many other young Canadian men and women of her generation, the prospect of serving her country through service to the disempowered appeared "rewarding, worthwhile and exciting." Though unsure of her abilities to help the poor and dispossessed of one of Toronto's inner city neighbourhoods, Alice claimed that she was "feeling my way, but learning all the time."[2]

Despite the fact that Alice did not remain with the Company for very long – the Don project closed down and its volunteers transferred to other Toronto area projects within the year – Alice's experience both as a CYC volunteer and as a young woman involved in the social politics of the time was in many ways representative of larger themes of the period. As many histories of second-wave feminism have pointed out, membership in New Left and other social justice movements provided fertile political experiences for young women.[3] The CYC experience was no different. That said, few women volunteers, staff, or governing council members joined the Company with an explicit political agenda, let alone a feminist one. Many signed on for the same reason men did – they wanted to "do something" with their lives and they were influenced by the ethic of service and social justice that permeated the decade's politics. They spoke of following the civil rights movement or of being incensed by the injustice of Canada's own treatment of Indigenous peoples. Others latched onto the service idea of the Peace Corps or its Canadian equivalent, Canadian University Service Overseas. Barbara Hall, one of the original CYC recruits and later mayor of Toronto and commissioner of the Ontario Human Rights Commission, expressed the idea that the Company represented "a sense of movement ... importance and possibility." It was all "very seductive, and ... I really felt, that this was important work."[4] In this sense, the experiences of women in the Company informed their later politics and social activism, not because of the treatment they received as female volunteers – most of them grudgingly acknowledged their subordinate status as a "fact of life at the time" – but because of their experiences as social animators and community organizers.[5]

This chapter seeks not only to reassess the origins of second-wave feminism within the Canadian New Left, but also to more meaningfully examine the experiences of female CYC volunteers through the lenses of affect theory and the history of emotions to help us understand the link between women's thoughts, feelings, and emotions and their political and social activism.[6] In short, understanding what motivated women to undertake their service to the Company, as well as how they felt about their work as volunteers, will help us better understand how "the personal became political." As many histories of second-wave feminism have noted, emotions were at the very core of feminist pedagogy and practice. Indeed, consciousness-raising was not only about sharing one's personal experiences, but also, perhaps more importantly, about the emotions it evoked. Emotions became important building blocks of women's self-knowledge, as well as critical knowledge and understanding of the world around them that they hoped to change.[7]

Of course, as many affect theorists note, accessing exactly what those feelings and emotions really were is fraught with danger since a good deal of what people feel is not only beyond their consciousness, but is also often involuntarily expressed in socially and culturally acceptable ways according to dominant "emotional regimes" that exist across both time and space.[8] The task of accessing and making sense of those feelings remains even more difficult when the historical record is sparse. Although women consistently comprised more than a third of all CYC volunteers, occupied important field staff positions, and were likely responsible for the actual production of much of the archival record of the Company's activities (e.g., typing, recording minutes), those records speak almost exclusively in a male-dominated voice.[9] Access to CYC women volunteers' thoughts and feelings relies heavily on a careful parsing of the scarce documentary record, as well as on oral histories that rely on memories coloured and shaped not only by years of intervening life events, but also by the feelings these events evoked at various points along the way.[10]

Nonetheless, an examination of women's experiences in the Company of Young Canadians through the lenses of affect theory and the history of emotions allows us to foreground some of the key themes in the prefigurative feminist politics of the late 1960s and early 1970s.[11] Though few women entered, or perhaps even left, the CYC with explicitly feminist politics or agendas, the work they conducted as volunteer community organizers/social animators provided them with important knowledge and understanding of the problems they faced as women, as well as the means by which they could tackle them. As much as young women of the period were drawn into the excitement of the era, they were both scared and doubtful of their own abilities. While many entered the Company's service with great enthusiasm, they soon discovered the difficult emotional struggles that would accompany their work as social animators and community development workers. While some thrived on these challenges, others left the Company emotionally isolated, frustrated, and spiritually unfulfilled by their work as volunteers. But whether their work in helping their community organizations succeeded or not, their work with the Company was the early test of their physical courage and, perhaps most importantly, their mental and emotional endurance.[12]

CYC [Wo]Man?

Though one would hardly know it from most histories or even media coverage of the Company, women volunteers such as Alice McNeil and Barbara Hall were not the exception to the rule.[13] Between 1966, when the first volunteers arrived at St. Francis Xavier University's Crystal Cliffs training centre in Antigonish, Nova Scotia, and 1976, when Pierre Trudeau's government disbanded the Company, women represented between 30 and 50 percent of all CYC applicants and volunteers.[14] The invisibility of women's role in the Company was undoubtedly due in part to the fact that the leadership of the Company was overwhelmingly male, not just in numbers but also in attitude (as was made clear in some of the interviews I conducted with them). Like other New Left formations of the period, the CYC placed a premium on highly gendered forms of intellectualism – thinking, strategizing, and articulating, rather than sensing, connecting, and, at times quite ironically, organizing.[15] Until the appointment of former volunteer Maeve Hancey, in 1968, as executive assistant to the CYC's executive director, Claude Vidal, there were virtually no women at CYC headquarters in Ottawa, at least not in positions of leadership. Along with legal adviser Manon Venat, she was the only woman who occupied a significant position in the Company's governance structure until the arrival of Sharon Cunningham, as communications director, in 1970. That said, many women held key positions at the field level as staff or regional directors. These included Elaine Krause (later Husband) in Calgary; Marilyn Assheton-Smith, in the Northwest Territories; Nora Curry, in British Columbia; Clara Chicoine, in Montreal; and Judi Bernstein, in Toronto. By the 1970s, the Company began to recruit women in Indigenous communities who also became field supervisors, including Thelma Chalifoux (now Senator Chalifoux), who supervised CYC projects in the Métis communities of northern Alberta, and Ernestine Trudeau, from the Anishinaabe community near Sault Ste. Marie, Ontario. Many other women were hired as consultants or contractors, including Heather Sim, Joan Newman (later Kuyek), Joy Woolfrey, Myrna Wood, and Jeannette Corbière (later Lavell).

Some women became volunteers along with their spouses. In many instances, it is difficult to tell whether spouses (husbands or wives) were hired to maximize the monthly stipends paid to volunteers or because of their unique skill sets. In some cases though, it is clear that women's volunteer status was a means of extending financial support to their male partners.[16] For instance, Joan Jones, the spouse of Rocky Burnley Jones, became a CYC volunteer while her husband did not. Though Rocky had been involved with the initial discussions over the CYC's mandate, he believed the "revolution could not be won on the government's dime" and therefore he could not "in good conscience accept its money."[17] However, within a year, Rocky's project for African Canadian youth in Halifax – Kwacha House – was desperate for support. Though Rocky was himself unwilling to become part of the CYC, it was clear that his wife, Joan, could – and thus Kwacha House benefited from two years of Joan's volunteer stipend and access to CYC volunteers and other resources.[18]

There was also Alona Ericson, a young nurse who became a volunteer out of Antigonish and went to work at the Selkirk Mental Hospital project in Manitoba. However, when that project folded, she moved to the Slave Lake project, in northern Alberta, along with her new husband, Albert Burger, a fellow Antigonish trainee. Ericson's arrival marked a significant change in the fortunes of the Slave Lake project. In early 1967, Burger and fellow volunteer Jeremy Ashton had been run out of the northern Alberta project by the settler community for siding with the town's Métis community. After the Company and the community agreed on a temporary cooling off period, Burger returned with Ericson to Slave Lake and both became long-time members and activists within the community. According to Company records, Ericson's presence soothed the fears of local residents as it made her husband look more stable and reliable, which was particularly important for gaining the confidence of the Métis and First Nation communities, since they were wary of unmarried young men. Indeed, according to reports, Ericson became a "kind of mother to many children and teens in the community," and women and kids were once again constantly coming and going from the Burgers' residence but now without constant rumours and innuendo of impropriety. Further, she also brought "practical skills" to the project as a nurse.[19] Equally important, such partnerships afforded volunteers a supportive "emotional community" that the Company itself too often failed to provide during its lifespan.[20]

Nonetheless, the public face of the CYC was overwhelmingly male. "CYC Man" was "young, hip and radical," which in the context of the late 1960s meant more often than not the bearded beatnik represented by volunteer David DePoe. DePoe, whose exploits in organizing Yorkville residents to close the inner city Toronto neighbourhood to traffic in the summer of 1967 are well documented in the National Film Board production *Flowers on a One-Way Street*, became the face of the Company a year earlier by leading an antiwar demonstration outside the United States consulate in Toronto along with fellow bearded volunteer Lynn Curtis.[21] On the one hand, the confrontational politics represented by DePoe and Curtis came to be seen by some in the Company as the ideal or prototypical CYC volunteer "hard-core organizer" who could build "THE movement for social change."[22] On the other hand, others in the CYC considered the more ideal volunteer to be akin to the fabled American community organizer and activist Saul Alinsky, an image that even most women volunteers agreed was the model on which they grounded their community development theory and practice.[23] As Harry Stevens, one of the Crystal Cliffs attendees, wrote in an internal Company publication, "The Company wants supermen ya ya ... Where is it going to get them? Where are natural training grounds in our present society for producing this sort of mature, tough, radical person?"[24] Indeed, the image of the bearded beatnik/hippy radical became so predominant that women were not the only ones to complain about their invisibility as volunteers. As one Indigenous male volunteer, Isaac Beaulieu, from the Sandy Bay First Nation in Manitoba, noted, "You don't hear about the [Indian volunteers] because Indians can't grow beards."[25]

Another reason for the invisibility of women in the CYC was the fact that the Company ran very few explicitly women-oriented projects, particularly in the early years. After all, as Barbara Freeman notes, when the Company was formed in 1966, the nation's feminist movement had yet to transition from the more traditional women's clubs to the more youthful consciousness-raising groups of the second wave.[26] Indeed, even the Royal Commission on the Status of Women would not be appointed until February 1967.

By the early 1970s, the CYC did sponsor women's centres, particularly in rural areas, including the first sexual health centre on Prince Edward Island and the Centre des Femmes du Saguenay in Chicoutimi, Quebec. Though many of its early anti-poverty projects grappled with particular aspects of female poverty, the Company's own second-wave projects during the 1970s, such as the Mother Led Union and the Parkdale Single Mothers' Association, focused more explicitly on specific communities of women. Eventually those projects branched out to include women-centred cooperatives in areas such as daycares and credit unions and, in rural areas, handicraft production to promote greater economic independence for women. In addition, the CYC was also crucial in First Nations' communities, supporting the foundation of the Ontario Native Women's Association and the Federation of Yukon Indian Women.

Still, one of the reasons for the shortage of explicitly women-oriented projects was that by the time second-wave feminism was on the rise in Canada, the federal government had established other programs to support women's groups and projects, such as Opportunities for Youth, the Local Initiatives Program, and, eventually, the Women's Program, which began in the lead-up to the International Year of Women, in 1975. The CYC's involvement with women-centred projects often occurred in conjunction with additional support from those other programs.[27]

Nonetheless, the basic work of the Company and its volunteers was fundamentally gendered. As historian Jennifer Frost's work on the Economic Research and Action Projects, sponsored by the American university group Students for a Democratic Society, reminds us, community organizing challenged traditional understandings of social activism by displacing traditionally male areas of production as the focus of organizing activity and concentrating on the reproductive sphere, on issues such as housing, food, health, and recreation. In addition, the nitty-gritty work of community organizing was in many ways a task that leveraged traditionally "female" traits and skills, particularly talking, listening, and commiserating with community residents, often around the kitchen table.[28] Indeed, as Judi Bernstein, Peggy Morton, Linda Seese, and Myrna Wood noted in "Sisters, Brothers Lovers ... Listen ...," their now infamous letter to their New Left brothers, community organizing was largely women's work. It was "tedious"; it "required patience, sensitivity, understanding and more patience." They concluded, "It is a sad commentary that so few men felt they could do this kind of work."[29]

Social animation not only leveraged "womanly skills," it also foregrounded the rise of feminist consciousness-raising. Social animation was intended to overcome discouragement, to motivate people who had lost hope to take responsibility for their plight. It could not do so without sparking their emotions – their anger, their desires, their sense of self-pride – and directing those emotions towards constructive action. In that sense, community organization or community development work is, by its very nature, what one might call "emotion work" or "emotional labour."[30] For one, although most think of communities in terms of geographical or physical and institutional structures, the very idea of community itself is more of an emotional than a physical construct. Community, as one of the founders of cultural studies Raymond Williams noted long ago, evokes a sense of "warmth" that, like motherhood, is rarely associated with anything other than positive feelings and emotions.[31] For another, one need only look at how the very communities targeted by the CYC and other social development and social action organizations, from Student Union for Peace Action to Summer of Service, were described as depressed, not just economically but, more importantly, emotionally and psychologically. Social animation was intended to overcome a sense of what early sociologist Émile Durkheim called "anomie" – a psychological state characterized by a sense of futility and lack of purpose, or, worse, by emotional emptiness and despair – not just of the communities they intended to help, but among the very volunteers themselves.[32] In short, social animation was to change mentalities, and hence the work of

CYC volunteers, both men and women, was primarily psychological and emotional. That said, for women, particularly the young women who joined the Company, community organizing often required skills and personality traits that deviated from dominant gender tropes of the period. Indeed, it often required a degree of assertiveness and self-confidence that many young women believed they neither possessed nor were socially permitted to assert.

Yours in the Company: An Emotional History of the CYC

Before assessing young women's experiences in the Company in light of affect theory and the history of emotions, we also need to understand the Long Sixties (1958–73) as fundamentally an emotional construct. Indeed, given the heated debates that have occurred within the literature of 1960s social activism, is it even possible to talk about this historical period and its social movements dispassionately? Most of the literature is dominated by emotional themes; one need only think of the subtitle of Todd Gitlin's memoir-cum-history, *Years of Hope, Days of Rage*, which has come to define the dominant narrative theme of the period – the declension thesis.[33] Other histories of the decade note that underneath the hope and idealism of the decade and its politics were deep currents of anxiety, doubt, and alienation. Much of this expressed itself through themes of authenticity, of wanting to be real – whatever that entailed. But authenticity was rarely a tangible thing; it was a structure of feeling that in many ways rejected rationalism and embraced more humanist understandings of the self and society that celebrated a broader range of human experience, including emotion.[34] Indeed, one could say that the sixties represented a break in what the historian of emotions William Reddy calls the dominant emotional regime of Western societies, which until then had tended to view emotion as something that needed to be suppressed and only released in controlled ways. What is odd is that until the 1960s, emotions were considered "*the key* to understanding virtually all political action that occurred outside [official] political institutions."[35] Nonetheless, the emotional nature of sixties social activism has been used both then and now to discredit the larger goals of the period's various movements for social and political change as immature or neurotic "children's crusades."[36] Still others have critiqued the New Left's rather emotional and "romantic" approach to supporting the dispossessed, be they racialized populations or the poor and working classes.[37] The highly emotional nature of 1960s social movements also emerges in the literature on the Company itself. Ian Hamilton, the CYC's information director between

1967 and 1969, noted in the introduction to his insider history that the CYC was an organization driven by emotion, one that left those who joined more often than not scarred by their experiences.[38] In many ways this should not be surprising given that as early as 1964, sixties student activist Jim Harding noted that the CYC's predecessor, Student Union for Peace Action, had "become a haven for neurotics and fanatics, people unable to cope with and manipulate reality." By the time the CYC formed two years later, drawing many former members of the Student Union for Peace Action into its ranks, the organization remained among other things a "quasi-therapeutic community for alienated kids."[39]

These problems revealed themselves from the start of the CYC and were made manifest at the Company's infamous inaugural training session, at Crystal Cliffs training facility. The six-week training session has been described by those who attended as a "mind-bending affair."[40] Before the session was half complete, two young women were hospitalized for emotional and psychological breakdowns. For those who survived, the professional trainers so successfully "turned on" the volunteers to feelings of the "beloved community" that many of them refused to leave that world to continue with the more prosaic concerns of learning how to deal with the day-to-day problems they would encounter as community development workers.[41] Those who worked in the field of social and community development warned Company organizers against creating a haven for those who were emotionally unstable or immature, particularly ones who could not distinguish between personal crises and community ones.[42] Others noted quite perceptively that "volunteers will offer themselves because, consciously or unconsciously, they will be seeking to meet their own ... emotional needs ... through a vicarious experience and will lack the emotional maturity and stability to function efficiently and selflessly in the type of work envisaged by the Company."[43] For that reason, community development experts emphasized above all else that volunteers should be selected based on their emotional maturity, since they would be living in the midst of constant conflict.[44]

Unfortunately, in the Company's early years these initial assessments about volunteer motivations were all too true. For many volunteers, the commitment and the zeal of the Company for the dispossessed and disadvantaged remained a potent attraction. But for many others, joining the CYC was an attempt to find themselves and their place in the world. A number of volunteers spoke of joining the CYC because "where else can one go to be real?"[45] As historian of the American New Left Douglas Rossinow has noted, this emphasis on authenticity and its link to social activism lay at the roots of much of sixties youth politics.[46] Caught in what historian William Rorabaugh has called the "shiny abyss of materialism," young men and women sought to redeem themselves through commitment and action for the downtrodden.[47] Early volunteer Dorothy Hill noted that she joined the CYC because she was afraid she was becoming "too materialistic" and hoped that her service in the Company would reawaken her spiritual side.[48] In that sense, membership in the Company became a rite of passage on the road to personal development. In volunteer Kim Moore's words, "you learn and then you drop out ... it's the healthy people who are planning to leave. I sort've feel I've passed through the Company stage. I'm so happy. Now I know what I want to do."[49]

Volunteers in Antigonish still found it difficult to leave the training environment behind for the hard life of their projects. Again, Kim Moore spoke on behalf of many volunteers when she claimed that the T-Group training sessions were some of the most intense and memorable experiences of her young life.[50] As she remembered,

> We were packed so close ... we were standing part inside each other's shells. The only way out was to expand the mind. And my mind opened a little further. The months since, in comparison, are diffused bloodless things. A lot has happened for me, but moments of intense feeling or of understanding are more random and scattered ... Wake up ... With all its faults, the training session was where the real brewing happened ... let things happen ... Don't rip apart the aimless-seeming growth of talk and exchange between people ... let people come close together ... let them stay there and in love with one another ... wonder for christsake let the new volunteers stay together for a time. Don't destroy.[51]

While others were not as poetic as Moore, they did evoke the "richness" of the training session experiences and the intense desire to continue those experiences by "all remain[ing] together in one big happy project."[52] These intense feelings of community, however, could just as often disable rather than enable volunteers to do their work. As one field supervisor noted, "What I'm concerned with is how effective they can be, not with their feelings about everything. [Company projects aren't] a resting place for neurotics."[53] As a result, of the first fifty volunteers the Company recruited, only half finished their two-year term.

Despite the casualties of the Crystal Cliffs training sessions, many of the accounts of women volunteers asserted that they were chosen because of their emotional maturity and stability. Barbara Hall noted in an interview, "I was seen as, sort of, as together, or strong, or that kind of thing, which is how I tend to project even if I am falling apart."[54] Similarly, *Globe and Mail* reporter and soon-to-be CYC communications director Michael Valpy described Dorothy Hill, a twenty-seven-year-old nurse, as the Company's "Den mother, the rock upon which the Company would be built." As she told Valpy in his interview with her, "I don't like flighty people." As such, she hoped to be posted to a project with single mothers because they "need someone who can handle women under stress."[55] Marilyn Assheton-Smith, who worked as the Company's field organizer for northern Alberta and the Northwest Territories, also relished the challenge of working in the difficult and isolated conditions of northern and largely Indigenous communities. She remembered that she should have looked back on her experience as distinctly "un-feminist." However, she also claims that

> I came into [community development work] with such a strong personal background that I don't think being a woman had much to do with anything. I was older than many of [the CYC volunteers and staff] and had [a] lot more experience. I was the only person who knew my turf. The fact that we were women in the CYC wasn't any different than being women anywhere else. At our age (mid-20s) and with our experience, we had learned to be a little bit tough ... and ... how to manage our world despite those problems.[56]

Once in their communities, the personal reactions of working as a CYC volunteer ran the gamut of emotions from excitement, happiness, and pride to anger, frustration, fear, and sadness. Like their male colleagues, women volunteers joined the CYC out of a sense of excitement. After successfully completing the six weeks of training in Antigonish, CYC volunteer Judy Yaworsky moved to her project placement in Vancouver, where she worked with seniors. Her letters to the prime minister's secretary described her work as "exhausting" and even at times "depressing." Nonetheless, she claimed that she had "never felt richer before." Despite any difficulties she had faced, she continued to "have great faith in the Company" and was certain that "we [CYC Volunteers] will not fail the Prime Minister or the people of Canada."[57] Others spoke of "falling in love" with their communities or their target groups.

However, those euphoric experiences often soon wore off when the hard and uncertain work of organizing took over. Women working with the

Company's Kingston project spoke of their work as "very frustrating." These young women had little or no previous contact with people "in their hopelessly powerless position, and ... found [themselves] shocked and bewildered by the sheer drudgery of their lives." "The myth of the powerless," they noted, "quickly disappeared."[58] Others became trapped or, as the phrase went in those days, hung up, by fear. Patricia Paul, who volunteered in the Cape Breton project, remembered that her first few weeks were "torturous" as she worked up the courage just to knock on doors: "Knock Knock Knock. Social Change? Not to-day, thank you. Slam!"[59] Paul, like other women in the Company, feared that what they were doing was not enough. The enormity of the problems facing the communities they worked in often made their own contributions appear insignificant. Others worried that their roles as CYC volunteers, particularly when they were employed in traditional feminine roles as teachers or recreation providers, were similarly insignificant. Kate Barlow, who was posted to the Oak River First Nations community in Manitoba, noted in her resignation,

> They asked for and expected a nursery school teacher and, in fact that is what they got ... but ... I am not a nursery school teacher [and] I don't want to be a nursery school teacher. I am trapped, and I am prolonging a myth and because I am fake, because I feel as though I am doing nothing but playing a part for which I am ill cut I have a very guilty conscience much of the time.[60]

However, the most prevalent issue for women in the Company was a sense of isolation. Such feelings expressed themselves in many different forms. First, there was the sheer geographic isolation of many Company projects where volunteers were placed far from home and, more importantly, Company support. In the early days, with only fifty trained volunteers, it also meant that volunteers served alone in their projects. For example, Barbara Hall worked as a single volunteer in the tiny community of Three Mile Plain, Nova Scotia, and received very few visits from Atlantic Canadian staff over her two-year term. And though the Oak River Reserve boasted two woman volunteers, the community itself was 270 kilometres from Winnipeg. As a result, volunteer Kate Barlow remarked, "I've never felt so alone in my whole life. I just long for someone to talk to. I'm completely isolated as I have no car and the nearest centre is twenty miles away ... I haven't seen a soul from CYC out here yet ... and I'm beginning to think I have been forgotten."[61]

Feelings of isolation among women volunteers were not always a function of geography. Brenda Pellier, who worked with the Ottawa project, mere steps from the CYC head office at 12 Chapel Street, felt isolated as "the only girl [on the project]." As she wrote in one of her reports,

> There is sometimes a feeling of exclusion or discrimination that as a female I'd better be good or else it'll be a pat on the shoulder, a kiss on the cheek (or forehead) and bye-bye in a month that could have been expected anyway. I may be paranoid. [Bob] Holmes you're not alone in problems. You're black [but] damn it, I'm a woman.[62]

Sometimes this loneliness as a single female volunteer expressed itself in other ways, particularly in terms of sexual relationships. After all, these were young women seeking excitement, but they also had to consider their responsibilities to the Company and to their communities in an era when open female sexuality was heavily stigmatized. The first two volunteers to enter the Cape Breton Project in Glace Bay, Susan McLean and Patricia Rose, found this out very quickly when they showed up wearing jeans rather than skirts, which was enough to sink the project due to the community's "moral concerns."[63] Nonetheless, Patricia Paul, who followed on in Cape Breton less than two years later, remembered "I could have stayed longer but the solitude and isolation of Cape Breton left me yearning for a little excitement. Well to be honest, I was horny as hell." Paul recalled that Skip Hambling, a fellow Cape Breton project volunteer, "used to suggest a fleet of flying whores with a picture catalogue so you could put in your order. If men were included it would have been ideal for lonely outposts like Cape Breton."[64]

The Company soon overcame some of the problems associated with the sheer physical isolation of volunteers by hiring them from within communities rather than by parachuting them in from afar. As a result, there were far fewer casualties due to emotional and psychological exhaustion. However, volunteers, particularly women, continued to feel a sense of isolation and vulnerability just by virtue of the community groups with which they worked. Donna Skeoch, who was recruited by the Company to run a youth drop-in centre – The Torchlight – in Guelph, Ontario, recalled that her physical safety was threatened on more than a few occasions by the centre's clientele, who often arrived drunk or high. Such physical confrontations left her feeling very "uneasy," and by the end she was "not big enough, not brave enough, or crazy enough to put myself in this position [again]."[65]

For others, such as Ernestine Trudeau, who managed the Sault Ste. Marie project, such vulnerability came in the form of personal attacks on her credibility by the focus groups she was working with, particularly a rival group seeking to control the city's newly formed Native Friendship Centre. As one CYC official noted in a visit to Sault Ste. Marie's projects, "The [p]ower plays, gossip, [and] drag down system ... which was personal and vicious ... created an emotionally charged environment" for Trudeau and very much undermined her leadership.[66]

Even when personal feelings of isolation and fear were not involved, volunteers often assimilated the feelings of isolation and helplessness of the community groups with which they worked. This was true in the case of the volunteers with the Mothers on a Budget project, which organized single mothers on social assistance in Thunder Bay, Ontario. The volunteers reported that their biggest task was to help project members overcome the isolation of poverty and to develop a degree of self-confidence. As one of the project reports noted, "Too many women on Welfare or Family Benefits are looked down upon as bums who are living off the taxpayers, [which] gives women the feeling of total failure that they cannot take care of their families." The volunteers noted that the stigmatization of poverty, particularly female poverty, was not only degrading, but often "very personal ... [and] frightening."[67] Volunteers working with the Centre des Femmes, in downtown Montreal, argued that their project was crucial not only because women's issues were central to the daily lives of area residents, but also because "ces femmes ressentaient la nécessité de sortir chez-elles car elles souffraient vivement l'isolement et d'ennui."[68] Similarly, a group in Toronto known as the Mother Led Union noted that many of the women in the organization sought refuge in the city's various mental institutions from the daily exactions of poverty. As one volunteer noted, "It seems that they had just had enough. Two of them were too tired and 'needed rest' from the continuing struggle that life had become for them. It sounds horrifying, but the mental institution was the safest place for them. They were tired of coping with an existence, which for them, was fraught with fear."[69] Indeed, they "feared ex-husbands ... sexual assault, [and many] even fear to take public transit. Of course all of this fear means that they have unlisted phone numbers which makes it difficult to keep in touch." She concluded, "The only thing these women don't seem to fear is death and official authority."[70]

The daily struggles of poverty, disenfranchisement, and disempowerment took a toll on the emotional reserves of volunteers. Though many looked back fondly on their experiences, it was also clear that by the end of their two-year term of service many were both emotionally and physically exhausted. Marilyn Assheton-Smith, who worked for the Company first as field staff in Yellowknife and later as a consultant and part of the Company's governing council, spoke about her time in the CYC as feeling like she "went to war." She was glad to have survived in what she remembers as "the midst of all kinds of death." Although she later realized her successful management of key projects in northern Alberta and the Northwest Territories was a significant accomplishment, she really "did not want to talk about it afterwards."[71]

As she recounted in an interview: "I can look back on it now and see the value, but at the time all I could see were the personal costs."[72] Assheton-Smith's comments also speak in many ways to the cyclical nature of community development and social action. Former volunteers, both men and women, spoke of not being able to continue living the life of an organizer in large part because of the tremendous material sacrifices demanded, but more importantly because of the emotional energy required to sustain their projects through the natural ups and downs of a community project. As Brenda Pellier lamented, "The limited work I did ... was exhausting in that it required extensive output with very limited input. I sound arrogant and forgive me, but I'm a selfish person. The pats, strokes, and ego-feeding type of support is needed because I'm so goddamned insecure and inferiority-complex-ridden. And I guess that support wasn't blatant enough in Ottawa South."[73] Even Patricia Paul, whose weeks of door knocking eventually developed a strong community project to clean up the Sydney Harbour, noted, "It was comforting and egotistically satisfying to be known as anti-establishment and protector of the poor. But I no longer had the energy or drive to commit myself to a group of people. I was no longer prepared to deal with the personal struggles involved with the day-to-day existence of a community organizer."[74] As such, Pellier's and Paul's experiences confirm observations about community development in Canada during this period. Community development expert Jim Lotz concludes that too often community development resulted in nothing more than "activities of isolated individuals" for whom "community development became merely an episode in their lives." As a result, Lotz notes, "They expected to be able to help others and reach the heights of human ecstasy. Instead they learned the limits of their own abilities after plunges into the darkest depths of their souls."[75]

Conclusion

If this analysis of women's emotional experiences as Company of Young Canadian volunteers appears rather negative, we should be cautious. Like many former male volunteers, almost universally the CYC women interviewed for this project spoke of the richness of their experiences and of their participation as a building block for their future careers and their activism in a range of social and political causes. As Rorabaugh has noted, the breaking down of barriers in the 1960s, whether they be of race, class, or gender, was an intensely personal experience. For many young women volunteers, their service in the CYC tested their emotional reserves and resolve.[76] Revealingly, staff member Marilyn Moreton wrote in a final assessment of one Calgary CYC project that all her volunteers had been "exposed to the most incredible situations imaginable" and even though they would "not now organize a pile of paper bags for a million dollars," their "excellent, if depressing, experience [as volunteers] would benefit them greatly in whatever future activities they undertake."[77] Indeed, if we view the centrality of emotional labour to the work of volunteers, we should not be surprised at the descriptions of burnout and dissatisfaction.[78] Although such demands would have affected both male and female CYC volunteers, women volunteers were under far greater pressure because of gendered expectations for them to remain "bright," "energetic," and "breezy," rather than "angry," "sullen," or, worse, "aggressive."[79]

These negative emotional experiences were also likely to have been enhanced by the feelings of isolation experienced by women volunteers. Such personal isolation is a prominent theme in the histories of early second-wave feminism. All too often young women believed their dissatisfaction, their feelings of disempowerment, and the blatant disregard and disrespect of their male colleagues were singular and personal rather than pervasive and systemic. Indeed, as volunteer Cynthia Chambers recounted, despite all the positive work she did in cooperation with the Dene Tree of Peace project she left the Company "indignant" at the way her work had largely been ignored or taken for granted. "I had things to say" and was "tired of not having a voice."[80] In the Company, such isolation was enhanced by, of all things, a lack of community among volunteers and CYC staff across the country. Indeed, despite its work in community development, the Company itself seemed unable to develop, nurture, or animate a sense of community among its own volunteers.

Despite these difficulties, many CYC women volunteers put down substantial roots in the various communities they served. Many of these roots were physical or tangible as women established countless institutions such as food cooperatives, daycares, and women's health and drop-in centres. Though often derided as mere band-aids, the building of such counter-institutions was a means of overcoming the malaise that seemed to set in to most projects when the initial excitement wore off.[81] Maeve Hancey did not initially conceive of her work in Vancouver's Strathcona Park housing project as "women's work" or as a feminist concern. To her, Strathcona Park residents' plight was first an issue of housing, poverty, and welfare rights; it "just so happened," she remembered, "that the people who were most affected by these issues were women." Only discussions with fellow volunteer Lynn Smith, who would go on to become a British Columbia Supreme Court Justice and founding director of Canada's Women's Legal Education and Action Fund, eventually brought Hancey to see some of these issues in light of women's rights/feminism.[82] So even though community organizing often operated without explicit feminist context, much of their work was feminist or led to feminism by challenging women's subordinate status. Further, it often represented an assertion of women's needs for respect, self-determination, and, eventually, greater autonomy that those like Cynthia Chambers too often found wanting in their service with the Company.[83] But perhaps more importantly, such institutions helped to create the emotional communities that would be crucial to nurturing and sustaining future movements for women's social and economic justice.

Notes

1 At its most basic level, community development seeks to empower communities (both geographic and identity based), particularly disadvantaged and disempowered ones, to effect social, political, and economic change through collective action. To do so, community development practitioners engage in politics, leadership, power attainment, group dynamics, learning, and social change, taking a multidisciplinary approach that draws from political science, sociology, social psychology, social work, and adult education. In Quebec, community development was known as animation sociale, and it generally took the same approach with some subtle differences. There, social animation was more overtly political and interventionist, and it privileged concepts of self-determination. For more on the theory of community development and social animation, see J. Draper, ed., *Citizen Participation* (Toronto: New Press, 1971); E. Hamilton, *Adult Education for Community Development* (New York: Greenwood Press, 1992); J. Lotz, *Understanding Canada* (Toronto: New Canada Publications, 1977); A. Tan, "Community Development Theory and Practice: Bridging the Divide between 'Micro' and 'Macro' Levels of Social Work" (paper, North American Association of Christians in Social Work Convention, Indianapolis, IN, October 2009); and K. Brushett, "Combler le fossé entre les deux solitudes:

L'animation sociale, le développement communautaire et la Compagnie des Jeunes Canadiens, 1965–1975," *Bulletin d'histoire politique* 23, 1 (2014): 62–81.

2 Alice MacNeil, cited in Peter Ward, "Alice in Cabbagetown," *Toronto Telegram*, n.d., Library and Archives Canada (LAC), Company of Young Canadians (CYC) fonds, RG 116, vol. 42, file B-2-1, Clippings 1968.

3 The literature is now immense, but the classic statements belong to Sara Evans, *Personal Politics: The Roots of Women's Liberation in the Civil Rights Movement and the New Left* (New York: Knopf, 1979); Ruth Rosen, *The World Split Open: How the Modern Women's Movement Changed America* (New York: Viking, 2000); and Rebecca E. Klatch, *A Generation Divided: The New Left, the New Right, and the 1960s* (Berkeley: University of California Press, 1999). The Canadian experience is less well documented; see Judy Rebick, *Ten Thousand Roses: The Making of a Feminist Revolution* (Toronto: Penguin Canada, 2005); and Myrna Kostash, *Long Way from Home: The Story of the Sixties Generation in Canada* (Toronto: James Lorimer, 1980).

4 Barbara Hall, interview (telephone) with author, March 14, 2011.

5 That sexism was a fact of life for CYC women volunteers was confirmed by interviews with Barbara Hall, Marilyn Assheton-Smith, Maeve Hancey, and Cynthia Chambers. Rebecca Klatch's analysis of women's involvement in American New Left and New Right organizations suggests the experiences of women in the CYC were common. Klatch, *A Generation Divided*, 165–73.

6 The distinction between affect theory and the history of emotions remains somewhat fuzzy, but generally most scholars of both agree that affect, which is preconscious if not biological, is not the same as feeling or emotions that are expressed through language. As Eric Shouse notes, recalling the work of social theorist Brian Massumi, "Feelings are *personal* and *biographical*, emotions are *social*, and affects are *prepersonal*." Cited in Eric Shouse, "Feeling, Emotion, Affect," *M/C Journal* 8, 6 (2005): para. 1, https://doi.org/10.5204/mcj.2443 (emphasis in original). See also Aleksondra Hultquist, "Introductory Essay: Emotion, Affect, and the Eighteenth Century," *The Eighteenth Century* 58, 3 (2017): 273–80, https://doi.org/10.1353/ecy.2017.0024.

7 Megan Boler and Michalinos Zembylas, "Interview with Megan Boler: From 'Feminist Politics of Emotions' to the 'Affective Turn,'" in *Methodological Advances in Research on Emotion and Education*, ed. Michalinos Zembylas and Paul A. Schutz (Switzerland: Springer, 2016), 20–22.

8 On emotional regimes, see Peter N. Stearns, with Carol Z. Stearns, "Emotionology: Clarifying the History of Emotions and Emotional Standards," *American Historical Review* 90, 4 (1985): 813–36; and Jan Plamper, "The History of Emotions: An Interview with William Reddy, Barbara Rosenwein, and Peter Stearns," *History and Theory* 49, 2 (2010): 237–65. See also Nicole Eustace, Eugenia Lean, Julie Livingston, Jan Plamper, William M. Reddy, and Barbara H. Rosenwein, "*AHR* Conversation: The Historical Study of Emotions," *American Historical Review* 117, 5 (2012): 1487–531, https://doi.org/10.1093/ahr/117.5.1487; and Ruth Leys, "The Turn to Affect: A Critique," *Critical Inquiry* 37, 3 (2011): 434–72.

9 There are very few documents explicitly authored by women volunteers in the CYC archives housed at Library and Archives Canada. Equally important, transcripts of meetings indicate that even when women volunteers were present they participated very little in discussions. For example, in a twenty-four page transcript of a CYC

Working Group held on December 3 and 4, 1966, women volunteers spoke a total of only four times and most were no more than sentence-long interjections. By contrast, male contributions to the discussions were often pages long. Perhaps also telling was the fact that women's contributions were flagged by their first names (e.g., Barb, for Barbara Hall, or Maeve, for Maeve Hancey), whereas those of male volunteers and staff were flagged by their last names (e.g., Salter, for Rick Salter, or Skippon, for Ronald Skippon). Ironically, the meeting focused on the anxieties and emotional "hang ups" of volunteers in their first few months on their respective projects. See CYC Working Group held December 3 and 4, 1966, LAC, CYC fonds, RG 116, vol. 25, file 120-W1-3.

10 Oral interviews conducted by the author occurred both in person and by phone depending on the availability of the subject. These interviews were conducted with both female and male volunteers, staff members, and members of the governing council of the Company of Young Canadians. The subjects were largely free to discuss their experiences in the Company as volunteers or staff, with the author interjecting for clarification or expansion.

11 On prefigurative politics, see Wini Breines, *Community Organization and the New Left, 1962–1968: The Great Refusal* (New Brunswick, NJ: Rutgers University Press, 1989).

12 Evans, *Personal Politics*, 68–70.

13 The two main histories of the CYC cover only its early years. See Ian Hamilton, *The Children's Crusade: The Story of the Company of Young Canadians* (Toronto: Peter Martin, 1970); and Margaret Daly, *The Revolution Game: The Short Unhappy Life of the Company of Young Canadians* (Toronto: New Press, 1970).

14 Barbara Frum, "Is the Company of Young Canadians Doing Any Good," *Saturday Night*, n.d., LAC, RG 116, vol. 42, file B-2-1, Clippings 1968; Profile of CYC Applicants, 1966, LAC, RG 116, vol. 312-4-4; Company of Young Canadians, *Annual Report 1973–74*. The percentage of female volunteers in the CYC compares favourably with the numbers of women who volunteered to work with Students for a Democratic Society's Economic Research and Action Projects. See Jennifer Frost, *"An Interracial Movement of the Poor": Community Organizing and the New Left in the 1960s* (New York: New York University Press, 2001).

15 For more on the highly gendered conceptions of the ideal community organizer, see Rosen, *The World Split Open*, 119; Evans, *Personal Politics*, 140–41; and Frost, *Interracial Movement of the Poor*, 23–25.

16 CYC volunteers were hired for a term of two years. They were paid a monthly stipend of fifty dollars, and the Company also paid for their housing costs. In some cases, the Company also provided volunteers with transportation, either Company vehicles or it covered the costs of rental vehicles or public transportation.

17 Burnley Rocky Jones, "Power to the People" (presentation, The Sixties Canadian-Style: Where Have All the Sixties Gone?, St. Catharines, ON, November 4, 2010).

18 Rocky later related that despite his misgivings, the CYC never interfered with the Nova Scotia Project. Burnley "Rocky" Jones and James W. St.G. Walker, *Burnley "Rocky" Jones Revolutionary: An Autobiography* (Halifax: Roseway Publishing, 2016), 74–75.

19 Memo to Project Planning Research and Evaluation Committee from Richard Salter, Re: Faust Project Evaluation, December 1967, LAC, RG 116, vol. 133, file 652; Alona Burger, "A Can of Beans," *Canadian Nurse*, July 1968, 30–32.

20 For more on the concept of "emotional communities," see the work of Barbara H. Rosenwein: "Worrying about Emotions in History," *American Historical Review* 107, 3 (2002): 821–45; "Problems and Methods in the History of Emotions," *Passions in Context: International Journal for the History and Theory of Emotions* 1, 1 (2010): 1–32, https://www.passionsincontext.de/uploads/media/01_Rosenwein.pdf; and in Jan Plamper, "The History of Emotions: An Interview with William Reddy, Barbara Rosenwein, and Peter Stearns."

21 For more on DePoe and his activities in Yorkville, see Stuart Henderson, *Making the Scene: Yorkville and Hip Toronto in the 1960s* (Toronto: University of Toronto Press, 2011); Daly, *Revolution Game*, 109–114; and Hamilton, *Children's Crusade*, 46–58.

22 On the conception of "CYC Man," see "Working Group Meeting, December 3–4, 1966," LAC, RG 116, vol. 25, file 120-W1-2 (emphasis added).

23 Saul Alinsky was an American community organizer who began his work in Chicago during the 1930s. Alinsky would go on to found the Industrial Areas Foundation, which became a training centre for community organizers. He later synthesized his ideas about community organization in two books, *Reveille for Radicals* (New York: Vantage Books, 1972) and *Rules for Radicals: A Primer for Realistic Radicals* (New York: Vantage Books, 1969) that became de facto bibles of sixties movements. Community development scholar and practitioner Eric Shragge has commented that in his experience many of his female students have trouble identifying with the charismatic style of leadership often associated with Alinsky. Shragge, *Activism and Social Change: Lessons for Community Organizing* (Toronto: University of Toronto Press, 2013), 57.

24 Harry Stevens, cited in Daly, *Revolution Game, 62.*

25 Isaac Beaulieu, cited in Lyn Schankerman, "Beaulieu Brings Out Humor in Indian-Metis Problem," *Winnipeg Free Press*, February 17, 1968, LAC, RG 116, vol. 72, file 700-2-3.

26 Barbara M. Freeman, *The Satellite Sex: The Media and Women's Issues in English Canada, 1966–1971* (Waterloo, ON: Wilfrid Laurier University Press, 2001), 22–23.

27 On the Women's Program, see Leslie A. Pal, *Interests of State: The Politics of Language, Multiculturalism, and Feminism in Canada* (Montreal/Kingston: McGill-Queen's University Press, 1993), 216–42. From a feminist and insider's perspective, see Sue Findlay, "Feminist Struggles with the Canadian State, 1966–1988," *Resources for Feminist Research* 17, 3 (1988): 5–9. Nancy Adamson's history of the second-wave feminist movement in Ontario highlights the way that federal funding was used to establish women's centres. Adamson, "Feminists, Libbers, Lefties, and Radicals: The Emergence of the Women's Liberation Movement," in *A Diversity of Women: Ontario, 1945–1980*, ed. J. Parr (Toronto: University of Toronto Press, 1995), 252–80.

28 J. Frost, *Interracial Movement of the Poor*, 24, 82–83.

29 Judi Bernstein, Peggy Morton, Linda Seese, and Myrna Wood, "Sisters, Brothers, Lovers ... Listen ...," in *Women Unite! Up from the Kitchen, Up from the Bedroom, Up from Under* (Toronto: Canadian Women's Educational Press, 1972), 38. Both Wood

and Bernstein worked for the CYC between 1966 and 1968. Those men who were successful, such as Bernard Muzeen, in the Calgary Project, often adopted a more low-key approach. "To Reach People He Used the Back Door," Victoria Park Residents' Association Newsletter, LAC, MG 31, Bernard Muzeen fonds, K37, vol. 1, series 1, file 1.

30 Arlie Russell Hochschild, *The Managed Heart: Commercialization of Human Feeling* (Berkeley: University of California Press, 1983).

31 Raymond Williams, *Keywords: A Vocabulary of Culture and Society*, rev. ed. (New York: Oxford University Press, 1983), 76.

32 The idea that poverty was rooted in a pervasive sense of personal despair was popularized at the time by anthropologist Oscar Lewis's concept of the "culture of poverty," in which the poor and the marginalized had become not only disengaged from the larger society, but also resigned to their fate. Oscar Lewis, "The Culture of Poverty," *Scientific American*, 215, 4 (1966), 19–25. However, many social scientists of the period also worried about a similar disengagement by young people. By the mid-1960s, American psychologist Kenneth Keniston was also concerned about a puzzling new alienation that had gripped the youth of the nation and left them deeply ambivalent towards the value of the adult world and its values. What was most puzzling to Keniston was that this new alienation was not imposed by their society on them, but a chosen response to it. Kenneth Keniston, *The Uncommitted: Alienated Youth in American Society* (New York: Harcourt Brace, 1965), 4–6.

33 Todd Gitlin, *The Sixties: Years of Hope, Days of Rage* (New York: Bantam, 1987). For a critique of the declension thesis, see John McMillan and Paul Buhle, eds., *The New Left Revisited* (Philadelphia: Temple University Press, 2003); Wini Breines "Whose New Left?," *Journal of American History* 75 (1988): 528–45; and Van Gosse, "A Movement of Movements," in *Companion to Post-1945 America*, ed. J.-C. Agnew and R. Rosenzweig (New York: Blackwell, 2007), 276–302.

34 The classic statement on the centrality of authenticity to the decade's political and social movements is Douglas Rossinow, *The Politics of Authenticity: Liberalism, Christianity, and the New Left in America* (New York: Columbia University Press, 1998).

35 Jeff Goodwin, James M. Jasper, and Francesca Polletta, "Why Emotions Matter," in *Passionate Politics: Emotions and Social Movements*, ed. Jeff Goodwin, James M. Jasper, and Francesca Polletta (Chicago: University of Chicago Press, 2001), 2 (emphasis added).

36 Hamilton, *Children's Crusade*.

37 For more on the way the romance of the poor by the New Left tended to inhibit action and analysis rather than sharpen it, see Richard Ellis, "Romancing the Oppressed: The New Left and the Left Out," *Review of Politics* 58, 1 (1996): 109–54; Breines, *Community Organizing and the New Left*, 139–46; and Jeremy Varon, *Bringing the War Home: The Weather Underground, the Red Army Faction, and Revolutionary Violence in the Sixties and Seventies* (Berkeley: University of California Press, 2004).

38 Hamilton, *Children's Crusade*, iv.

39 Jim Harding, cited in Doug Owram, *Born at the Right Time: A History of the Baby Boom Generation* (Toronto: University of Toronto Press, 1996), 231.

40 Michael Valpy, "Stress and Strength at Crystal Cliffs," *Globe and Mail (The Globe Magazine)*, August 6, 1966, 5; and P.N. Mussallem to Alan Clarke, n.d., 2, York University Archives, Alan Clark fonds, vol. 21, file 30.
41 Art Stinson, "What Happened at Crystal Cliffs?," p. 1, McMaster Archives, CYC fonds, vol. 4, file 13. The term "beloved community" was popularized by Rev. Martin Luther King Jr. during the civil rights movement of the 1960s to denote a society based on the core values of love, trust, peace, justice, and reconciliation.
42 Project Planning Evaluation and Research Committee Report, Pacific Regional Projects, Sept 30, 1967, p. 6, LAC, RG 116, vol. 13, file 120 C12 – Committee Project Planning, Evaluation and Research.
43 Memo to CYC Organizing Committee from Bert Marcuse, MSW, Exec Director of Calgary Family Service Bureau, August 19, 1965, LAC, RG 116, vol. 18, file 120 – 01, Organizing Committee – General.
44 Interdepartmental Committee on Community Development – Norbert Prefontaine, Survey of Training Programs Related to Community Development in Canada – Summary of Findings. March, 1966, LAC, RG 116, vol. 14, file 120 J3.
45 Kim Moore, cited in *The Package – Ontario Region* (newsletter), April 13, 1967, York University Archives, Alan Clarke Fonds, vol. 21, file 19.
46 Rossinow, *Politics of Authenticity*.
47 W. Rorabaugh, *Kennedy and the Promise of the Sixties* (Cambridge: Cambridge University Press, 2002), 5.
48 Dorothy Hill, cited in Michael Valpy, "The Yearnings of Young Canadians: 'I'm Tired of Narrow-Minded People,'" *Globe and Mail*, August 6, 1966, A10.
49 Kim Moore, cited in *The Package – Ontario Region*, April 13, 1967, York University Archives.
50 T-Grouping is a form of sensitivity training developed by psychologist Kurt Lewin and was widely employed in the 1960s as a team-building exercise. Since such groups focused on process rather function, individuals were encouraged to examine the emotions released by the words and actions of others in the group, including their own emotions. See Carole Robin, "The Power of T-Groups," accessed October 15, 2017, https://www.gsb.stanford.edu/sites/gsb/files/files-fpp/42436/article-idftp-power-tgroups-experiential-learning.pdf.
51 Kim Moore, cited in *The Package – Ontario Region*, April 13, 1967, York University Archives.
52 Murray Martin, *Feedback – To Be the Way for Those without a Way* (CYC Volunteer Newsletter), March 4–10, 1967, McMaster University Archives, CYC Fonds, vol. 4, file 8.
53 Cited in Barbara Frum, "Is the Company of Young Canadians Doing Any Good," *Saturday Night*, n.d., 4, LAC, RG 166, vol. 42, file B-2-1 Clippings 1968.
54 Hall, interview.
55 Valpy, "The Yearnings of Young Canadians"; Dorothy Hill, cited in Valpy, "The Yearnings of Young Canadians."
56 Marilyn Assheton-Smith, interview (telephone) with author, June 22, 2011.
57 Judy Yaworsky to Miss Annette Perron (private secretary of Lester Pearson), September 18, 1966, LAC, MG 26, N4, Pearson Papers, PMO, vol. 148, file 353.2, part 1 November 1965 to December 1966.
58 Kingston Community Project Report, 1966, 33–34, LAC, RG 116, vol. 122, file 579.

59 Patricia Paul, cited in CYC What's New, March 1971, LAC, RG 116, vol. 52, file 160-1.
60 Kate Barlow to Alan Clarke, March 7, 1967, LAC, RG 116, vol. 133, file 655.
61 Kate Barlow to Bernard Muzeen, n.d., LAC, MG 31 D37, Bernard Muzeen fonds, vol. 1, file 4.
62 Brenda Pellier, Progress Report #1, January 31, 1969, LAC, RG 116, vol. 126, file 597.
63 G.D. Colford to Campbell Mackie, November 14, 1966, LAC, RG 116, vol 75, file 730-6.
64 Patricia Paul, cited in CYC What's New, March 1971, LAC, RG 116, vol. 52, file 160-1.
65 Donna Skeoch to B.T. Dale, Medical Officer of Health, Guelph, January 29, 1971, LAC, RG 116, vol. 122, file 576.
66 Ben Baich, Staff Report on Sault Ste. Marie Visit, November 6–8, 1972, January 24, 1973, LAC, RG116, vol. 122, file 580. On the emotional power of gossip in community organizing, see Rosemary Hennessy, "Open Secrets: The Affective Cultures of Organizing on Mexico's Northern Border," *Feminist Theory* 10, 3 (2009): 309–22.
67 Colleen Miller, Project Submission, Mothers on a Budget, LAC, RG 116, vol. 123, file 584.
68 Rapport du projet – Centre des Femmes, n.d., LAC, RG 116, vol. 99, file 333.
69 Mother Led Union Report, n.d., LAC, RG 116, vol. 127, file 600.
70 Mother Led Union Report, n.d.
71 Assheton-Smith, interview. Assheton-Smith helped establish and manage the CYC's Great Slave Lake project, which eventually went on to become the Dene Nation under the leadership of CYC volunteer Georges Erasmus. In addition, the oral history project of CYC volunteer Roy Daniels conducted among the region's Indigenous peoples was central to their opposition to the Mackenzie Valley pipeline and to the decisions rendered by the Berger Commission. See René Fumoleau, *As Long as This Land Shall Last: A History of Treaty 8 and Treaty 11, 1870–1939* (Calgary: University of Calgary Press, 2004); John David Hamilton, *Arctic Revolution: Social Change in the Northwest Territories, 1935–1994* (Toronto: Dundurn Press, 1994); Kerry Abel, *Drum Songs: Glimpses of Dene History* (Montreal/Kingston: McGill-Queen's University Press, 1993).
72 Assheton-Smith, interview.
73 Brenda Pellier to Bob Holmes, March 8, 1969, Confidential, LAC, RG 116, vol. 126, file 597.
74 Paul, cited in CYC What's New, March 1971, LAC.
75 Jim Lotz, "The Moral and Ethical Basis of Community Development: Reflections on the Canadian Experience," *Community Development Journal* 17, 1 (1982): 29.
76 Evans, *Personal Politics*, 68–70. Even male volunteers recognized that being a community organizer "demanded a great deal of emotional investment." See Lyon Malt, "CYCer Seeks Challenge, Freedom," *Manitoban*, October 6, 1967, LAC, RG 116, vol. 42, file, B-2-1, Clippings 1968.
77 Marilyn Moreton, Report on Calgary Municipal Housing Tenants' Association, 1974, LAC, RG 116, vol. 136, file 691.

78 C.M. Brotheridge and A.A. Grandey, "Emotional Labor and Burnout: Comparing Two Perspectives of 'People Work,'" *Journal of Vocational Behavior* 60, 1 (2002): 17–39, doi:10.1006/jvbe.2001.1815.
79 See Hochschild, *The Managed Heart.*
80 Dr. Cynthia Chambers, interview (telephone) with author, June 12, 2017.
81 Kingston Community Project Report, 1966, LAC, RG 116, vol. 122, file 579.
82 Maeve Hancey, interview with author, July 12, 2011.
83 See Frost, *Interracial Movement of the Poor;* Breines, *Community Organization and the New Left*; and Evans, *Personal Politics.*

5

Tears and Tiaras
Affect, Beauty Pageants, and Protests

PATRIZIA GENTILE

In an August 1969 *Saturday Night* article, journalist Satu Repo briefly alluded to a protest by radical feminists, the Toronto Women's Liberation Group, against an "Outdoor Bikini Contest" in 1968, organized and sponsored by a local appliance store. According to Repo, a "beautiful sister" infiltrated the beauty contest and proceeded to stun the "organizers and onlookers by emerging fully clad under her borrowed furs, with a sign: I Have A Mind."[1] The promoters of the contest responded by offering her a "Mind" prize for her trouble, but she declined. The winner, a McMaster University philosophy student, however, was left confounded by the protest. When asked to comment on whether she was disgusted by being treated as a sex object, she responded, "That's what a girl wants most."[2]

This incident was just one of many challenges to beauty pageants in the 1960s. More widely known, for example, is the protest against the 1968 Miss America Pageant, in Atlantic City. Organized by New York Radical Women, that protest drew over one hundred women liberationists from across the United States and became one of the defining moments of second-wave feminism.[3] The theatrics of the protest garnered national coverage. Some protesters "chained themselves to a life-size Miss America puppet to emphasize women's enslavement to 'beauty standards.'"[4] Others succeeded in disrupting the pageant during the broadcast by unfurling a large banner that read "Women's Liberation."

In the late 1960s, feminists grappled with the meaning of pageants, often targeting them for their objectification of women's bodies and as a symbol of women's oppression within a heteropatriachal system. This chapter examines three specific incidents: the rejection of the industry by Linda Douma, Miss Canada 1965; the participation in Miss Canadian University 1970 beauty pageant by Janiel Jolley, an official protest candidate from Simon Fraser University; and the radical feminist protest against the Miss Canada 1976 pageant in November 1975. Together, these incidents reveal the beauty pageant as a central site of Canadian second-wave feminist activism and resistance. In addition, these stories open up an opportunity for rethinking what we mean by protest in the context of the second wave – from "dropping out" as an individual act of resistance to the use of beauty to infiltrate pageants. These three acts of resistance also illuminate the changing nature of that protest, from a trajectory of individual feminist consciousness to collective action, to fraying collectivities.

In analyzing these incidents, I draw on Sara Ahmed's figure of the feminist killjoy to illustrate the connection between affect and feminist activism. For Ahmed, feminists "kill joy" because "they disturb the very fantasy that happiness can be found in a certain place."[5] Ahmed's theoretical configuration of the feminist killjoy as the "troublemaker ... who violates the fragile condition of peace" by "not finding the objects that promise happiness to be quite so promising" is based on the rejection of what Ahmed calls "happy objects" or "scripts."[6] For Ahmed, the feminist killjoy "is a spoilsport because she refuses to convene, to assemble, or to meet up over happiness."[7] The killjoy constantly questions and critiques existing social norms and structures of oppression such as the ideal of the happy housewife. As affective power used to sustain heteropatriarchy, the happy housewife is a key target of the feminist killjoy, who destabilizes the feelings of joy and fulfillment that this role allegedly promises women by not only demonstrating the myth behind this ideal but by also refusing and resisting the affective power of happiness it promises.

Like the happy housewife, the beauty queen holds an affective power. The figure of the beauty queen affectively personifies that "meeting up over happiness." Her affective power is based on good and happy feelings: wholesomeness, beauty, poise, and orchestrated sexual innocence predicated on the settler logic of white femininity as good, pure, and superior.[8] Those rejecting the beauty pageant industry were thus the killjoys who destabilized the affective power of the beauty queen figure. While second-wave feminists protesting these contests did not mobilize behind the racial logic at the heart of settler societies like Canada, these beauty pageants were not disentangled from these logics and the affective powers they generate.

The concept of the killjoy is closely connected to the emotional concept of anger. In questioning the ideal of the beauty queen, killjoys both incited anger by their actions and embodied the anger that underlay much of the political action in these beauty pageant incidents. Beauty pageants became a significant target for feminist activism and anger. Considered vile representations of sexism and symbols of the pinnacle of heteropatriachy, beauty pageants ignited feminist consciousness. In the context of the 1960s counterculture, resisting, protesting, and disrupting beauty contests can be seen as a radical strategy, whether this involved massive disruption such as the 1968 Miss America protest or defiance by a former beauty queen.

Protest through Buddhist Enlightenment: Miss Canada 1965

The pre-television Miss Canada pageant was, in many ways, a mom-and-pop operation, owned and operated by S. Radcliffe Weaver and his wife, Edith. The Weavers were based in Hamilton, Ontario, and owned a beauty salon, a steam bath, and a Palomino stable.[9] When they bought the Miss Canada franchise from the Miss America organization in 1946, the Miss Canada title was considered an insignificant venture, but the Weavers saw potential. While the Weavers were able to gather largely local support from businesses and organizations in the southern Ontario region to promote their investment, they were never really able to access the national and international funding sources needed to secure the Miss Canada pageant significant visibility. Indeed, Miss Canada's involvement in the Miss America Pageant proved an annual but fleeting moment of fame. Under the Weavers, the Miss Canada contest suffered numerous mishaps and controversies that nearly brought it to total collapse.[10]

It was not until 1962, when Walter Pasko and Tom Reynolds of MCP Talent Associates took over the franchise, that the Miss Canada beauty contest began to emerge as a viable advertising and entertainment investment for companies like Air Canada, Yamaha, and Samsonite.[11] In 1963, MCP Talent Associates produced the first televised *Miss Canada* pageant, thereby introducing Miss Canada as a potentially lucrative advertising gimmick: wholesome girl-next-door sex appeal wrapped up in white Canadian nationalism. Despite their rocky start, Pasko and Reynolds transformed the pageant into an internationally recognized franchise with support from corporate money and the television industry.[12]

Pageants, however, are tricky businesses to manage because their success is built on the ability of the winner to *sell* the right balance of beauty, sexual innocence/appeal, and a settler logic of whiteness. Luckily, the new managers caught a break when Linda Douma, of Sidney, British Columbia, won the Miss Canada 1965 competition in the fall of 1964. As the first "full-time" Canadian beauty queen heralded immediately as "Canada's Sweetheart," Douma quickly helped establish the pageant as a viable and reliable business entity. The organizers labelled the pageant "a unique, all-Canadian institution" with "tremendous merchandising and promotional potential."[13] Douma proved to be a major asset not only because she was a popular domestic symbol of white femininity, poise, and beauty, but also because she promoted Canadian nationalism abroad.

Douma, however, offers one of the more fascinating cases of pageant protest. While there is no evidence that she identified as a feminist, her actions following her reign as Miss Canada 1965 occurred amid the aftermath of the publication of Betty Friedan's *The Feminine Mystique*, a book that spoke to the "problem that has no name," a phrase used by Friedan to indicate the collective pain women experienced as an oppressed class.[14] After her reign, Douma returned to Victoria in 1966 to finish the third year of her bachelor of arts degree. But as she explained to Shirley Culpin, a reporter for *The (Sidney) Review*, "When I visited the Orient [*sic*] during my year as Miss Canada ... I'd been tremendously attracted to the culture and the Zen temples there."[15] Once in India, she said that she felt a "sense of peace and gentleness that is in that land" and decided to visit a "Buddhist temple when I was out exploring one day, and I immediately felt at home there."[16] Douma's transformation from a beauty queen to a Buddhist living in a hut in Nepal by 1967 may not seem particularly extraordinary if not for the fact that she understood it to be a rejection, at the material and affective levels, of all that the Miss Canada pageant represented. Douma appeared to push back at the beauty mystique, the feminine ideal, and the commercial consumerism, by rejecting the so-called charm and poise that gave her access to a world full of financial opportunities. She refused to engage in the corporate culture that the title was supposed to foster, and she abandoned potential careers in show business, modelling, or public relations. This differed from many of her predecessors who viewed the beauty contest as a stepping stone to singing and acting careers in the movies, in television, and the theatre.[17] Their subsequent successes in these various pursuits bolstered the cachet of the title for potential contestants and for the audiences who gazed upon them. Douma's personal choice to embrace a path diametrically opposed to fame and glamour led her into obscurity. Despite her massive success and popularity as Miss Canada, coverage of her Zen practice and her new life in Nepal was scarce to nonexistent.[18]

It is in the surviving correspondence between Douma and June Dennis, her chaperone and personal manager during Douma's reign as Miss Canada, that we most directly encounter her resistance and rejection of the title and what this beauty queen considered its excesses. We also glimpse the disbelief and deep disappointment experienced by Dennis when she realized that her protegé had had a change of heart. The emotional pleas and replies in Dennis's letters and diary entries give us a sense of how anger, rejection, disappointment, and anxiety about the future shaped the way Dennis came to terms with the rebellious Douma. Understanding the affective history behind this rebellion requires an exploration of how June Dennis vicariously experienced her own feelings of success and failure through Douma.

Dennis was one the few female radio personalities working in Canada in the postwar period. She "was offered her first radio job after making an impressive plea on a wartime charity broadcast and before long, ranked as one of Canada's most heard and best-paid women."[19] It is unclear whether Dennis considered herself a feminist, either liberal or radical, but given her work and own career trajectory, it is clear that she was committed to the "uplifting" of women in society. While Dennis never achieved the career prominence of June Callwood or Barbara Walters, she did establish herself in a historical moment when women had very limited access to careers in the media or as publicists.[20] After seventeen years as a radio show host, Dennis quit in 1963. She pursued various careers, including as a novelist, publicist, and editor of *Quill & Quire* (a Canadian trade journal for publishers), but it was her work as personal manager to Miss Canada 1965 that seemed to inspire her letter writing, diary entries, preserved newspaper clippings, and a draft of an introduction to an unfinished book about Douma.[21] It is in these materials that we encounter the affective discourse behind Dennis's protective feelings and disappointment about Douma's decision to move to India and embrace Buddhism as a religion and way of life.

In a winter 1973 diary entry, for example, we learn of Dennis's frustration with Douma and her partner, Shakya's, commitment to Buddhism and, perhaps, of Dennis's final realization that any attempts to bring Douma back to her senses were futile, writing in her diary that "they are both utterly convinced of Buddhism, reincarnation and the necessity for meditation and practice ... It is difficult for a Westerner to grasp the reasons for philosophies of the East."[22] Resigning herself to the quotidian practices of Buddhism and one of its basic precepts, reincarnation, was part of the reconciliation process that Dennis might have been able to accept; however, this entry also reveals that Dennis had difficulty embracing that Douma's new path was a significant turn away from Dennis's own identification as a westerner. In many statements, Dennis's orientalism and sense of racial superiority surfaces. Her inability to "grasp" Eastern philosophies, and her characterization of these philosophies as "junk," underscored her frustration with Douma's decision. Dennis bound these orientalist feelings with what she perceived as a rejection of Western culture and values by Canadian youth such as Douma. In her introduction to an unfinished book on Douma, Dennis mapped the contours of what she described as the "unsettling phenomena" wherein white, middle-class youth defy their role as "inheritors" of what we can only surmise is Dennis's idea of the "promise" of the West.[23] Dennis's attempt to make sense of the rise of the counterculture was at root a struggle to understand the decisions of her young friend and former protegé. Douma's rejection was the underlying affective trauma with which Dennis struggled – a struggle only thinly veiled by the epistemic violence of her orientalist filter.

Undeterred by Dennis's resentment of the unfolding events, Douma wrote her response in a May 1969 letter that explained the surge in youth rebellion and implicated herself in the explanation:

> You showed great concern over the growing occurrence of world-wide student revolt. I guess that all of these young people are feeling pretty insecure and dissatisfied with their present lot. Many of them recognize that there is something missing in our highly materialistic and mechanized progressive society. But few of them seem to know with what new system they want to follow up the present one. Some of these few do know what the west needs but realize that it cannot be forced, but must come gradually with the natural evolution of things. I have met a number of these young people in India doing the same thing as myself. They have found as have I, that all the questions being asked by our Western scientists, psychologists, philosophers and theologians were answered by the Buddha over 2,500 years ago.[24]

Douma's attempts to negotiate the affective field between Dennis and herself introduced an opportunity for Douma to comment on a significant political and historical moment and offer a more personal explanation as to why the rebellious nature of youth culture resonated with her experiences and feelings. Yet in this letter, Douma's own orientalism is revealed since she seems to suggest that westerners who have understood the east know the answers being sought by the "insecure and dissatisfied." But we also learn how Douma used this orientalist filter to come to terms with her own motivations for rejecting the "highly materialistic and mechanized progressive society" and embracing Buddhism. We do not know if this explanation satisfied Dennis since we do not have her response, but given Dennis's book and diary entries we can surmise that she felt little comfort.

As a former beauty queen, Douma's decision to reject a glamorous lifestyle and a future in the entertainment industry created tension (however short-lived) not only for the Canadian pageant industry but also for her personally. A promising symbol of Canadian white youth, femininity, and beauty, Douma seemed to contradict her former life with her ideals about how to live and engage with the world, but her story is indicative of how women began to resist sexist and oppressive forces within the larger context of the counterculture. Their actions often resulted in generational conflict, as illustrated in the correspondence between Dennis and Douma. The rejection and disenchantment with consumer culture and the materialism it magnified was emblematic of the disempowerment that many women, such as the female volunteers of the Company of Young Canadians whom historian Kevin Brushett describes in Chapter 4 of this volume, felt in the 1960s and 1970s. Coupled with the counterculture movement and its anti-establishment rhetoric, feelings of disenchantment could lead to resistance against life trajectories that bolstered more of the same. The impact on Dennis of Douma's decision to drop out of Western society also illuminates this form of resistance as a radical act, as well as the impact of the feminist killjoy at a personal level.

Battle at Waterloo: Miss Canadian University 1970

Within the confines of her mountain retreat, Linda Douma was part of an emerging counterculture embraced by many youth in the West. Accompanying that movement was a rising tide of activism, particularly on university campuses. While Douma did not take part in campus activism, the influences of this generational shift were at the heart of the tensions with Dennis. This shift is often marked by the May 1968 mass movement and strike initiated by French university students protesting capitalism, imperialism, and their limited rights as students.[25] Canadian campuses also experienced an upsurge in youth radicalism against "the establishment." Some notable examples include the occupation and protest of a building at the Sir George

Williams University (now Concordia University), in Montreal, by Black student activists in April 1968 and the events at the newly minted Simon Fraser University that led to the forceable eviction of students occupying the president's office in December 1968.[26] Protesting the 1970 Miss Canadian University pageant, to be held at Waterloo Lutheran University, was part of this youth radicalism, not only stirring the emotions of the protest candidate and participating beauty contestants but also invoking the power of feminist anger and consciousness-raising against pageants as a whole.

The protest against the Miss Canadian University pageant was preceded, in 1969, by the actions of the Kingston Women's Liberation Movement, which disrupted a local contest associated with homecoming at Queen's University.[27] This successful campaign was facilitated by six women from the Kingston group who infiltrated the pageant as contestants. "While the audience waited for the show to begin, several [of these] women dressed in black wrapped another sister up in a white sheet and, gobbing her with cosmetic and hair accessories, proclaimed her 'Miss Consumer Product,' as other sisters passed around flyers explaining our protest."[28] Moreover, each of the six Kingston Women's Liberation Movement members (forming a majority of the contestants) made speeches denouncing the pageant. The master of ceremonies reacted by insulting the contestants as frustration with the feminists' presence increased. As a result, no queen contests, that is, contests associated with homecoming, sports events, or student society festivities, were ever again organized at Queen's University; however, despite the protest, one contestant was crowned Miss Queen's University and continued on to the Miss Canadian University pageant in 1970.

Janiel Jolley would stand as a challenge to this network of university beauty pageants. As a member of the Vancouver Women's Caucus, a women's liberation group founded at Simon Fraser University and the feminist organization that organized the Abortion Caravan from Vancouver to Ottawa in the spring of 1970 to advocate for the legalization of abortion, Jolley was positioned to not only disrupt the university beauty contest circuit but also to use the circuit as a platform for feminist rage.[29] On January 30, 1970, Jolley, the official protest candidate for Simon Fraser University, caused a huge headache for the Waterloo Lutheran University winter carnival committee. In the middle of the contest, Jolley stood up at the back of the auditorium and walked towards the stage while her supporters stood up and raised their fists, singing "Solidarity Forever."[30] Amid shouts of "let our women speak" from supporters in the audience, Bill Walker, master of ceremonies and organizer of the pageant, gave the microphone to Jolley. Jolley pulled no punches:

> I demand to speak here tonight as I represent a growing tendency in Canadian women to object to the dehumanizing nature of beauty contests and I demand to speak because I am the legitimate candidate of my student body who have raised a great deal of money to send me here to be heard ... We have been divided for centuries over such a superficiality as who is the prettiest. I appeal to you to join us in our protest. Let there be no losers in this auditorium tonight.[31]

At the time of Jolley's action, the Miss Canadian University Beauty pageant was celebrating its ninth year of success.[32] Jolley's plan was not to antagonize her "sisters" but to explain to them the manner in which beauty contests objectify and exploit women and their bodies.

She insisted that her aim was not to battle with other women but to destroy the vehicle of their oppression, that is, the contests themselves. In partnership with the Vancouver Women's Caucus and the Simon Fraser Student Society, Jolley gained support and popularity as her protest gained momentum. In a letter she wrote to other feminist and student groups, Jolley explained her belief that as a protest candidate "this [would be] the first time in North America that women's liberation has had this opportunity to expose the dehumanizing nature of beauty contests from the inside."[33]

Jolley believed that the recent Miss America Pageant protests in Atlantic City went too far by attacking the individual contestants and that "the direction our protest will take will be to expose the institutions that force women to make themselves into more desirable sexual commodities rather than attack the women who have been victimized by their socialization. We want to be able to offer the women in Canada an alternative."[34] The notion that the Miss America protesters in 1968 went too far developed into a common critique of the action.[35] Yet, the Canadian alternative was actually no different from that of New York Radical Women protesters, who also believed they were supporting their "sisters" who were participating in the contest. Despite her interpretation, Jolley was still deemed what Ahmed called a spoilsport.

In a poster titled "Janiel Jolley Day," Simon Fraser University organizers outlined their reasons for sending a protest candidate.[36] Although feminist student groups hitherto had boycotted university pageants, the Vancouver Women's Caucus and Jolley were convinced of the need for more drastic action to deliver the message that beauty contests, and the figure of the beauty queen, were degrading and dehumanizing for women. Their argument is particularly important for developing an affective history of feminist protest. Underlying the assertion that the figure of the beauty queen, like the happy housewife, is degrading and dehumanizing for women is the idea that to leave happiness is to become alive. As Ahmed argues, "the concept of feminism as 'becoming alive' was crucial to second wave feminism."[37]

The 1970 Miss Canadian University protest was one of the few times that a women's liberation group in Canada used a beauty contest as a platform to communicate a broader message about women's rights and social status from the inside. As stated in a poster, the Vancouver Women's Caucus rightly saw the political potential of beauty pageants, which reached thousands of women because of their status as highly publicized entertainment programs: "Beauty contests are one of the few platforms open to women, through which we can reach other women, and the public at large. Hopefully, this action may help explain the ideas of women's liberation to thousands of people who have never heard them before."[38] The Vancouver Women's Caucus (and the Miss America protesters) simply took over, and for a moment, reversed the message.

Jolley's approach and methods proved instrumental in disrupting the Miss Canadian University pageant, but not in the way she originally envisioned. The ideal situation, perhaps, would have been for the contestants to rise up and join her in protest by walking off the stage with her, singing "Solidarity Forever." This did not happen. Instead, her success and the success of the women's liberation groups that supported her lay in creating enough bad publicity to agitate the sponsors of the pageant. Jolley disrupted the figure of the beauty queen as a happy object and disrupted the pageant as a common space to convene happiness. This was a major feat, considering that the feminist movement could not do the same for the Miss Canada pageant. Sponsors involved in the Miss Canadian University pageant such as Visa and Ford Motors considered this institution to be a serious business venue.[39] Large corporations would participate in pageants by donating expensive prizes like round trips to sunny destinations, cars, fur coats, and jewellery only if they believed the pageants to be financially profitable, which meant capturing large audiences engaged in what Ahmed calls the "sociality of happiness" or the idea that we share a "social bond if the same objects make us happy."[40]

An important strategy behind the 1970 protest of the Miss Canadian University pageant, therefore, was an attack on its sponsorship and the sociality of happiness it depended on, embodied in the figure of the beauty queen. When Jolley sent her first nomination as Miss Simon Fraser University to the winter carnival committee at Waterloo Lutheran University, she was completely transparent about her intentions as a protest candidate. Officials first accepted her application, stating that "any representative from any university, protest or otherwise, will be welcomed in the same manner as in past years."[41] But this decision was reversed two weeks before the pageant was to take place. There were several reasons for Jolley's disqualification. The Queens Committee officials at Waterloo Lutheran claimed that she was not enrolled as a full-time student at Simon Fraser, that she did not represent the main body of students at her university, and that she was married (which was considered taboo in the context of beauty contests since this shattered the fantasy of sexual innocence). Also included in this list of reasons to disqualify Jolley was the issue of the financial support from the pageant's sponsors that covered the transportation and accommodation costs of the thirty-five contestants from across Canada.[42] The idea of funding a protest candidate, a professed feminist killjoy, who had the potential to disrupt the pageant and garner negative attention aggravated the sponsors, forcing pageant officials to disqualify Jolley. Jolley would only be able to attend if she could secure funds by a different means. In the end, support from various campuses and women's liberation groups enabled her to continue with her plans.

In an article she penned for the *Vancouver Sun*, Jolley explained how the pageant operated as a vehicle for the sponsors to sell their products, whatever the cultural cost to young Canadian women.[43] At the core of the protest against the Miss Canadian University pageant was the feminist critique that pageants constitute part of a system that commercialized and exploited women's bodies for economic gain. Indeed, in her speech on the night of the pageant, Jolley addressed "her sisters" onstage, asking them not to allow themselves to be manipulated for profit by those who "oppressed them the most, cosmetic and fashion corporations."[44] Working from within the pageant system, Jolley aimed to disrupt what was considered by many as a perfectly fun and harmless event. Jolley and her compatriots attacked sponsors to expose the multifaceted relationship among ideals of beauty, the sexual exploitation of Canadian women, and the selling of products and profit-making. More important, the protests were, on some level, successful, resulting in the cancellation of the Miss Canadian University pageant.

Why was this feminist protest of campus pageants so successful where others failed? The answer to this question lies in recognizing the strength of feminist mobilizations on Canadian campuses in the 1960s and early 1970s. The official story of its demise was that sponsors pulled their support for Miss Canadian University, sealing the fate of the contest since Waterloo Lutheran's administration would no longer foot the bill. Sponsors deserted the pageant because of the negative publicity generated by the feminist protest organized by Jolley and the Vancouver Women's Caucus. In addition, the protest succeeded in branding beauty contests as archaic relics of a time when women were supposed to be submissive objects for display. Perhaps this tactic was more successful because of the university context. As institutions geared to promoting the ideal of enlightenment, the argument that beauty contests were antithetical to this philosophy probably had more traction in a university environment. What was certain was that beauty contests as legitimate events on Canadian campuses suffered greatly once feminist attacks against them increased, but this was not necessarily the case in other contexts such as at the national level. For the Miss Canada pageant, which had a much broader audience, the popularity of the pageant model persisted even as it faced feminist mobilizations.

Smash Sexism: Miss Canada 1976 Protest

Despite protests such as the one orchestrated by Jolley, beauty contests, homecoming queens, and competitions where women competed for a title (such as wet T-shirt contests) retained popularity across university campuses and elsewhere. In response, feminists continued to disrupt and protest their existence. The protest in 1975 against the Miss Canada 1976 pageant by a group of Toronto-based second-wavers is illustrative. The national and international attention garnered by the Miss America Pageant protest not only put feminist anger and its killjoy proponents on the map, but also transformed beauty contests. From their inception, modern beauty contests have always been controversial, but the protest at the Miss America Pageant in 1968 challenged the institution's exalted position as the arbiter of American female ideals.[45] From that date on, it was not the internal controversies that made the news, it was the ideological and affective clashes between the feminist movement and beauty contest organizers, producers, supporters, and participants. The new story of beauty pageants was not just whether they could *adapt* to the modernization of society as they had in mid-century, but whether they could compete with the alternatives to the female ideal put forth by the increasingly formidable women's movement.

The only Canadian version of a radical feminist protest similar to the 1968 Miss America mobilization occurred in Toronto, organized by ten women who were members either of the Women's Anarchist Group or of the Radical Feminist Lesbian Group. The Miss Canada 1976 pageant protesters first arrived in taxis in an effort to appear as just another group arriving to enjoy the show. After their first failed attempt to gain backstage access, they returned, eluded the first security officer, and ran towards Studio 6 with officers in pursuit.[46] As they ran into the studio, they threw leaflets to the audience that read "Happy I[nternational] W[omen's] Y[ear]" and "Smash Sexism." They arrived precisely at the moment when the announcer was introducing Miss Canada 1975, Terry Lynne Meyer. Footage of the event captures the screams of surprise from the audience, protester Adrienne Potts raising her fist and yelling at the contestants, "We are not here to attack you!," and the expressions of shock and gasps of surprise emanating from the contestants, with one exclaiming, "Oh my God!" Several women physically fought with the security guards and police officers, who struggled to reach two of the protesters who had jumped onstage.

As anarchists, radical lesbians, and socialist feminists, the ten protesters passionately believed this radical action – the disruption of a beauty contest – to be a manifestation of their feminist anger towards sexist big business. However, the protesters used the action to pursue other ends. They believed they could use the protest to communicate their dissatisfaction with the tone of International Women's Year, specifically that the women's movement was losing its radicalism by developing partnerships with the state. In the protesters' minds, the women's movement was being co-opted by willingly partnering with the government concerning their International Women's Year initiatives.[47] In a post-protest interview, some of the protesters explained that the radical action against the beauty contest was a way for them to bring this issue of co-optation into the spotlight given the high profile of the televised event.[48] In addition, at least one of the women who participated in the protest did so because she wanted to use the action as a springboard to finally come out as a lesbian.[49] Ann Russell, a member of Wages for Housework, said that she had been "fantasizing" about this protest in the same way that she had fantasized about "walking down the street and beating up pricks."[50]

The multiple aims of this direct action highlight the tensions surfacing throughout the women's movement – both ideologically and strategically – in the mid-1970s. Feminist scholars have recorded the internal schism that developed in the middle of International Women's Year, a momentous event for feminists around the world who wanted to bring women's issues to the forefront of political, social, and economic agendas. As the movement grew, various grassroots factions began to move away from the influence of white and middle-class institutional feminists who were quickly positioning themselves as the legitimate voice of women's liberation in Canada.[51] Radical feminists, and especially those that protested the Miss Canada 1976 pageant, were partly resisting this association between the feminist movement in Canada and the legitimization of institutional feminists as the only true voice of women.

Thus, if the disruption of the Miss Canada 1976 pageant was a display of feminist anger, that anger was directed not just at the beauty contest industry but at other feminist "sisters." Ahmed's reading of affect is not solely based on the emotional outlet of a subject, but also based on what that affect can tell us about the political and cultural pulse that drives some forms of feminist mobilization. Ahmed's turn to the affective allows us to see the connective tissue between the subject's emotion and the way it is used as a political outlet during this historical incident.[52] In the case of the disruption, the frustration and anger towards what this set of feminist killjoys understood as the commodification of women's bodies and the co-optation of other feminists by the state translated into a protest against structural power and its acceptance by some sections of the second wave.

Conclusion

At first glance, using beauty contests to shed light on the history of emotions and protest within the context of the history of the second wave might seem counterintuitive. Beauty contests and beauty contestants were considered the antithesis of feminist activity. These institutions measured women's value based on their bodies, exposing women once again to the male gaze to be exploited sexually and as a profit-making venture. Yet beauty contests made feminists angry, and when pageants became the targets of feminist protest, everyone else got angry with the feminists. This anger was significant. It turned on the feeling that feminist protest disrupted the idea of beauty contests and contestants as a power source of good feelings – of embracing agreed upon happy feelings. In this sense, protests in the context of beauty contests during the second wave are a critical entry into understanding the affective turn in the history of second-wave feminism.

Linda Douma, Janiel Jolley, and the radical feminists who disrupted the Miss Canada 1976 pageant illuminate various forms of feminist resistance. Douma, for example, rejected the rewards associated with beauty and white hyperfemininity, turning away from the celebrity status and material comforts available to beauty queens during and after their year-long reign.

She refused to remain the "happy object" so central to the making and sustainability of the beauty queen persona. Jolley used her ability to pass as a beauty queen – she exhibited the white, wholesome, and youthful looks attributed to beauty queens in this period – to disrupt the Miss Canadian University pageant in 1970. In this example of organized feminist anger, Jolley could use the rhetoric of solidarity as a feminist and a beauty queen to exact an affective result from the other contestants, while effectively bringing the Miss Canadian University pageant to an end. Finally, the radical feminists who protested the Miss Canada 1976 pageant used their action to send a message about the systemic workings of heterosexism as well as their concerns about the ways in which partnership with the state during International Women's Day organizing might diminish the radical aims of feminists.

In refusing to embrace the culture of the beauty pageant, protesters became, in Sara Ahmed's more modern language, feminist killjoys. They disrupted the script that equated beauty pageants with happiness, as sites of enjoyment, and as affirmations of a certain expression of womanhood. In doing so, they provoked a variety of emotions: disappointment, shock, outrage. Central to their activities was anger: protesters often deployed anger in their mobilizing efforts and evoked anger with their actions. For Ahmed, both activities constitute core feminist aims.

Notes

1 Satu Repo, "Are Women Necessary?," *Saturday Night*, August 1969, 30. According to Nancy Adamson, the first protest of a Canadian beauty contest was in 1968 by Toronto's Women's Liberation Group against a "winter bikini" contest. Apparently, "the protesters displayed meat-cutters' charts to show that the contestants were involved in marketing their flesh." See Adamson, "Feminist, Libbers, Lefties, and Radicals: The Emergence of the Women's Liberation Movement," in *A Diversity of Women: Ontario, 1945–1980*, ed. Joy Parr (Toronto: University of Toronto Press, 1995), 252–80.

2 Repo, "Are Women Necessary?," 30.

3 According to Echols, the Miss America Protest "marked the end of the movement's obscurity because the protest – the movement's first national action – received extensive press coverage." Alice Echols, *Daring to Be Bad: Radical Feminism in America, 1967–1975* (Minneapolis: University of Minnesota Press, 1989), 93.

4 Echols, *Daring to Be Bad*, 93.

5 Sara Ahmed, *The Promise of Happiness* (Durham: Duke University Press, 2010), 66.

6 Ahmed, *Promise of Happiness*, 60, 65.

7 Ahmed, *Promise of Happiness*, 65.

8 The link to settler logics of white femininity, nationalism, and beauty contests is explored in my book titled, *Queen of the Maple Leaf: Beauty Contest and Settler Femininity* (Vancouver: UBC Press, 2020). I draw on Patrick Wolfe's work on settler logics and settler colonialism.
9 Marilyn Reddick, "My, uh, Dazzling Career as Miss Canada," *Maclean's*, September 15, 1954, 19.
10 For more on the history of the Miss Canada pageant under the Weavers, see Patrizia Gentile, *Queen of the Maple Leaf.*
11 *The Courier*, circa 1967, p. 1, Library and Archives Canada (LAC), MG 31, D191, vol. 1.
12 For more on a history of television, see Paul Rutherford, *When Television Was Young: Primetime Canada 1952–1967* (Toronto: University of Toronto Press, 1990).
13 "Miss Canada Pageant," promotional booklet, LAC, RG 69, vol. 177, file 4-1-59.
14 Betty Friedan, *The Feminine Mystique* (New York: W.W. Norton, 1963), 15.
15 Linda Douma, cited in Shirley Culpin, "Future Path for Ex-Beauty Queen May Lead Back to India," *The Review*, September 12, 1979, 5.
16 Douma, cited in Culpin, "Future Path for Ex-Beauty Queen," 5.
17 For a good illustration of a beauty pageant titleholder's experience, see Marilyn Reddick, "My, uh, Dazzling Career as Miss Canada," *Maclean's*, December 14, 1954, 15, 19, 104–107. See also a much more scathing account of the commercialism behind the Miss Canada pageant and the unattainable "dreams" it fostered, in Valerie Miner Johnson, "Meet Miss Canada; Or, the Rape of Cinderella," *Saturday Night*, February 1973, 15–16, 18–20.
18 A newspaper search for the years 1966–1980 shows that there seemed to be no coverage of Douma's move to Nepal. An article published in the *Province* is the only article I found other than the Culpin piece that appeared in *The Review*. See Shirley Lynn, "Beauty Queen Happy Exile," *Province*, July 16, 1974, 22. According to this article, Douma's "frequent" letters to her mother "tell of a completely happy life, not at all 'monastic,'" and that her friends are "many of the young Canadians and Westerners working and living in India." It seems that by 1974, Douma was working in India (we don't know where or what kind of work) but not being paid.
19 George Gamester, "Names in the News," *Toronto Star*, February 27, 1980, D17.
20 Barbara Freeman has written extensively about the challenges and obstacles that female journalists experienced in the early and mid-twentieth century in the Canadian context. See Barbara M. Freeman, *The Satellite Sex: The Media and Women's Issues in English Canada, 1966–1971* (Waterloo, ON: Wilfrid Laurier University Press, 2001).
21 June Dennis deposited these materials at the Library and Archives Canada. See MG 31 D191, vol. 2, June Dennis file. The titles of her books include *A Mike for Marion* (1962) and *TV Career Girl* (1964). I was unable to determine from the records that were available to me as to why Dennis was hired as Miss Canada's chaperone by the pageant's new owners, MCP Talent Associates. It is possible that her profile as one of the few female public personalities in the 1960s with substantial experience and expertise in the world of public relations and the media made her a desirable choice for the job. Televising the Miss Canada pageant meant that the organization had to pivot the beauty contest as a marketable and highly publicized event requiring

people with publicist skills, like Dennis, to navigate advertisers, corporate interests, and journalists.

22 June Dennis, diary entry, LAC, MG 31, D191, vol. 2, file 2-9, Douma, Linda, Clippings, notes and introduction to unfinished book by June Dennis, n.d. 1971–1979. There are only a few references to Shakya. We do know that Shakya was Douma's male companion, also training as a Buddhist monk for several years.

23 Linda Douma, Clippings, notes and introduction to unfinished book by June Dennis, n.d., LAC.

24 Linda Douma to June Dennis, May 4, 1969, LAC, MG 31, D191, vol. 2, file 2-9, Douma, Linda, Former Miss Canada, Correspondance, n.d., 1968–1982.

25 Kristin Ross, *May '68 and Its Afterlives* (Chicago: University of Chicago Press, 2002), engages with the historiography of this massive movement. I would like to thank Susan Prentice for sending me the information on the Simon Fraser University protest candidate for the Miss Canadian University pageant.

26 For an excellent account of the Sir George Williams University occupation (the largest in Canadian campus protest history), see Chapter 7 of David Austin's, *Fear of a Black Nation: Race, Sex, and Security in Sixties Montreal* (Toronto: Between the Lines, 2013); and see Doug Owram's *Born at the Right Time* (Toronto: University of Toronto Press, 1996) for more on the campus strikes that shifted the balance of power between students and faculty on the one hand, and the administration on the other.

27 Nancy Adamson, "Feminists, Libbers, Lefties, and Radicals," in *A Diversity of Women: Ontario, 1945–1980*, ed. Joy Parr (Toronto: University of Toronto Press, 1995), 262.

28 Adamson, "Feminists, Libbers, Lefties, and Radicals," 262–63.

29 For a brief history of the Vancouver Women's Caucus, see Christabelle Sethna and Steve Hewitt, "Clandestine Operations: The Vancouver Women's Caucus, the Abortion Caravan, and the RCMP," *Canadian Historical Review* 90, 3 (2009): 463–95.

30 "Janiel Jolley Shows 'em the Way," *The Peak* (Burnaby, BC), February 4, 1970, Simon Fraser University Archives and Records (SFU Archives and Records), Women's movement collection, Marge Hollibaugh collector, 1969–1970, F-73, item 2, Beauty pageant scrapbook.

31 Janiel Jolley, cited in "Janiel Jolley Shows 'em the Way," SFU Archives and Records.

32 Candidates from universities across the country, including University of British Columbia, Simon Fraser University, University of Alberta, University of Manitoba, University of Toronto, York University, University of Western Ontario, Waterloo Lutheran University, University of Windsor, Carleton University, University of Ottawa, Queen's University, Laval University, Loyola University, Sudbury University, St. Mary's College, Ryerson University, Acadia University, Mount Allison University, Dalhousie University, University of New Brunswick, Prince Edward Island University, and Memorial University, participated in the event.

33 Janiel Jolley to feminist and student groups, January 17, 1970, SFU Archives and Records, F-73. Jolley's assertion was not entirely accurate when we consider the action taken by the KWLM. Nevertheless, for more, see the two-page letter. Judy Darcy, a prominent Canadian union activist, has retold her own story as York University protest candidate in the same pageant. Judy Darcy, quoted in *Ten Thousand*

Roses: The Making of a Feminist Revolution, ed. Judy Rebick (Toronto: Penguin Canada, 2005), 10–11.

34 Janiel Jolley to feminist and student groups, January 17, 1970, SFU Archives and Records.

35 For a wonderful analysis of the media-generated discourse on agency during the Miss America protest, see Bonnie J. Dow, "Feminism, Miss America, and Media Mythology," *Rhetoric and Public Affairs* 6, 1 (2003): 127–60.

36 "Janiel Jolley Day," poster, n.d., ca. January 1970, SFU Archives and Records, F-73, item 2. By the time Janiel Jolley and her supporters mounted their protest, other universities had begun to boycott the Miss Canadian University pageant.

37 Ahmed, *Promise of Happiness*, 78.

38 "Janiel Jolley Day," poster, SFU Archives and Records.

39 "Queen's Agenda," n.d., and "Major Prizes," n.d., SFU Archives and Records, Women's movement collection, Marge Hollibaugh collector, F-73, item 2. Included in the roster of sponsors were Visa Marketing, Fairweather Fashion Council Stores, Electrohome, McBrine Luggage, Vic Tanny's, Dobbie Industries, Lyons of London, Greb Industries, Diamond Knitting Ltd., Bulova Watch Company, and Ford Motor Company.

40 Ahmed, *Promise of Happiness*, 56.

41 Pat Doyle, Co-chairman, Queens Committee, to Norm Wickstrom, President Student Society, Simon Fraser University, November 25, 1969, SFU Archives and Records, Women's movement collection, Marge Hollibaugh collector, F-73, item 2.

42 Pat Doyle to Norm Wickstrom, November 25, 1969, SFU Archives and Records.

43 "SFU Protester 'Overcomes' University Beauty Contest," *Vancouver Sun*, January 31, 1970, SFU Archives and Records.

44 "Janiel Jolley Shows 'em the Way," *The Peak*, February 4, 1970, SFU Archives and Records.

45 Modern beauty contests have been plagued by controversies since their inception in the North American context. From debates over appropriate displays of women's bodies and Victorian ideals of respectability in the mid-nineteenth century (such as Phineas T. Barnum's first attempt, in 1854, to organize beauty contests) to the exploitative relationship between these contests and for-profit business ventures from 1921 onwards, beauty pageants have been a source of distaste, spectacle, and entertainment. For more on this see, Gentile, *Queen of the Maple Leaf*.

46 The *Toronto Star* reported that this guard had broken ribs as a result of the protesters forced entry, but I have no evidence to support or dispute this story. See "Feminists Storm Stage at Miss Canada Contest," *Toronto Star*, November 4, 1975, A3.

47 "Interview," *The Other Woman*, December/January 1976, 3, Canadian Women's Movement Archives (CWMA). There are two versions of the interview I mention in the text. The long version is a taped interview conducted by Pat Leslie, former editor of *The Other Woman*, which I transcribed for my purposes here. The short version that appeared in *The Other Woman* is in some ways radically different, not only because it is a truncated version, but also because the reorganization of the interview by Leslie or the editors of the feminist newspaper changed the tone of the original taped version. The taped version can be found at "Interview of the Women

Who Protested the Miss Canada Pageant," for *The Other Woman*, Sound Recording (S/R), 11/13, CWMA.

48 "Interview of the Women Who Protested the Miss Canada Pageant," for *The Other Woman*, CWMA.

49 "Interview of the Women Who Protested the Miss Canada Pageant," for *The Other Woman*, CWMA. The woman identified in *The Other Woman* was Audrey Donaldson.

50 "Interview of the Women Who Protested the Miss Canada Pageant," for *The Other Woman*, CWMA. Wages for Housework in Toronto was part of a global movement founded in the early 1970s dedicated to fighting for women's right to work outside the home as well as for women who work in the home as mothers and wives to receive a salary. One of the main tenets of this global movement was the link between the division of labour along gendered lines and the survival of industrial capitalism/class society.

51 Nancy Adamson, Linda Briskin, and Margaret McPhail, *Feminists Organizing for Change: The Contemporary Women's Movement in Canada* (Toronto: Oxford University Press, 1988), 54. These grassroots factions included radical feminists, lesbian feminists, and socialist feminists. As the decade progressed, issues integral to the survival of immigrant, Indigenous, and Black women were also affecting the ability of the Canadian women's movement to claim one unified voice.

52 Sara Ahmed, *The Cultural Politics of Emotion* (Edinburgh: Edinburgh University Press, 2004), 176.

6

"Jesus Is Not Part of This Collective" Secular Passions and Religious Alienation among the Sisterhood

LYNNE MARKS, MARGARET LITTLE, MARIN BECK, EMMA PASZAT, AND TAYLOR ANTONIAZZI

During the 1980s when Sandy tried to stock Christian books in her feminist bookstore collective or to talk about her faith at meetings, she was firmly told, "Jesus is not part of this collective."[1] As an evangelical Christian she believed it was possible to be both religious and a feminist, but the other members of Everywomans Books in Victoria, BC, did not agree. For many feminists in Canada, during the 1960s to 1980s feminism and religion were simply incompatible. "We didn't like religion," recalled Brooke, a Vancouver lesbian and feminist whose work in feminist groups in the 1970s and 1980s ranged from organizing International Women's Day parades to welfare rights protests. "Religion was seen as the patriarchy ... Women were really put down in most religions. So as a feminist you cast off the dogma of the church. I knew not one feminist who went to church ... or if they did, they hid it."[2] To explore the role of religion in feminist activism in Canada from the 1960s to 1980s, we conducted archival research and fifty qualitative oral history interviews with women activists. Of the interviews, twenty-five were with white radical and socialist feminists, including several white Jewish feminists, and twenty-five interviews were with racialized immigrant women activists. All interviewees had lived in Ontario or BC during this era. We define these white radical and socialist feminists as mainstream, or what Chela Sandoval calls "hegemonic feminists."[3] While these women may not define themselves as mainstream, we define them this way because of the leadership roles they played in the most influential feminist groups of this era such as the National Action Committee on the Status of Women, the abortion and reproductive rights movement, the International Women's Day collectives, women's shelters, and feminist bookstores.

In this chapter we show that feminism, religion, and the rejection of religion evoked a host of emotions and could create what American historian of emotions Barbara Rosenwein calls "emotional communities."[4] These communities could produce a range of emotions including anger, pain, love, wonder, joy, and hope.[5] And, at times, these emotions could conflict, creating both contradictions within, and exclusions from, these emotional communities.[6] In some ways, this hegemonic feminism replaced religion and carried a similar religious zeal. Some described a strong anger against religion and other institutions that were viewed as patriarchal. Others described a powerful love of those who were committed to the same causes and the same feminist and secular ways of understanding the world. This strong emotional attachment to a certain type of feminist politics could feel intoxicating, creating an emotionally intense community that created strong boundaries of inclusion and exclusion. And as our archival and interview evidence will show, this emotionally intense community could be challenging for white Christian and Jewish feminists and often felt particularly exclusionary to racialized immigrant women activists.

While the relationship between religion and feminism was a central focus for scholars of nineteenth- and early-twentieth-century English Canadian feminism,[7] we know very little about the relationship between religion and feminism in English Canada in the 1960s–80s period. What we do know, and explore here, suggests that the relationship was challenging at best. We know that many of the women involved in the pacifist Voice of Women, founded in 1960, came from Quaker, Unitarian, and other religious social justice backgrounds. We are also aware that some Christian and Jewish second-wave feminists sought to challenge patriarchy within their denominations, demanding equal rights within religious institutions and more inclusive liturgy and ritual practices.[8] African Canadian women had been working on women's rights, civil rights, and other social justice issues within their churches since the nineteenth century, and some African Canadian women continued to do so during this era.[9] Other feminists completely abandoned traditional denominations in this period but sought alternative forms of feminist spirituality.[10]

The various ways in which many Canadian second-wave feminists related to religion and spirituality are important and require further study. However, they are not the focus of this chapter. Brooke's comment makes clear that some second-wave feminism was marked by significant disdain for, and rejection of, organized religion. Indeed, the popular assumption has been that second-wave feminism was largely secular. Yet this claim has not been the focus of historical study in either Canada or the United States.[11] In this chapter we begin exploring the secularity of English Canadian second-wave feminism, examining its silent assumptions, its inclusions, and, most importantly, its exclusions (particularly in relation to immigrant women activists) and the emotions it evoked.

The strongest anger and hostility against religion existed within white radical feminist and socialist feminist groups, as well as lesbian feminist groups (who may or may not have defined themselves as radical feminists). These groups tended to create tight emotional communities, with shared values and ideals. Liberal feminist groups also shared values and norms, although their connections may not have been as intense. These liberal groups appeared increasingly over the 1970s and 1980s to assume a basic secularism among their members, but there was more willingness to accept religious feminists within their ranks than was the case with other white mainstream feminist groups.[12]

Women who worked with immigrant women in these decades were often from immigrant and/or racialized communities themselves, and even if they were not, were much more likely to recognize the intersecting oppression of gender, race, class, and immigrant status than other feminists. These immigrant women activists also had a more complex relationship with religion and the secular, with some remaining religious and those who had rejected religion themselves recognizing its importance for the immigrant women with whom they worked. These activists, both secular and religious, felt the need to engage with religion and the cultures associated with it, in a much more complex and nuanced way than was the norm among primarily white feminists. Scholars have identified many of the tensions between racialized feminists and white feminists in Canada in the 1980s and 1990s, but religion and the secular have not been a central focus of study.[13]

As Sara Ahmed, Elspeth Probyn, Barbara Rosenwein, and other scholars have argued, feminism evokes a wide range of emotions – among them a feeling of alienation from the everyday world and a deep desire to build a community.[14] In fact, becoming a feminist can parallel feelings evoked by a religious conversion experience among evangelical Christians. It can be intoxicating, with a flood of emotions as one feels included, enveloped into an "emotional community." But as with many religious organizations, feminist groups can also encourage conformity. Ahmed has noted the frequent tendency within feminism to create "natives and strangers" – those who fit within a particular feminist culture, world view, and set of values and those who do not. As Ahmed explains, "To be identified as a stranger is to be identified as not being from here, or not being entitled to be here; you are identified as *someone who endangers who is here*."[15] She also underscores the feelings of anger and alienation associated with being made "strangers."[16] Probyn focuses on the morality associated with feminism and the deep reproach and shame this can produce.[17] While involvement in feminist organizations united some women from different religious backgrounds, our research shows that to fit within many of these organizations – to be truly part of the community – one had to abandon any religious beliefs in favour of a largely unspoken but powerful shared secularism. These secular assumptions reinforced a sense of difference and of alienation – of creating natives and strangers – between primarily white feminists and immigrant women activists.

Religion and the Secular among Institutional and Grassroots Feminists

While almost all of the white feminist activists we interviewed became secular, most had some religious upbringing, with some being devout Catholics, Anglicans, and Jews, and some being occasional attenders of church or synagogue. A few had been raised in families with no religious upbringing. A minority of both Christians and Jews had parents who were active in social justice work – for the Christians and a number of Jews from a religious social justice perspective – while other Jews emerged from a more secular, left-wing framework.

Most of these women had drifted away from religion during their late teens, a fairly common phenomenon in Canada during the late 1960s and 1970s. Scholars have noted major secularizing trends emerging at this time, with the number of those leaving the churches and religion itself increasing dramatically from the late 1960s onward. Some scholars have argued that secularizing trends were accelerating because, for the first time, women were almost as likely as men to abandon religious faith and practice. As feminist ideals of women's personal autonomy and independence became more accepted within the larger culture, more women abandoned Christian norms of feminine piety and domesticity and, often, the churches themselves.[18] American gender historian Joan Scott argues that this reflects the way many women, and feminists more generally, were adopting the dominant liberal secular narrative of the modern autonomous individual.[19]

However, many feminists we interviewed would see their secularism as going beyond these dominant liberal narratives.

These feminists did not just leave the churches and Christian norms behind but more actively and passionately rejected them. Organized religion was the enemy: it was associated with the patriarchal and homophobic institutions these women were struggling against. The churches, they argued, oppressed women, lesbians, and gay people and opposed reproductive choice and many other feminist goals. A number of the women interviewed noted that this was both their own individual perspective and dominant within the larger feminist movement, particularly within the more radical grassroots lesbian feminist, radical feminist, or socialist feminist movements.[20]

Some of the women were very clear that their feminism had replaced any religious faith and practice, that they had transferred from one emotional community to another. Anita Roberts was perhaps the most explicit, stating that "it was almost like feminism was our religion, and our collective chosen religion."[21] Another woman noted, "I had a kind of religious zeal about feminism. So you know, you could find a congruence with religion and all that's good about believing in something." She also spoke of the "quasi-bliss of feminist activism" as being very close to spirituality for her.[22] Marilyn Callahan spoke about "the passion ... of the organizing ... it ... [was] so ... exhilarating. For so many women. It was like a whole brand new world." She agreed that it was perhaps "like a religion in itself."[23] A number of women spoke of this excitement, passion, and energy in feminist activism. In her early work, Sara Ahmed identified these intense positive, hopeful, and joyous emotions of the feminist movement as it worked towards visions of a better future.[24] What we wish to probe is how these emotions may be equivalent to a religious zeal, or what Ahmed later calls the sensational nature of feminism – the big emotions and deep desire to build community.[25]

The positive emotions of being part of feminist communities emerged very clearly in the interviews. Enise Olding said that she had not felt much in common with many other women until she found the women's movement and was excited "to discover a community of women who had so many of the same issues ... [with] whom I could relate."[26] These feelings could be particularly intense for lesbian feminist women.[27] Reva Hutkin spoke of knowing that she was a lesbian from the 1950s on but of having no context for herself, no community until the 1980s, when she spoke of the joy and excitement of discovering "her tribe." Her words echoed the joy and emotion of a religious conversion experience when she said, "It blew my mind to be at a dance with women's music and women dancing, and I thought somebody had dropped me into another world, literally." She noted that the only time before that she had felt part of a "tribe" had been when she was active in a left-wing Zionist youth group for several years as a teenager, which also felt like "they were my tribe, my people."[28]

In addition to the joys of belonging, another potential parallel between religion and feminism can be found in the moralism of certain religious and feminist communities, a tendency to create rigid rules that those who wished to be part of the community had to accept. Kate Nonesuch, who had been actively involved in an evangelical church as a teenager, made these links explicitly. She said that in being a feminist, "it helped to have been a Puritan in a former life ... I saw a [lot] of similarities between being a feminist and being a Christian." She spoke of how self-righteous she now thinks her feminist group was and how they "were really trying to live a life according to a [certain] politics."[29] Another lesbian feminist said she was "purged" from the Marxist feminist organization, Wages for Housework, "for individuation" and "being still too into lesbian feminism." She said that being suspended was "kind of like being in purgatory, and people didn't want to talk to me."[30]

While not all feminist politics was as extreme as Wages for Housework, many feminist organizations, particularly grassroots organizations of this period, shared a number of powerful spoken and unspoken rules that could, as Probyn has noted, create shame in those who did not follow the norms and dictates of feminist community politics.[31] As Campbell, Dawson, and Gidney note in the Introduction to this volume, Probyn speaks about both the negative *and* the positive aspects of shame and how shame can be evoked to create connection and communication with others. But we heard more of the negative aspects of shame. This phenomenon mirrored that of religious communities with strict norms of belief, morality, and dress. For example, certain conservative Mennonite communities used to shun those who wore brown rather than black shoes.[32] Lesbian feminists of the 1970s and early 1980s looked down on those wearing overly butch or femme attire.[33] Another polarizing issue among lesbian feminists and other radical feminists was the question of male children, who were often not welcome at feminist events or spaces.

No one has yet explored the unwritten, and generally unspoken, norms of secularism within many English Canadian feminist organizations. When asked if religion was an issue in any of the feminist organizations they belonged to, almost all the white lesbian radical and socialist feminists said no, it didn't come up. When pushed a bit further, a number of them said that it would not have been acceptable to be actively religious, particularly Christian, in their organizations, noting that Christianity was associated with patriarchy, with being anti-choice, and with everything feminists were fighting against. This attitude was particularly strong within white radical, lesbian, and socialist feminist organizations in larger cities, but it was not confined to these groups. Nonesuch, a white lesbian feminist in Vancouver who believed that the self-righteousness of feminism had Puritan echoes, was also very clear that "it wouldn't have been acceptable" for women active in the feminist organizations she was involved in "to be religious."[34] Similarly to Nonesuch, a heterosexual Marxist feminist from Toronto said that,

> I have no recollection of any of my networks being tied to religion in that period ... I think most of us were indifferent to religion, or hadn't thought about it, or saw the institutions as problematic ... The other interesting question is whether people who were religious in that period, if they felt that it was unsafe to say so. They might have been, because I can imagine us all [saying] – you what? And not being very supportive.[35]

Another interviewee, Jen Moses, who was an organizer for a feminist union and also volunteered with a range of other predominantly white lesbian and feminist organizations, recalled, "I didn't know any religious people at the time. Nobody in my circle was out ... about being religious. Nobody was heading into religious institutions ... churches, temples, synagogues. There was no talk about any of that."[36] Anita Roberts, who spoke of feminism as being her religion, said, "I would say the band that I ran with, my gang – my tribe, better word – were flying in the face of so many traditional things, that religion was a part of that. And I don't even know if I knew personally one woman who was religious."[37] These bands, "tribes," circles, and networks mentioned by the interviewees above were all tight feminist communities, sharing common values and a powerful sense of belonging and joy and excitement about changing the world. Being religious did not fit within the norms of these secular feminist communities.

Yet this hostility to religion led to pushback from some older feminists. Many of the women who were active in Voice of Women, for example, did not appreciate the growing hostility to religion among many feminists from the late 1960s onward. One such conflict was evident in the Toronto feminist magazine *Broadside*. In early 1980, Bernadette Maxwell wrote to challenge an article by Susan Cole, which had attacked the legitimacy of religion. Maxwell argued, "I know of many people who arrived at their anti-sexist, anti-racist, anti-capitalist, anti-militarist positions through a radical understanding of the Christian message." Maxwell noted that her friends within the Voice of Women included "some Quakers, some Unitarians and … radical Catholics" and argued that the self-righteously anti-religious stance of *Broadside* was alienating her and other Christian feminists.[38] *Broadside* tried to be somewhat conciliatory, publishing other articles by Christian feminists about their efforts to transform the churches, as well as a fairly even-handed article on Judaism and feminism by Susan Cole.[39] However, *Broadside* also published an editorial pointing to the antifeminist nature of religion, as well as an article viciously hostile to Maxwell's arguments.[40] The author of the latter piece, Kris Furlought, attacked Maxwell, claiming that "only in the minds of the feeble, the brainwashed and the fascist does the notion of a male-god have any significance!" Furlought concluded by arguing that "being a 'feminist' and a 'Christian' at one and the same time are mutually exclusive. Christian ideology is savagely anti-feminist."[41]

The deep anger fuelling such anti-religious attitudes among many white feminists may have been intoxicating, and it helped to construct strong feminist communities, but it also created barriers. Such anger can take the form of what Sara Ahmed calls "the feminist killjoy," the troublemaker, the one who feels alienated when she names injustice and inequality that others consider inappropriate for critique.[42] But this anger can also exclude, creating very distinct boundaries between who is a member of feminist communities and who is a stranger.[43] And feminists can block or refuse to hear the anger of others through a defence of their own positionality.[44] Thus feminists can become involved in legitimizing certain feelings of anger and pain and delegitimizing others. Ahmed's understanding of mainstream feminists' delegitimization and exclusion of feminists of colour is applied by political scientist and race scholar Malinda Smith to feminists in the Canadian academy and by historian and race scholar Funké Aladejebi in Chapter 10 to understand Black women teachers' experiences in Ontario.[45] It is also relevant for our study.

Clearly, a number of Christian feminist activists were identified as strangers by many feminists of the time. A white lesbian feminist who fought for same-sex benefits in her professional union said, "I suffered as a lesbian in the Christian community, I also experienced discrimination as a Christian in the lesbian community."[46] Linda Sproule-Jones, a white heterosexual feminist and a practising Anglican involved in churches with a social justice focus said, "Sometimes people would make snide remarks [about religion] … but I would just say … well, that's not my experience."[47] Jane, a white, heterosexual, middle-class woman who was active in Victoria's Status of Women Action Group, a primarily white activist group, revealed during the interview that she defined herself as a "pro-life feminist." She said she was "a great believer in women making their own choices," but this strongly held personal belief emerged from the religious values of her Anglican upbringing, although she was not an actively practising Anglican as an adult. When asked if she had revealed her pro-life personal views while in the Status of Women Action Group, she said, "No way," and noted that she had previously not told anyone except her husband about her views on this subject.[48] Support for abortion rights was (and remains) a litmus test for feminists, and one of the many sources of feminist hostility to organized religion has been the refusal of many religious institutions to accept women's right to abortion. At the same time, an unwillingness to be open to feminists with Christian views certainly led to at least some alienation that came with the personal self-censorship of women of faith within second-wave feminist groups. It was certainly one of the many ways of creating natives and strangers within the women's movement.

While feminists who were active both in large cities and in smaller communities expressed hostility to organized religion, those in smaller communities were sometimes more open to religious differences. As other scholars have suggested, the smaller pool of feminists from which to draw in these communities may have led to an acceptance of a greater diversity of views.[49] United Church women were very active and supportive in the early years of Kingston's transition house. The staff collective of the transition house in the small city of Vernon, BC, included some women who, for religious reasons, opposed abortion, but as long as they did not seek to impose their views on others, they were accepted.[50]

Transition houses in smaller cities often made compromises with local churches. For example, Louise noted that no one on the staff collective of the feminist transition house in Ottawa was religious, or at least openly religious, again because "religion was a force that oppressed women ... So if you were strongly religious ... you wouldn't have felt ok to talk about it." At the same time, the transition house had "a lot of churches that supported us." For example, the transition house received regular bread deliveries from one church. And some churches supported families when they left transition homes. The transition house in Vernon, BC, dealt with similar contradictions in that most staff members opposed religion as patriarchal, but the transition house building itself had been donated by the local Anglican church, "because they [the churches] do good works."[51]

Most of the mainstream feminist organizations that accommodated religion only acknowledged Christianity. Bobby Kovar, who was involved with a transition house in Victoria, recalled that "there were women from Muslim countries, but I can't remember anyone saying at 5 o'clock in the morning, 'Oh, I have to put my prayer rug out to pray.' They may not have felt that comfortable doing that in a place that was predominately white women."[52] Kate Nonesuch, who was involved in the Ottawa transition house in its early phase, noted that "if somebody had come wearing a hijab, that would have been fine, but we wouldn't have known to offer her halal food unless she first said, 'I can't eat what you're giving me; you need to give me something else.' In that case, we would have found something else for her, but we wouldn't have known. We wouldn't have thought about those things beforehand."[53]

During the 1970s and into the 1980s, very few Muslim women were involved in the feminist organizations that we have been discussing thus far, other than as clients of feminist anti-violence services. However, one group of women from non-Christian backgrounds was active in a broad range of feminist organizations. In many ways, the Jewish women who were actively involved in feminist organizations shared the political and secular values that we have been discussing. However, some tensions did emerge between Jewish and non-Jewish feminists, given the definition of the secular that was assumed within these organizations. As scholars of religion and irreligion have noted, the definition of the secular used in Western societies tends to be a very Christian one, but in a powerfully unmarked way.[54]

Since religion was to be rejected and ignored in feminist groups, it is not surprising that most secular feminists from Christian backgrounds were oblivious about dates of non-Christian holidays, often setting meetings on such days. This speaks to the shallowness that is sometimes found in feminist inclusion. Ahmed cautions that sometimes feminists reify feminist ideals. "Such a reification of political ideals would position some feminists as 'hosts' who would decide which others would receive the hospitality of love and recognition, and would hence remain predicated on a differentiation between natives and strangers."[55] Thus inclusion can be more token than meaningful integration and respect. Such was the case with non-Christian holidays. Active secular Jewish feminist women like Debby Yaffe and Reva Hutkin would challenge their sisters when events were set for Jewish holy days, although neither woman would enter a synagogue on that day. As Yaffe recalled,

> They would have stuff on Rosh Hashanah, they would have stuff on Yom Kippur, and I would say, "You know, these are the holiest days in the Jewish calendar; what are you doing?" And they would just look at you, like, "Huh? Who cares?" They just had never heard of it. And, even though I personally, like, I don't observe Sabbath, I don't really do anything for Rosh Hashanah, for Yom Kippur, I just feel, you know, in principle ... that should be respected. Just like I would for other religions. If it's a big religious holiday, you don't schedule things. It's just respect.[56]

Yaffe and Hutkin harboured considerable anger and frustration about the obliviousness of their sisters.

At the same time, secular feminists from Christian backgrounds did not see any problem with celebrating Christmas and Easter as "secular" holidays that everyone should participate in. Jews saw things differently. Christmas and Easter have religious and exclusionary connotations for most people from non-Christian religious backgrounds. As Yaffe noted, at Everywomans Books each year "there was a Christmas potluck ... People don't realize how much Christmas is not a secular holiday. [The women who held these events] weren't religious ... They were what I would call secular Christians, like I'm a secular Jew. But they don't think of themselves that way because they don't have to."[57]

The inability of most secular feminists from Christian backgrounds to understand the concerns of Jewish feminists about the celebration of secular Christian holidays could cause frustration and some temporary alienation. At other times the explicitly anti-religious impetus of second-wave feminism could be more emotionally damaging. Dorothy Elias had been raised with no knowledge of her Jewish background, because as Holocaust survivors her parents sought to protect themselves and their children from further anti-Semitism. When she discovered her Jewish heritage she was already a feminist, and she became involved in a culturally Jewish feminist social group that celebrated Jewish holidays in a progressive way. This was a very positive experience for her, reclaiming her heritage in the context of a supportive Jewish feminist community. As Elias tells it, her first serious experience of anti-Semitism came from an anti-religious feminist. She described this as her "first, on-my-skin experience of anti-Semitism. A woman was arguing with me that it was not okay to claim being a Jew because Jews had prayers about being glad they weren't born women and separated the women out, and so you couldn't support that. You couldn't be part of that if you were a feminist." From this encounter, Elias understood that this woman clearly had no interest in, or understanding of, differences between cultural Judaism and Orthodox religious Judaism. In fact, this feminist was engaged in what Probyn calls the shaming of those she considers outsiders.[58] As Elias explained, "She thought you were either-or" – a completely secular, pure feminist or a Jew who accepted a patriarchal religion. Elias noted that this woman "was one of those hardliners who was holier than thou about absolutely everything."[59] The language here is telling. The moral certainty of individual feminists in this period has clear parallels to the religious dogmatism they rejected as patriarchal and damaging to women. This incident demonstrates how such secular moralism could be emotionally damaging to feminists who were not from secular Christian backgrounds and how it could most definitely construct fully secular "natives" and religious "strangers" in very stark and exclusionary terms.[60] The tensions and frustrations faced by Jewish women, who in many ways were insiders within secular feminism, were exacerbated for immigrant women activists in a range of ways.

Immigrant Women Activists, Feminism, Religion, and the Secular

There has been increasingly good work on the history of immigrant women by Canadian historians.[61] But there has been less work on immigrant women's organizations from the 1960s to 1980s. In the postwar era, there was a significant increase in immigration to Canada, primarily from Europe. From the 1960s on, as immigration regulations changed, more immigrants began to arrive from Asia, the Caribbean, Latin America, and the Middle East. Where 90 percent of all immigrants prior to 1961 were European-born, this declined to 25 percent by the 1980s.[62] Multiculturalism became official Canadian state policy in 1971, and Canada reinvented itself as a welcoming nation for people of different ethnicities. But this multicultural policy was a new way of managing difference, transforming racial identities into cultural differences that contained and preserved "ethnic" cultures in a primitive and backward past while asserting whites as superior, tolerant, and progressive.[63] In the 1970s and 1980s, as immigrant women faced racist and sexist policies and practices in their new country and communities, they began to unite to assert the need for services for themselves and other female immigrants.[64]

The majority of the immigrant women activists interviewed came from religious backgrounds, and most of these women believe this religious heritage gave them a social justice education that they later transformed into feminist politics. Debbie Douglas was pivotal in the early days of Zami (the first Canadian group for Black and West Indian gay and lesbian persons), Lesbians of Colour (a group formed in Toronto in 1984), and Samaroo House (the first immigrant and racialized women's shelter in Toronto). She believes her family's religious background gave her examples of how women could play leadership roles. "I was born in Grenada. And interestingly, my family was Seventh-Day Adventists. And the first Seventh-Day Adventist Church in Grenada was founded by my grandmother. So I come from a long line of feisty, take-control women."[65] Deb Barndt, a white academic and activist focusing on Latin American and migrant workers' issues, also explained her religious upbringing and its influence on her activism: "I grew up as a daughter of a minister and was very influenced by the social justice Christianity ... It was a living faith; it was not about dogma. It was more about relationships and commitment to social change."[66] Similarly, Patsy George, an immigrant from India who was involved in a range of political activism including welfare rights and immigrant women's issues, believes familial religion influenced her politics. "Both my parents were very active politically. We were taught the social teachings of the Catholic Church, which is very progressive ... And my parents were very strong about that. They were trade unionists ... And I think that came from the social teachings of the Catholic Church."[67]

While many of the immigrant women activists had been steeped in religious traditions during their youth, the majority had drifted away from religion when they became activists. Several defined themselves as atheists during this era. Others defined themselves as spiritual in a nonspecific way.[68] Douglas remembers this era as an anti-church time. "We were all too busy bashing the church ... I think many of us that come out of a church tradition or a mosque tradition or a temple tradition were totally busy recovering. So we didn't have very good things to say" about religion.[69]

At the same time, like the white feminists discussed above, some of the immigrant women activists who had left religion behind saw parallels between a religious and a feminist sense of community. Many emotions were evoked as these immigrant women activists formed emotional communities of their own. As one immigrant woman activist recalled, "It was exhilarating. There was so much energy. After our political meetings and our organizing we did not want to go home ... There was a sense of connectedness, of community." This woman thought this sense of community was particularly appealing to immigrant women activists whose families and communities might be far away. "It was expansive, all encompassing. There was a feeling of being rooted in Canada, of belonging."[70] Another immigrant woman activist saw a parallel between religion and feminism in both inclusion and exclusion from a community. "That's what we do if someone's politics is not like ours. We shun them ... That's very much like religious shunning to me."[71] However, any shunning or other tensions did not appear to be about secular norms. The immigrant women activists seemed to be much more accepting of religion than other feminists, even if it was not part of their world view in this period.

Many of these activists worked closely with religious leaders and organizations. Samaroo House, a transition house for immigrant and racialized women, had been created in response to immigrant and racialized women's experiences of racism and a lack of culturally and religiously appropriate services at more mainstream transition houses. Samaroo House staff worked with relevant religious communities.[72] Douglas explained how Samaroo House pursued public education through religious organizations.

> We didn't organize around religion. But at Samaroo House we recognized the importance of faith communities. Because we knew that if we were going to engage communities in talking about the eradication of violence against women we had to engage faith leaders. Because that's where folks get their information that they see as legitimate. So we talked to ministers or imams or Hindu priests. We felt that was important. And I think we were probably one of the very few women's shelters who saw public education and policy as part and parcel of the work that we did on violence against women. It wasn't only about counselling and women's right to leave.[73]

While some of the more mainstream shelters received charitable support from the churches, as discussed above, the white secular women who ran them did not appear to see a need to reach out to religious leaders as a way to support their clients.

Occasionally immigrant women activists would receive support from various religious leaders. Judith Ramirez recalls a priest quietly supporting the work of the immigrant women's centre:

> I was on the Italian radio station getting publicity for the immigrant women's centre. A priest heard me and called our office, and he asked if I would go and speak with him. And of course I said yes to everybody; you're trying to build community support ... And he said to me, "You know, we're Catholic here. I'm running a parish. And we don't approve of abortion. But a lot of the women here can't afford to have another child. They already

> have several. Their husbands work hard. They come home, they're drunk, they beat them. So, we'll send you the ones who need help. But of course, you'll never know they come from here." I said, "It doesn't matter. You send them any way you can, we'll help them." And I wouldn't know, however he sent them. Some circuitous route, it was not direct. Of course, you know, he needed plausible deniability [laughing]. After all, he's the parish priest! But he was very sympathetic. And, you know, these ladies were in his flock.[74]

Similarly, another immigrant woman activist, Fatima Filippi, recalled several discussions with the local Catholic leadership. She was instrumental in supporting immigrant women through the Working Women's Community Centre and the Rexdale Women's Centre and recalls having important conversations with the local Catholic priests,

> We had one Portuguese priest come to us and accuse us of trying to split up the family. And I remember at that time saying to him, "So you endorse men beating up on their wives and sometimes killing them?" And he didn't know what to say. And I said, "You need to address it ... You need to tell women about their rights, and you have to tell men that their behaviour's unacceptable."[75]

Filippi believes it was really important to talk with religious leaders about violence. "I don't know of any religion that advocates abuse."[76] And Judith Ramirez recalls that the Catholic archbishop of Toronto was very supportive of INTERCEDE, an organization for immigrant domestic workers. "He was wonderful. I would go in and talk to him and explain what we were trying to do. And we always knew that he would lend his considerable prestige of his office to write letters to the government," to advocate for legislative improvements for immigrant domestic workers.[77]

Some immigrant women activists worked for, or with, religious organizations. For instance, Deb Barndt worked for eight years with the Jesuit Centre for Social Faith Justice on a project to bring activists together. Even though she never identified as Catholic she worked closely with the Jesuits.[78] Barndt is not the only immigrant woman activist who expressed great respect for the Jesuits and their focus on social justice.[79]

Most of the immigrant women activists, whether religious themselves or not, spoke about the need to recognize religious or cultural diversity when providing services to immigrant women. They generally found mainstream feminists unsympathetic towards immigrant women's distinctive needs. They suggested that whereas mainstream feminists tended to focus on gender as the most important, if not the only, form of oppression, immigrant women activists saw gender oppression interlinked with a range of other problems facing immigrant women in Canadian society – including poverty, racism, limited social services, and the racist and sexist nature of immigration laws. In addition, immigrant women's material circumstances, as well as their cultural and religious beliefs, meant that mainstream feminist solutions did not always fit with immigrant women's lives. As Filippi explained, "You know religion plays a big role in many people's lives, immigrant women, racial minority women, and others." Activist women like Filippi did not assume that religion was just oppressive for these women. She went on to say that it is important to "learn ... to understand what religion means within that context, how religion can be empowering for some women."[80]

One example of such empowerment concerns the case of the Portuguese women who worked as cleaners in downtown Toronto offices. They preferred this work to working in hotels, because it meant that they could have Sundays off to attend church and spend time with their families and that they could work evenings or nights when their husbands were home to care for their children. Although they were seen as very docile Catholic women, in fact, with the support of immigrant activists, they were involved in militant strikes in Toronto in the 1980s, both to prevent contracting out and to increase their very low wages. Suşana Miranda, who advocated for Portuguese immigrant women in Toronto, noted that their Catholicism did not preclude their militancy, and that, in fact, "at one particular strike in 1985, at First Canadian Place, it lasted six weeks, and these Portuguese women were on the picket line downtown six weeks. And a lot of these women ... said, 'Jesus gives me the strength to continue fighting.' You know, they really used their religion ... it gave them strength."[81]

In addition to supporting immigrant women workers in unionizing and striking, immigrant women activists provided a variety of other services and supports. Some of this work was similar to mainstream feminist activism in demanding employment opportunities, protection from violence, and reproductive health. But the majority of the work done by immigrant women activists was distinctly tailored to the everyday lives of immigrant women and supported their religious and cultural concerns.

The white mainstream feminists we interviewed seemed sympathetic to immigrant women, but they were not generally aware of some immigrant women's particular religious and cultural needs in relation to food.

Yet almost every immigrant woman activist we interviewed stressed the importance of food in any support services for immigrant women. One director of Samaroo House recalls why culturally and religiously appropriate food is vital. "We had a big food budget. Food is comfort. When you are in crisis it is good to have something that is familiar – food can be that. So it is important to have the right food."[82] And Douglas recalls some of the misunderstandings around the need to provide culturally appropriate food. "Some people worried that we were forcing everyone to eat halal meat or to become vegetarian because most Hindus are vegetarian. So it was that kind of ignorant nonsense. But you know, when you talk about equity it doesn't mean treating everybody the same."[83]

As the founder of INTERCEDE, Ramirez remembers organizing meetings around immigrant women's work responsibilities and religious practices. "They were off on Sunday, most of them, because they were all very devout. So they would go to church and we would hold the meetings right after lunch. They go to church, go to lunch, and came to the INTERCEDE meetings in their beautiful church hats and everything."[84] Some of the activists who helped to build and manage immigrant women's shelters and community centres spoke of how they reserved a space for prayer. "I tried to set up a prayer room, a free room for Sunni women to pray five times a day, and during Ramadan," explained Tomoko Okada, who immigrated from Japan and helped found the Cowichan Valley Intercultural Society. Okada also advocated for women and children who were fasting during Ramadan. "The women's energy levels would be very low, so we tried to educate the mainstream service providers to understand the issues. And we received so many calls from the school, teachers complaining during Ramadan that the children weren't participating in physical education."[85]

Other immigrant women activists tried to accommodate the religious holidays of their staff. These staff were not paid for the time they took from work for religious holidays but accommodation was generally made.[86] This contrasts with what appeared to be the situation in more mainstream feminist organizations. In addition to the Jewish women who struggled over the issue of religious holidays, one Sikh feminist activist noted similar problems in working with white feminists. Rita Kholi pointed out that with Christianity being the dominant religion, they had to fight to have their religious days recognized. She noted that "there were a significant number of women activists who were refugee and racialized, who fought for those."[87]

In some immigrant women's groups they avoided discussing religion, not because the women were secular but because they were not, and the activists realized that it might have created tensions if women from different religious backgrounds discussed religious issues. "We avoided talking about religion because we didn't want to offend anybody," recalls Filippi.[88] Others organized a number of religious or cultural celebrations within their organizations. "We sort of exchanged cultures and shared our cultures with one another ... It was all opening up and trying to get people out of their ethnic ghettos," explained Beverly Nann, who founded the Pacific Immigrant Resources Society, in Vancouver.[89] Hortensia Houle, a racialized immigrant activist who was an executive director of an immigrant women's group in Duncan, BC, explained, "When there was a [religious] festival, the women would bring the food to our centre ... Sometimes they would celebrate by dancing and they would show us how to do it."[90]

Religious Tensions in the Sisterhood

Some immigrant women activists recall explicit tensions between immigrant women and white mainstream feminists over religious and cultural issues. "In feminist spaces there's always that tension between religion and politics. And in some spaces, if you were to say anything religious you were seen as anti-feminist, that the two things couldn't co-exist," said Douglas.[91] A number of immigrant women activists who had ties to religious communities found this challenging. One immigrant woman activist said, "It was interesting because at the time I knew a whole bunch of really radical nuns who were lesbians, and I dated one!"[92] Others argued against feminist anti-religious moralism, noting that religious organizations could be supportive of their work with immigrant women. Ramirez noted that churches "gave money. People would come to our demonstrations. We would go and speak to them. And they were motivated by ideas that are part of their theological thinking, which are about basic justice ... We're talking about the more progressive elements in all of these groups. But they were very good supporters."[93]

While the immigrant women activists found religious organizations and leaders supportive at certain moments, they found this to be less true of most white feminists. Instead, as critical race scholars explain, white mainstream feminists would include these immigrant activists in a token manner that required little effort or attention. Ramirez recalls the 1960s and 1970s as an era when most feminists were often indifferent to the struggles of immigrant women. "It was more like benign neglect. When you really need their strength and their resources and their megaphones, and it's just not there. And when you look around for allies, and you see the ones who should be there and they're not, it feels like betrayal."[94] Such views reinforce existing scholarship that suggests the National Action Committee on the Status of Women and other feminist organizations largely ignored the politics of immigrant women's groups until the mid- to late-1980s.[95] "We worked so separately," explained Ramirez. "There was not a lot of support. There was not a lot of oppression ... It wasn't dramatic enough to be terrible or wonderful." But Ramirez felt there was an undercurrent. "They didn't understand why we needed our own groups, why we couldn't just join a feminist group that already existed."[96]

There were various reasons for organizing separately, but secularism was certainly one of them. While most white mainstream feminists did not see their secularism as a problem as it was invisible to them, it could create barriers to working in a meaningful way with immigrant women activists. The latter understood the role of religion in a more nuanced way. Immigrant women activists saw religion as patriarchal but recognized the important role it played in the lives of many of the immigrant women they worked with. They also believed it could serve as a positive cultural and spiritual resource in a foreign and racist world. While immigrant activists recognized this, even if they themselves were atheists, this reality was not intelligible within the profoundly secular world view of most white feminists.

Abortion was an issue where religion, race, and class could create major tensions between immigrant activists and white mainstream feminists, as well as sometimes creating complexities for immigrant women activists themselves. Immigrant activists had a broader focus here than many white feminists, arguing that reproductive rights should mean the right to have children, to challenge forced sterilizations and abortions, as well as to choose abortion.[97] Douglas recalls supporting young women, some of whom were pregnant:

> We were trying to empower the women ... And so we wanted to just support them through the process and giving them the message that your life doesn't end here at seventeen because you have a child. And so we were really fighting the system ... We wanted them to have choice – real choice. [Not the mainstream feminist] choice which meant you had to have an abortion.[98]

While many immigrant women supported reproductive choice, for other immigrant women religious opposition to abortion could be a dividing line that separated them from the women's movement. For example, although the Portuguese women cleaners worked closely with immigrant activists in Toronto in unionizing and striking, one of our interviewees noted that they were "very Catholic and, so, not comfortable with abortion."[99]

Conclusion

The immigrant activists who worked with immigrant women recognized the need to respect the religious values of immigrant women, even when they came into conflict with strongly held feminist beliefs. These issues were clearly emotionally charged for the immigrant women activists, but their recognition of the importance of religion for the women they served made such work possible. The intense secularism of most white feminists, however, made it harder for these hegemonic feminists to see, understand, and respect the religious views of some immigrant women.

There were many reasons why white mainstream feminists remained separate from the immigrant women's movement even though they shared political values, mutual passions to improve women's lives, and even a tendency to move away from the religious values of their youth. Many of these reasons have been well documented by other scholars. We suggest in this chapter that another issue that has not received much attention, that of the religious and the secular, created further divisions and misunderstandings. For most feminists, a rejection of religion was one of the touchstones of membership in feminist communities. In some cases feminism replaced religion, as feminists felt included and enveloped into this new emotional community. But some of these emotions of inclusion encouraged conformity and a delineation between natives and strangers. This new, exciting, passionate, and secular feminist community made it more difficult for many feminists to understand and respect immigrant women, for whom religion was often deeply enmeshed in who they were and how they understood and navigated an often hostile and racist world. Immigrant women activists were also feminists, but they were not limited by secular blinders. They were much more willing to accept the complexities of religious world views and even to work closely with religious leaders to provide the support needed to improve immigrant women's lives, on their own terms and within familiar religious contexts. While the rejection of patriarchal religion is not surprising as part of the feminist challenge to gender oppression, the unbending hegemonic secularism of much of the second-wave women's movement was one more way in which deeply felt divisions were created and many potential sisters were defined as strangers to the intense feminist communities of the time.

The tensions and divisions created by the rigid secularism of much of second-wave feminism is not just a question of historical interest. As Joan Scott has argued recently, the most current version of Western secularism, strongly inflected with secular feminism, is complicit in the othering of Muslim women and their cultural and religious values, and it contributes to some of the central political divisions of current times.[100] We must address how white mainstream feminism has a history marked by significant distain for, and rejection of, organized religion. Feminism, religion, and the rejection of religion evoked a host of emotions that both contributed to the creation of emotional communities and excluded certain women, particularly certain immigrant women, from these secular communities. This emotional inclusion and exclusion from second-wave feminism on the basis of religion continues to haunt contemporary feminist politics.

Notes

1 Sandy is a pseudonym. This is the story of her experience, as recalled by another member of the feminist bookstore collective. Debby Yaffe, interview with authors, Victoria, July 19, 2016.

2 Brooke Ferguson (pseud.), interview with authors, Victoria, June 28, 2016.

3 Chela Sandoval, *Methodology of the Oppressed* (Minneapolis: University of Minnesota Press, 2000), 41–42.

4 Barbara H. Rosenwein, "Worrying about Emotions in History," *American Historical Review*, 107, 3, (2002): 842.

5 There are other emotions we could cite, but anger, pain, love, wonder, joy, and hope are the ones that Ahmed mentions in describing feminism. We find them also applicable to religion. See Sara Ahmed, *The Cultural Politics of Emotion*, 2nd ed. (New York: Routledge, 2015), Chap. 8.

6 Rosenwein, "Worrying about Emotions in History," 844–45.

7 For literature on feminism and religion among first-wave feminists see, for example, Wendy Mitchinson, "Canadian Women and Church Missionary Societies in the Nineteenth Century: A Step towards Independence," in "Part 2: Conference Issue," ed. Linda Christiansen-Ruffman, special issue, *Atlantis* 2, 2 (1977): 57–75; and Mariana Valverde, *The Age of Light, Soap, and Water: Moral Reform in English Canada, 1885–1925* (Toronto: University of Toronto Press, 2008).

8 Although there has been very little work on the relationship between religion and second-wave feminism in Canada, a few examples are: Christine Gervais, *Beyond the Altar: Women Religious, Patriarchal Power, and the Church* (Waterloo, ON: Wilfrid Laurier University Press, 2018); and Rosa Bruno-Jofré, Heidi Macdonald, and Elizabeth Smyth, *Vatican II and Beyond: The Changing Mission and Identity of Canadian Women Religious* (Montreal/Kingston: McGill-Queen's University Press, 2017). For the US context see, for example, Ann Braude, "A Religious Feminist – Who Can Find Her? Historiographical Challenges from the National Organization for Women," *Journal of Religion*, 84, 4 (2004): 555–72.

9 For the American context, see Evelyn Brooks Higginbotham, *Righteous Discontent: The Women's Movement in the Black Baptist Church, 1880–1920* (Cambridge, MA: Harvard University Press, 1993); and Martha S. Jones, "Overthrowing the 'Monopoly of the Pulpit': Race and the Rights of Church Women in the Nineteenth-Century United States," in *No Permanent Waves: Recasting Histories of U.S. Feminism*, ed. Nancy A. Hewitt (New Brunswick, NJ: Rutgers University Press, 2010), 121–43. There is very little in the Canadian context, but see Jane Rhodes, *Mary Ann Shadd Cary: The Black Press and Protest in the Nineteenth Century* (Bloomington: Indiana University Press, 1998); and Tamari Kitossa, "Criticism, Reconstruction and African-Centred Feminist Historiography," in *Back to the Drawing Board: African-Canadian Feminisms*, ed. Njoki Nathani Wane, Katerina Deliovsky, and Erica Lawson (Toronto: Sumach Press, 2002), 85–116.

10 For a discussion of alterative feminist spiritualities see, for example, Cynthia Eller, *Living in the Lap of the Goddess: The Feminist Spirituality Movement in America* (New York: Crossroad, 1993).

11 Very little has been written about the apparent secularism of the women's movement in the American context either, although recently a few women's studies scholars have begun to acknowledge the gulf between feminist religious studies and mainstream and very secular feminist studies. See Dawn Llewellyn and Marta Trzebiatowska, "Secular and Religious Feminisms: A Future of Disconnection?," *Feminist Theology* 21, 3 (2013): 244–56; and Niamh Reilly, "Rethinking the Interplay of Feminism and Secularism in a Neo-secular Age," *Feminist Review* 97, 1 (2011): 5–31. Also see Kathleen Sands, "Feminisms and Secularisms," in *Secularisms*, ed. Janet R. Jakobsen and Ann Pellegrini (Durham, NC: Duke University Press, 2008), 308–29. Most recently, Joan Scott has taken an interest in the relationship between secularism and women's rights, although her main focus is on the shifting attitudes within mainstream Western society between secularism and women's equality/autonomy. See Joan Wallach Scott, *Sex and Secularism* (Princeton, NJ: Princeton University Press, 2018).

12 The National Action Committee on the Status of Women, the umbrella group of Canadian feminist organizations, certainly included some religious women's groups.

13 See, for example, Vijay Agnew, "Canadian Feminism and Women of Colour," *Women's Studies International Forum* 16, 3 (1993): 217–27; Himani Bannerji, "Organizing Exclusion: Race, Class, Community and the White Women's Movement," *Fireweed* 17 (1983): 57–65; Mary Jo Nadeau, "Rebuilding the House of Canadian Feminism: NAC and the Racial Politics of Participation," in *Opening Doors Wider: Women's Political Engagement in Canada*, ed. Sylvia Bashevkin (Vancouver, UBC Press, 2009), 33–48; Roxana Ng, "Finding Our Voices: Reflections on Immigrant Women's Organizing," in *Women and Social Change: Feminist Activism in Canada*, ed. Jeri Dawn Wine and Janice Ristock (Toronto: Lorimer, 1991), 184–97.

14 Sara Ahmed, *Living a Feminist Life* (Durham, NC: Duke University Press, 2017), 48. There is a growing scholarship on emotions and our research is particularly influenced by the following: Sara Ahmed, *The Promise of Happiness* (Durham, NC: Duke University Press, 2010); Ahmed, *Cultural Politics of Emotion*; Ahmed, *Living a Feminist Life*; Megan Boler, *Feeling Power: Emotions and Education* (New York: Routledge, 1999); Elspeth Probyn, *Blush: Faces of Shame* (Minneapolis: University of Minnesota Press, 2005); Rosenwein, "Worrying about Emotions in History," and

Ann Cvetkovich, *An Archive of Feelings: Trauma, Sexuality, and Lesbian Public Cultures* (Durham, NC: Duke University Press, 2003).

15 Sara Ahmed, *Living a Feminist Life*, 117 (emphasis added).

16 Sara Ahmed, "Feminist Attachments," in *Cultural Politics of Emotion*, especially 178.

17 Probyn, *Blush: Faces of Shame*, 76 and 106.

18 See, for example, Callum Brown, *The Death of Christian Britain: Understanding Secularisation, 1800–2000* (London: Routledge, 2001); Brown, *Religion and the Demographic Revolution: Women and Secularisation in Canada, Ireland, UK and USA since the 1960s* (Woodbridge, UK: Boydell Press, 2012); and Brown, *Becoming Atheist: Humanism and the Secular West* (London: Bloomsbury, 2017).

19 Scott, *Sex and Secularism*.

20 See Diana Smith, interview with authors, Victoria, May 18, 2017; Dorothy Elias, interview with authors, Victoria, May 18, 2017; Nancy (pseud.), interview with Tina Block, Toronto, October 12, 2016; and Darlene (pseud.), interview with Tina Block, Vancouver, October 3, 2016. Both of the latter interviews are part of the Oral Histories of Unbelief collection. Interviews for the Oral Histories of Unbelief project, Tina Block, PI, were conducted in Kamloops, Vancouver, Sudbury, and Toronto between 2015 and 2017. The interview transcripts are currently in possession of Block and will be archived in Thompson Rivers University's open access digital repository, TRUSpace, at the completion of the project. Pseudonyms are used throughout to protect the anonymity of participants.

21 Anita Roberts, interview with Liza Tom, Vancouver, June 16, 2016.

22 Caroline (pseud.), interview with Steve O'Reilly, Kamloops, BC, June 9, 2015, Oral Histories of Unbelief interview collection.

23 Marilyn Callahan, interview with authors, Victoria, May 26, 2016.

24 Ahmed, "Feminist Attachments."

25 Ahmed, *Living a Feminist Life*, Chapter 1, "Feminism Is Sensational," 21–42.

26 Enise Olding, interview with Liza Tom, Victoria, June 14, 2016.

27 Scholars have written about the intense closeness of lesbian feminist communities, but potential parallels with religious communities have not been explored. See Becki Ross, *The House That Jill Built: A Lesbian Nation in Formation* (Toronto: University of Toronto Press, 1995); Francis Wasserlein, "'An Arrow Aimed at the Heart': The Vancouver Women's Caucus and the Abortion Campaign, 1969–1971" (master's thesis, Simon Fraser University, 1990); and Liz Millward, *Making a Scene: Lesbians and Community across Canada, 1964–1984* (Vancouver: UBC Press, 2015).

28 Reva Hutkin, interview with authors, Victoria, May 8, 2017.

29 Kate Nonesuch, interview with authors, Victoria, May 16, 2017.

30 Ellen Woodsworth, interview with authors, Vancouver, August 16, 2016.

31 Probyn, *Blush: Faces of Shame*.

32 Annalee Lepp, personal communication with Lynne Marks, March 2, 2016. For discussion of the strict policing of the boundaries of earlier religious communities see, for example, Lynne Marks, "Railing, Tattling, General Rumour and Common Fame: Speech, Gossip, Gender and Church Regulation in Upper Canada," *Canadian Historical Review* 81, 3 (2000): 380–402.

33 Jan Trainor, "The Personal and the Political: Canadian Lesbian Oral Histories, 1970–2010" (master's thesis, University of Victoria, 2015), 20, 28.

34 Kate Nonesuch, interview with authors, Victoria, May 16, 2017.
35 Nancy (pseud.), interview with Tina Block, Toronto, October 12, 2016, Oral Histories of Unbelief interviews.
36 Jen Moses, interview with Liza Tom, Vancouver, July 12, 2016.
37 Anita Roberts, interview with Liza Tom, Vancouver, June 16, 2016.
38 Bernadette Maxwell, letter to the editor, *Broadside* 1, 6 (1980), 3. responding to Susan Cole, "Resurrection of God," *Broadside* 1, 4 (1980), 3.
39 Susan Cole, "Daughters of the Covenant," *Broadside,* 1, 9 (1980), 4.
40 Broadside editorial, "The Church's One Foundation," *Broadside,* 1, 9 (1980) 2.
41 Kris Furlought, "Christianity – the Controversy Rages On," *Broadside* 1, 8 (1980): 19. Also see *Broadside* 1, 9 (1980) for a variety of articles on feminism and religion, including Cole's article on Judaism and feminism, "Daughters of the Covenant."
42 Ahmed, *Living a Feminist Life*, 36–42.
43 Ahmed, *Living a Feminist Life*, 117.
44 Ahmed, *Cultural Politics of Emotion*, 178.
45 Malinda S. Smith, "Gender, Whiteness, and 'Other Others' in the Academy," in *States of Race: Critical Race Feminism for the 21st Century*, ed. Sherene Razack, Malinda Smith, and Sunera Thobani (Toronto: Between the Lines, 2010), 37–58.
46 Cited in Trainor, "The Personal and the Political," 83.
47 Linda Sproule-Jones, interview with authors, Victoria, June 14, 2016.
48 Jane, (pseud.), interview with authors, Victoria, May 17, 2017.
49 See, for example, Nancy Janovicek, *No Place to Go: Local Histories of the Battered Women's Shelter Movement* (Vancouver: UBC Press, 2007).
50 Wendy Burton, telephone interview with authors, August 17, 2017; Enise Olding, interview with Liza Tom, Victoria, June 14, 2016.
51 Louise (pseud.), interview with authors, Victoria, May 8, 2017; and Enise Olding, interview with Liza Tom, Victoria, June 14, 2016.
52 Bobby Kovar, interview with authors, Victoria, May 16, 2017.
53 Kate Nonesuch, interview with authors, Victoria, May 16, 2017.
54 See, for example, Andrew Gow, "Secularism: A 'Work in Progress' or an Ideological Obfuscation?" (public lecture, Centre for Studies in Religion and Society, University of Victoria, February 2016); Laura Schwartz, *Infidel Feminism: Secularism, Religion and Women's Emancipation, England, 1830–1914* (Manchester: Manchester University Press, 2013), 21–26; Scott, *Sex and Secularism*; and Sands, "Feminisms and Secularisms."
55 Ahmed, *Cultural Politics of Emotion*, 178.
56 Debby Yaffe, interview with authors, Victoria, July 19, 2016. Also Reva Hutkin, interview with authors, Victoria, May 8, 2017.
57 Debby Yaffe, interview with authors, Victoria, July 19, 2016.
58 Probyn, *Blush: Faces of Shame*, 106.
59 Dorothy Elias, interview with authors, Victoria, May 18, 2017.
60 This anti-Semitic incident foreshadows more recent tensions between some secular white feminists and Muslim women who are declared to be oppressed for wearing the hijab and following other Muslim customs. See Scott, *Sex and Secularism*.
61 See, for example, Franca Iacovetta, *Gatekeepers* (Toronto: Between the Lines, 2006); and Marlene Epp and Franca Iacovetta eds., *Sisters and Strangers: Immigrant,*

Ethnic, and Racialized Women in Canadian History, 2nd ed. (Toronto: University of Toronto Press, 2016).

62 Yasmeen Abu-Laban, "Keeping 'em Out: Gender, Race, and Class Biases in Canadian Immigration Policy," in *Painting the Maple: Essays on Race, Gender, and the Construction of Canada*, ed. Veronica Strong-Boag, Joan Anderson, Sherrill Grace, and Avigail Eisenberg (Vancouver: UBC Press, 1998), 69–82. For a detailed discussion of the points system, see Sedef Arat-Koc, "NAC's Response to the Immigration Legislative Review Report: 'Not Just Numbers': A Canadian Framework for Future Immigration," *Canadian Woman Studies* 19, 3 (1999): 18–23.

63 Sara Ahmed, *Strange Encounters: Embodied Others in Post-Coloniality* (London: Routledge, 2000), 104.

64 There are quite a few publications produced in the immigrant activist community about immigrant women and organizing in the 1970s and 1980s, including Karen Lior, ed., *Making the City: Women Who Made a Difference* (Halifax: Fernwood, 2012); and Tania Das Gupta, *Learning from Our History: Community Development by Immigrant Women in Ontario, 1958–1986; A Tool for Action* (Toronto: Cross Cultural Communication Centre, 1986).

65 Debbie Douglas, interview with authors, Toronto, February 9, 2017.

66 Deb Barndt, interview with authors, Toronto, March 21, 2016.

67 Patsy George, interview with authors, Vancouver, July 25, 2016.

68 Interestingly, a few of the immigrant women activists interviewed have returned to religion in mid-life, although they tend to practice at more progressive churches than the ones they rejected as young activists. Therefore, although they may have defined themselves as atheists or irreligious during this second-wave era, they may define themselves differently today.

69 Debbie Douglas, interview with authors, Toronto, February 9, 2017.

70 Maria (pseud.), interview with authors, Toronto, March 2016.

71 Dorine (pseud.), interview with authors, Toronto, May 2017.

72 Rita Kohli, interview with authors, Toronto, March 21, 2016.

73 Debbie Douglas, interview with authors, Toronto, February 9, 2017.

74 Judith Ramirez, interview with authors, Toronto, February 4, 2017.

75 Fatima Filippi, interview with authors, Toronto, March 1, 2016.

76 Fatima Filippi, interview with authors, Toronto, March 1, 2016.

77 Judith Ramirez, interview with authors, Toronto, February 4, 2017.

78 Deb Barndt, interview with authors, Toronto, March 21, 2016.

79 Maria (pseud.) interview with authors, Toronto, March 2016.

80 Fatima Filippi, interview with authors, Toronto, March 1, 2016

81 Susana Miranda, interview with authors, Toronto, March 2016.

82 Maria (pseud.), interview with authors, Toronto, March 2016.

83 Debbie Douglas, interview with authors, Toronto, February 9, 2017.

84 Judith Ramirez, interview with authors, Toronto, February 4, 2017.

85 Tomoko Okada, interview with Liza Tom, Victoria, June 28, 2016.

86 Debbie Douglas, interview with authors, Toronto, February 9, 2017; Franca (pseud.), interview with authors, Toronto, May 2017; Maria (pseud.), interview with authors, Toronto, March 2016.

87 Rita Kholi, interview with authors, Toronto, March 21, 2016.

88 Fatima Filippi, interview with authors, Toronto, March 1, 2016.
89 Beverly Nann, interview with Liza Tom, Vancouver, July 25, 2016.
90 Hortensia Houle, interview with Liza Tom, Victoria, June 6, 2016.
91 Debbie Douglas, interview with authors, Toronto, February 9, 2017.
92 Dorine (pseud.), interview with authors, Toronto, May 2017.
93 Judith Ramirez, interview with authors, Toronto, February 4, 2017.
94 Judith Ramirez, interview with authors, Toronto, February 4, 2017.
95 After the mid-1980s, relations between mainstream feminists and immigrant and racialized women became more intense and, in some contexts, much more difficult. See, for example, Nadeau, "Rebuilding the House of Canadian Feminism."
96 Judith Ramirez, interview with authors, Toronto, February 4, 2017.
97 For example, in 1977, the Immigrant Women's Centre in the downtown Toronto area stated, "Many of us, both immigrant and native born are forced to have abortions because we cannot afford to have the children we want ... For us, the 'right to choose' can never be only the right to abortion, but must also be the right to have all the children we might want." Statement by Immigrant Women's Centre, May 10, 1977, Immigrant Women's Centre, Ontario Archives, Immigrant Women's Organizations files, DSC 00920093.
98 Debbie Douglas, interview with authors, Toronto, February 4, 2017.
99 Susana Miranda, interview with authors, Toronto, March 2016.
100 Scott, *Sex and Secularism*.

7

Intense Times

Love, Fear, and Pride as Guides to Lesbian Feminist Organizing

LIZ MILLWARD

Reflecting on her lesbian activism during the 1970s and 1980s, Jan Trainor recalled, "Of course, through all of this time we're facing various different political issues. We're mating up a storm, we're breaking up, making up, finding new partners, serial monogamy ... I mean, it was a very intense time – it was an extremely busy time intellectually and emotionally and culturally and physically."[1] For lesbian activists whose community-building efforts were informed by feminism, this level of intensity reflected, at least in part, the experience of "paradox, contradiction, and tension" that accompanies the transition from one "emotional community" to another.[2] These women were moving from dominant heteropatriarchal emotional communities, which might even be considered "emotional regimes,"[3] into newly emerging lesbian feminist emotional communities. They were simultaneously creating, and interacting with, the latter, some of which bore the hallmarks of their own emotional regimes.

The development of these new emotional communities went hand in hand with the creation of the physical lesbian scene. The 1970s saw an explosion of lesbian community-building at local, regional, national, and transnational levels. In Canada, a buoyant economy, the rise of the women's movement and second-wave feminist theory to explain women's oppression, and the 1969 omnibus bill that proposed to decriminalize homosexuality generated momentum for experimenting with new ideas and new ways of being in the world. Most of the women involved in lesbian feminist organizing were young, although older women were also galvanized by its possibilities. Women wrote about and published accounts of their experiences trying to find community and their feelings about situating themselves – sometimes uncomfortably, sometimes with a sense of unparalleled joy – within a community once they had found it. This chapter draws on those accounts from unpublished letters held in the Canadian Women's Movement Archives and the Saskatchewan Archives Board and from letters and accounts published in community newsletters and magazines during this period.

During the 1970s, lesbians across Canada found that community through their access to a scene which they were in the process of making up as they went along. The scene comprised community centres, private members' clubs, women-only spaces, community groups that held regular meetings, festivals, and conferences, women-only land or houses, and, of course, bars, beer parlours, and house parties.[4] Many (mostly young) women dedicated their time and energy to creating and maintaining this scene. They found spaces to rent, negotiated with landlords, applied for permits and grants, put up posters, dragged sound equipment and vinyl records onto rickety stages, and hauled crates of beer to obscure venues. They stole time and resources from their employers to type up minutes or articles for newsletters. They snuck material through Gestetner copiers or photocopiers, only afterwards noticing the grammatical or spelling errors and thinking, frequently enough, that rules of grammar and spelling – like *Robert's Rules of Order* – were patriarchal impositions, anyway.

Women's reasons for getting involved in developing and sustaining the many components of the lesbian scene were manifold, but certainly the desire to meet other women was a major motivating force. In February 1973, for example, a woman in Regina wrote to the Gay Community Centre of Saskatchewan asking for their assistance.

> I am a gay woman looking for companionship and a sense of joy and purpose in life. Would you know of any Gay group in Regina where I could meet others who are like myself? I have tried to find out but have been unable to find anything – and I'm afraid the reactions from most people I've had has been most unkind etc.[5]

This request worked on the assumption that other women had already created the space where she could find community. However, such spaces were far from stable or well established. They were not only in constant flux as volunteer energy fizzled, landlords increased the rent, or internecine strife prompted dramatic and irreconcilable splits within groups; they were also in the process of becoming, of being imagined and created. Historian Valerie Korinek's detailed analysis of community-building on the Prairies provides a rich and nuanced account of these processes.[6]

Many of the varied components of that scene – the buildings, rooms, decor, music, entrance restrictions, presence or absence of alcohol, drugs, children, men, or straights – were either physical or created an atmosphere that affected the physical space. But emotions were also crucial building blocks in this process. They provided some of the energy that kept women involved in the hard graft of social, cultural, and political work. Just as women had to reach out and try to locate the "others who are like myself,"[7] they also had to negotiate their often very strong emotions, interpreting what the feelings meant and trying to fit those emotions into a schema that was informed by feminist analysis.

Stakes could be high in emotional communities representing shared values and signifying belonging. Since the lesbian feminist emotional community was nascent, its shared values were up for debate. Although in reality there were different, overlapping emotional communities, to some women trying to feel that they belonged there seemed to be one authentic community, which was exceedingly hard to access. In articles written for a lesbian audience, at conferences and in private discussions, lesbians who were using feminist organizing techniques to carve out a new world for themselves expressed a powerful range of emotions and often used these to guide their political action and to help them define themselves. Many lesbians attempted to create new emotional frameworks through which a resolutely nonpatriarchal lesbian community could thrive. In this sense their emotional community had a distinctly political cast, although the parameters of the community were difficult to establish. Feminist scholar Rosemary Hennessy suggests that "to argue that we must pay attention to the passionate politics of political education is to recognize that unmet needs do indeed haunt our imaginations, our ability to dream another world, and our labour to make possible its realization."[8] Nelly, a member of the WomanShare Collective, which was an intentional land community and was part of a loose cluster of lesbian and feminist communities located in Oregon, confirms Hennessy's argument. She wrote in 1976, "I find we must imagine the new world we wish to create before we can actively work on its creation. There is a time lag between recognizing the need for change and the beginning movements toward that change when we seem to continue acting in old ways."[9] The political labour these and other women expended to make another world possible was an integral part of the scene and precipitated plenty of passionate feelings, as women (and men) worked together or against each other and debated their goals and the means to arrive at them. Lesbian emotional communities thus emerged in the combination of this political organizing, new physical spaces that communicated community values and aesthetics, and a heady sense of erotic and political possibility.

Although there was obviously not a single lesbian emotional community, certain common experiences solidified what being lesbian in this context meant. Coming out to oneself and finding a community to join (or at least a partner) were the most basic components. But beyond that, part of the problem that vexed women was knowing what lesbian community really was. Reflecting on "the invisible community" in Toronto in 1980, Val Edwards asked, "What is a community anyway?" She suggested that,

> most of us would agree that something called a lesbian community exists. Which reminds me of the judge who once refused to venture a definition of obscenity, but simply stated, "I know it when I see it." Likewise a community lesbian: we recognize one when we meet her, but damned if we know exactly what it is that she has in common with the rest of us.[10]

Edwards decided to attempt to identify the three attitudes that she felt defined the lesbian community. The first was that "although we are homosexuals, we consider ourselves different, in more than a physical sense, from gay men." The second presumed that "we all identify ourselves as feminists," while the third attitude was that "we think of ourselves as more enlightened and well-rounded human beings than those lesbians who call themselves 'gay' and who don't give two rips about feminism, ie, the bar dykes."[11] This particular version of community, then, was organized around a theoretical approach and a sense of emotional and intellectual superiority to both gay men and gay women (as opposed to lesbians) who, by these measures, were likely perceived as working-class and uneducated in feminist praxis. This sense of difference and superiority dictated (loosely speaking) both how a woman should interpret her emotions and which emotions she should actually have – or at least be willing to admit that she had.

Sharing Emotions

At the beginning of the 1970s there were very few places where women could go to meet "the others who are like myself"[12] and thus members of this emotional community. Beer parlours, softball diamonds, and private house parties had provided the best opportunities to meet gay women, but these were few and far between, and access to them typically depended on being in the know. In any case, the new emotional community reflected a lesbian feminist politics that could not be squeezed into those pre-existing locations. In the early 1970s, second-wave feminist analysis and books and articles about lesbianism coming out of the United States, such as *Sappho was a Right-On Woman*, by Sidney Abbott and Barbara Love, and *Lesbian/Woman*, by Del Martin and Phyllis Lyon, started to circulate in Canada.[13] Young women attending university encountered feminist ideas and feminist pedagogy in new women's studies classes. These encounters helped them to name and understand their experiences as commonplace – rather than exceptional – under patriarchy. The style of teaching borrowed heavily from consciousness-raising practices and encouraged women to overcome their nervousness about speaking in front of others or taking up space. Indeed, consciousness-raising in general emboldened women to see their fears (of being too much, or of admitting to feelings of alienation or loneliness) as the outcome of patriarchal conditioning, whereby women were persuaded that it was unfeminine and inappropriate to take up space or airtime or to talk about themselves, instead of politely and supportively listening to men.

The excitement of sharing experiences with other women and the thrill of watching women speak confidently was compelling. Having had a taste of it, many women wanted more. It was important to share emotions rather than treat them as something personal or individual. As the Victoria-based Feminist Lesbian Action Group (FLAG) wrote in their Statement of Purpose, in the late 1970s, "When several people become aware of the fact that they are experiencing similar kinds of loneliness, frustration, and oppression, one of the more positive choices open to them is to form a strong, cohesive support group."[14] Dian Wagner, Carol Osmer-Newhouse, and Billie Miracle, three of the women who went on to establish the WomanShare Collective, all belonged to a consciousness-raising group in Montreal, in 1973. Trying to articulate the process that politicized them, "the three of them always say that their consciousness-raising group helped them make the changes necessary to become lesbians. Through many hard struggles the women in the consciousness-raising group became very close. Together they discovered their mutual oppression as women and reached a common solution ... lesbianism."[15] The process of consciousness-raising could lead women to take their place within an emotional community whose parameters were being drawn through that process itself.

Consciousness-raising groups and organizations like FLAG created the space in which women could acknowledge and explore their emotional

Sharing emotions: Meeting of the Lesbian Caucus of the British Columbia Federation of Women, Doran Road, North Vancouver, 1974 or 1975. (Photographer Linda Hancock. Photo courtesy of Cy-Thea Sand.)

reactions to everything from everyday sexism to workplace dynamics, and from their sexual desire for other women to their fear of that desire. These groups also provided a context through which women could situate those feelings in a political framework. This transformed the emotions from being personal or individual responses to particular life experiences into lesbian feminist perspectives on love, patriarchy, and power. Both the more formal consciousness-raising groups and the informal consciousness-raising that occurred when lesbians got together and started discussing their lives provided fuel for that emotional community.

In turn, these shared emotions, or the correct political response to those emotions, could be established through commitment to community values. Historian Barbara Rosenwein argues that "insofar as both values, and also the objects/ideas to which those values are attached, differ, emotions (for example, what people get angry at and how they express their feelings) will differ as well."[16] This was tricky ground: on the one hand, lesbians were committed to shared political values based, loosely, on a critique of patriarchy and the way that their heterosexual sisters – in their view, falsely – aligned their interests with it. On the other hand, maintaining a sense of a distinctive lesbian community with its own shared values that therefore constituted an emotional community was a struggle because it was hard to pin down exactly what made lesbians into a community. Val Edwards, writing about the lesbian community in Toronto in 1980, for example, commented, "I would rather live in the straight, patriarchal world, and try to make a few changes to make my life easier, than to repudiate a lifestyle and system of values which are part of me."[17] Noting that fewer lesbians now imagined an alternative to patriarchy (compared to the heady days of early to mid 1970s–organizing), Edwards mourned the loss of that imagination and considered its impact on the idea of community.

> As the drive to develop a distinct lesbian culture dissipates, so too does our only real hope of creating something that can be properly called a community. For without separatism, however loosely we define it, there is no such thing as lesbian politics – our only hope of attaining a powerful common denominator – for the simple reason that there are no purely lesbian issues.[18]

She went further to suggest that "Toronto's lesbian community has no political or cultural character to express, and our emotional needs are being served adequately by a web of interlocking social circles."[19]

In terms of setting the community values that would indicate whether a specific woman "belonged" or not, in an undated letter written to the Broadside Collective, the group which published the feminist newspaper *Broadside*, one woman considered what impact it would have on her if strippers performed at the women's dances hosted by Womonspace, in Edmonton. In the spring of 1983 this was being considered, although in the end the Womonspace Board ruled that since strippers performed at other venues in the city, there was no need to have them at Womonspace events.[20] Explaining her position, the letter writer wrote, "As a lesbian, the Womonspace dances give me a beautiful environment where love and good feelings flow freely. I feel strengthened by seeing hundreds of lesbians gathered in one place, the energy is positive and I always leave jubilant and rejuvenated."[21] Bringing a feminist analysis to bear on her emotions, she suggested that she would have to give up that wonderful experience if strippers were present, because she would be unable to see them as harmless entertainment. The letter writer was informed by her reading of the documentary *Not a Love Story: A Film about Pornography*, which came out of the National Film Board of Canada's

Studio D in 1982. Written and directed by Bonnie Sherr Klein, the film represented strippers as being situated at one end of a spectrum that, further along, included pornography and violence against women. This documentary was highly influential, setting the terms for the feminist debates over the pornography industry in Canada for at least a decade. Clearly influenced by Klein's analysis – yet cautious to acknowledge that her views were her own and not necessarily shared by other women – the letter writer argued that the presence of strippers at the Womonspace dances would put her in a position where she would "cry with sadness and rage."[22]

This letter indicates the intense emotions attached to the experience of the scene where large numbers of lesbians gathered in one space. The stakes were very high, and for this woman at least a shift in the political tone of the dances would completely alter her emotional life for the worse. In effect, she was anticipating what would have been an untenable shift in her emotional community. Although she took the time to write a letter to express her feelings, her acknowledgment that others might not agree with her suggests that perhaps her anticipation was tinged with a sense of powerlessness. For Rosenwein, "emotions are about things judged important to us. Emotions overwhelm us only because something has been presented to us or happened to us that matters to our sense of well-being: emotions are the result [*sic*] our values and our assessments."[23] The letter writer's expectation that her emotions would now shift from jubilation to sadness and rage speak directly to Rosenwein's point about well-being. The space was vitally important to this woman (and to many others). Altering the dominant values in the space meant that the writer would no longer find it rejuvenating: instead, it would now be a place that gave rise to negative and draining emotions and thus itself become the cause – like patriarchal and homophobic spaces – of the need for rejuvenation. In spite of these doubts and disappointments about whether a lesbian community really existed or what values its members shared, for the women who were attempting to situate themselves within a larger political framework three emotions seemed to dominate their discussions and writing. These were love, fear, and pride.

Framing Belonging and Authenticity

Desire and love for other women were, of course, at the heart of any lesbian emotional community. Those feelings that had often been the source of shame, doubt, or confusion in an individual woman's life now had to be honoured and acted on in order for a woman to feel that she legitimately belonged. Certainly, feelings of love and joy at experiencing a sense of community were frequently remarked upon. Anne Fulton, from Halifax, for example, reflected on the time she spent at a lesbian conference in Ottawa. "The tremendous emotional support and euphoria I felt in being with these women is something which yet amazes me, and has stayed with me."[24] Similarly, in *Sapphistry: The Book of Lesbian Sexuality*, the American author Pat Califia explained the impact of falling in love with a woman. The two were never lovers:

> But the intensity of that passion was all I needed to tell me I was indeed a lesbian. It was so incandescent, so all-consuming, that I could not possibly have mistaken my feelings for mere affection. Knowing I was a lesbian transformed the way I saw, heard, perceived the whole world. I became aware of a network of sensations and reactions that I had ignored my entire life ... The system doesn't simply deny women economic or political power. It denies them a vision of their own fury and glory, the feeling that each of them is a thundering river pouring into and joining other women until they are a flashflood that will carry everything in its wake. The world denies us a chance to be heroes for one another, to rescue and care for and worship each other.[25]

These remarks by both Fulton and Califia are fairly representative: many women shared a similar sense that lesbian love, which they were newly discovering and acknowledging within themselves, was also profoundly political. It linked them to a community whose power to transform women's lives seemed to have been deliberately and systematically hidden. However, in the context of a lesbian feminist politics those feelings also had to be exhaustively interrogated for any evidence of possessive patriarchal influence. For example, two members of the WomanShare Collective bravely articulated their thoughts on this process of self-examination in what reads as unadorned self-criticism. Carol and Billie worked hard at trying to explain to themselves, as well as to other interested lesbians, the meaning of being lovers. "We approve of couple energy and the intensities that accompany it, but we also feel the need to change our culturally conditioned attitudes about jealousy, possessiveness, and exclusiveness."[26] Indeed, the WomanShare Collective as a whole considered that "we are moving closer to our goal of being able to love women in ways that are not as jealous, possessive, or self-destructive as the ways of loving taught us by the patriarchy. We have some methods we would like to share ... ways that helped us through heavy situations."[27] Love, then, was complicated by the need to consider which emotions were authentic and which were part of an oppressive emotional regime that had to be unlearned.

Attempting to maintain open relationships with multiple lovers was a challenge. In trying to analyze why these could be very painful, women acknowledged that they might well see themselves (unfavourably) in competition with newer lovers and that sexual love incorporated the potential for a complex power dynamic. As they processed how to manage the painful emotions, they remarked that

> remaining open and not withdrawing one's emotional support is another way of equalizing power within a triangle. By remaining open here we mean that the old lover remains responsible ... loyal to the woman with whom she shared love ... and not closed off to her because of the excitement the new love brings. Even though responsibility in this case may mean having to deal with a heavy load of anger and pain.[28]

If anger and pain were present alongside love, so was fear. Fear, in fact, loomed large. Women were afraid to be visible, to lose their jobs, homes, and children. One woman who wrote to the Gay Community Centre of Saskatchewan in January 1973 clarified, "Please ~~do not~~ keep this confidential. But I'm sure interested in meeting others like myself. Would you please phone me as soon as possible between 9 and 4.30 as that is when I am alone and I want to keep this confidential. If possible, have a female call, as I am very shy with men."[29] The combination of underlining for emphasis and the crossing out of the phrase "do not" in this letter points to conflicted emotions and the desire to somehow become visible to other similar women without being exposed: a paradoxical desire to be seen and simultaneously to not reveal oneself. The writer's request to be contacted during the period when she was alone and to only speak to another woman, if possible, also suggests that she was actively trying to manage her fears. Some years later, a woman reflecting on her process of coming out as a lesbian remarked that it was "no easy task for someone who a mere six years ago froze paralyzed to her chair when asked by a womyn for a dance."[30] She explained that she spent years trying to rationalize that reaction, unable to link it to her barely acknowledged desire for women. During her slow journey towards lesbianism, "during all this mental activity, my feelings would occasionally manage to make themselves known. Again, with hindsight, I am able to see that very often my feelings are operating, giving me messages, yet I simply don't recognize it on a conscious level."[31] These women's reactions suggest high levels of fear and anxiety coupled with ambivalence and desire. To fully enter the emotional community of lesbians meant aligning the subconscious feelings, expressed through physical paralysis, with the intellectual interpretation of those feelings.

This fear of exposure was certainly rational in the context of a patriarchal, homophobic, and sexist society and was an emotion shared by many lesbians. In their Statement of Purpose, FLAG suggested that "lesbians will have the opportunity to become strong, self-respecting women. Non-lesbians perhaps will lose some of the fear and pain of prejudice."[32] To that extent fear formed a recognizable part of the emotional community. But this was a fear of external attack and the power of the dominant "emotional regime" to define lesbians as deviant, sick, and criminal. FLAG argued that one of their main objectives was to "try to effect social change by dispelling the age-old myths that surround the word lesbian, so that ultimately all lesbian women need no longer be afraid or ashamed."[33] Reporting on the May 1981 Lesbian Conference in Vancouver, two Toronto-based attendees, Maureen Fitzgerald and Daphne Morrison, wrote that "we are sometimes afraid but mostly we are not."[34]

Another source of fear was internal. Women expressed concerns over whether they could fit into this hard-won community. For some, their fear was that they were not lesbian enough and would not find the sense of home and belonging that they hoped might sustain them. They were afraid of oppressing their sisters through their words or behaviour, or of not understanding the political nuances of lesbian existence as determined by "a core group of vocal, articulate women – women who considered themselves political activists and who spoke as such. Women without that sense of themselves and that experience may well have felt intimidated, nervous and on the periphery."[35] As Sue, a member of the WomanShare Collective, wrote in 1976, "I think we each feel very strongly about our ideas and beliefs about 'Lesbian Nation,' and, at the moment, our ideas are like stone walls between us. Disagreement is taken as nonsupport. Our political differences seem harder to deal with when other things in our individual and collective lives become difficult."[36] Both of these points speak to the challenges of negotiating a new political identity.

Historian William Reddy claims that "emotional styles are enforced, that penalties and exclusions fall on those who do not conform to them. 'Style' becomes 'regime' when the sum of the penalties and exclusions adds up to a coherent structure, and the issue of conformity becomes defining for the individual."[37] This accurately captures the sense of a demarcated set of expectations that influenced lesbians' emotional lives. What is particularly interesting about this period is that the women who were trying to conform to this emotional regime based their claim to it on "authentic" lesbianism. They were very often women who would diligently, even relentlessly, interrogate their own and each other's statements, use of language, and feelings of desire and possessiveness for evidence that they held the "correct" approach. They were searching for the key that would signal their belonging. In other words, authenticity was a nebulous concept only achieved through painstaking effort, and there was considerable fear associated with meeting the criteria of authenticity and of conforming, or failing to conform, to the emotional regime that was in the process of solidifying at this time.

In addition to the pressures to conform to a new emotional regime and the associated fear of failure, women had to manage feelings of fear over how best to articulate their lesbianism and to overcome the reluctance to speak openly about being lesbian. Sue remarked that there was an emotional place "where as a long-time lesbian you don't believe that being a lesbian is right at all – and so you'll take the crumbs off the table."[38] Reflecting on a poetry workshop at the 1981 Lesbian Conference in Vancouver, Maureen Fitzgerald and Daphne Morrison remarked that the participants at that workshop "lingered for a while on the agony and audacity of writing from their experience as women and as lesbians ... they confronted the fear that comes from the change that underlies their experience and that can be precipitated by their writing."[39] The fear associated with being in a known lesbian (and/or gay) space was also something to dwell on and process afterwards. For example, in 1978, a woman sitting in a church in Calgary one Sunday morning reflected on her experiences at Myrt's. This was a gay club she had been at the night before, where she had noticed a woman who was obviously making her first venture into the lesbian scene. The anonymous churchgoer wrote,

> This entrance was not exactly a pleasant experience for her. Her body was tense. I could feel her fear across the room ... I wished to go over to this woman. I wanted very badly to help her skip some of the agony I went through coming out. But, I was afraid. Would it look like I was making a pass? Would it look like I was trying to pick her up? Would I only make her fear worse? Would she panic if I went near her table? I felt helpless. I wanted so much to help. I didn't know how.[40]

This fear was paralyzing, but in a different sense to that which had frozen another woman to her chair. Here the fear was multilayered and complex. At one level was fear of being misinterpreted as predatory, which was a common fear for lesbians who had to negotiate dominant homophobic narratives that suggested lesbians preyed on vulnerable women. On another level was the desire to prevent fear, to intervene in the new woman's coming-out process in order to circumvent the fear and agony that often (but not always) accompanied that process. A third area of concern was that she would actually generate more fear, would contribute to the agony, and potentially drive the new woman away, not provide the support that was motivating her desire to intervene in the first place. In the end, she did nothing, dissuaded from taking any action by her lover who rationalized the inaction by suggesting that "she has to come out when she is ready. She has to learn the hard way. She has to make the first move to be friendly with others."[41] All of these different forms of fear were paralyzing, preventing women from acting in the first place or freezing them in alarm or even panic as they situated their own feelings in a wider homophobic context, where misinterpretation was both rife and highly likely.

Another form of fear was present for members of the WomanShare Collective, struggling over opening up their relationships sexually to other women. This fear focused on the potentially devastating and destructive forces of jealousy and loss of romantic partners. While any couple who decides to make their relationship open and to introduce new sexual partners into their dynamic would risk feelings of jealousy, insecurity, loss of control, and even loss of the relationship if the new lover replaced them, for lesbians the stakes were particularly high. After all, finding a partner in the first place was frequently a major challenge. It was not uncommon for two women to stay together in an unhealthy relationship if they believed that there were no alternatives.[42] In this context, attempting to live a politics of nonpossessive and, therefore, nonpatriarchal love came with significant risks. For example, Carol wrote about the possibility of having an open relationship and recalled, "I was thinking about it, but it really scared me, so I put it away for a few days, and then I talked about it with Billie and it scared her too. But then we decided to open up!"[43] For Carol's new lover Susann, fear operated in a different way:

> Well, here I am alone in Carol's room. She is off sleeping with Billie tonight. I felt depressed for about two hours but I feel better now that she's actually there ... Last night I thought we should sleep together every night, but I am afraid of declaring our love for each other to death ... or so to speak.[44]

Another member of the WomanShare Collective, Dian, reflected that "living collectively has increased my understanding of emotions and relationships. I have learned to speak some awful angry words instead of hiding my feelings. And i [*sic*] now see that when i do that, i open the way for the other woman (or women) to speak to me."[45] In other words, the lesbian feminist framework made it possible to articulate powerful fears and other emotions.

Feeling Proud

In spite of the complications around love and fear, lesbians also took pride in the world-changing potential of politicized lesbianism. They wrote and spoke of the motivation for change precipitated by feelings of anger and rage. In Calgary, in 1978, one woman seemed to capture the significance of feeling proud when she wrote,

> Yes, I'm a lesbian. I'm just learning to be proud of that fact. The pride has been acquired at great cost but I can assure that it will be well worth it. I am now able to be what I am, rather than the cardboard character that the world expected me to be. I am freer in many ways than I've ever been before.[46]

Assertions of pride seemed to have a specific resonance and indicated that a woman was defining herself for herself, had attained a politicized understanding of lesbianism in the context of feminist critiques of patriarchy, and was somewhat visible as a lesbian.

To feel proud was, therefore, to have achieved a certain visible level of self-possession. In 1973, Ellen, one of the nineteen women who put together the lesbian issue of the Toronto-based revolutionary feminist newspaper *The Other Woman*, stated this succinctly when she explained that "the thing about dressing like a dyke is that it challenges the assumptions that if you dress like a dyke you're trying to be a man. We can be what we want to be. We're proud of being strong-looking and dykey."[47] An anonymous piece entitled "My Name Is Gay Woman," in the same issue, also drew attention to the link between pride, self-definition, and self-confidence. The author asserted that "we must fight to regain ourselves – to rediscover our own minds and bodies – to know that it can be a good thing to love another woman. To learn how to deal with our feelings for one another, for the longer we say no to one another, the longer we negate ourselves."[48] These comments signal that feeling proud was multilayered and could incorporate a strong sense of resistance to patriarchal and homophobic definitions of lesbianism.

For some lesbians, their pride was noticeably distinct from the version espoused by gay men. These lesbians refused to just add a women's version to a general vision of gay liberation. Reporting on Toronto's Gay Pride week, held in August 1973, a writer in *The Other Woman* critiqued the emphasis given to the week's events by the Community Homophile Association of Toronto. "We didn't want to put energy into something that presents itself in a trippy, apologetic way when we're feeling serious and defiant about being lesbian. Bake sales and pot luck suppers sounded like the Women's Auxiliary again." Instead, the lesbian feminists' approach to the Saturday march emphasized pride over begging for tolerance. The anonymous author explained that "we went as a group of lesbian feminists to the march and shouted: 2468 gay is so much better than straight, whilst all the Official Megaphone Carriers (OMCs) were instructing everyone to shout 2468 gay is JUST AS GOOD as straight. We don't want to apologise for believing in who we are." After some initial hostility, other marchers and the OMCs began to use the lesbian feminists' chant, and in the end the other marchers "joined with some of the women who had previously marched separately and we all shouted and sang together. It was a great feeling of sisterhood, walking down the middle of the street arm in arm. The march made us feel how strong women can be together. But that says little for Gay Pride and much for Lesbian Pride."[49] This form of lesbian pride combined individual feelings of self-definition with the collective experience of shared values. Moreover, when the other women joined in the unapologetic chant and linked arms with the original group of lesbian feminists, all the women, at least according to this author, received the benefits of belonging in that moment to the emotional community, and "it was a great feeling."[50] Pride was catching.

Conclusion

Sometimes the emotions involved seemed unendurable for women who were trying to create a satisfying lesbian community and sustain themselves and their needs within it. In 1973, Dian, Carol, and Billie were travelling from Montreal to British Columbia, looking for land to buy in order to create a lesbian community and eventually establish the WomanShare Collective. Carol and Billie were a couple and Dian struggled with her feelings about the situation in which she found herself. As they searched for suitable land and negotiated with Dian's father over access to some stocks with which they could purchase the land, emotions began to run high. As Dian recalled,

> The emotional atmosphere among the three of us had become unbearable. In our travels searching for land we had had a very hard time of it. There had been lots of tears, hysteria, and recriminations along the way. Billie and Carol were lovers and i [*sic*] couldn't help but feel left out most of the time. Self-hate and doubt were consuming me and i wasn't sure i could live with the two women and stay sane, let alone put their names on the [property] deed.[51]

The language here speaks of feelings which were incredibly intense, leading Dian to not only doubt her own emotional reactions but to also question whether continuing to commit to the emotional community that the three women were trying to inhabit would, in fact, seriously and negatively affect her mental health. By contrast, in 1980, Val Edwards wrote about the positive feelings of inclusion that could accrue to members of the community. She explained that inclusion in the category of "we" applied to "every woman who has derived even a modicum of emotional support or happiness from the group of lesbian-feminists that resembles and calls itself a community."[52]

Certainly, some women during the decade struggled over the promise of an emotional community that was in the agonizing process of forming and perhaps simultaneously developing the characteristics of an emotional regime. In its latter state, members felt the pressure to conform to a nebulous and often-changing standard of authenticity and feared the potential penalties of no longer belonging to a lesbian community that they had fought so long and hard to find in the first place.

The emotions were intense, and for many of the women involved who left a record of their feelings the stakes were very high. Sexual desire, love, jealousy, and the overwhelming need to find a place of belonging motivated women to keep struggling with difficult feelings of fear, as well as love and the rewards attained by having pride in one's sexuality. The promise that lesbian community would provide a rich and satisfying emotional life kept many women hopeful and committed to the movement of trying to achieve it. Writing from Halifax in the inaugural issue of *Lesbian Canada Lesbienne*, Anne Fulton expressed her optimism for a nationwide lesbian movement:

> I would like to see us all communicate and keep that warmth and closeness going, which we experienced in Ottawa [...] There are so many things we

> have to say to each other, so much to listen to from each other. I hope that this dialogue continues to happen. If it does, by God, we'll all make it to Lesbos some day. Once we start to move, I don't think there's anything that can stop us.[53]

Feminism gave many of these women the political language through which they could frame their tumultuous emotions.

Notes

1 Jan Trainor, personal interview with Liz Millward, April 29, 2012.

2 Jan Plamper, "The History of Emotions: An Interview with William Reddy, Barbara Rosenwein, and Peter Stearns," *History and Theory* 49, 2 (2010): 257.

3 According to historian William Reddy, any given community will have its own set of accepted and expected emotional styles. These can cohere into an emotional regime when they are reinforced through "penalties such as gossip, exclusion or demotion." Reddy, cited in Plamper, "The History of Emotions," 243.

4 Liz Millward, *Making a Scene: Lesbians and Community across Canada, 1964–1984* (Vancouver: UBC Press, 2015).

5 Letter to Gay Community Centre of Saskatchewan, February 5, 1973, Saskatchewan Archives Board (SAB), Neil Richards Papers, S-A 821 IV. 20 Correspondence, 1971–1982 (2 of 2) (Restricted).

6 Valerie J. Korinek, *Prairie Fairies: A History of Queer Communities and People in Western Canada, 1930–1985* (Toronto: University of Toronto Press, 2018).

7 Letter to Gay Community Centre of Saskatchewan, February 5, 1973, Saskatchewan Archives Board (SAB), Neil Richards Papers, S-A 821 IV. 20 Correspondence, 1971–1982 (2 of 2) (Restricted).

8 Rosemary Hennessy, "Open Secrets: The Affective Cultures of Organizing on Mexico's Northern Border," *Feminist Theory* 10, 3 (2009): 311.

9 Nelly, cited in Sue Deevy, Nelly Kaufer, Dian Wagner, Billie Miracle, and Carol Osmer-Newhouse, *Country Lesbians: The Story of the WomanShare Collective* (Grants Pass, OR: WomanShare Books, 1976), 183.

10 Val Edwards, "The Invisible Community," *Broadside* 1, 10 (1980): 4.

11 Edwards, "The Invisible Community."

12 Letter to Gay Community Centre of Saskatchewan, February 5, 1973, Saskatchewan Archives Board (SAB), Neil Richards Papers, S-A 821 IV. 20 Correspondence, 1971–1982 (2 of 2) (Restricted).

13 Sidney Abbott and Barbara Love, *Sappho Was a Right-On Woman: A Liberated View of Lesbianism* (New York: Stein and Day, 1972); Del Martin and Phyllis Lyon, *Lesbian/Woman* (New York: Bantam, 1972).

14 Statement of Purpose, Feminist Lesbian Action Group, Canadian Women's Movement Archives (CWMA), box 28, Feminist Lesbian Action Group (FLAG, Victoria, BC), Correspondence and statement of purpose, 1973–1980.

15 Deevy et al., *Country Lesbians*, 62.

16 Barbara Rosenwein, cited in Plamper, "History of Emotions," 251.
17 Edwards, "The Invisible Community," 4.
18 Edwards, "Invisible Community," 4.
19 Edwards, "Invisible Community."
20 Noelle M. Lucas, "Womonspace: Building a Lesbian Community in Edmonton, Alberta, 1970–1990" (master's thesis, University of Saskatchewan, 2002), 97–99.
21 "On the Question of Having Strippers at Our Dances," undated letter, CWMA, box 6, *Broadside* (Toronto, ON), Correspondence 1979–1989.
22 "On the Question of Having Strippers at Our Dances," undated letter, CWMA.
23 Barbara Rosenwein, cited in Plamper, "History of Emotions," 251.
24 Anne Fulton, "Comments," CWMA, *Lesbian Canada Lesbienne*, 1977, n.p.
25 Pat Califia, *Sapphistry: The Book of Lesbian Sexuality*, 3rd ed. (Tallahassee, FL: Naiad Press, 1988), 165.
26 Carol and Billie, cited in Deevy et al., *Country Lesbians*, 75.
27 Deevy et al., *Country Lesbians*, 98.
28 Deevy et al., Country Lesbians, 99.
29 Letter to the Gay Community Centre of Saskatchewan, January 17, 1973, SAB, Neil Richards Papers, S-A 821 IV. 20 Correspondence, 1971–1982 (2 of 2) (Restricted). (Emphasis in original.)
30 "Looking in the Mirror on the Closet Door," *Images*, 9, 11 (1982): 10. The use of the spelling "womyn" rather than "woman" situates this writer squarely in the lesbian feminist camp, given that this spelling and other similar alternatives, such as "womon" and "wimmin," deliberately remove "men" and "man" from references to women.
31 "Looking in the Mirror on the Closet Door," 10.
32 Statement of Purpose, Feminist Lesbian Action Group, CWMA.
33 Statement of Purpose, Feminist Lesbian Action Group, CWMA.
34 Maureen Fitzgerald and Daphne Morrison, "Lesbian Conference: Agony and Audacity," *Broadside* 2, 9 (1981): 4.
35 Fitzgerald and Morrison, "Lesbian Conference," 4.
36 Sue, cited in Sue et al., *Country Lesbians*, 129.
37 William Reddy, cited in Plamper, "History of Emotions," 243.
38 Sue, cited in Sue et al., *Country Lesbians*, 169.
39 Fitzgerald and Morrison, "Lesbian Conference," 4.
40 Anonymous, "Lesbian Centre," *Gay Calgary* 2, 3 (1978): 4. SAB, Neil Richards Papers, Gay Information and Resources (Calgary), 1977–1983, A595 II.83. For more on "catching" feelings see Anna Gibbs, "Contagious Feelings: Pauline Hanson and the Epidemiology of Affect," *Australian Humanities Review* 24 (2001): 1–9, http://australianhumanitiesreview.org/2001/12/01/contagious-feelings-pauline-hanson-and-the-epidemiology-of-affect/.
41 "Lesbian Centre," SAB.
42 Millward, *Making a Scene*, 242.
43 Carol, cited in Deevy et al., *Country Lesbians*, 77.
44 Susann, cited in Deevy et al., *Country Lesbians*, 90.

45 Dian, cited in Deevy et al., *Country Lesbians*, 137.
46 "Lesbian Centre," *Gay Calgary*.
47 Ellen, cited in "A Conversation," *The Other Woman*, September/October 1973, 4.
48 "My Name Is Gay Woman," *The Other Woman*, September/October 1973, 6.
49 "Gay Pride," *The Other Woman*, September/October 1973, 18.
50 "Gay Pride," 18.
51 Dian, cited in Sue et al., *Country Lesbians*, 66.
52 Edwards, "Invisible Community," 14.
53 Fulton, "Comments."

8

Resisting Red Hot Video
Feminism, Pornography, and the Political Utility of Emotion

ERYK MARTIN

In late November 1982, a clandestine force of nine women firebombed three locations of the pornographic video chain Red Hot Video. A new addition to the sexual entertainment industry in British Columbia, Red Hot Video had first opened its doors to the public in February 1982. It quickly established seven outlets across the province within a month. By October, it had added eight more locations, bringing the total to fifteen stores in eight months. Victoria, Kelowna, Prince George, and the greater Vancouver area were all hosts to its expanding commercial operations. Throughout 1982, anti-pornography activists responded with a campaign to shut down the chain, with feminists at the centre of this political project. Reflecting the concerns of anti-pornography feminists in other communities across Canada and the United States, activists in BC focused on Red Hot Video's dissemination of films that depicted coercion and violence against women and children. And, like their colleagues elsewhere, they suggested that the violence they saw in pornography both reflected and contributed to other patterns of male violence against women and girls, including rape, battering, and pedophilia. This emphasis on gendered violence led to a situation in which activists linked struggles against

Content note: This chapter contains graphic descriptions of pornography, including violence against women and girls. This content is included because it is essential for understanding feminist anti-pornography activism in the 1970s and 1980s.

pornography to a wider array of feminist anti-violence projects, including public education initiatives, legal advocacy, policy reform, community organization, direct action, women's self-defence, and the expansion of women's shelters and transition houses.

It was in this wider context that the nine women – calling themselves the Wimmin's Fire Brigade (WFB) – firebombed Red Hot Video. For two of the women involved – Ann Hansen and Juliet Belmas – participating in the WFB was also an offshoot of their work in Direct Action, an anarchist group that had bombed controversial industrial projects in both BC and Ontario earlier in the year. While these earlier actions reflected Direct Action's environmental, anti-militarist, and anti-imperialist politics, the group also supported feminist organizing and activism in Vancouver. For Hansen and Belmas, joining with seven other women to form the WFB was an extension of their anarchist-feminist commitments, as well as a contribution to the longer feminist campaign against Red Hot Video and a violent pornography industry.

The day after their attack on the stores, the WFB reiterated the arguments that feminists had been making for months. They explained that Red Hot Video's collection of films showed women and children being physically assaulted and emotionally "humiliated." Maintaining that the state had done little to address these issues despite the province-wide movement against the stores, the WFB concluded that "we are left no viable alternative but to change the situation ourselves through illegal means." As such, they declared, the arsons had been an "act of self-defense against hate propaganda!"[1]

Although the WFB arsons were certainly militant, it would be a mistake to see them as isolated events. Rather, as the WFB communiqué itself argued, they were one of many political actions in the local campaign against Red Hot Video and, in turn, part of a larger feminist anti-pornography movement embedded in the wider history of late-twentieth-century feminism in North America. To date, there has been little historical scholarship that explores feminist anti-pornography activism in Canada.[2] In this chapter, I undertake this work with a focus on the struggle against pornography in Vancouver in the 1970s and 1980s, situating the actions against Red Hot Video in a wider context of feminist anti-pornography politics in British Columbia and beyond. I argue that feminists' analyses and claims to emotion were central to their anti-pornography politics. Specifically, the chapter demonstrates first that feminists built their arguments against pornography on critical analyses of its changing emotional dynamics and themes in this period. Then, it traces how feminists sought to mobilize claims to emotional experience, both individually and collectively, as tactics to contest directly the pornography industry. Overall, this discussion underscores the political utility of feminist claims to emotion, while offering a new history of anti-pornography activism as part of the wider feminist movement in the late-twentieth century.

A Crucible for Conflict: Feminism in the Golden Age of Pornography

In the 1960s and 1970s, feminists and pornographers were generally perceived to be mutually exclusive groups who not only held conflicting views on gender and sexuality, but who also mobilized these perspectives for very different objectives. Put simply, the intentions of feminists in these years were to fight for a diverse and open-ended project of women's liberation and to connect these aspirations to other forms of social, economic, racial, sexual, and environmental emancipation. In contrast, most pornographers' aims included economic reward and industry expansion. While specific products varied by pornographers' sexual politics and cinematic tastes, political economy mattered. Misogyny and capitalism would flourish together so long as the former was economically viable. And in the shifting landscape of post-1960s sexual culture, misogyny was very much big business for them.

While these very different beliefs clearly accounted for much of the animosity between feminist activists and the pornography industry, the intensity and timing of their conflicts were also shaped by a historical context in which both groups were attaining heightened levels of political and cultural influence. Although feminism and pornography were not new phenomena, they were remade in the social, cultural, and political transformations of the 1960s, 1970s, and 1980s. For feminism, this period is associated with the often-contested notion of a second wave, which signalled significant changes in feminism's political and cultural contours and a dramatic increase in its social influence.[3] The same era is commonly described as pornography's so-called golden age, a moment in which porn became both culturally chic and an extremely lucrative mass commodity.[4]

The simultaneity of these developments had much to do with the shifting terrain of gender and sexuality during the Long Sixties and in its wake. On the one hand, there was a significant connection between changing social expectations of sexuality and activist politics. The 1960s, broadly defined, are often regarded as a period of sexual transformation, in which changing cultural perspectives and access to reliable oral contraceptives ushered in more progressive approaches to gender and sexuality. For example, the political radicalism of the New Left broadly challenged the conservative sexual mores of the mid-twentieth century, including assertions that sexual liberation was a key facet of social revolution. Here, leftist movements and culture took inspiration from popular academics such as Herbert Marcuse and Wilhelm Reich, who combined Marxism and Freudian analysis in order to challenge the idea that personal sexual desires necessitated, in Carolyn Bronstein's words, "constant repression for the maintenance of civilized society."[5] Instead, they suggested that sexual liberation was an essential pillar in the quest for a better world.[6]

On the other hand, while feminism drew heavily from the New Left's emphasis on participatory democracy and the idea that liberation was both a social and personal process, it was also motivated by the New Left's own patriarchal politics. New feminist projects developed, in part, to address the sexism that women often faced as activists and the dismissal of gender and sexuality as worthy categories of political analysis within the student and antiwar movements of the Long Sixties.[7] Capturing much of this dissatisfaction, Judy Bernstein, Peggy Morton, Linda Seese, and Myrna Wood wrote to their colleagues in the Student Union for Peace Action, in 1967, stating "it is our contention that until the male chauvinists of the movement understand the concept of liberation in relation to women, the most exploited members of any society, they will be voicing political lies."[8]

Reflecting similar concerns, the emergence of women's liberation in Canada sought to contest long-standing patterns of women's oppression in general, as well as their more recent subjugation in the context of the New Left. Between 1968 and 1970, women's liberation organizations took root in cities such as Vancouver, Toronto, Regina, and Fredericton, and soon expanded nationwide. Often starting within the confines of New Left–inspired student movements, their activities quickly outgrew campus boundaries.[9] In Vancouver, feminists active within the student community at Simon Fraser University moved off campus with the 1969 formation of the Vancouver Women's Caucus.[10] As a number of historians have noted, the Vancouver Women's Caucus played an important role in the creation of new feminist initiatives, the most well known being a caravan that travelled from Vancouver to Ottawa to advocate for women's access to, and personal control over, abortion services.[11] Activists within the caucus also worked to create innovative forms of feminist activism such as the Working Women's Workshop and Working Women's Association – groups that fostered a growing emphasis on workplace organizing through an explicitly socialist feminist perspective.[12]

As pivotal as these activist projects were, the history of feminist activism in the decades after the 1960s also expanded well beyond issues surrounding women's waged and unwaged labour. The issue of pornography is a critical example of this. Feminists in British Columbia carried out sustained forms of anti-pornography organizing, beginning in 1976. The fact that feminists had an expanding pornographic industry to contest was itself a product of the historical moment. While the growing cultural appeal of pornography may have reflected the broader liberalization of sexual consumption in popular culture – including more sexual content in media such as billboards and commercial signs, print journalism, television, literature, and film – legal changes in the regulation of sexually explicit material in the decades following the Second World War were also a factor. In both the United States and Canada, courts struck down charges of obscenity in a series of cases in the 1950s and 1960s. Although most of these involved literary depictions of sex – in works such as D.H. Lawrence's *Lady Chatterley's Lover* (1928), Henry Miller's *Tropic of Cancer* (1934), and the anonymously published *My Secret Life* (1888) – other mediums of sexual representation, including films and magazines, also benefited from the shifting legal terrain.[13] This new legal and cultural environment created what the sociologist Dany Lacombe has called a "glasnost of the erotic."[14]

Technological change also factored into the expansion of pornography, particularly from the late 1970s on. In this period, the development of Video Home System (VHS) technology increased the marketability, dissemination, and production of pornography. This in turn enabled new opportunities for consuming pornography at home, while the infrastructure that fed this consumption – video retailers specializing in the sale or rental of pornographic material – expanded pornography's public presence at the community level. Pornographic retail outlets became visible markers of industrial expansion and sexual politics.[15] The stores also worked in conjunction with other distribution systems, including print and postal services. American publications such as *Adam Film World Magazine* produced guides that reviewed pornographic films and provided information on how to order them through the post. These guides were available in Canada and featured prominently in the debate over Red Hot Video, since at least some of the stores in BC carried copies of the publication. A 1983 edition of *Adam Film World's X-Rated Movie Handbook*, confiscated by feminists in BC, suggests that that much of the growing pornographic catalogue was American in its origin.[16] This is not to say that there were not Canadian films too, but rather that the role of international production – particularly in the United States – was incredibly important in shaping and promoting the consumption of pornography in Canada.[17]

The arrival of new sexually explicit publications, including Larry Flynt's *Hustler* (1974) and Bob Guccione's *Penthouse* (1965), demonstrated the growing diversity of, and expanding commercial rewards for selling, sexual imagery. *Hustler* and *Penthouse* also signalled a shift towards more explicit sexual genres, taking pornographic forms often referred to as "hardcore." One of the most important expressions of this shift was the 1972 film *Deep Throat*. Indeed, pornography scholars such as Bronstein maintain that the film's incorporation of high-quality cinematography, a developed plot line, and graphic sexual content – including oral sex, vaginal penetration, and male ejaculation – "broke the mould for adult films." In doing so, it set new standards in both production value and sexual content, while its international popularity worked to normalize the consumption of pornography as a "hip" or "chic" form of leisure during the 1970s and after.[18]

Hardcore pornography was also marked by its graphic representation of violence. For example, *Hustler*'s comic strip, "Chester the Molester," repeatedly depicted the kidnapping, manipulating, assaulting, and raping of women and girls. The magazine's June 1978 cover, which featured a woman's naked body being put through a meat grinder, did nothing to alleviate activists' growing concerns about hardcore pornography's celebration of misogyny and violence.[19] Another prominent example was the 1975 film *Snuff*. Produced by the American filmmaker Allen Shackleton, *Snuff* depicted one of the film's female participants being tortured, killed, and disembowelled on camera. Rather than being a gruesome act of fiction, this killing was presented to the viewer as an act of real violence. While these claims of authentic murder were eventually proven to be a hoax, the film's emphasis on violence against women enraged feminists across North America and helped to catalyze the growing anti-pornography opposition.[20]

The 1970s, then, saw the expansion of both feminism and the pornography industry. As the latter shifted into violent hardcore, feminists formed part of a diverse anti-pornography opposition in Canada and the United States. As part of this political turn, activists analyzed pornography to develop supported and sustained critiques of hardcore pornography. In doing so, they drew on the emotional character of women's reactions to pornography as a tactic of resistance. By leveraging their emotional experiences, activists created analyses of how pornography worked and what was at stake, while also mobilizing emotion to contest pornography at the community level.

Feminism, Violence, and Emotional Assessments of Pornography

To aid their efforts to contest the industry, activists analyzed the content of pornography and sought to communicate its significance to a broader audience. While they developed various methods for analyzing the objectification and commodification of women's bodies, feminists frequently articulated their concerns with pornography by tracing its changing emotional codes. More specifically, these activists emphasized the place of hatred, revenge, terror, and anger as features of the new pornography. In doing so, they used these affective assessments as foundations for their political organizing against the growing industry.

Given the connections between violence and hardcore pornography, it is not surprising that feminist analyses of pornography in the 1970s and 1980s maintained that pornography expressed emotional themes of revenge, terrorization, and hatred against women. For American activist Andrea Dworkin, the violence of pornography was, at least in part, an act of revenge against the growing power of feminism. Situating this in the specific context of New Left misogyny, she suggested that this political affect was explained by the failures of radical men. Rather than joining with feminists to overturn the dominant patriarchal order, they had chosen to ally themselves with a wider assortment of men in a quest to crush feminism. "Only in this alliance," she wrote in the late 1970s, "could they find the social and political power that could compensate them for their waning virility. Only in this alliance could they gain access to the institutionalized brute force necessary to revenge themselves on the women who had left them."[21] Dworkin argued that pornography was "the perfect vehicle" for this political project since it served two overarching male objectives: the need to make money and a desire to use sexualized violence as a mechanism for "terrorizing women into silence."[22]

Similarly, another American feminist, Beverly LaBelle, argued that pornography functioned as a form of propaganda in which hatred against women played a prominent role. In doing so, she argued that hate was significant because it had the power to bind men together in their opposition to women. "Hatred," she maintained, "is one of the most powerful unifying emotions, since it permits feelings which are usually suppressed to be brought to the surface and expressed stridently. Women are the enemy in pornography – they are the group to be subdued and vanquished."[23] In these ways, Dworkin, LaBelle, and others suggested that pornography's emotional codes supported the maintenance and extension of a violent patriarchal order. Moreover, the common argument that "pornography is the theory, and rape the practice" articulated the view that what happened within the pages of *Hustler* or *Penthouse* had real-life implications for women and girls.[24] This gave debates over pornography an intense sense of urgency and connected anti-pornography struggles with feminist projects combatting violence against women in other settings.

At the same time as these American women were analyzing the emotive dynamics of pornography, so too were their colleagues north of the border. Addressing similar issues and engaging with each other's work, neither national community was separate from the other. Canadian feminists, for example, were keen participants in the Feminist Perspectives on Pornography Conference that took place in San Francisco, in 1978. As one of the first mass gatherings of anti-pornography activists in North America, the conference was a foundational political event. As such, it drew a strong contingent of anti-pornography feminists from BC, including activists connected to the BC Federation of Women, Vancouver Status of Women (VSW), the media collective Women in Focus, and other feminist organizations. According to the VSW newspaper, *Kinesis*, conference organizers also drew on the work of their member Debra Lewis, who had spent the previous several years formulating a feminist definition of pornography that hinged on categories of sexualized violence and oppression rather than on representations of sex alone.[25] In this work, Lewis was part of a current of feminist anti-pornography activism in BC that began in 1976 and expanded rapidly thereafter.

While British Columbian feminists were active in this work, they certainly were not the only Canadian feminists fighting against violent pornography. In 1977, feminists in Toronto incorporated anti-pornography actions into a national day of protest against violence against women. Struggles against pornography in Toronto also helped to catalyze the creation of new feminist organizations in the city, including a branch of Women Against Violence Against Women.[26] In 1978, Calgary Status of Women organized a Women in a Violent Society conference that drew participants from across the country and included a display and workshop on pornography and activism.[27] Every year the issue of pornography seemed to grow in its prominence. By the end of 1982, feminist periodicals such as *Kinesis* were arguing that "porn was undoubtedly the issue which has generated the greatest response in the broadest range of women."[28] Therefore, while feminists in BC were among the first in the nation to make concerted efforts to organize against pornography, it did not take long for anti-pornography campaigns and actions to develop into a national issue for Canadian feminists.

As important as these international and national activities were, much of the work against pornography was firmly rooted in local acts of analysis and resistance. This could take many forms, but one important element of this work in BC involved feminists' critical consumption of pornography. Activists watched pornographic films in order to educate themselves and the public about a range of issues connected to the industry. Sometimes they screened films publicly to foster discussion and debate at conferences and community events.[29] In other instances, these viewings took place privately among individuals or small groups. Participants in these sessions often produced written analyses of the films that could then be used for public campaigns against the industry. For historians, these reviews are now fruitful sources for investigating feminists' understanding of pornography in this period.[30]

In these feminist pornography reviews, activists sought to understand, assess, and communicate the content and significance of pornography with a focus on its affective themes. For example, in their struggles against Red Hot Video in Victoria, Women Against Pornography (WAP) watched and critically reviewed numerous examples of the company's materials. Agreeing with a wider feminist assessment of the industry, WAP argued that the pornography they watched was defined by patriarchal politics in which the theme of "male dominance/female submission" was ever present. However, unlike critics who focused on one or two dominant emotional themes, such as hate or terror, WAP did not associate the industry with any specific emotions, suggesting instead that it was broadly "characterized by images which objectify, demean, and stereotype women."[31]

This general commentary did not mean that emotion had no specific role in their assessment of pornography. To define and explain pornography, WAP juxtaposed the genre against other forms of sexual representation, including what they called "erotica." If pornography had no specific overarching emotional standard, then erotica had several. For WAP, erotica was the representation of sex according to two basic characteristics: first, the absence of violence, coercion, and inequality; and second, the presence of "mutual pleasure." Furthermore, WAP maintained that erotica involved other emotional themes, including "tenderness, humour, caring, and mutuality."[32] By implication, pornography was marked by the absence or opposite of these. Using this definition, four members of WAP then reviewed the film *Talk Dirty to Me* – a title stocked by Red Hot Video. They concluded that the film qualified as pornographic because it objectified women and because it lacked an overarching pattern of eroticism as defined by the collective. While there was one slight exception to this assessment – a seven-minute scene that reviewers suggested contained both "humor" and "caring" – the film's overall sexist content nullified the significance of this erotic affect.[33] In the end, WAP could "only conclude that the message of this film about women and about female sexuality, is consistent with that of any other porn film: women are mere objects, receptacles, for the use of men."[34]

WAP was not the only feminist group reviewing pornography. The Vancouver activist Regina Lorek spent six months of 1983 watching and analyzing pornographic films for the BC Federation of Women (BCFW).[35] During this period, Lorek had access to fifty-two VHS tapes. A sympathetic video merchant in Richmond had purchased this collection from a Vancouver Red Hot Video outlet and then turned them over to the BCFW to support their campaign against pornography.[36] Lorek viewed and analyzed most of these films. Like other feminist critics, she commented on how the emotional dynamics of these films were connected to patriarchal politics, particularly violence against women. However, because the BCFW collection included so many films, Lorek's analysis took on a greater scope than most feminist pornography reviews. And because the collection included a wide array of films produced between the 1960s and the 1980s, Lorek had a body of evidence that she could use to construct a historical analysis of how and why pornography's affect had changed over time.[37] The result was an assessment that sought to recognize the complexity of emotion in pornography while at the same time creating a clear analysis that would be politically useful for feminist organizers.

In a talk delivered to a public forum on pornography in Vancouver and reprinted in *Kinesis*, Lorek argued that the content of pornographic films had changed between the 1960s and the 1970s. While she certainly did not suggest that the films of the 1960s were unproblematic, she found that they were more likely to be humorous and to involve female characters who were in control of their own sexuality. In contrast, she argued, by the 1970s the emotional landscape of pornography had changed. While humor was still present, she maintained that it accompanied greater amounts of sexualized violence and rape. "What they usually do in the movies," she noted, "is soften you up with one of the funny or consensual scenes, and then throw in a little violence later. It makes the violence more acceptable, and leaves you with a lot of confused feelings."[38]

Moreover, she maintained that this violence came with a shift in emotional content in which women were more likely to be "humiliated" on camera. Lorek argued that this transformation had taken place to control women who, thanks to feminism, had been making significant steps in challenging patriarchal power over the previous several decades. In this way, she reiterated a common feminist critique that understood pornography as a form of propaganda and an instrument of social control. Built into this notion was the idea that changing emotional representations and experiences in the films reflected changing collective, societal standards about sex and violence off the screen. By tracing the affective changes in pornography over time, Lorek proposed that pornography was growing more violent and more sexist and that society was becoming more violent and sexist as a result.[39] Such an assessment reflected a number of interconnected concerns within late twentieth-century feminism about the impact of pornography for both individuals and communities. These included the idea that pornography taught men to equate sexuality and violence, particularly through the practice of rape; that pornography was a form of emotional abuse and patriarchal manipulation of women carried out through popular culture and intimate relationships with men; and that pornography was also a direct form of exploitation of the individual women and girls who appeared in films, magazines, and other media.[40]

Taken together, these feminist analyses were marked by common attention to the changing emotional standards of pornography in the late-twentieth century. In reviews and other public discussions of pornography, these activists highlighted the place of hatred, terror, and revenge and an absence of tenderness or humour as markers of the problematic nature of the industry. In doing so, their critiques of emotion helped to historicize the transformation of pornography, theorize how it worked, and comment on what was at stake in a changing industry and society.

The Emotions of Resistance

Feminist assessments of emotion onscreen were not the only way in which affect worked its way into the struggle against pornography. Activists also emphasized personal experience – how pornography made them feel as women. More specifically, activists used individual and collective claims to emotion to communicate the personal stakes of their political work. At the same time, since the personal was simultaneously political, they made such assertions publicly in order to support community-organizing projects against pornographic retailers, including Red Hot Video. In this sense, narratives of emotional experience ought to be seen as a feminist strategy of resistance, as these activists attempted to leverage personal feelings to achieve political change. This is not to suggest that political usefulness meant that feminists' claims to feeling were dishonest, exaggerated, or superficial. Rather, it is to underscore how affect functioned within the context of activist work, and what that can tell us about the relationship between feminist politics and pornography.

Given the violence and misogyny that women identified in pornography, anger was among the most common and important affective responses. However, anger could exist alongside, and in difficult relationship to, a wide range of feelings. This was certainly true for Regina Lorek, who situated her analysis of the pornography industry in a complicated mixture of emotions. Commenting in *Kinesis*, she argued that "I have been scared by some of the pornography I have seen, bored by some, amused by some, horrified by some, turned on by some and angered by lots. I have been walking around in a state of rage." But Lorek also emphasized that this "state of rage" was fraught and personal, reaching into the most intimate corners of activist life. After watching these films, she explained,

> [I] went home to my friend and lover, and fought with him harder than I ever had, demanding that he and I prove right now – right here in this bed – that pornography does lie about my sexuality and oh, please, let it be true that pornography also lies about his. But it's not that simple. Sometimes it does, and sometimes it doesn't.[41]

Such explanations highlight how difficult anti-pornography work could be, while also indicating how emotional experiences were useful for acting against pornography. Lorek's state of rage situated a personal conflict with her partner as a political struggle, for example. This anger was a force for action, one that initiated an act of sexual resistance against the power of pornography. The fact that Lorek told this story to the wider feminist community via the press also integrated this personal act into a wider public campaign.

Suzanne Gerard, a member of the Women in Trades Association of BC, similarly mobilized her personal anger to initiate a discussion of pornography in Vancouver in the pages of *Kinesis* in 1982. "The other morning I lost my temper," Gerard told her readers in her opening sentence. On a trip to a drugstore in East Vancouver, she confronted a display of objectionable pornographic magazines. Normally, she explained, she would have ignored them. However, that morning she was "more aware and less accepting" because she had recently attended a screening of Bonnie Sherr Klein's

Conflicting graffiti on the matter of pornography, painted near Fraser Street and Durward Avenue, Vancouver. (*September 19, 1984, Porn Lies! ON MY BED/Location: Northeast Corner, Fraser Street and Dunward Avenue.* Photographer Gordon E. McCaw. SFU Library, Digitized Collections, Gordon E. McCaw Vancouver Street Art Photography Collection.)

National Film Board documentary, *Not a Love Story: A Film about Pornography*. Motivated by her engagement with Klein's anti-pornography film, Gerard broke her silence and engaged in an act of public condemnation. She "yelled," "shouted," and "rant[ed]" at the woman who worked in the store, as well as at a male customer, for their apparent tolerance of the magazines. Waving one of the items at the man, she loudly proclaimed, "Look! There's another future pervert." With this final act of defiance, she walked out of the store.[42]

As with Lorek, Gerard's rage served as the narrative starting point for political action. In the wake of her exit from the retailer, she imagined further actions that she and other women could take in response. "I wanted every woman in hearing distance to volunteer to go back with me and scatter the magazines all over the streets; to plaster a sign saying Payless Drugs Encourages the Sexual Abuse of Women, and to write letters to the owner of the store."[43] Although she stopped short of attacking property, Gerard explained that she continued to visit retailers that sold pornographic magazines in the months following her initial outburst. In these visits, she again mobilized anger to explain and describe her conflicts with retail workers and customers about the presence and significance of pornography, including being kicked out of a London Drugs over a "furious" denunciation of *Penthouse*.[44] In this and other confrontations, she read the magazines aloud and showed the images to customers and staff. In doing so, she highlighted the argument that such material reflected and contributed to violence against women and girls.[45] Where Lorek's confrontations took place in the context of a romantic relationship, Gerard mobilized her fury against the commercial infrastructure of pornography. Yet despite their differences, these two instances of resistance were clearly linked by how anger functioned as an impetus for feminist action. In both cases, affect was a resource, a form of political ammunition that activists could use in the struggle against their opponents. Where feminist pornography reviews used emotional assessments as analysis, Lorek and Gerard's experiences reveal how feminists used emotional experiences as tactics for political resistance.

The Take Back the Night marches organized in Vancouver during the late 1970s and early 1980s were another example where feminist resistance engaged with the struggle against pornography through mobilizing affect. The marches were part of a larger array of political actions in North America and Europe beginning in the 1970s in which women sought to take back or reclaim public space in their communities through marches, demonstrations, and other collective events. As the organizers of the first Take Back the Night event in Vancouver, in 1978, argued, by gathering at midnight and marching through the streets of the city, women would express their "right to be out on the streets at any time without being subjected to harassment, and without having recourse to the 'protection' of men."[46] In this way, Take Back the Night demonstrations expanded the affective scope of feminist politics to include militant joy, rage, and the absence of fear. For the Fly By Night Collective that organized the 1978 march, for instance, part of the purpose of Take Back the Night was to create an event that could resist fear. Positioning that emotion as an immobilizer of women's agency, organizers argued that marching at midnight was a strategy to "celebrate our strength together as women, to exorcise fear from our spirits and take hold of the power we have."[47] Collective action and support enabled the casting aside of fear, which in turn provided room for a blossoming of power and political action. Other activists involved in the 1978 event maintained that the march was also an "exciting" event, where women "felt good" about their political connections with other women. Summing up the important and positive effects of such feelings, one participant in the 1978 march concluded,

"Perhaps there is a time and place for women to be outrageous, and this was it. It may have gladdened some people's hearts."[48]

Although the feminist press did not elaborate on what such "outrageous" activity might have entailed or its possible relationship to anti-pornography work, oral testimony from a participant in the 1978 event provides further detail. For Jill Bend – a long-time Vancouver activist – Take Back the Night marches were opportunities for militant confrontations, solidarity, and direct action. While not every march was like this, the inaugural event in 1978 was. To begin with, organizers did not take out a permit for their march but, rather, assembled in Vancouver's downtown without civic authority. Carrying banners and flaming torches, they proceeded along the main thoroughfare of Granville Street until they reached a strip of "sex shops" that sold, among other things, pornographic magazines. Bend and others entered the stores and plastered the magazines with feminist stickers, some of which read, "Why be a wife?" Others depicted the Queen of Hearts proclaiming, "Off with their heads!," a reference to Lewis Carroll's militant monarch in *Alice's Adventures in Wonderland*. Meant to be funny (to feminists) and irremovable, the stickers were an easy and entertaining way to cause physical damage to patriarchal media. Besides causing a ruckus for retailers and defacing their property with feminist propaganda, women also spray-painted graffiti as they made their way through the city streets. When the police attempted to arrest some of the painters, crowds of women descended on the officers. As Bend recalled, "The other women would not let the cops take them. We fought with the cops, we surrounded them, we held arms, and fought, yelled, and the women got away ... It was wild." For Bend, this confrontation was an important example of "being brave" in the face of state power.[49] Such an assessment meshed seamlessly with Fly By Night Collective's desire to "exorcise fear" from the hearts of women. Encompassing claims to both feminist humour and bravery, Bend's recollections provide another example of how emotions were layered into the work of feminist action in these years. Even though she spoke about these events some three decades after they were over, the durability of emotional claims in her analysis speaks to the significance of feminist affect in understanding its political activity.

When the Red Hot Video stores began opening in Vancouver in early 1982, feminists drew from this longer pattern of affective analysis of, and confrontation with, pornography to campaign against the video chain. Some activists used their assessments of particular films carried by the stores to pressure the police and the Crown to prosecute Red Hot Video.

North Shore Women's Centre activist Jancis Andrews was central in this organizing, relentlessly writing letters to civil officials on the North Shore, to Crown council, and to the Attorney General to oppose the expansion of the franchise. Andrews's main argument was that many of its films were illegal because their sexual violence contravened provincial and federal regulations on pornography. Although that assessment was legally debatable, it was politically powerful because it suggested that the state was not staying true to its own laws. As a result, when the police and Crown dragged their heels, activists escalated their resistance against Red Hot Video.[50]

By the early fall of 1982, a growing number of women's groups began to directly act against Red Hot Video through a campaign of public protest that included marches, rallies, and pickets. In September, Women Against Pornography organized a Take Back the Night march in Victoria that brought approximately one hundred women into the streets to protest pornography and violence against women. Later in the month, WAP activists organized private viewings of the film *Snuff* for politicians and members of the media. When the film was over, they took the videotape into the street and burned it in front of the media's cameras.[51] At the same time, the BC Federation of Women increased its pressure against the pornography industry by creating the Action Committee to Stop Red Hot Video, which organized pickets outside a number of the video store's locations.[52] The following month, a manager at Red Hot Video complained about the growing harassment of the stores by members of the public. In addition to pickets, this resistance included more sticker attacks, stink bombs, and a failed – and unclaimed – arson of one of the company's outlets in Vancouver.[53]

Two months after WAP destroyed pornographic material in the streets of Victoria and the BCFW initiated a coordinated campaign to shut down Red Hot Video, the Wimmin's Fire Brigade struck Red Hot Video with their own acts of sabotage in November 1982. In her autobiography, Hansen claims that there was widespread support within the women's movement for more militant responses to Red Hot Video and that this "harmonized perfectly" with Direct Action's commitment to sabotage. The WFB was created out of this evolving resistance. And here again, activists such as Hansen mobilized affect – particularly anger – as a way of explaining the politics of anti-pornography activism. Much of this anger was directed against the state. As Hansen recalled, "The women whom we did speak to were universally outraged at the government's inactivity."[54] At the same time, she also highlighted that participants in the WFB experienced anger and disgust towards the pornographic industry for the content of its films. Referencing the idea that pornography taught men and boys that it was "acceptable to rape and torture women," a fellow activist in the WFB told Hansen that her own viewing of Red Hot Video films proved to her that attacking the retail outlets was the right thing to do.[55]

With this in mind, the nine women gathered together to plan their attacks against Red Hot Video. This was to be a one-time action, modelled on an urban guerrilla hit-and-run strategy. The women would break into three separate groups, synchronize their attacks, burn the stores down, and then disband.[56] Generally, this strategy worked well for their aims. The attack on the company's North Vancouver location destroyed part of the store, while the arson at the Surrey location incinerated the entire location. However, the WFB was unsuccessful in setting a fire at the Coquitlam outlet, as the device they used failed to ignite a blaze. In addition to this, Hansen was also badly burned in the process of starting one of the fires.[57] The following day, the group released a short statement that claimed responsibility for the attacks. As noted at the beginning of this chapter, the WFB explicitly framed their actions as a form of self-defence against misogynist hate. Tied to this affective critique of patriarchy was the understanding that Red Hot Video was also guilty of economic exploitation. In this way, the arsons were positioned as "another step towards the destruction of a business that promotes and profits from violence against women and children."[58]

While there was no single feminist response to the WFB actions, the women's movement in Vancouver generally responded with sympathy. On the day after the attack, the BCFW issued a statement that read, in part,

> While we did not participate in the fire bombings of November 22 1982 in the Lower Mainland, we are in agreement with the frustration and anger of the women who did. We noted and appreciated their efforts to see that no one was hurt. We insist that [Attorney General] Allan Williams take action immediately to prevent rich men profiting from Red Hot Video's hate literature about women and children. The women of BC are being driven to desperate acts.[59]

Such commentary not only reflected the great extent to which feminist organizations in the province accepted a militant solution to the expansion of pornography but also reiterated the central political utility of emotion within the campaign. In this short statement, the BCFW echoed the emotional assessment of pornography as one rooted in hatred of women, sympathized with the anger they saw within the WFB's actions and analysis, and proposed that such activity was to be understood through the affective language of desperation and appreciation.

Although the WFB attacks on Red Hot Video were proportionally different from other actions taken against the company, they were not incongruous. From Gerard's fantasies of trashing drugstore pornography, to WAP's symbolic acts of sabotage against individual films, to Bend's recollections of stickering and graffiti, and, finally, to the varied strategies of direct action against Red Hot Video in the fall of 1982, the WFB's decision to firebomb three stores in November were part of a long pattern of feminist activism that utilized a diversity of tactics in which emotion, in various forms, was always central. These acts of resistance, in which emotions such as anger, disgust, sympathy, and desperation played an important role, shaped the struggle over pornography in the province. Soon after the arsons, in early 1983, the state finally took action. In early January, the police raided twelve pornography stores across BC, confiscating hundreds of videotapes and charging at least one Red Hot Video store with obscenity.[60] While some stores closed as result of this campaign, neither the punitive power of the state nor the power of community activism ultimately diminished the presence of pornography in Canadian society. Nevertheless, the struggles against pornography in Vancouver and elsewhere were a crucial component of late-twentieth-century feminism.

Conclusion

When the Wimmin's Fire Brigade firebombed three locations of Red Hot Video in November 1982, they framed the arsons as an act of self-defence against the violence of pornography – violence that they positioned as inseparable from the industry's humiliation and hatred of women. They were far from alone in this affective commentary, as the wider history of anti-pornography feminism during the 1970s and 1980s demonstrates. However, there was no single or straightforward use of emotion within this political work. Indeed, what feminist action in both Vancouver and elsewhere revealed were the multiple, overlapping, and diverse affective expressions that were significant in projects targeting pornography in these years. In their emotional assessments of the industry and in their personal claims to emotional experience, activists were not simply angry but, rather, placed that anger within a broader emotional activism that included hate, terror, humiliation, joy, humour, and bravery.

This political affect was complicated in other ways too. As powerful as these assessments and claims to emotional experience were, not everyone in the feminist community agreed about the definition and significance of pornography. Indeed, in the years and decades to follow, feminist communities would often take deeply divergent views on these issues. While the concept of the "Porn Wars" would not come into popular usage until later, the activism of the late 1970s and early 1980s saw instances of these emerging debates.[61] As one example, we might consider the controversy raised by a 1982 classified advertisement in *Kinesis* that read, in part, "Lesbian photographer seeks S/M lesbians to be photographed for positive, healthy images of sex."[62] Writing in response, one reader expressed "disbelief" that the feminist press would run this advertisement. Their objection reflected a broader critique, shared by some feminists, that sado-masochism was inherently violent and oppressive. Following this assumption, the reader maintained that since "men should not be free to circulate pornography which validates sado-masochism," the reader believed it was hypocritical for women to tolerate it in their own communities. This was based on the perception that sado-masochism was "not an expression of love," they explained, but rather "an expression of power imbalance, oppression and societal sickness. We must not condone this even when the participants are women."[63] In this way, the author mobilized a critical component of feminist affective analysis from the wider pornography debate: the acceptability of sexual representations defined not only through expressions of power, but also through claims to emotion, particularly the perceived absence or presence of love. Writing to contest this objection, a different reader suggested that there was nothing inherently wrong with "S/M behavior" and that this ought to be left up to "personal preference and analysis." While they agreed that personal choices were also political choices, they were "concerned that feminist analyses might become so rigid that the radical complexity of individual experience and identity will be lost."[64] Such an astute warning would take on added political significance in the years to come, in the context of escalating debates over the acceptable boundaries of feminist sexuality and the pushback from queer activists over the definition, meaning, and significance of pornography within their own communities. In this sense, when firebombs ripped through Red Hot Video in November 1982, the feminist politics of pornography and their connections to histories of emotion were already significant but at the same time were only just beginning.

Notes

I am very grateful to Lara Campbell, Michael Dawson, and Catherine Gidney for their support and excellent feedback on this chapter and for the dedication they gave to the collection as a whole. Sincere appreciation is also due to the anonymous reviewers for their comments and suggestions. I would like to thank my fellow contributors who provided insightful advice on an early draft. Finally, I am very much indebted to Laura Ishiguro for her wise recommendations for the chapter. Research for this piece was supported by funding from the Social Sciences and Humanities Research Council of Canada.

1 Wimmin's Fire Brigade, "Wimmin's Fire Brigade Communiqué," November 22, 1982, reprinted in Ann Hansen, *Direct Action: Memoirs of an Urban Guerrilla* (Toronto: Between the Lines, 2001), 483.
2 Studies of pornography in Canada are more frequently found outside the discipline of history. See, for example, Dany Lacombe, *Blue Politics: Pornography and the Law in the Age of Feminism* (Toronto: University of Toronto Press, 1994); Kristen Johnson, *Undressing the Canadian State: The Politics of Pornography from* Hicklin *to* Butler (Halifax: Fernwood, 1995); and Brenda Cossman, Shannon Bell, Lisa Gotell, and Becki L. Ross, *Bad Attitude/s on Trial: Pornography, Feminism, and the* Butler *Decision* (Toronto: University of Toronto Press, 1997).
3 For a critical engagement with the metaphor of feminist waves, see Nancy A. Hewitt, ed., *No Permanent Waves: Recasting Histories of U.S. Feminism* (New Brunswick, NJ: Rutgers University Press, 2010).
4 Susanna Paasonen and Laura Saarenmaa, "The Golden Age of Porn: Nostalgia and History in Cinema," in *Pornification: Sex and Sexuality in Media Culture*, ed. Kaarina Nikunen, Susanna Paasonen, and Laura Saarenmaa (Oxford: Berg, 2007): 23–32.
5 Carolyn Bronstein, *Battling Pornography: The American Feminist Anti-Pornography Movement, 1976–1986* (Cambridge, MA: Cambridge University Press, 2011), 26–27.
6 Herbert Marcuse, *Eros and Civilization: A Philosophical Inquiry into Freud* (London: Routledge, 1998); Wilhelm Reich and Therese Pol, *The Sexual Revolution: Toward a Self-Regulating Character Structure* (New York: Farrar, Straus and Giroux, 1986).
7 Marcy Toms, interview with author, February 8, 2012.
8 Judy Bernstein, Peggy Morton, Linda Seese, and Myrna Wood, "Sisters, Brothers, Lovers ... Listen ...," in *Open Boundaries: A Canadian Women's Studies Reader*, ed. Barbara A. Crow (Toronto: Prentice Hall, 2000), 95.
9 Ian McKay, *Rebels, Reds, Radicals: Rethinking Canada's Left History* (Toronto: Between the Lines, 2005), 198–99.
10 Marcy Toms, interview.
11 See Frances Jane Wasserlein, "'An Arrow Aimed at the Heart': The Vancouver Women's Caucus and the Abortion Campaign, 1969–1971" (master's thesis, Simon Fraser University, 1990); Christabelle Sethna and Steve Hewitt, "Clandestine Operations: The Vancouver Women's Caucus, the Abortion Caravan, and the RCMP," *Canadian Historical Review* 90, 3 (2009): 463–95; and Gorden Hak, *The Left in British Columbia: A History of Struggle* (Vancouver: Ronsdale Press, 2013), 134–35.

12 See Julia Smith, "An 'Entirely Different' Kind of Union: The Service, Office, and Retail Workers' Union of Canada (SORWUC), 1972–1986," *Labour/Le Travail* 73, 1 (2014): 23–66.

13 Bronstein, *Battling Pornography*, 66–67; Lacombe, *Blue Politics*, 155–56.

14 Lacombe, *Blue Politics*, 156.

15 The way in which VHS technology circumvented the state's ability to regulate pornography was an important issue in the campaign against Red Hot Video. See Gail Peain, "Video Chain Expands despite Outcry," *Kinesis*, October 1982, 1, 18. For a glimpse into how feminist organizations used VHS in their public education work, see Leslie Dixon, "Awareness through Video," *Kinesis*, September 1975, 6. For anonymously authored pieces on this topic, see "Women in Focus," *Kinesis*, May 1976, 10; and "What's Out There? Audio-Visual," *Kinesis*, August 1976, 12.

16 *Adam Film World's X-Rated Movie Handbook*, University of Victoria (UVIC), Anarchist Archives, AR543, Ann Hansen Papers, box 2, file 2.3.

17 The summary report of the *Special Committee on Pornography and Prostitution* argued in 1985 that significant coordination was required between the RCMP, customs, and the postal service in order to achieve effective regulation of material originating outside of the country. See Canada, *Pornography and Prostitution in Canada: Report of the Special Committee on Pornography and Prostitution: Summary* (Ottawa: Minister of Supply and Services Canada, 1985), 20–24.

18 Bronstein, *Battling Pornography*, 74–75.

19 Lacombe, *Blue Politics*, 26; Bronstein, *Battling Pornography*, 154–55.

20 Bronstein, *Battling Pornography*, 85–87. For an exploration of the ways in which snuff films have influenced feminist thinking and the significance of those interpretations for anti-pornography activism, see Lisa Downing, "Snuff and Nonsense: The Discursive Life of a Phantasmiatic Archive," in *Porn Archives*, ed. Tim Dean, Steven Ruszczychy, and David Squires (Durham, NC: Duke University Press, 2014), 249–61.

21 Andrea Dworkin, "Why So-Called Radical Men Love and Need Pornography," in *Take Back the Night: Women on Pornography*, ed. Laura Lederer (New York: William Morrow, 1980), 153.

22 Dworkin, "Why So-Called Radical Men Love and Need Pornography," 153–54.

23 Beverly LaBelle, "The Propaganda of Misogyny," in Lederer, *Take Back the Night*, 177.

24 The phrase "pornography is the theory, and rape the practice" as used here comes from Robin Morgan's well-known essay, "Theory and Practice: Pornography and Rape," in Lederer, *Take Back the Night*, 139.

25 "Pornography: Developing Our Definition," *Kinesis*, February 1979, 10.

26 "Violence against Women: A National Day of Protest," *Kinesis*, December 1977, 4; "Women against Violence," *Kinesis*, May 1978, 9.

27 Jillian Ridington and Gene Errington, "Women in a Violent Society," *Kinesis*, June 1978, 13.

28 "The Year in Review," *Kinesis*, December/January 1983, 1.

29 See "Porn Forum Toughens Fightback," *Kinesis*, April 1983, 1.

30 For a collection of reviews based on these feminist-activists' private viewings of pornography films, see the materials produced by Women Against Pornography, UVIC, Anarchist Archives, AR543, Ann Hansen Papers, box 2, file 2.1.

31 Women against Pornography, "'Talk Dirty to Me': A Feminist Review," 1, UVIC, Anarchist Archives, AR543, Ann Hansen Papers, box 2, file 2.1.
32 Women Against Pornography, "'Talk Dirty to Me': A Feminist Review," 1.
33 Women Against Pornography, "'Talk Dirty to Me': A Feminist Review," 2.
34 Women Against Pornography, "'Talk Dirty to Me': A Feminist Review," 3.
35 Regina Lorek, "Porn: Who's Hurt? Who Benefits?," *Kinesis*, April 1983, 8.
36 Lorek, "Porn: Who's Hurt? Who Benefits?," 9.
37 Lorek, "Porn: Who's Hurt? Who Benefits?," 9.
38 Lorek, "Porn: Who's Hurt? Who Benefits?," 9.
39 Lorek, "Porn: Who's Hurt? Who Benefits?," 9.
40 For a range of feminist perspectives on the harms of pornography, see the collected essays in section two of Lederer, *Take Back the Night*, 55–118.
41 Lorek, "Porn: Who's Hurt? Who Benefits?," 9.
42 Suzanne Gerard, "Porn Is Winning," *Kinesis*, September 1982, 19.
43 Gerard, "Porn Is Winning," 19.
44 Gerard, "Porn Is Winning," 19.
45 Gerard, "Porn Is Winning," 19.
46 "Taking Back the Night," *Kinesis*, July 1978, 2.
47 "Reclaim the Night Evaluated," *Kinesis*, October 1978, 8.
48 "Reclaim the Night Evaluated," 21.
49 Jill Bend, interview with author, February 28, 2012.
50 North Shore Women's Centre, "Proliferation of Hardcore Pornography," June 1, 1982, p. 1–2, UVIC, Anarchist Archives, AR543, Ann Hansen Papers, box 2, file 2.2.
51 "WAP Schedule – Sept/82 to Mar/83," n.d., p. 1, UVIC, Anarchist Archives, AR543, Ann Hansen Papers, box 2, file 2.1.
52 "Chronology of Struggle against R.H.V.," n.d., p. 2, UVIC, Anarchist Archives, AR543, Ann Hansen Papers, box 2, file 1.25.
53 Ted Emery to Jancis Andrews, October 28, 1982, p. 2, UVIC, Anarchist Archives, AR543, Ann Hansen Papers, box 2, file 2.2.
54 Hansen, *Direct Action*, 329.
55 Hansen, *Direct Action*, 332.
56 Ann Hansen, interview with author, September 8, 2011.
57 Hansen, *Direct Action*, 340–45.
58 Wimmin's Fire Brigade, "Communiqué," in Hansen, *Direct Action*, 487.
59 British Columbia Federation of Women, "News Release," November 22, 1982, UVIC, Anarchist Archives, AR543, Ann Hansen Papers, box 1, file 1.25.
60 "Anti-pornography Organizing Boosted by Police Raids," *Kinesis*, February 1983, 1.
61 Bonnie Sherr Klein's 1981 documentary film *Not a Love Story* and its reception, as well as the 1992 Canadian Supreme Court decision *R v Butler*, were two key events in the escalation of the pornography debate. See Rebecca Sullivan, *Bonnie Sherr Klein's "Not a Love Story"* (Toronto: University of Toronto Press, 2014); and Cossman et al., *Bad Attitude/s on Trial*.
62 "Lesbian Photographer," *Kinesis*, February 1982, 36.
63 "Taking Issue with S/M," *Kinesis*, May 1982, 19.
64 "S & M Illustrates Complexity of Individual Experience," *Kinesis*, June 1982, 19.

9 An Assumption of Shared Fear
Feminism, Sex Work, and the Sex Wars in 1980s *Kinesis*

EMMA MCKENNA

In the 1980s, a routine tactic of anti-pornography feminist activism throughout Canada and the United States involved staging "tours" through sex-worker strolls, where feminists would be "exposed" to "the thriving pornography industry."[1] Reflecting on these tours, Marie Arrington, a founding member of Vancouver's sex-worker activist group, the Alliance for the Safety of Prostitutes, noted that the women employed in the public sex industry found these kinds of feminist tours to be "intimidating or degrading."[2] In 1985, Arrington summarized this view in the Letters section of the feminist magazine, *Kinesis*:

> We don't need saving, we need what all women need, decent and affordable housing, money, jobs, food to cook and a way out of the everlasting circle of poverty ... The meaningful and fundamental change that needs to be made is *money* to survive. An end to our poverty and hopelessness. That will not be accomplished by well-meaning and well fed, white middle class women who only know about our lives by observation and by hanging out in bars, who are able to return to their own homes out of the area.[3]

Forced to endure criticism, moral condemnation, and a patronizing concern about their livelihoods while they were working, sex workers were shamed and humiliated by the feminist appropriation of their workplaces for political agitation.[4]

Feminist anti-pornography tours formed part of feminism's broader attempt to bring awareness to the commercialization of women's bodies.[5] After 1977, pornography became increasingly available through home video distribution, and as films moved into private homes, their content included more violence.[6] As Eryk Martin's chapter in this collection shows, the firebombing of three Red Hot Video locations in Vancouver, BC, in November 1982, marked a turn in emerging feminist debates about sexual representation and pornography. Factions of the feminist movement became preoccupied with unveiling "the sexist values" of pornography and especially its "glamorization of sexual violence against women."[7] Remembered now as the feminist "sex wars," the debates that took place in the 1970s and 1980s about the role of sexuality in determining or enabling women's oppression and liberation preoccupied feminist theory and activism, with particular emphases on violence, sexual identity, and sex work.[8] This chapter examines how the sex wars played out within the pages of the popular feminist periodical *Kinesis* and shows how second-wave feminist analyses of pornography were interconnected with feminist views and attitudes towards prostitution.

Feminist perspectives on commercial sex brought second-wave feminism into collusion with the Canadian state as the feminist movement pressed for legal interventions that would regulate and criminalize pornography, with the ultimate goal of abolishing both pornography and prostitution. Most feminists understood the sex industry as an oppressive institution that stemmed from, and contributed to, actual violence against all women.[9] As a result, rather than attending to the political and economic context of sex work on sex workers' terms, feminists theorized pornography as a hypersexualization of women with harmful material effects, in particular sexual and gender-based violence. This approach not only contributed to the exclusion of sex workers from second-wave feminism, but also lent itself to a growing criminalization of prostitution that increased harm and violence against sex workers.

By attempting to draw women into a wider feminist emotional community where all women were seen as victims of the violence caused by the objectification and commodification of women's bodies, anti-pornography feminism developed a discourse of fear and anger that silenced the actual women working within the pornography industry. At the same time, a small but diverse movement of indoor and outdoor sex workers, sex-worker activists, and allies was emerging in Canada.[10] Often opposed to the kind of feminist intervention suggested in *Kinesis*, and directly affected by the increasing criminalization of the state, this movement asserted that sexual labour in exchange for money was legitimate work, challenged the dehumanization of sex workers, and demanded the decriminalization of sexual labour.[11] Insisting on the significance of sex workers' analyses to the development of feminist theory on the sex wars, this chapter points to the way in which sex workers laboured to broaden and intervene in these discourses as feminist scholars and activists in their own right.[12]

Second-Wave Feminist Writing

Drawing on Barbara Godard and Tessa Jordan's research on second-wave feminist periodicals in Canada, the feminist periodical is a site of discursive cultural production that promotes a shared feminist vision of how to transform women's oppression.[13] I suggest that the periodical actively shapes and influences how feminists should respond to debates about the sex wars in their own communities, often strategically prioritizing some women's issues over others. Publications about the sex wars in *Kinesis* reflected a movement in process, meted out in theoretical writing and mobilized through direct action and state lobbying. Produced in Vancouver, British Columbia, between 1974 and 2001, *Kinesis: News about Women That's Not in the Dailies* was published by the grassroots feminist organization Vancouver Status of Women (VSW) and was both local and national in its journalistic scope. *Kinesis*'s content included news articles; position papers; music, film, and book reviews; a community bulletin; a Letters section; and, after 1985, advertisements. Beginning in 1978, and throughout the 1980s, its coverage of pornography and prostitution was mainly found in news items, position papers written by *Kinesis* employees or volunteers, and letters contributed by readers.

Kinesis's writers and readers were part of a broader women's liberation movement that had been under way across North America since the late 1960s.[14] As Benita Roth has demonstrated of the American context, the second-wave women's movement developed through diverse women's political communities that shared a commitment to gender equality but held varying opinions on the primacy of gender oppression as a theoretical framework.[15] The privileging of gender above race, class, or sexual oppression also characterized the more mainstream segments of the second-wave movement in Canada, reflecting the dominance of white, middle-class, heterosexual women.[16] For example, Vijay Agnew argues that the white women's movement reinforced systemic forms of racism against women of colour via "exclusionary practices of the 1970s," the "marginalization of the 1980s," and enduring "difficulties in forming alliances and solidarities" into the 1990s.[17] Adherence to a shared goal of women's liberation encouraged varying sectors of the women's movement to organize across race, class, and sexual differences, with varying benefits for marginalized women.[18]

The emergence of a largely white, heterosexual, middle-class, anti–violence-against-women framework gained momentum in Canada in the 1970s and was foundational to feminist theorizing on pornography and prostitution.[19] This anti-violence framework, particularly as it was developed within *Kinesis*, drew on broader theoretical trends regarding the issue of violence against women in the 1970s.[20] High-profile, white American feminist authors such as Susan Brownmiller, Andrea Dworkin, and Susan Griffin were also working to link violence and sexuality with prostitution and pornography.[21] In Canada, white women with class status were also at the helm of the debate, with the 1977 publication of *Rape: The Price of Coercive Sexuality* positioning authors Lorenne M.G. Clark and Debra J. Lewis as experts on the relationship of violence to pornography;[22] in turn, Lewis was a regular contributor to the anti-pornography discourse in *Kinesis*.

Historian Nancy Janovicek demonstrates that this feminist anti-violence theorizing was a critical force in moving discussion away from the "gender-neutral analysis of family violence" and drawing attention to how patriarchal violence sustained male dominance.[23] In building transition houses and services for women fleeing violence, for example, the movement challenged the common-sense belief that the home and the family were safe places for women and children. However, Janovicek cautions that reluctance to examine structural issues of racism and poverty as endemic to gendered and sexual violence contributed to the movement's "exclusivity" as it "promoted solutions that centre the experience of white, heterosexual women."[24] It is this white, heterosexual framework of anti-violence that underscored most feminist discourses on pornography and prostitution in Canada and which stymied analyses of race, class, and sexuality in the sex work industry both within the pages of *Kinesis* and beyond.

Defining Pornography and Prostitution as Violence

The foundation for what would become *Kinesis*'s preoccupation with the sex wars was laid during the 1970s.[25] On February 7, 1978, the Supreme Court ruled 9–0 that the Criminal Code be amended to criminalize solicitation if it could be found to be "pressing and persistent."[26] The court's decision in *R v Hutt* brought the question of street prostitution into public discourse as "residents groups, politicians, and police" sought to assert control over street prostitution.[27] A month later, in March of 1978, the Parliamentary

Committee on Justice and Legal Affairs held public forums to discuss Criminal Code amendments to pornography. From 1978 onwards, VSW members and *Kinesis* contributors were roused by the possibility of increased criminal sanctions against pornography and prostitution, with distinct – and varying – feminist positions crystallizing in response to both. On September 26, 1978, Lewis – who was also a VSW member – wrote and delivered to Parliament a brief on Pornography and Prostitution that would set the tone of the debate in *Kinesis*.[28] This brief was the touchstone of two subsequent articles on pornography and prostitution published in the magazine.

In 1978, Lewis published two *Kinesis* position papers on pornography and prostitution that would typify feminist analyses in the coming decade.[29] Lewis framed pornography and prostitution as distinct but connected phenomena in the oppression of women. Lewis theorized pornography as harmful not only in its unrealistic representation of women, sexualization of violence, and promotion of rape as a form of male fantasy, but also for its potential to cause real violence against women. Lewis described pornography as "a threat" to all women's sexualities, relationships, and bodily integrity, which "made acceptable the use of coercion and violence towards women and children in the name of individual male rights."[30] She theorized prostitution as an effect of sexual, economic, and social oppression of women and an alternative to a lack of economic opportunities for women.[31] Lewis advocated for closer relationships between feminism and the state, and while she was "opposed to any changes in the criminal code which would put an increased responsibility on prostitutes," she argued that both pornography and prostitution should be abolished by criminalizing male producers, proprietors, and consumers.[32]

Lewis's work on behalf of VSW and *Kinesis* helped to lay the groundwork for feminist perspectives on pornography and prostitution and to shape not just feminist discourse but also the state's approach to legislating against prostitution and pornography. In 1985, the newly elected federal Progressive Conservatives introduced Bill C-49, which ushered in a draconian anti-soliciting law that criminalized all forms of "communication" about soliciting.[33] Soon after, the federal government tabled two bills, in 1986 and 1987, both of which attempted to expand the definition of pornography and increase the prohibitions against it.[34] Bill C-54 (1987) incorporated a feminist perspective of obscene materials as "dehumanizing and degrading" to women.[35] As the public battle over pornography made its way into the courts, the landmark *R v Butler* Supreme Court ruling, in 1992, solidified the determination of obscenity as harmful to women and the place of feminist ideology as a carceral force.[36]

Both pornography and prostitution became significant focal points of feminist analysis in *Kinesis* in the 1980s, reflecting a commitment made by members of VSW to "prioritize" debates on these issues.[37] The vast majority of position papers on pornography and prostitution advocated for abolition, were penned by white women engaged in the anti-violence movement, and were detached from the perspectives of those working within the sex industry. The two topics were understood as interconnected, but they were not treated exactly the same. Analyses of pornography nearly doubled those of prostitution: approximately fifty-five news articles versus twenty-four, and seventeen position papers versus eight. This particular interest in pornography was likely due in part to its increasing commercial visibility. However, another reason was the racial, class, and sexual differences that separated feminists and "heterogeneous" street-level sex workers.[38] As VSW echoed in their 1984 brief to the Fraser Committee on Prostitution, a disproportionate number of women working outdoors were poor and women of colour.[39] In contrast, commercial pornography existed – at least partially – as an imaginary, where ideals of white femininity prevailed.[40] The white, middle-class, and heterosexual majority of the women's movement saw themselves as imagined victims of pornography but didn't see themselves as sex workers.[41] Bolstered by assumptions of race, class, and sexuality, this refusal of identification was the linchpin on which feminist anti-pornography activism in Canada colluded with the state in the increased criminalization of prostitution.[42] In a sense, because feminists were distracted by the spectacle of pornography as both an object and an idea, the possibility of its potential criminal regulation helped usher in anti-prostitution legislation that harmed marginalized women. The prohibitionist perspective enabled certain feminists to imagine themselves as the victims of pornography, as only feminist activists who wished to eradicate the sex industry were recognized as knowing subjects capable of reason, theory, and action.

Anti-pornography writing in *Kinesis* attempted to draw women together through a shared identification as the "victims" of sexist and violent pornography.[43] Grounded in first-person experience, feminist writers in *Kinesis* used an accessible and emotional language that invited readers to feel the fear and anger of being objectified as women, together.[44] This emotional strategy relied on writers and readers, as assumed outsiders to the sex industry, to share not only ideological beliefs about commercial sex, but also norms about gender, race, class, and sexuality. One rhetorical strategy by which feminists warned readers of the dangers of pornography was through describing women as "objects" who are "for sale" as "commodities" within a representational frame where "men are the surveyors" and "women are the surveyed."[45] Notably, the first position paper on pornography in the 1980s appeared under the heading of "Violence against Women," as members of Women Against Violence Against Women argued that a rise in violent pornography was a kind of backlash to the women's movement.[46] Feminists extended the analysis of women as objects into a critique of the pornography industry as both profiting off women and promoting violence against women through the economic "possession of the woman."[47] This perspective equated all forms of media objectification and sexist advertising as pornography that fostered violence against women. As Jan Barnsley and Megan Ellis, members of the Working Group on Sexual Violence, declared in 1983, "What is being sold is power; for a mere $29.95, one acquires control of the product and the masculine potency to gain possession of the woman. Possession of the women is acquired by the sexual taking of her. So the ad promises gratification on two levels, economic and sexual."[48]

Writers in *Kinesis* transformed a collective disgust and disbelief that through prostitution a woman could be "bought" and "sold" into their anger towards pornography. In equating prostitution and pornography as tools for patriarchal violence and domination, feminists nurtured their visceral feelings of pain and frustration into diverse action-strategies to eradicate pornography.[49] Indeed, in a 1985 article, Vancouver Rape Relief workers Lee Lakeman and Joni Miller argued that "porn is also a way to make violence against women turn a profit."[50] "Pornography," they argued, "is a great improvement on the age old scam of pimping, because a man can now vastly increase the potential for profits by selling one woman's body many more times to a much bigger market. He pays her only once, if at all."[51] In their indictment of local business owner Jim Pattison, Lakeman and Miller invoked the spectre of sexual violence to mobilize feminists as potential victims into a collective force opposing pornography, asking, "Who is this man? And why is he trying to *rape us*?"[52] While exposing the local entrepreneur as a man with strong economic investments in both pro-pornography and anti-prostitution legislation, their writing relied on emotional appeal to convey their urgency and meaning. A follow-up article by Lakeman and Miller took the coercion argument further with its claim that prostitutes are "*forced* to star in hard-core films or pose for publications."[53] Prostitution and pornography were thus presented as interlocking systems of violent sexual exploitation of women, where men – and critically, not women workers – profited from women's sexual commodification.

Lakeman and Miller's papers reflected the tone of a collectively authored position paper, in 1983, "Prostitution: An End to the Invisibility," which suggested that prostitution exposes "the foundations of sexual power and barter in our society."[54] The *Kinesis* writers asserted that prostitution "affects all of us," as every woman is confronted by the combined effects of "economic oppression" and the "exploitation of sexuality for [male] profit." Acknowledging that because "all of us" are victims of sexual inequality feminists should "support" prostitutes, the authors still insisted that prostitution and pornography were interconnected systems of oppression, remarking, "Pimps and Johns are to prostitution what pornographers are to pornography."[55] What can at first be read as a level of solidarity with prostitutes quickly bleeds into an argument for abolition, equating "pimps and johns" with "pornographers," all of whom were defined as men who "exploit" women "for profit."[56] Notably, the authors once again elide women working in pornography. Instead, the economic realities – and differences – of prostitution and pornography became caught up in an abstracted discourse of harm, where all men are in control not only of the bodies of women who work in the sex industry, but also of *all* women's bodies.[57] This jump from solidarity with an imagined victim of prostitution to "all of us" reified a problematic vision of who the "rightful feminist of the nation" was by ignoring differences in race, class, and sexuality for both men and women.[58]

An additional feminist rhetorical strategy involved imagining all women as victims of misogyny by theorizing pornography as "the ideological arm of violence against women."[59] This perspective sympathized with women for using their bodies and sexualities "as a form of bargaining power" by expanding pornography to include all (hetero) sexual relations that are "potentially coercive" including "virginity, monogamy, and marriage."[60] Influenced by her community work at the Vancouver Battered Women's Services, Lewis linked pornography to everyday sexual and gender-based violence. The view that pornography *causes* sexual violence was regularly articulated by feminist opponents of pornography who sought its abolition, as also demonstrated in a 1983 position paper by Regina Lorek, a volunteer at Vancouver Rape Relief and an activist in the movement against BC's Red Hot Video chain.[61] In disclosing her experience of being coerced into taking nude photos when she was sixteen years old and looking for a modelling job, Lorek observed that

> most of the violence done to women is not done in the making of pictures or movies. It is done by men who rape women, men who pressure women into sexual acts as a result of pornography, and men who less and less frequently see rape as aberrant anti-social behavior. I'm sure some men are encouraged to rape by watching or using pornography.[62]

Like the American feminist anti-pornography perspective, Canadian feminist analyses theorized pornography as *evidence of* sexual and gender-based violence and as *responsible for* increasing forms of sexual and gender-based violence.[63]

In emphasizing a causal link between sexual violence and pornography, the hegemonic feminist position sought to emphasize violence against women as the central issue at stake in the regulation of pornography. In yoking together all *women* who were potential *victims* of the violence of pornography, this feminist perspective on pornography exploited the emotion of fear. The emphasis on the threat of violence was an effective, if questionable, way to inspire action at the presumed subordination of women as objects and victims of pornography. In so doing, women's very real fear of sexual and gender-based violence helped feminists organize collectively around the shared affects of fear and anger in relation to pornography.

But who is entitled to feel fear? And what does this fear entail? Sara Ahmed has argued that "fear is overdetermined," particularly in how fear is experienced differently by different subjects.[64] Racism, Ahmed explains, is one way in which fear of the "other" is created and reinforced by privileging the bodily integrity and emotional safety of subjects already privileged within fraught affective encounters. In effect, this relegates subjects who are entitled to experience fear as white people, versus those who are objects of fear as people of colour. Ahmed notes that feminist discourses have tended to interpret fear less as "an immediate body response to an objective danger," and more as a "response to the *threat* of violence," which validates some narratives of violence over others.[65]

Building on Ahmed, I argue that the feminist fear of sexual violence was not solely what spurred anti-pornography activism; rather, as Amber Cooke, a sex worker and sex-worker activist attested, some feminists were also afraid of the *women* working in the sex industry.[66] Again, in connecting anti-pornography feminism to an imagined or real exposure to street-level prostitution, it is clear how feminists were faced with the viability of a diverse workforce composed of many racially, economically, and sexually marginalized women.[67] The presumption of shared fear of commercial sex solidified a collective "we" of feminists who were joined not only in their opposition to pornography, but also by their investment in gendered race, class, sexual, and labour norms. This marked the women located within the images, representations, and workplaces of the sex industry as outside of a feminist collective, a community to which women could only really belong if they understood sex work as inherently violent and took action to abolish it.

The dedication of the foundational American collection *Take Back the Night: Women on Pornography* succinctly captured this ideology, reading: "To the thousands of women in this country and abroad who recognize the hatefulness and harmfulness of pornography, and who are organizing to stop it now."[68] Not only were these feelings supposed to be shared between women encountering pornography – the recognition that pornography produces both hate and harm against women – but it was also through this shared recognition that a specific feminist "emotional community," warranting particular feminist actions, was formed.[69]

Marginalizing Sex Workers

Equating sex work with violence against all women and advocating for the prohibition of commercial sex as a feminist priority contributed to the marginalization of, and feelings of, profound exclusion among sex workers. This feminist perspective on sexuality, violence, and labour elevated noncommercial sexual exchanges and relegated prostitution as always already inferior to other noncommoditized sexual acts. As Ross and Sullivan point out, feminists were sex workers' "logical allies," but their "ambivalence toward, if not outright opposition to, the exchange of sexual services for money" hindered their support.[70] From this vantage point, pornography comes to be seen as an exploitative industry targeting all women, with women working in both industries held complicit with reproducing the sexual oppression of all women. As one *Kinesis* reader declared in 1988, it is "the phenomena themselves, not the women who work in them" that "bring in their wake countless harmful effects on the images and self-images of girls and women and the way we are treated in our everyday lives."[71] Yet pornography and prostitution can only be seen as abominable *without blaming women* by ignoring those same women's labour and experiences. It is no accident that prostitutes were figured as "the most blatantly exploited victims of sexism" while women working in pornography were rarely – if ever – mentioned at all.[72] While prostitutes were produced as victims within feminist discourses, women working as prostitutes nonetheless resisted this ascription of victimhood and insisted on their own agency in their labour, activism, and writing. Women working in pornography, however, were virtually silent in the pages of *Kinesis,* their experiences and subjectivities assumed – and subsumed – by feminists.[73]

Without acknowledging the economic inequality that women experience in various kinds of employment, prohibitionist feminists ignored the reality that sex workers exhibit agency and pursue financial gain by working in their respective industries. By equating pimps with pornographers and charging both as responsible for women's exploitation, the material conditions of poverty, racism, classism, homophobia, transphobia, etcetera, are obscured. Moreover, the woman's body that is sold in pornography becomes a metonym for all women, everywhere, subject to omnipresent pornographers, which both universalizes and invisibilizes a woman's particular subjectivity and her sexual labour. Taken out of the context of a commercial exchange of services for capital, sex workers' labour ceases to matter on its own terms.

While the cause-effect theory of sexual violence became a touchstone of anti-pornography feminist analysis, this sentiment remains its most debatable conviction, because it assumes that representation is equivalent to actual material harm.[74] Indeed, anti-pornography feminist theory was not solely preoccupied with opposing sexual images of violence against women per se.[75] Rather, pornography became an overarching concept employed to define *all* forms of commodified public sexuality as violence. Hence, this emergent second-wave feminist politic was not only harnessed to a fear of actual material violence, but also to an anxiety about the sexualization of women in the public sphere taking place in an exchange for money. This latter anxiety demonstrates a discomfort with, and opposition to, forms of women's labour that resist sexual, class, and racial ideals of white, middle-class, heterosexual womanhood. A discomfort with the labour aspect of sex work is reflected in the reluctance of anti-pornography feminists to address pornography as an industry, an inattention that persists.[76] Indeed, there is a disconcerting lack of attention to the actual women working in the sex industry given the feminist preoccupation with their workplaces and the products of their labour, as the industry tours mentioned in the introduction illuminate.

As feminist analyses of violence, sexuality, prostitution, and pornography converged, the connection between commercial sex and violence was forged in ways that increasingly alienated sex workers from mainstream feminist communities. As a catch-all for male domination and patriarchy, pornography was a readily available object of feminist resistance; as a result, the structural and material conditions of violence against women – particularly classism, racism, homophobia, and transphobia – were subordinated to this critique. This focus on pornography as the object of patriarchal violence par excellence had the effect of short-circuiting critiques of capitalism and the analysis of sex work as work. Oversaturated with the sensational linkage between violence and sexuality, early second-wave anti-pornography critiques downplayed analyses of political economy, in particular an analysis of the pornography industry alongside other media industries in the increasingly neoliberal market economy.[77] As a result, women's experiences of labour within the sex industry, and their own assessments of the conditions of their labour, were obscured.[78]

While coverage of pornography and, to a lesser extent, prostitution were significant themes in *Kinesis,* sex workers and sex-worker activists were generally not provided with the discursive space to write about their experiences as *legitimate feminist subjects* within the periodical. In turn, news and position papers on pornography did not include the voices of women employed in the pornography industry, while coverage on prostitution sought to include interviews with women working in prostitution, as well as with sex-worker activists. Thus, the voices of sex workers and sex-worker activists were most discernible in the quotations of news articles focused on prostitution, and also as contributors to the Letters section at the back of the paper. The limited space for sex workers' perspectives in the periodical reflect *Kinesis*'s and VSW's stance on prostitution and pornography: while feminists ultimately sought the long-term abolition of both, they made some efforts to push back against the state surveillance of prostitutes in the short-term.[79] As prostitutes were the targets of state surveillance, they were engaged in a daily struggle to work in a hostile and criminalized environment. Sex-worker activists articulated this into a political problem of a right to live and work free from violence. Evidence of VSW's sporadic efforts to support prostitute rights speaks to the important efforts sex-worker activists undertook to engage feminists in their struggle, despite the dominant feminist position on prostitution's overall harms.[80]

At the same time, these efforts by sex workers, and the more limited support of their feminist allies, were overshadowed by local feminist activism directed against pornography. Both prostitution and pornography were situated within feminist, media, and state discourses of sex and morality, rather than the discourses of economics and materiality. The lack of a labour analysis from feminists was reflected in the outright neglect of women working in pornography, figuring pornography as a representational politic that demanded specific legal intervention as opposed to a site of women's labour.[81] The refusal to recognize pornography as a labour industry can be characterized as an "exceptionalist approach" that positions pornography as "qualitatively different from other forms of culture."[82] Efforts to eradicate pornographic video stores from Vancouver neighbourhoods, for example, fed into the state's logic of moral hygiene, where the affective tone of feminist rhetoric was recycled by the media into catchy bylines that distilled the feminist concerns over violence against women into concerns about sexual morality.[83] In positioning themselves as guardians of sexual values seeking state intervention, feminist activism against the violence of pornography easily doubled as action against sexual repugnancy.[84] As a result, the emotional energy of feminist attempts to abolish pornography was channelled into the moralistic fervour of the state to sanitize society, which simultaneously enhanced feminism's legitimacy as a valid political perspective.[85]

Despite feminists' awareness of the dangers employed in state tactics to "clean up the streets," feminist anti-pornography activism undermined feminist solidarity with prostitutes.[86] In privileging their own experiences of fear and anger over the lived experiences of sex workers, feminists asserted their emotional, philosophical, and civil authority on pornography and prostitution.[87] This tension is apparent in the way in which sex workers' were represented in *Kinesis*: at once present and peripheral, vocal and stifled, and visible and marginalized, it would be too generous to suggest that sex workers were given fair representation but too reductive to suggest that they were completely silenced. Rather, their presence in *Kinesis* nuances Ross and Sullivan's sense that most feminists "steered clear of a concerted commitment to prostitutes' rights, and to a broad campaign of sexual liberation."[88] As *Kinesis* writers increasingly covered news relating to violence against prostitutes in the mid-1980s, interviews with sex workers frequently informed the scope and tone of the article.[89] However, feminists maintained control of the discourse as the writers and editors of news items and opinion pieces, positioning prostitution and pornography as abstract "political" issues.[90] And yet, by incorporating sex-worker activist perspectives into their coverage of prostitution issues, a counter-discourse emerged in *Kinesis* where sex workers vocalized resistance to the violence that affected them; paradoxically, these inclusions maintained violence against women as a feminist priority.

Occasionally, *Kinesis* also published sex-worker perspectives that were critical of feminism, though these interventions were generally relegated to the back pages of the periodical in the Letters section. One letter, in

Members of Women Against Pornography (Victoria branch) performing street theatre in front of a Red Hot Video Outlet in Vancouver. (University of Ottawa Archives and Special Collections, Canadian Women's Movement Archives Collection (10-001), references 10-001-S3-I402 and 10-001-S3-I403, photographer unknown.)

particular, captures the emotional impact of this double-edged sword, the hypervisibility and invisibility of women working as prostitutes within the Vancouver women's movement, in addition to highlighting the peripheral status of sex-worker writing in *Kinesis*. In 1988, the sex-worker activist group P.O.W.E.R. (Prostitutes and Other Women for Equal Rights) responded with a feeling of "absolute rage" to the "racism, whorephobia, and whatever else?" of a *Kinesis* op-ed.[91] The column, penned by staff writer Nora Randell, had included disparaging remarks about the clothing and sexualities of sex workers and their allies at a sex worker–led demonstration organized to protest the violent murder of a local woman working as a prostitute.[92] P.O.W.E.R.'s collective voice in the Letters section articulated the affective pain of being stereotyped, caricatured, and depoliticized by a feminist writer in an act of "horizontal hostility" that reflects discursive violence and a lost opportunity for political solidarity.[93] The women from P.O.W.E.R. lamented, "It has been with hard work and great difficulty that we attempt to form alliances or ask for support from the women's movement, as we get trashed while spilling our guts."[94] The affective tone of P.O.W.E.R.'s letter documents the exclusion of sex workers in *Kinesis* and in the broader women's movement at large, and their struggle for legitimacy as feminist subjects.

Indeed, writing by sex workers and sex-worker activists complicated the feminist approach to commercial sex in *Kinesis* by providing moments of intervention that insisted on the political framework that "prostitution is a job" embedded within structural and social contexts.[95] At the same time, the jarring lack of representation in *Kinesis* of women working in pornography was a glaring absence that sustained pornography as an abstracted object of shared fear and anger. Without pornography workers to force feminists to clarify, nuance, or reconsider their perspectives on pornography as an industry, pornography was tethered to a theoretical conceptualization of violence affecting *all women* and not grounded as a site of *particular women's* labour. Pornography remained the domain of objectified women in the second-wave feminist imaginary; in the freeze-frame of audio-visual representation, women working in pornography were symbols of sexual oppression. These silenced subjects became the commodities of a hegemonic feminist theory that defined itself in the uneven distancing of some women as objects, some women as victims, and some women as agents in their own liberation.

In 1988, dryly aware of how the sex industry had become a preoccupation in popular, state, and feminist discourses, sex worker and activist Kairn Mladenovic accurately predicted that prostitution "will continue to be a 'hot' feminist issue and debate for a few years to come."[96] In the sole position paper authored by a sex worker in *Kinesis*, she argued:

> Unfortunately, feminists have had more of a say about our lives than we have had. Often the theories have been based on assumption, with no direction from or accountability to women working in the sex trades. Far too often this leaves us in separate corners, fighting each other, while men are literally getting away with murder. It is crucial that we build on our commonalities. It is also crucial that our differences are not ignored and explained away by the common myth that we are ignorant women playing into men's sexism. Poverty and racism are the realities for women working the streets.[97]

Mladenovic acknowledged violence against women was an important issue but insisted that the violence experienced by sex workers was distinctive; in particular, prostitutes' status as marginalized and criminalized subjects led to their systematic targeting by the state and the police.[98] She explained, for instance, that since the 1986 passage of Bill C-49, twenty-one women working as prostitutes in British Columbia had been murdered, and reported incidents of rape with weapons had drastically increased.[99] At the same time, Mladenovic emphasized the economic context facing poor women and women of colour as significant factors in their daily lives, regardless of their employment in the sex industry.

Mladenovic then shifted her focus to list the structural changes that all poor women required: "decent, affordable housing; affordable universal daycare; job training programs, with good paying jobs afterwards; welfare rates increased above the poverty line; decriminalize prostitution; end violence against all women" and finally, the abolition of "racism and class oppression."[100] Sex-worker feminist theorizing demonstrated an economic analysis of sex work that accounted for intersecting forms of oppression and located prostitution as a specific form of labour targeted by the state, the police, and feminists.[101] Critically, Mladenovic emphasized that the "differences" between women could not be absorbed into shared "commonalities," noting that forms of violence against women were both general and specific.[102] In drawing attention to the economic context wherein poor women labour in varying conditions of state-sanctioned violence, the author echoed the voices of other sex-worker activists who intervened in (and continued to resist) the second-wave feminist perspective that subordinated economic critiques of women's subordination to that of male violence.

Conclusion

At once a history of fiery feminist activism and new forms of collectivity, feminist organizing against prostitution and pornography is also a history of sexual normativity and morality, racial privilege, and economic inequality. A close reading of *Kinesis* offers a window into the shaping of a public feminist discourse on pornography and prostitution in 1980s Canada. Most coverage of the feminist sex wars in *Kinesis* rested on a shared view of pornography as feminism's decried object. Anti-pornography feminist analyses perpetuated a view of pornography as "exceptional" rather than as a new media industry subject to the norms and conditions of "other work under capitalism."[103] Feminist perspectives on prostitution overwhelmingly positioned prostitutes as victims of patriarchy, poverty, and racism, struggling to recognize sex workers' agency and resistance to these conditions. In sustaining sexual and gender inequality as the primary oppressors of all women and dismissing the assertions of their complex realities by sex workers, hegemonic feminist perspectives on pornography and prostitution universalized violence against women without specifying how women were unevenly targeted by structural and individual forms of assault. The exhaustive efforts of some feminists to eradicate pornography sidestepped economic analyses of women's participation in pornography and marginalized the women labouring in the sex industry in favour of emotional analyses informed by fear and anger.

This necessarily partial history of the Canadian feminist sex wars also attests to the ways in which feminist discourses are easily incorporated into state mechanisms of control.[104] Relying on state regulatory structures to transform gendered sexual relations for some women reinforced the domination of others. These events affirm that second-wave feminism did not imagine its subjects as equally deserving of freedom. Instead, the pages of *Kinesis* reveal discrete emotional communities in which some feminist subjects were included because of their shared fear and anger at pornography, while others were excluded, left to create their own communities of support. At the same time, this chapter has shown how sex workers were also crucial contributors to this discourse, developing a counter-discourse of resistance that asserted their place as knowing feminist subjects.

The hegemonic feminist goal to abolish both prostitution and pornography neglected sex worker–led strategies of economic and resource redistribution that might have improved the material conditions of sex workers' experiences and bodily safety. The refusal to privilege the desire for economic justice and bodily integrity of women working in the sex industry over feminist ideals of womanhood has had fatal effects that reverberate into the present. Refusing to make sex workers' lives *a feminist priority* contributed to a vexed relationship between sex workers and feminists that continues to limit which subjects feel "at home" within feminism.[105] Reflecting on the second-wave Canadian feminist sex wars is a reminder of the ongoing struggles for sex workers' self-determination and the uneven efforts of feminists to create – and sustain – relations of solidarity with marginalized women and workers.

Notes

This chapter draws on research supported by the Social Sciences and Humanities Research Council.

I acknowledge and appreciate the generosity of Becki L. Ross in enabling me to cite my research files created during my research assistantship in 2010.

1 Laura Lederer, ed., *Take Back the Night: Women on Pornography* (New York: William Morrow, 1980), 15.

2 Marie Arrington, "Community Organizing," in *Good Girls/Bad Girls: Sex Trade Workers and Feminists Face to Face*, ed. Laurie Bell (Toronto: The Women's Press, 1987), 106.

3 Marie Arrington, "Ask the Street Women What *They* Need," *Kinesis*, September 1985, 36 (emphasis in original).

4 Priscilla Alexander, "Interview with Nell," in *Sex Work: Writings by Women in the Sex Industry*, ed. Frederique Delacoste and Priscilla Alexander (San Francisco: Cleis Press, 1987), 54.

5 Carol Leigh, a.k.a. Scarlot Harlot, "Inventing Sex Work," in *Whores and Other Feminists*, ed. Jill Nagle (New York: Routledge, 1998), 226–27.

6 The creation and subsequent ease of distribution of the VHS transformed the pornography industry. Georgina Voss, *Stigma and the Shaping of the Pornography Industry* (New York: Routledge, 2015), 29; Jennifer C. Nash, *The Black Body in Ecstasy: Reading Race, Reading Pornography* (Durham, NC: Duke University Press, 2014), 62.

7 Rebecca Sullivan, *Bonnie Sherr Klein's* Not a Love Story (Toronto: University of Toronto Press, 2014), 5.

8 Suzanna Danuta Walters, "Introduction: The Dangers of a Metaphor – Beyond the Battlefield in the Sex Wars," *Signs: Journal of Women in Culture and Society* 42, 1 (2016): 2

9 Dany Lacombe, *Blue Politics: Pornography and the Law in the Age of Feminism* (Toronto: University of Toronto Press, 1994), 17.

10 Emily van der Meulen, Elya M. Durisin, and Victoria Love, *Selling Sex: Experience, Advocacy, and Research on Sex Work in Canada* (Vancouver: UBC Press, 2013), 8.

11 Elya M. Durisin, Emily van der Meulen, and Chris Bruckert, "Contextualizing Sex Work: Challenging Discourses and Confronting Narratives," in *Red Light Labour:*

Sex Work, Regulation, Agency, and Resistance, ed. Elya M. Durisin, Emily van der Meulen, and Chris Bruckert (Vancouver: UBC Press, 2018), 3–24. In particular, the authors highlight the "the sex-work-is-work paradigm" as defined by international sex-worker movements (10–14).

12 Sex workers examined the politics of gender and sexuality on their own terms. Frederique Delacoste and Priscilla Alexander, eds., *Sex Work: Writings by Women in the Sex Industry* (San Francisco: Cleis Press, 1987); Margo St. James, "The Reclamation of Whores," in Bell, *Good Girls/Bad Girls*, 84. "The division between women is essentially that of good girl/bad girl. It worries me then to hear non-prostitute women use the word feminist to refer to themselves and not to me. I've always thought that whores were the only emancipated women" (St. James, 84).

13 The feminist periodical was a vehicle for feminist politicization. Barbara Godard, "Feminist Periodicals and the Production of Cultural Value: The Canadian Context," *Women's Studies International Forum* 25, 2 (2002): 209; Tessa Jordan, "Branching Out: Second-Wave Feminist Periodicals and the Archive of Canadian Women's Writing," *ESC: English Studies in Canada* 36, 2–3 (2011): 73.

14 The second-wave women's movement has been well documented in the United States, with a growing field of scholarship in Canada. Alice Echols, *Daring to be Bad: Radical Feminism in America, 1967–1975* (Minneapolis: University of Minnesota Press, 1989); Judy Rebick, *Ten Thousand Roses: The Making of a Feminist Revolution* (Toronto: Penguin Canada, 1995).

15 Benita Roth, *Separate Roads to Feminism: Black, Chicana, and White Feminist Movements in America's Second Wave* (Cambridge: Cambridge University Press, 1994).

16 Alissa McDonald, "Kinesis Survey Results Now In," *Kinesis*, October 1988, 3. As a 1988 membership survey of *Kinesis* subscribers reported, the majority of *Kinesis* readers were white, middle-class women in their late thirties. A qualitative study by Benita Bunjun further demonstrates the demographics of the collective at this time. Benita Bunjun, "Organizational Colonial Encounters: A Critical Intersectional Analysis of Entitlement and Nation Building," *The International Journal of Organizational Diversity* 13 (2014): 5. Prior to an affirmative action policy at Vancouver Status of Women (VSW), in 1992, white, middle-class women also composed the majority of paid positions at *Kinesis* and VSW in the 1980s.

17 Vijay Agnew, "Canadian Feminism and Women of Color," *Women's Studies International Forum* 16, 3 (1993): 221.

18 Bronwyn Bragg, "Deconstructing 'Hegemonic Feminism': The Emergence of 'Second Wave' Feminism in Canada (1965–1975)" (master's thesis, University of Toronto, 2011), 96. See, for instance, a shared concern over violence against women in the working relationship between Vancouver Rape Relief and the Indian Mahila Organization.

19 The anti-violence movement was a precursor to feminist organizing on pornography and prostitution. Krin Zook, "Rape Relief Debate: Why Institutions Do Nothing to Stop Rape," *Kinesis*, December–January 1979–1980, 12; Deb Friedman, "Rape Relief Debate: Should We Increase Convictions, or Lower Expectations?" *Kinesis*, February 1980, 14. For a historical examination of the relations of Victorian norms of sexuality to sexual and domestic violence in Canada, see Karen Dubinsky, *Rape and*

Heterosexual Conflict in Ontario, 1880–1929 (Chicago: University of Chicago Press, 1993).

20 "WAVAW Completes Research Project, Holds Open House," *Kinesis*, March 1980, 24; Kinesis staff writers, "Rape Relief Takes Us on a Tour of the Local War Zone," *Kinesis*, April 1980, 18; and Margo Dunn, "Is There a Place for Men Inside the Women's Movement?," *Kinesis*, November 1980, 9. Recent scholarship on Vancouver Rape Relief affirms that the early anti-violence movement in Canada was galvanized by a shared concern over rape. Margo Goodhand, *Runaway Wives and Rogue Feminists: The Origins of the Women's Shelter Movement in Canada* (Halifax, NS: Fernwood, 2017), 43.

21 Susan Brownmiller, *Against Our Will: Men, Women and Rape* (New York: Simon and Schuster, 1975); Andrea Dworkin, *Woman Hating: A Radical Look at Sexuality* (Boston: E.P. Dutton, 1974); Susan Griffin, *Rape: The Power of Consciousness* (New York: Harper and Row, 1979). See also Janet Reche, "Women Against Violence: Kate Millet Speaks of Violence against Women in *The Basement*," *Kinesis*, March 1980, 24.

22 Lorenne M.G. Clark and Debra J. Lewis, *Rape: The Price of Coercive Sexuality* (Toronto: Women's Press, 1977).

23 Nancy Janovicek, *No Place to Go: Local Histories of the Battered Women's Shelter Movement* (Vancouver: UBC Press, 2007), 9.

24 Janovicek, *No Place to Go*, 14. Janovicek notes in contrast that Indigenous anti-violence activists resisted the white feminist model that saw gender as the primary cause of women's inequality, arguing that this theory relied on omitting structural issues of racism, colonialism, and classism and exposed how individual violence was related to state violence such as the Indian Act, residential schools, and the Sixties Scoop (Janovicek, 12–13). See also Kate Baxter, with Eliza Sasakamoose, Darlene Little, and Jean, "Ducking Bullets: Women from Ahtahkakoop Cree Nation Work to End Violence," in *Listening to the Thunder: Advocates Talk about the Battered Women's Movement*, ed. Leslie Timmins and Jan Barnsley (Vancouver: Women's Research Centre, 1995), 281–97.

25 On September 5, 1974, and October 16, 1974, VSW's community cable television show, *Woman Alive*, on Cable 10, aired two episodes on prostitution. See the VSW Index of Annual Reports 1974, Vancouver Status of Women Archives (VSW Archives), Personal Collection of Becki Ross, VSW Archives Off-Site Storage, box: Annual Reports, file: Index of Annual Reports, 1974–1986.

26 Quoted in Deborah R. Brock, *Making Work, Making Trouble: Prostitution as a Social Problem* (Toronto: University of Toronto Press, 2009), 45.

27 Emily van der Meulen and Elya M. Durisin, "Sex Work Policy: Tracing Historical and Contemporary Developments," in Durisin, van der Meulen, and Bruckert, *Red Light Labour*, 31.

28 Vancouver Status of Women Brief on Pornography and Prostitution, VSW Archives, Personal Collection of Becki Ross, VSW Archives Off-Site Storage, box: Minutes, file: Minutes to be sorted.

29 Debra J. Lewis, "Pornography: Developing Feminist Perspectives," *Kinesis*, October 1978, 10, 12, 13; Debra J. Lewis, "Prostitution: A Difficult Problem for the Movement," *Kinesis*, November 1978, 6–7.

30 Lewis, "Pornography," 12.

31 Lewis, "Prostitution," 6.
32 Lewis, "Prostitution," 6.
33 Van der Meulen, Durisin, and Love, introduction to *Selling Sex*, 9. Bill C-49 contravened the recommendations in 1984 of the Fraser Committee on Pornography and Prostitution to reduce restrictions related to prostitution. Valerie Scott, "C-49: A New Wave of Oppression," in Bell, *Good Girls/Bad Girls*, 100–3. Bill-C49 increased the criminalization of and violence against sex workers, as well as criminializing their political organizing with one another.
34 Lacombe, *Blue Politics*, 104–16.
35 Brenda Cossman and Shannon Bell, introduction to Cossman, Bell, Gotell, and Ross, *Bad Attitude/s on Trial*, 19. See also Becki L. Ross, "'It's Merely Designed for Sexual Arousal': Interrogating the Indefensibility of Lesbian Smut," in Cossman, Bell, Gotell, and Ross, *Bad Attitude/s on Trial*, 193.
36 Cossman and Bell, *Bad Attitude/s on Trial*, 27. Cossman and Bell argue that obscenity laws intensified the systematic targeting of LGBTQ representations throughout the 1990s; see also, Lacombe, *Blue Politics*, 134.
37 General Info: welfare, prostitution, pornography, VSW Archives, Personal Collection of Becki Ross, VSW Archives Off-Site Storage.
38 Becki Ross, "Sex and (Evacuation from) the City: The Moral and Legal Regulation of Sex Workers in Vancouver's West End, 1975–1985," *Sexualities* 13, 2 (2010): 109. Sex workers in Vancouver were diverse. Becki Ross and Rebecca Sullivan, "Tracing Lines of Horizontal Hostility: How Sex Workers and Gay Activists Battled for Space, Voice, and Belonging in Vancouver, 1975–1985," *Sexualities* 15, 5/6 (2012): 605. Ross and Sullivan also emphasize the gender diversity of sex workers in Vancouver's West End prior to 1984, a community which included gay men, transgender and transsexual women, and cisgender women.
39 VSW Brief on Prostitution to Fraser Committee, VSW Archives, Personal Collection of Becki Ross, VSW Archives Off-Site Storage, box: VSW, files-Briefs.
40 Mireille Miller-Young, "Putting Hypersexuality to Work: Black Women and Illicit Eroticism in Pornography" *Sexualities* 13, 2 (2010): 226.
41 Melissa Gira Grant, *Playing the Whore: The Work of Sex Work* (Brooklyn, NY: Verso, 2014), 18. Grant argues that in the dawning consciousness of second-wave feminists, "the wretched prostitute is one myth they refused to denounce entirely," 18.
42 Lee Lakeman and Joni Miller, "Who Is This Man? And Why Is He Trying to Rape Us?," *Kinesis*, June 1985, 18.
43 Grant, *Playing the Whore*, 41. The victim strategy serves prohibitionist feminists by using sex workers – in particular pornography workers – as "mute icon[s]" of the anti-violence cause, 41.
44 Suzanne Gerard, "Porn Is Winning," *Kinesis*, September 1982, 19, 22.
45 Marion Barling, Mickey McCaffrey, and Suzanne Perreault, of Women Against Violence Against Women, "Reclaiming Ourselves: A Feminist Perspective on Pornography," *Kinesis*, June 1980, 20.
46 Barling, McCaffrey, and Perreault, "Reclaiming Ourselves," 8.
47 Megan Ellis and Jan Barnsley, of the Working Group on Sexual Violence, "What Can We Do about Pornography?," *Kinesis*, March 1983, 3.

48 Ellis and Barnsley, "What Can We Do about Pornography?," 3.
49 Kinesis Staff Writers, "Letter Lobby Night," *Kinesis*, September 1982, 1. For example, *Kinesis* writes that anti-violence feminists "brought their pens, their paper, and their rage" to the tasks of lobbying the state for change ("Letter Lobby Night," 1).
50 Lakeman and Miller, "Who Is This Man?," 14.
51 Lakeman and Miller, "Who Is This Man?," 15.
52 Lakeman and Miller, "Who Is This Man?," 14 (emphasis added).
53 Lee Lakeman and Joni Miller, "Jim Pattison: Who Is This Man?," *Kinesis*, July/August 1985, 14 (emphasis added).
54 Kinesis Staff Writers, "Prostitution: An End to the Invisibility," *Kinesis*, May 1983, 13.
55 "Prostitution: An End to the Invisibility," 13.
56 "Prostitution: An End to the Invisibility," 13.
57 "Prostitution: An End to the Invisibility," 13.
58 Bunjun, "Organizational Colonial Encounters," 6.
59 Debra Lewis, "Pornography: A Feminist Analysis, Misogyny, Pornography, and Violence against Women," *Kinesis*, April 1983, 6. See also Clark and Lewis, *Rape: The Price of Coercive Sexuality*.
60 Lewis, "Pornography: A Feminist Analysis," 6.
61 Regina Lorek, "Porn: Who's Hurt? Who Benefits?" *Kinesis*, April 1983, 8. Lorek was also a member of the British Columbia Federation of Women's Committee to Stop Red Hot Video.
62 Lorek, "Porn: Who's Hurt? Who Benefits?," 9.
63 For key foundational American texts, see Andrea Dworkin, *Pornography: Men Possessing Women* (New York: G.P. Putnam, 1981); Catherine A. Mackinnon, "Pornography, Civil Rights, and Speech," *Harvard Civil Rights-Civil Liberties Law Review* 20, 1 (1985): 10–68.
64 Sara Ahmed, *The Cultural Politics of Emotion*, 2nd ed. (Edinburgh: Edinburgh University Press, 2015), 62, 68.
65 Ahmed, *Cultural Politics of Emotion*, 69, 70 (emphasis in original).
66 Amber Cooke and Laurie Bell, "Sex Trade Workers and Feminists: Myths and Illusions," in Bell, *Good Girls/Bad Girls*, 197.
67 Kairn Mladenovic, "Reader Insulted," *Kinesis*, April 1988, 21. Sex worker and activist Kairn Mladenovic argued that "racism plays a major role in the sex trade," where "50% of women on the streets in Vancouver are women of color" and many women are also lesbians (Mladenovic, 21).
68 Lederer, *Take Back the Night*, 5.
69 Barbara H. Rosenwein, "Problems and Methods in the History of Emotions," *Passions in Context: International Journal for the History and Theory of Emotions* 1, 1 (2010): 11.
70 Ross and Sullivan, "Tracing Lines of Horizontal Hostility," 205.
71 Helen Forsey, "Sex Trade: Let's Consider 'Conversation' Efforts," *Kinesis*, February 1988, 17.
72 Lewis, "Prostitution: A Feminist Analysis," 6. For a rare exception to the invisibility of pornography workers, see Laura Lederer and Jane Jones, "Then and Now: An Interview with a Former Pornography Model," in Lederer, *Take Back the Night*,

57–70. See also Linda Lovelace, *Ordeal: An Autobiography,* with Mike McGrady (New York: Citadel Press, 1980). Note that both narratives of former porn workers are reformist and abolitionist.

73 Pat Feindel, "Feminists Step Up Anti-porn Fight Back," *Kinesis,* September 1983, 3. Feindel notes that in 1983, Victoria's Women Against Pornography (WAP) published a letter in the *Times Colonist* to oppose the filming of a pornographic movie in Victoria. According to WAP, one of the six female performers in the film later contacted WAP to say that she was suing the film's producers. Whether this ever happened is unclear, as this is the only mention of communication between a woman working in pornography and feminists I encountered in either VSW or *Kinesis.*

74 Miller-Young, "Putting Hypersexuality to Work," 223.

75 See Lederer, *Take Back the Night.*

76 Clarissa Smith and Feona Atwood, "Anti/Pro/Critical Porn Studies," *Porn Studies* 1, 1–2 (2014): 15.

77 Alan McKee, "Pornography as a Creative Industry: Challenging the Exceptionalist Approach to Pornography," *Porn Studies* 3, 2 (2016): 109.

78 See Mary Johnson, "CABE and Strippers: A Delicate Union," in Bell, *Good Girls/Bad Girls,* 113; and International Committee for Prostitutes' Rights, "International Committee for Prostitutes' Rights World Charter and World Whores' Congress Statements," in *Sex Work: Writings by Women in the Sex Industry,* ed. Frederique Delacoste and Priscilla Alexander (San Francisco: Cleis Press, 1987), 308. For recent discussions of pornography and labour, see Heather Berg, "Labouring Porn Studies," *Porn Studies* 1, 1–2 (2014): 77; and Jiz Lee and Rebecca Sullivan, "Porn and Labour: The Labour of Porn Studies," *Porn Studies* 3, 2 (2016): 104.

79 Jillian Ridington, "Letter to the Editor," *Vancouver Sun,* April 23 1983, n.p., VSW Archives, Personal Collection of Becki Ross, VSW Archives Off-Site Storage, file: VSW Correspondence: January 1983–December 1983. In 1983, Vancouver municipal representatives pressed Vancouver City Council to support the federal government in increasing the criminalization of prostitution. VSW responded with an open letter to City Hall, publicly denouncing the mounting attacks on prostitutes. VSW also spoke on this at City Council. Lorri Rudland and Cole Dudley, "Prostitution Recommendations Spark Heated Debate," *Kinesis,* June 1983, 10. Shortly after publishing their open letter, VSW feminists supported the Alliance for the Safety of Prostitutes in their opposition to the motion at a Council meeting at Vancouver City Hall; these perspectives were also reflected in their presentation to the Fraser Committee. "Brief on Prostitution to the Fraser Committee of Pornography and Prostitution," VSW Archives, Personal Collection of Becki Ross, VSW Archives Off-Site Storage, file: Correspondence/Briefs. VSW and *Kinesis* feminists submitted a brief to the Fraser Committee on Prostitution on January 13, 1984, demanding the repeal of Sections 193 (communication in public for the purpose of prostitution) and 195.1 (keeping of a bawdy house) of the Criminal Code.

80 For reporting on sex-worker activism in *Kinesis,* see Kinesis Staff Writers, "Prostitutes March on Vancouver City Hall," *Kinesis,* May 1983, 1; Cole Dudley, "The Alliance for the Safety of Prostitutes," *Kinesis,* May 1983, 14, 15; and Rudland and Dudley, "Prostitution Recommendations Spark Heated Debate," 10.

81 Steve McClure, "The Heat Is On at Red Hot," *Vancouver Courier*, December 15, 1982, 6. A woman employed in 1982 at a Red Hot Video store stated to a feminist protester a month after the firebombing, "You don't understand the industry" (McClure, 6).
82 McKee, "Pornography as a Creative Industry," 107.
83 See Linda Hossie, "Porn: Women's Anger Is Justified," *Vancouver Sun*, November 26, 1982, A5; Keith Morgan, "Porn Man Fears for His Life," *Province*, November 24, 1982, A4; and "Red Hot Plays Hide 'n' Seek," *Vancouver Sun*, December 13, 1982, A12.
84 Pat Hercus and Jean Bennett, "Red Hot Video Picket: An Analysis," *Kinesis*, June 1983, 8, 9. Hercus and Bennett declared that a weeklong picket of Red Hot Video was "one way of emphatically stating our belief that there is a direct connection between the pornographic image and the real-life violence against women" (Hercus and Bennett, 8).
85 Minister of Supply and Services, *Pornography and Prostitution in Canada: Report of the Special Committee on Pornography and Prostitution* (Ottawa: 1985). Known as the Fraser Committee Report on Pornography, it outlined the feminist perspective as follows: "The position of most feminist groups, and some church organizations, was that erotica, which they described as sexually explicit material which contains no violence or coercion and in which participants were there by choice, was acceptable. They were totally opposed however, to violent pornography, which they defined as material with a sexual content combined with violence, degradation and abuse, with men shown as the aggressor and women as the subordinate or victim" (Minster of Supply and Services, 63). National feminist groups took a different approach to prostitution recommendations than the general perspective on pornography. Brock, *Making Work, Making Trouble*, 51. At the same time, presentations to the Fraser Committee by feminist groups including the National Action Committee on the Status of Women, the Elizabeth Fry Society, and the National Association of Women and the Law advocated for partial decriminalization, recommending the removal of soliciting from the Criminal Code and the loosening of bawdy-house laws.
86 Lori Rudland, "Views Change on Prostitution," *Kinesis*, February 1984, 3.
87 Megan Ellis, "Prostitution and Men: Is the Demand for Sex or Power?," *Kinesis*, September 1986, 12, 13. Ellis's piece summarizes the feminist position on prostitution in *Kinesis*: "And while it is important to work to increase protection against dangers faced by women who do that labour, that is not the same thing as working to protect their jobs. The issue of prostitution is not just about conditions of work, it is also about the nature of the work, and the consequences of the work for all women" (Ellis, 13).
88 Ross and Sullivan, "Tracing Lines of Horizontal Hostility," 616. Support for sex workers fluctuated but was never the priority of *Kinesis* and VSW. Staff Meeting Minutes, October 1982, VSW Archives, Personal Collection of Becki Ross, VSW Archives Off-Site Storage, file: Staff Meeting Minutes, April 1–82/March 31–83. For instance, VSW rejected the Alliance for the Safety of Prostitutes' request to use their office phone line on October 19, 1982.
89 See Esther Shannon, "Prostitution Law: First Victims," *Kinesis*, April 1986, 1; Esther Shannon, "Vancouver Prostitutes Fear Increasing Violence," *Kinesis*, September 1986, 3; and Sonia Marino, "Hallway Justice for Hookers," *Kinesis*, December–January 1986–1987, 5.

90 Cooke, quoted in Bell and Cooke, "Sex Trade Workers," 199. As Cooke points out, "survival and politics are two different things," as feminists have the "luxury" to theorize the sex industry, while sex workers are actually engaging in sexual labour in exchange for money (Cooke, 199).

91 P.O.W.E.R., "Horizontal Hostility," *Kinesis*, June 1988, 20.

92 Nora Randell, "A Night in the Streets," *Kinesis*, May 1988, 10.

93 P.O.W.E.R., "Horizontal Hostility," 20.

94 P.O.W.E.R., "Horizontal Hostility," 20.

95 Kairn Mladenovic, "Many More Women Will Be Working the Streets," *Kinesis*, July/August 1988, 8.

96 Mladenovic, "Many More Women," 8.

97 Mladenovic, "Many More Women," 8.

98 Mladenovic, "Many More Women," 8.

99 Mladenovic, "Many More Women," 8. Scholarship on this period supports Mladenovic's observations. John Lowman, "Deadly Inertia: A History of Constitutional Challenges to Canada's *Criminal Code* Sections on Prostitution," *Beijing Law Review* 2 (2011): 33–54. Lowman notes how Justice Canada's review of the communicating law in 1989 revealed that in Toronto and Vancouver – the cities with the highest rate of street-level prostitution – as well as in Calgary, Regina, and Winnipeg, the law had not reduced street prostitution. Rather, since 1985, between two hundred and three hundred women working on the streets have been murdered (Lowman, 33).

100 Mladenovic, "Many More Women," 12.

101 Brock, *Making Work, Making Trouble*, 197n86. The Toronto-based sex-worker organization, the Coalition for the Rights of Prostitutes, joined the National Action Committee on the Status of Women as a pressure group in 1985. For the following four years, the prostitute subcommittee – composed of women working in the sex industry and allies – engaged the National Action Committee to develop a policy on prostitution that supported decriminalization, labour rights, and anti-racism. Valerie Scott and Peggie Lee, "Emergency Resolution for NAC, 1986," University of Ottawa, Canadian Women's Movement Archives, CORP fonds 10-001, box/file: 11-1, item 26.

102 Mladenovic, "Many More Women," 8.

103 McKee, "Pornography as a Creative Industry," 116; McKee encourages a comparison of sex work to other categories of labour to reduce "exceptionality," while Berg argues that anti-pornography feminists are reluctant to examine exploitation as inherent in all forms of waged labour. Berg, "Labouring Porn Studies," 77.

104 Clare Hemmings, *Why Stories Matter: The Political Grammar of Feminist Theory* (Durham, NC: Duke University Press, 2011), 139.

105 Bunjun, "Organizational Colonial Encounters," 2.

10 Emotional Scripts of Difference
Black Women Teachers and Feminist Mobilization

FUNKÉ ALADEJEBI

> Now, unions keep us with the people that we have. It's our responsibility. We're teachers, to challenge their [unions'] beliefs, to challenge their [unions'] value system. As a board, that's our job to challenge that white privilege thing ... We do it through our hiring practices, we do it through the way we treat children and staff, the way our unions support the staff. We do it in so many different ways. We have to make changes. I don't know how. But one of the ways in starting is to challenge where we are at right now.[1]

When principal Donna Lockette remembered her experiences in the 1970s with her teachers' union, the Federation of Women Teachers' Associations of Ontario (FWTAO), she expressed her belief in the collective responsibility of all educators and school boards to challenge white privilege within Ontario's school systems. Her critique, largely shaped by her experience of mandatory membership in the FWTAO, alluded to a longer history of systemic privilege and racial discrimination within unions.[2] While the federation advocated for the professional status of women teachers in Ontario, Lockette felt that the role of the union should go further: it should not only represent the diverse racial dynamics of its membership but should also challenge broader social expectations that positioned whiteness as a marker of privilege and power.

Indicative of broader discourses within second-wave feminism and women's organizing in Canada at the time, Lockette's experiences reveal the challenges Black women faced as they tried to find their place within Canada's women's movement. As second-wave feminists and consciousness-raising groups politicized the emotions of anger and discontent to mobilize collective action, they also shaped the parameters and boundaries of who could articulate and tell the story of gender inequality. By creating a narrow, exclusive, and universal understanding of pain and anger, white women prioritized their feelings and emotional scripts as legitimate, negating Black women's diverse articulations of emotional expression. These "legitimate" feelings would characterize many women's organizations in the late-twentieth century.

While feminist scholars are increasingly embracing affect theory, the emotional lives of Black women is in need of further analysis. Indeed, scholars such as Sara Ahmed and Claudia Garcia-Rojas ask us to theorize affect in ways that centre race and counter dominant structures of emotion.[3] These scholars conceptualize how systems of power are recreated through the writing of emotions. Building on their ideas, this chapter documents the ways in which Black Canadian women created a different set of values and emotional scripts based on their own experiences and needs. Sometimes these scripts responded to the isolation and exclusion these women experienced within mainstream (white) feminist organizations; at other times, these scripts were a reflection of the collective needs of diverse Black Canadian communities. As historian Barbara Rosenwein argues, within society there exists multiple, sometimes contradictory, emotional communities.[4] As such, even within Canadian women's organizations, individuals moved through society with a variety of "guidelines, standards and expectations for emotional expression."[5] Consequently, as white feminists fashioned the language of gender equality and women's liberation through their advocacy work, increasing union participation, and their push for legislative changes, Black Canadian women's intersectional experiences rendered an alternative articulation of emotion within second-wave feminist organizations.

Drawing on oral interviews, school board and FWTAO minutes, and newspapers, this chapter contends that as Black Canadian women moved between their professional and cultural communities, mainstream women's organizations viewed their emotions as out of place and just outside the boundaries of (white) women's liberation. The federation's brand of feminism, based on white middle-class ideals, left little room for Black women educators, who searched for other avenues to obtain equality based on their multiple forms of oppression.[6] My analysis of this professional organization, then, highlights the complexities of women's organizing as it related to Black women teachers and education more broadly. Ultimately, I problematize the relationship between racism and feminism as it existed for some Black women educators, revealing how these women understood themselves as occupying in-between spaces, where they built alliances, borrowed discourses, and strengthened identities unique to their personal experiences as Black women. In doing so, I highlight the uneven and conflicting ways Black women's emotions were part of, but also stood separate from, larger social justice movements in the late-twentieth century. As Black women educators like Donna Lockette searched for representation within their professional unions, the need to organize on the basis of their multiple identities and experiences not only revealed the relationships between power and privilege inherent in the women's movement, but also reflected the existence of a hierarchy of emotions that characterized second-wave feminist organizations.[7]

"The Duality of the Damnation for the Black Woman": FWTAO and the "Other Others"

The Federation of Women Teachers' Associations of Ontario offers a unique lens for understanding how professional unions shaped Canada's women's movement.[8] Although the FWTAO was largely concerned with women's working lives in the profession, by the late 1970s the organization became increasingly politically active and was part of a larger movement for women's rights. Advocating a liberal feminist agenda by lobbying for legislative changes, FWTAO was one of many organizations that worked to promote women's increased access to education and equal pay through its emphasis on gender equality within school systems and its assertion of women's special capabilities as leaders in Ontario schools.

Founded in 1918 to address the unique interests of female elementary educators in Ontario, the FWTAO would eventually include all female elementary school teachers through mandatory membership with the passage of the Teaching Profession Act of 1944. The male counterpart to this association was the Ontario Public School Men Teachers' Federation which was created in 1920 to represent male public school teachers until 1998, when the Elementary Teachers' Federation of Ontario became the umbrella organization that represented all elementary educators in the province regardless of gender. Conversely, high school teachers belonged to the Ontario Secondary School Teachers' Federation, which was created in 1919.

The FWTAO evolved out of splinters within locally based teachers' organizations as female educators began noticing discrepancies on the basis of gender, largely around pay. As a result of systemic gender biases, women teachers created separate female teacher associations to lobby for professional recognition and work improvements.[9] The FWTAO emerged as a provincial coalition of these smaller local associations with the explicit goal of obtaining "financial equality with men, a reasonable pension in old age and greater opportunities within the education system."[10] By the middle of the twentieth century, the FWTAO was the only affiliate of the Ontario's Teachers' Federation that specifically represented female elementary educators.[11] Its mandates were firmly rooted in the development and increased status of teaching as a profession, supporting campaigns for greater opportunities for professional development, maternity leave, improved pensions, equal pay, as well as a variety of other concerns, including preventing violence against women and the creation of subsidized daycares.[12]

Yet, despite the growing number of racially diverse professionals and students in Ontario, the federation consistently presented the model female educator almost exclusively as a member of its majority constituency, which was white, Protestant, and middle class.[13] Indeed, in her examination of the ways in which employment equity affected racial minority women teachers before the advent of racially inclusive legislation in 1992, education scholar Dolana Mogadime argues that the FWTAO's commitment to advocating for the advancement of all women teachers was undermined by its universalizing vision of all its constituents as white women.[14] According to Mogadime, the federation failed to engage in discussions of race, neither attempting to find the precise numbers of minority women within its membership nor making concerted efforts to interrogate the ways in which racial minority women experienced policies such as employment equity.[15]

As a result of the ways the FWTAO prioritized white women's issues, some Black women teachers felt excluded from the organization; this exclusion was manifested through the ways Black women felt they could approach the federation for assistance and the continuation of racial discrimination within individual school settings. Although racialized educators were small in number, they represented a growing and regularly paid membership base in the teaching community.[16] Fundamentally, the ways in which mainstream women's movements advocated for gender equality hinged on notions of whiteness as a signifier of power; this hierarchy affected Black women, not only those who were informed by, and also participated in, the women's movement but also those who abandoned mainstream women's organizations in search of a broader, more inclusive view of Canadian womanhood.

This hierarchy that focused on a particular kind of gender equality was also reflected in other Canadian social and educational institutions. In her examination of gender, race, and academic access, political scientist Malinda S. Smith contends that there was a shift in the definitions of equity within the Canadian academy in the 1970s and 1980s. Smith argues that the category of "woman" became the primary focus of equity policies, transforming gender into *the* signifying marker of difference. According to Smith, Canadian equity-focused approaches, as shaped by feminist advocacy in academic spaces, engendered a dividing practice that privileged white women as "the Other" and further marginalized non-whites as the undifferentiated "other Others."[17] According to Smith, it meant that as white women gained access and power in academic spaces, created policies, and produced empirical data to support their everyday experiences, white feminists shifted the gaze from equity (then broadly defined) to gender equity. As such, equity for white women was an achievable goal, while equity for other groups (racial minorities) was envisioned as too challenging and thus something that could be deferred until later.

Similarly, while women's organizations in Ontario moved towards creating gender-equitable spaces for (white) women, those spaces became less open for Black women teachers, who gained some support by virtue of their gender but struggled to find organizations that addressed their intersectional experiences. This silence on race-based issues within teacher-union leadership was evident in FWTAO reports and surveys in the 1970s. Indeed, on the rare occasion that issues of race were discussed by the FWTAO, they were often treated as tokenistic forms of inclusion or conveyed as unimportant to its white majority membership – a trend that frustrated the FWTAO's minority members.

While the expression of emotion embedded in social and institutional practice is often difficult to uncover in written documents, a report about a 1972 FWTAO incident illuminates both the progressiveness of FWTAO's leadership and its significant racial divisions. That year, the FWTAO invited Gloria Steinem, the founding editor of *Ms. Magazine*, and Margaret Sloan, an African American lesbian, civil rights advocate, and editor at the magazine, to give a keynote address at its annual dinner assembly. While the FWTAO disassociated itself from the more radical elements of the women's movement, Steinem and Sloan's joint appearance marked the organization's progressive focus on coalition-building in the women's movement.[18] In a piece for the

Educational Courier titled "The Night Women's Lib Came to Dinner," reporter Edward Lynas wrote that Steinem discussed the historical divisions between men and women in North America, highlighting gender discrimination within Canadian schools as demonstrated through the visibility of men in administrative posts and women as teaching staff. Lynas wrote that Steinem received resounding applause from the audience when she stated, "Women are beginning to realize that it is not they who are crazy. That it is the system that is crazy. And when they do they get angry. We should use that anger to change our situation and that of our sisters."[19]

Margaret Sloan's speech, however, seemed to generate a different response and divided teacher-delegates at the dinner assembly. Lynas reported that Sloan's address, in which she spoke openly about the plight of Black women in mainstream society, was not well received by dinner attendees. While Lynas described Steinem as revolutionary, intellectual, and attractive, he characterized Sloan as "emotional, forceful and 'dead-on.'"[20] He wrote that Sloan was not afraid to call "a spade a spade" but that most people found her difficult to follow and that she polarized the audience. "First she chastised the Minister [of Education] for his jokes, then she chastised the women for their dressed-up outfits. She talked of the duality of the damnation for the black woman especially," Lynas explained. "And as she wound-up one particularly deadly, salvo against men, she let fly with the most familiar old English copulative adjective. That did it."[21]

Sloan not only tackled women's liberation on the basis of gender, but also encouraged her audience to consider a multiplicity of experiences. For example, her critique of the minister of education, Thomas Wells, served to directly confront mainstream schooling institutions that limited Black bodies though racial discrimination and reinforced male dominance and power.[22] Here, Sloan focused her attention on larger institutions that inadequately responded to the needs of racial minorities and their experiences of systemic racism. Sloan also chastised the women teachers at the event who were "dressed up" and highlighted class-based assumptions about respectable and, in this case, professional womanhood.[23] Finally, Sloan's comments remained grounded in feminist arguments about patriarchy and sex difference through her criticism of men more broadly. In this sense, Sloan's vision of women's liberation and consciousness-raising sought to encompass a broader understanding of equality that considered dimensions of race, class, and sexuality.

After Sloan's speech, Lynas reported that while a few members in the audience yelled in approval of her points, many others chuckled, left in anger, or were offended. Reporting that the evening ended with a question period, Lynas noted that few audience members seemed converted to women's liberation and concluded that the session ultimately widened the gaps among attendees. Sloan's frank insertion of race and other forms of oppression, including class, sexuality, and gender, challenged women's liberation as it was conceived by many Ontario educators. The responses from dinner attendees were not only a result of Sloan's unabashed ability to call a spade a spade, but also a direct result of her challenges to white womanhood as promoted by mainstream feminists.[24]

Sloan's reception at the dinner indicated that although the FWTAO was strongly influenced by the second wave of the women's movement, the organization also had its internal struggle with how best its goals and objectives should be represented. Educational historian Rebecca Coulter contends that the federation's desire for professional status in the twentieth century served to "contain women's potential to act for radical change."[25] According to Coulter, members of the FWTAO articulated a style of "domesticated professionalism," which emphasized feminine behaviour and appearance. This meant that members often pushed against what they perceived to be radical factions in the broader women's movement and instead maintained existing social orders within the association. At times, this focus also reflected hierarchal emotional scripts that excluded Black women from feeling like they belonged in the organization. For example, in her oral histories of FWTAO members in the twentieth century, Coulter cites the story of Hannah, a former FWTAO member who maintained the belief that women's union activism should not disrupt goals of professionalism. In discussing a one-day walkout staged by teachers in 1973, Hannah recalled FWTAO protests as "always very well controlled. We never got into any fisticuff, fights or anything like that. I thought it was done in a very professional way."[26] Hannah's distinction is important for the ways she positions women's advocacy work in the FWTAO as connected to "proper" and "professional" styles of activism.[27] As such, the kinds of militancy that Sloan called for would demand a different set emotional scripts that moved beyond the status quo.

Placed within this context, Lynas's report of Sloan's unfavourable reception indicates an important way that emotion can be understood as relational and can situate boundaries of separation and subordination. In this instance, the way the FWTAO's dinner participants received both speakers revealed a hierarchy of emotions, where some feelings were prioritized over others.[28] Steinem's use of anger served as a call to action and indeed worked to politicize women and their emotional journeys as educators. Such anger moved some women beyond the universalizing emotional experience of pain and closer towards feminist action.[29] However, while the use of anger became an important tool for feminist mobilization, it became equally important to "hear the anger of others, without blocking [that] anger through a defence of one's own position."[30] It is here, through this (in)ability to hear the anger of others, that the reception and management of some emotions can be attached to conditions of subordination.

Moreover, the way Sloan's speech was perceived by the FWTAO's membership also indicated that when anger was articulated through an intersectional body, this emotional expression was likely to be met with ambivalence, to be ignored, or to be met with prescribed cursory inclusion. The very act of highlighting these silences reflected a different set of political expressions rooted in Sloan's experience as a Black queer woman. Here, then, was tangible evidence that the FWTAO's organizational focus was not ready to fully align itself with Black feminist discourses about race. However, amid this clear omission, the FWTAO actively worked to invite and support some of the most prominent speakers of the second-wave feminist movement, including the first president of the National Action Committee on the Status of Women, Laura Sabia, indicating the organization's desire to remain connected to women's liberation more broadly.

"White Women Who Were Very Mean": Limits of Interracial Collaboration

By the late 1970s, the federation became more focused on its campaign to increase the pay and authority positions of female employees in Ontario schools. Its demand for more women in administrative positions at schools identified legitimate concerns that needed to be addressed by education administrators.[31] Working to recruit women into positions of responsibility throughout Ontario schools, the FWTAO launched summer leadership courses for its members as early as 1969 and engaged in a variety of other initiatives to equip and encourage women to apply for promotions. When the provincial government introduced policies to improve the representation of women at senior levels of the civil service in 1973, the result was an increase in the number of women in leadership roles in the Ministry of Education.[32] By 1979, the ministry had established an employment equity unit that worked to address issues facing all women in education with a specific focus on women in administration.[33] Thus, it seemed that the ministry was responding to the advocacy work done by women's organizations and that these legislative gains would improve the status of many female teachers. With the success and progress of various equity programs, such as the Equal

Opportunity/Affirmative Action Unit at the Ministry of Education, the equal pay for equal work platform became especially important to the FWTAO, and the organization used it to advocate for promotions and increased salaries for female educators.[34]

For some Black women, this push for increased women's participation in administrative positions created some space for interracial and cross-gender collaboration, fortified relationships with other female educators, and elevated their social and economic status. For example, educator Marcia Lambert remembered the increasing expansion of the North York school board, in the 1970s, where she built positive relationships with several female teachers. The board allowed her to work with diverse groups of women and, while she did not consider herself a feminist at the time, her fight for women's equal treatment in the workforce reflected the influence of a growing feminist consciousness arising in the late-twentieth century. Lambert believed that as all young women worked towards equal pay and status in educational institutions, avenues for support and collaboration were solidified through women's advocacy in the teachers' unions. Reflecting on her experience with the North York school board, Lambert recalled that "it was women who were coming into their own. Because at the time the feminist movement was very powerful, and so there was a large group of women who considered themselves feminist in thought, if not necessarily in action. They were feminists in their thought. And so the women supported each other actually and encouraged each other."[35] According to Lambert, even though not all women were involved in activist organizations, her consciousness, as well as those of other women, was changed by the awareness of women's rights and liberation. Furthermore, Lambert fondly remembered the ways in which this growing female consciousness encouraged by women's liberation facilitated partnerships across racial lines to promote gender and, on occasions, racial equality.

While working to build a Black educators' group within the North York school board in the early 1970s, for example, Lambert recalled being supported by the school director and other women who were fighting for equal representation:

> And then the women in the system, all women, not just Black women, also were pushing to have themselves represented within the system's hierarchy, so women supported other women. [It] didn't matter if you were Black, white, blue or yellow. They supported each other. And so the two [race and gendered critiques of board limitations] were happening at the same time.[36]

The mobilization occurring in Black Canadian communities and the growing activism in the women's movement created some avenues of mutual understanding and support among women who were advocating for equality within the education system. The increasingly prevalent language of human rights promoted by both women's and Black cultural organizations also contributed to these spaces of collaboration and support.[37]

Still, Lambert noted that the bonds of "sisterhood" as advocated by women's organizations were not always practised within school settings. Lambert felt that as she worked to move outside the classroom and into administration, she faced backlash from her white counterparts. She explained,

> There were a few women, of course, who saw you, if you were aspiring to go beyond the classroom or aspiring to be a consultant or a vice-principal or principal, who saw you as a threat. And I think they certainly [did]. I know there were some who saw me as a threat ... But I know that once I began to see other opportunities outside of the classroom, there were some white women who were very mean and very negative.[38]

Hinting at the difficulties in building alliances based exclusively on gender, Lambert revealed that some white women perceived Black women's chance at promotion and status with hostility and fear. Although it is possible that the limited access women had to administrative posts increased competition among eligible candidates, Lambert's recollections indicate that she was not perceived as a threat on the basis of just her Blackness or gender, but rather because of her positionality embodying both these identifying markers.

Fear (or perceived fear) can work to limit people from securing access to certain social spaces. As a result, the movement of some women into positions of responsibility and the perceived threat of others who could gain these positions, namely racialized women, revealed a more complex negotiation of collective activism. In this case, it reflected the dimensions of emotional hegemony that preserved dominant gender-based values and placed Black women at the receiving end of white women's anger and hostility.[39] Consequently, promotions under employment equity initiatives that focused on gender could both be used to delegitimize the credentials and expertise of Black women educators and also provide opportunities for their increased economic status. Implicit in this fear was that some Black educators were ostensibly less deserving candidates for these promotions.

In other instances, Black women were cognizant of the ways in which the white (colonial) gaze often rendered their feelings as either emotional excess (i.e., angry, hypersexual, and dysfunctional) or as invisible.[40] These contradictions within the women's movement were offensive and aggravating to many Black women teachers who desired more collaborative feminist action around gender and racial discrimination. As such, the boundaries for political action could be un-made and, at times, reconstituted, based on the place of Black women's feelings within mainstream women's organizations. For example, Canadian-born educator Tamara Mogrant felt that the women's movement, and feminism for that matter, was a waste of time. Mogrant asserted,

> We've [Black women] made them [white women] our girlfriends, our buddies. We share our ideas. And they come together? Never. They'll be your friend, but when it comes to this whole other business of job sharing, it ain't going to happen. And if it does, it's the exception. So I wasted a lot of time in feminism because I do believe in the idea. I do believe that doors should be open to women, I do believe that. And I was criticized by Black men. Black men hated the whole fact that Black women were involved in feminism because they said it subordinates that whole business of race. Well, I thought that was stupid because I can hold two ideas in my head at the same time. That was just ridiculous. So I see myself having wasted that time for other reasons.[41]

Mogrant's *in-between* space as a Black woman meant that she did not solely align with race or gender politics. Instead, she indicated how some broader social movements authorized selected feelings "while downplaying and even invalidating others."[42]

According to scholar Deborah Gould, Mogrant's recollection indicated the ways social movements made sense of affective states and provided the context, language, and categories by which people were made to feel. These restrictive boundaries left little room for Black women's emotion work and their desires for political activism. In Mogrant's case, building bonds around gender did not change the fact that women educators competed for the same jobs and limited administrative positions within school boards. The idea of unity based on a common gendered oppression became a superficial concept rather than a tangible move towards collaborative change. Instead, Mogrant's recollection emphasized the uphill battle that Black women teachers faced in trying to gain equal footing within mainstream institutions – an effort that also came at the risk of isolating themselves from Black men. Mogrant's resistance to containing her gendered politics under the umbrella of racial activism was an important indicator of not only her Black feminist perspective but also her expressions of betrayal by both the Black and women's liberation movements. Refusing to choose one category of difference, her reflection of time wasted spoke to a long and difficult battle balancing mainstream institutions and community expectations. Furthermore, Mogrant's articulation of an emotional culture that valued her own needs and experiences was indicative of Black experiences across the diaspora.[43]

Despite the fact that Mogrant also wanted, and benefited from, the legislative gains for which the federation advocated (particularly surrounding equal pay and access to positions of power), it seems that the federation's focus did not meet the priorities of several Black female educators at the time. These included priorities voiced by immigrant populations from the Caribbean, addressing drop-out rates among Black pupils, and access to professional jobs.[44] In fact, Mogrant only increased her involvement in the FWTAO in the late 1980s as a result of the organization's shift towards multicultural education and the creation of its Equal Opportunity committee, which focused on the development of anti-racist education.[45] As such, *when* and *why* Black women chose to participate in the FWTAO was important for understanding their subversive politics. Connected to Mogrant's delayed participation in the FWTAO are the ways affect remained deeply intertwined with broader social contexts. Therefore, Black women's social conditions in Canada shaped their feelings and desires to engage in political activism and to challenge systems of power that sought to erase their participation within mainstream organizations.

Although the Ontario Ministry of Education did not develop a formal policy on anti-racism and ethnocultural equity in education until 1993, prior to this period, racial minority educators played a central role in the implementation of anti-racist education. In addition to initiatives supported by Black educators such as Mogrant, increasing community pressure and changing student demographics pushed school boards and teacher organizations to implement diversity in teacher hiring and training practices, as well as to increase teaching materials and facilitate dialogues around "race relations" within various schools.[46] The Toronto Board of Education, for example, created the Equal Opportunity Office and Race Relations Committee in the 1980s, which demonstrated a growing push towards anti-racist education and an expansion of board-wide policies that included more discussions of racial diversity.[47]

"There Was Hurt": Black Women (Re)telling Stories of Pain

As a result of experiences of sexism in Black activist organizations and racism in feminist organizations, Black women's feelings of anger and frustration shaped their advocacy work and led to the creation of organizations geared towards their intersectional experiences. For those Black women who felt alienated from the mainstream women's organizations, the Congress of Black Women of Canada provided a place in which Black women from various socioeconomic, cultural, and educational backgrounds could gather and network with one another. Wrapped up in their collective feelings of anger and frustration was also a sense of solidarity and a desire for change. The Congress's ability to encourage Black women to recognize their position in Canadian society and search for ways to combat the oppression they faced from various mainstream sources exemplified how Black women used multiple avenues of expression and organizing to challenge subjugation.

Initiated in 1951, the Canadian Negro Women's Association (CANEWA) began as a social club for middle-class Black women.[48] The organization later changed to focus on social issues facing Black populations, particularly in late 1950s Toronto. Spearheaded by Canadian-born professional television and radio actor, Kay Livingstone, CANEWA worked to promote the "merits of the Canadian Negro" and to educate Black Canadian students through scholarships, organizing balls and festivals, and developing written texts about Black historical achievements.[49] In 1973, convinced that Black women needed a national voice, CANEWA organized the First National Congress of Black Women. The Congress quickly mobilized around two key political concerns: the fact that male-dominated organizations like the National Black Coalition did not adequately address Black women's concerns and the tendencies of white feminist groups to largely ignore issues of racism.[50]

The creation of the Congress of Black Women also stood alongside growing anti-racist discourse happening in the late 1970s. In the hopes of highlighting the experiences of all racialized women, both mainstream feminist organizations and racial minorities adopted the term "woman of colour" to acknowledge interlocking systems of oppression that racial minority women faced. However, this inclusion had its limitations and some Black female educators continued to feel disassociated from mainstream women's organizations. Such was the case of Enid Rubin, a principal in Toronto in the 1980s, who joined several mainstream women's organizations at the time but felt that there was a disconnect between white and Black women's organizing philosophies. Before leaving these mainstream women's organizations

National Congress of Black Women brochure, Toronto, April 1973. (Courtesy of Congress of Black Women of Canada.)

to join the Congress of Black Women of Canada, Rubin found herself constantly having to explain to her white counterparts the legacy of slavery and how racism impacted her life on a daily basis. Rubin soon grew tired of always having to talk about the scars of her lived experience and recalled,

> But it's like if you're Black and you're with some people, you always have to say, "Oh, well this happened to me." And after a while, you have to say, "Have you heard about racism? You must know that some ugly things happen[ed]. I don't have to give you everything that happened ... Come on, go read a book about slavery, read a book about racism and find out that people do hurt! And that nobody is blaming you. But we're saying it's a fact of life, so wake up and understand when I'm saying that there was hurt, that there was hurt."[51]

By the 1980s, the mainstream women's movement in Canada was experiencing multiple schisms: socialist feminists criticized the movement for not focusing enough on capitalism and patriarchy as systems which oppressed women; radical feminists wanted to eradicate prescribed gender roles in society and focused on sex stereotyping in literature and teaching materials, and Québécois women worked to connect their feminist demands with nationalist ideas.[52] For their part, racial minorities chastised the movement for excluding discussions of racism and created alternative organizations such as the Immigrant and Visible Minority Women of Canada, which included immigrant, Indigenous, South Asian, and Black women to develop anti-racist strategies and policies within the movement. Focusing on an anti-racist framework revealed the multiple political and social constructions of race that systematically left visible minorities disadvantaged.[53] Forcing the women's movement to examine definitions of universal sisterhood, anti-racist organizers demanded inclusion and the examination of the challenges they faced as visible minorities. Therefore, Black women's feelings of solidarity highlighted the importance of community care in their activist work.

In this context, Enid Rubin criticized women's organizations that tried to tackle issues of racism yet did little to actually increase the number of marginalized Black women within their membership. While her white colleagues suggested that they understood her struggle, Rubin remained adamant about their inability to truly understand life as a Black woman. Rubin's position as an "outsider within" meant that she was constantly being judged by her white feminist counterparts and forced to relive painful experiences for the sake of possible interracial collaboration rather than systemic change.[54]

Scholar Vijay Agnew describes such episodes as tokenism, where racial minorities are accommodated within mainstream institutions in order to give the appearance of inclusion and to avert accusations of discrimination. Agnew contends that while racialized women have been integrated into many organizations, their identities and concerns have been largely left unacknowledged, leaving many to feel as if they were part of somebody's private zoo.[55] Hence, when Rubin was included in (white) women's organizations, she did not feel like an integral part of the movement but rather that she served as a storyteller of wrongs done to Black women. Rubin's constant reliving and retelling of issues of racism served as a form of oppression in which her experiences were an object of display rather than a catalyst to force structural changes within the organization.

This type of "inclusion" became characteristic of some mainstream women's organizations in the late-twentieth century and demonstrates what Indigenous studies scholar, writer, and poet, Dian Million describes as a resistance to the emotional content of felt knowledge.[56] Under these circumstances, the (re)telling of stories of pain and grief, often connected to the historical disenfranchisement of African-descended peoples in Canada, fetishized Black women's experiences as the racialized other within women's organizations. Sara Ahmed charts a similar experience in her discussion of the labour of pain and the creation of difference between bodies. Accordingly, the sociality of pain allows for someone to feel empathy without sharing the same experiences of pain. "In this way," Ahmed argues, "empathy sustains the very difference that it may seek to overcome: empathy remains a 'wishing feeling,' in which subjects 'feel' something other than what another feels in the very moment of imagining they could feel what another feels."[57] In a similar sense, Rubin's retelling of her pain helped others within women's organizations to express empathy while also upholding spaces of difference.

In her discussion of women's anti-racist organizing in the 1980s, sociologist Sarita Srivastava describes what she calls the "let's talk approach," which produced a controlled space for the expression and suppression of knowledge and feelings about racism. According to Srivastava, this approach allowed for social movement activists to discuss anti-racism without making organizational changes in response to these testimonies. Like the sentiments expressed by Rubin, Srivastava argues, "Typically, non-whites are expected to disclose stories of racism, while whites share their feelings of being shocked, affronted, racist or non-racist, and so on."[58] Essentially, when Rubin was asked to tell her story, mainstream women's organizations shifted the dialogue from institutional change to talking and listening and thus limiting the potential for material change. These experiences also indicate how forms of domination were manifested through control over the (re)production of emotion within the second wave.[59] Hence, even in moments of so-called inclusion, some Black female educators still felt disconnected from, and perhaps even exploited by, various parts of the women's movement.

Moreover, some Black women educators were not simply disconnected from women's union activity because of ideological differences, but they also felt largely unsupported by the FWTAO. Donna Lockette tried to be active in the union but concluded that the union did not support her. Her recollection hinted at racial discrimination as the reason for this:

> I remember when I was at B--[school], there was a guy who really gave me some real issues, and I felt the union supported him and not me. I talked to the union about it, and I wasn't happy with the union's response. I got more support from my superintendent than from the federation. It was not a nice

> situation. Then, after he and I had a conflict, he went after the principal, who was a visible minority woman. He was horrible to her. He was awful. He would get his little cronies together and have secret meetings. They tried to get her kicked out of the school. It was absolutely ridiculous. I remember when I didn't feel like I was being supported I told the union. I said, "You know that white dude who is harassing me. You are supporting him. Black woman, you are not supporting me. We have a problem here."[60]

Lockette's critique of the federation's lack of support in the early 1980s highlights the multiple ways Black women teachers experienced discrimination within schools. While she felt that the FWTAO was supposed to protect her from all forms of harassment in the workplace, the tribulations of the principal, who was also a racial minority woman, further reveal the limitations of the FWTAO's ability to create equitable spaces for all women. Lockette's intervention also served to challenge the status quo as presented by the teachers' union and instead offered "subversive observations" about Black women's treatment within institutional structures.[61] Lockette would eventually participate in volunteer activities for the Elementary Teachers' Federation of Ontario once she saw that the union was conducting more anti-racist initiatives.[62] Her reminiscences reveal that she believed the federation neither took her intersectional experiences as a priority nor seemed to know how to address them adequately. The fact that Lockette remembered that the union did not support her as a Black woman is important for identifying the ways in which she felt disconnected from the organization. In her final thoughts about the association, Lockette explained that

> even though their [FWTAO] main statement has to do with, you know, at the beginning of all their meetings, they have a statement where no one will be allowed to be discriminated against, I didn't find that to be the case ... It wasn't something that I got a lot of strength from.[63]

Lockette's very personal sentiments expressed the contradictory ways the federation addressed some Black women teachers. Lockette voiced clear feelings of disillusionment (and disappointment) towards the federation, an organization that, on the one hand, created policies and platforms where she felt supported through anti-racist initiatives but, on the other, ignored forms of discrimination by not addressing her experiences as a Black woman.

Lockette was not alone in describing these feelings. Cecily Tremaine, who worked in a number of Toronto schools in the 1970s and 1980s, also recalled cases where the union did not represent its Black and white teachers equally.[64] In discussing workplace conversations, Tremaine alluded to an underlying perception and feeling among some Black female educators that the FWTAO did not equally support its racialized members. This reflection was dramatically different from white members in FWTAO who remembered positive experiences through their federation activities. Rebecca Coulter contends that several of the (white) women teachers in her study gained pleasure from the social relationships, fellowship, and camaraderie they gained through the federation. According to Coulter, "as they looked back on their work with the federation, they expressed considerable satisfaction, both personal and professional, with that part of their teaching careers."[65] The fact that some educators expressed little regret about their participation in the FWTAO suggested that the organization better spoke to mainstream (white) women's goals for gender equity. These same women also articulated feelings of sadness and loss as the federation became incorporated into the Elementary Teachers' Federation of Ontario, in 1998. The loss of a separate women's organization, no matter how fraught, was a painful event for women who felt better connected to the federation.[66]

Nevertheless, for many Black women teachers, automatic membership did not mean automatic inclusion and representation. Black women's sense of belonging within organizations like the FWTAO influenced their need for mobilization around gender and racial inequalities. This emotion work led to the creation of, and Black women's participation in, separate organizations such as the Congress of Black Women of Canada. That organization spoke specifically to the needs and concerns of Black women through its focus on assisting Black women and their families and implementing various programs to support Black education, health, housing, and employment, as well as addressing concerns surrounding racism, sexism, and human rights.[67]

Conclusion

Black women educators were conscious of, and affected by, various social movements appearing in Canada in the second half of the twentieth century. Utilizing the language of human rights, mainstream women's organizations advocated for gender equality while silencing racialized women. In some instances, mainstream organizations such as the FWTAO offered avenues through which some Black women educators could gain promotions, obtain equal pay for their work, and forge alliances with their white counterparts. In participating in the FWTAO, some women felt that the collaboration of Black and white women based on gendered concerns remained integral to their careers as professional women. However, similar to other mainstream women's organizations at the time, the FWTAO privileged a homogenous category of womanhood that was often white and middle class.

This meant that Black women had to build their own set of emotional expressions, which included calling attention to their intersectional experiences, articulating ambivalence at cursory forms of inclusion within broader organizations, and pursuing community service that stood outside of women's organizational mandates. While white women used emotions of fear and, at times, anger to mobilize feminist activism, they often did so from within their own frameworks, reflecting the relational nature of power and emotion within these organizations. The reception of Gloria Steinem and Margaret Sloan at the FWTAO's dinner in 1972 speaks to a specific hierarchy of emotion that situated white female anger as the primary motive for feminist politicization and action. Conversely, Black educators experienced varying forms of pain and alienation as the federation often failed to prioritize discussions of race-based issues and tokenized the few minority members within its organization.

While the FWTAO embraced a variety of precepts of second-wave feminism, it inadvertently promoted one kind of feminism and created a place where race was an invisible category that often went unacknowledged and was not interrogated. As a result, some Black female educators were ambivalent about participating in mainstream women's organizations and disclosed that they rarely actively participated in women teachers' unions. Their stories, then, reflected experiences of feminism and difference. Subsequently, while the FWTAO became branded as feminist, the various Black women's groups like the Congress of Black Women of Canada were understood as different, and separate, from the mainstream women's movement. Black women teachers dealt with these silences by developing their own set of emotional scripts in response to broader discourses within the women's movement.

Notes

1 All interviewees have been provided with pseudonyms. Donna Lockette, interview with author (audio recording), Windsor, ON, August 20, 2011.

2 As a result of the Teaching Profession Act of 1944, membership in a teaching federation was compulsory and the payment of federation dues was mandatory. All teachers in Ontario belonged to one of five teachers' associations, and the Federation of Women Teachers' Associations of Ontario (FWTAO) represented all female

elementary teachers employed by a public board in the province. Mario Spagnuolo and Larry A. Glassford, "Feminism in Transition: The Margaret Tomen Membership Case and the Formation of the Elementary Teachers' Federation of Ontario," *Historical Studies in Education*, 20 (2008): 59.

3 Sara Ahmed, *The Cultural Politics of Emotion* (New York: Routledge, 2004); Claudia Garcia-Rojas, "(Un)Disciplined Futures: Women of Color Feminism as a Disruptive to White Affect Studies," *Journal of Lesbian Studies*, 21, 3 (2017): 254–71.

4 Barbara H. Rosenwein, "Worrying about Emotions in History," *American Historical Review* 107, 3 (2002): 842, 844.

5 Susan J. Matt, "Current Emotion Research in History: Or, Doing History from the Inside Out," *Emotion Review* 3, 1 (2011): 119.

6 Rebecca Coulter argues that FWTAO primarily focused its energy on promoting opportunities for women in leadership positions and on developing materials to combat sex-role stereotyping in Ontario classrooms. She contends that liberal feminism, with some elements of radical/cultural feminism, was strongly promoted within the organization. Coulter explains that teacher federations like FWTAO provided the platform on which teachers would participate in a gender-equity agenda. Rebecca Prigert Coulter, "Gender Equity and Schooling: Linking Research and Policy," *Canadian Journal of Education* 21, 4 (1996): 437.

7 Ahmed, *Cultural Politics of Emotion*, 8.

8 While many women were still working as secretaries, nurses, clerks, and sales personnel, the high number of women in the education sector made it ripe for women's union participation and increased political action. In fact, between 1965 and 1975 the number of women in unions had increased by 144 percent allowing for the emergence of a more robust organizational structure to address various women's issues with increasing force. See Wendy Robbins, Meg Luxton, Margrit Eichler and Francine Descarries, eds., *Minds of Our Own: Inventing Feminist Scholarship and Women's Studies in Canada and Quebec, 1966–76* (Waterloo, ON: Wilfrid Laurier University Press, 2008), 11.

9 Spagnuolo and Glassford, "Feminism in Transition: The Margaret Tomen Membership Case," 59

10 Mary Labatt, *Always a Journey: A History of the Federation of Women Teachers' Associations of Ontario, 1918–1993* (Toronto: Federation of Women Teachers' Associations of Ontario, 1993), 6, quoted in Spagnuolo and Glassford, "Feminism in Transition: The Margaret Tomen Membership Case," 58.

11 Labatt, *Always a Journey*, 129.

12 Gail Cuthbert Brandt, Naomi Black, Paula Bourne, and Magda Fahrni, eds., *Canadian Women: A History* (Toronto: Harcourt Brace Jovanovich, 1988), 530.

13 See Shirley Stokes, *The Shortest Shadow: A Descriptive Study of the Members of the Federation of Women Teachers' Associations of Ontario* (Toronto: Federation of Women Teachers' Associations of Ontario, 1969), 80; and Leone Kirkwood, "Study Finds Ontario's Women Teachers Are Mostly WASCs (White, Anglo-Saxon and Canadian-Born)," *Globe and Mail*, August 13, 1969. In 1972, the Planning and Policy Analysis Unit of the Ontario Department of Education funded a study examining the characteristics of Ontario elementary school teachers in their schools.

Acknowledging that there was no single database detailing the entire elementary teacher force in the province, the unit collected data from various studies, records, and reports and discovered that most public elementary school teachers were white, Canadian, and Protestant. It reported that most separate school teachers were white, Canadian, and Catholic. More specifically, the report found that in the 1967–68 year, "87% of members of the Federation of Women Teachers' Associations of Ontario were of the Protestant faith and less than 5% came from countries other than Canada, the United States or the United Kingdom." Cicely Watson, Saeed Quazi, and Russ Jones, *The Elementary Teacher: A Study on the Characteristics and Supply/Demand Relations of Ontario Teachers*, Department of Educational Planning, Ontario Institute for Studies in Education (Toronto: Institute for Studies in Education, 1972), 5.

14 Dolana Mogadime, "Racial Differential Experiences of Employment Equity for Women Teachers: One Teacher's Narrative of Resistance and Struggle," *Journal of Black Studies* 39, 1 (2008): 90. In 1992, the *Stephen Lewis Report on Race Relations* found that there was a strong presence of anti-Black racism in Canadian institutions and called for a Cabinet Committee on Race Relations to meet with visible minority communities to implement system-wide racially inclusive policies. In the education sector, the government issued a policy directive titled, "Development and Implementation of School Board Policies on Anti-racism and Ethnocultural Equity," which required school boards to develop race relations policies and outlined ways to implement these policies. This led to an overarching move towards anti-racism initiatives throughout Ontario schools. George J. Sefa Dei, "Challenges for Anti-racist Educators in Ontario Today," *Orbit* 33, 3 (2003): 3. Also see Roxana Ng, Patricia Anne Staton, and Joyce Scane, eds., *Anti-racism, Feminism, and Critical Approaches to Education* (Connecticut: Bergin and Garvey, 1995).

15 Dolana Mogadime, "Racial Differential Experiences of Employment Equity for Women Teachers," 93.

16 It is difficult to find disaggregated data based on race and gender in school board records prior to 1980. On the grounds that so few sources exist documenting the number of visible minority educators on the basis of gender during this study period, I rely on contemporary reports, teachers' college yearbooks, and oral histories to highlight the racialized and gendered experiences of Black women teachers in the late-twentieth century. For example, in a larger national study examining the demographic characteristics of teachers in Canada, Jean-Guy Blais and Soundiata Diene Mansa Ouedraogo collected data between 1991 and 2001 and discovered that in Ontario in 1991, only 8 percent of the teaching population identified as visible minorities. By 2001, this number rose to 10 percent. Of the visible minority teacher population numbers collected for all of Canada, Blais and Ouedraogo found that 53 percent of these educators were female, and 43 percent were male visible minority educators in both 1991 and 2001. While Blais and Ouedraogo's data on racial minority educators stands largely outside of the historical time period for this study, they offer a glimpse into the number of minority educators in the province and also the imbalance of statistical reporting that categorized visible minorities and gender as separate and distinct points of analyses.

17 Malinda S. Smith adopts Sara Ahmed use of the term "other Others" to reveal everyday relationships of power and the process of privileging gender equality as experienced by white women. Malinda S. Smith, "Gender, Whiteness and the 'Other Others' in the Academy," in *States of Race: Critical Race Feminism for the 21st Century*, ed. Sherene Razack, Malinda Smith, and Sunera Thobani (Toronto: Between the Lines, 2010), 37.
18 Jane Gaskell and Sandra Taylor, "The Women's Movement and Canadian and Australian Education: From Liberation and Sexism to Boys and Social Justice," *Gender and Education* 15, 2 (2003): 6.
19 Edward Lynas, "The Night Women's Lib Came to Dinner," *Educational Courier* 43, 1 (1972): 18.
20 Lynas, "The Night Women's Lib Came to Dinner," 19.
21 Lynas, "The Night Women's Lib Came to Dinner," 19.
22 The use of "Black bodies" borrows from the work of geographer Katherine McKittrick, who situates the ways in which Black communities and spaces are often unseen and erased in the Canadian nation. According to McKittrick, Black people, their bodies, and their histories have been disavowed through a series of processes that characterize them as both un-Canadian and invisible. Using examples that include the *Code Noir* in eighteenth century New France, McKittrick outlines the ways Black bodies were legally marked as objects on the Canadian landscape. This chapter also considers the ways Black people, and their bodies, are used in specific moments throughout Canadian history to mark spaces of difference, making them both hypervisible and invisible within Canadian institutions. Katherine McKittrick, *Demonic Grounds: Black Women and the Cartographies of Struggle* (Minneapolis: University of Minnesota Press, 2006).
23 Lynas, "The Night Women's Lib Came to Dinner," 19.
24 It is important to note that Edward Lynas's account also reveals some sexism in his reporting, specifically his tendency to describe the physical attractiveness of speakers and the implicit racist undertones in his discussion of Sloan's "vernacular phrases." In addition, Lynas's report does not indicate if Steinem and Sloan were paid for their participation in the FWTAO dinner. Edward Lynas, "The Night Women's Lib Came to Dinner," 19.
25 Rebecca Priegert Coulter, "'Looking after Ourselves': Women Elementary Teachers and Their Federation," *Oral History Forum/Forum d'histoire orale* 24 (2004): 75.
26 Coulter, "'Looking after Ourselves,'" 76.
27 Coulter, "'Looking after Ourselves,'" 76.
28 Ahmed, *Cultural Politics of Emotion*, 3.
29 Ahmed, *Cultural Politics of Emotion*, 171, 174.
30 Ahmed, *Cultural Politics of Emotion*, 178.
31 An Affirmative Action memo submitted by the FWTAO in 1980 described the stark reality of gender discrimination in the education sector. FWTAO members cited the Ministry of Education 1978–1979 employment statistics, which reported that 3,262 males were employed as principals in the public and Roman Catholic elementary schools, while only 469 women were employed as principals that year. At the high school level, the differences were even greater; that year saw 560 male principals and

only 17 female principals throughout Ontario schools. *Teachers in Ontario by Employment Status, Sex and Type of Duty, 1978–1979,* from Table 20-20.01, Ministry of Education, Statistics Department, in Affirmative Action Memo, September 10, 1980, FWTAO.

32 R.D. Gidney, *From Hope to Harris: The Reshaping of Ontario's Schools* (Toronto: University of Toronto Press, 2002), 162.

33 Alison Taylor, "Employment Equity for Women: Toward a Revolution from the Ground Up," in *Women and Leadership in Canadian Education,* ed. Cecilia Reynolds and Beth Young (Calgary, AB: Detselig, 1995), 83.

34 See Cecilia Reynolds, "In the Right Place at the Right Time: Rules of Control and Woman's Place in Ontario Schools, 1940–1980," *Canadian Journal of Education* 20, 2 (1995): 141; Hanne B. Mawhinney, "Institutionalizing Women's Voices, Not Their Echoes, through Feminist Policy Analysis of Difference," in *Feminist Critical Policy Analysis I: A Perspective from Primary and Secondary Schooling,* ed. Catherine Marshall (London: Falmer, 1997), 224.

35 Marcia Lambert, interview with author (audio recording), Markham, ON, April 15, 2011.

36 Lambert, interview.

37 Although Lambert did not remember Black men being actively unsupportive at the time, she also made it clear that they were not particularly supportive of women's advocacy, alluding to possible tensions based on gender among Black educators. (Lambert, interview).

38 Lambert, interview.

39 Ahmed, *Cultural Politics of Emotion,* 69.

40 Aimee Carrillo Rowe and Francesca T. Royster, "Loving Transgressions: Queer of Color Bodies, Affective Ties, Transformative Community," *Journal of Lesbian Studies* 21, 3 (2017): 243.

41 Tamara Mogrant, interview with author (audio recording), Toronto, ON, July 26, 2011.

42 Deborah B. Gould, *Moving Politics: Emotion and ACT UP's Fight against AIDS* (Chicago: University of Chicago Press, 2009), 28.

43 In her work on African American life and religious expressiveness, Kimberly Philips argues that African American spiritual music reflected the emotional and participatory nature of working-class men and women's everyday lives and experiences. According to Philips, the expressive nature of gospel music also revealed "an emotional culture and a set of values that African American workers crafted from themselves, sometimes in oppositional settings." Kimberly Philips, "'Stand by Me': Sacred Quartet Music and Emotionology of African American Audiences, 1900–1930," in *An Emotional History of the United States,* ed. Peter Stearns and Jan Lewis (New York: New York University Press, 1998), 243.

44 See Lydia Foster, "Unemployed Teachers," *Globe and Mail,* September 8, 1970; "National Congress Held in Toronto: Women's Lib Aids Black Struggle, NDPer Says," *Globe and Mail,* April 9, 1973; Lotta Dempsy, "First Congress of Black Women Coming in April," *Toronto Star,* January 9, 1973.

45 Mary Labatt, *Always a Journey,* 169.

46 Paul R. Carr, "'Transforming the Institution, or Institutionalizing the Transformation?': Anti-Racism and Equity in Education in Toronto," *McGill Journal of Education* 34, 1 (1999): 59–61.
47 Paul R. Carr and Thomas R. Klassen, "Different Perceptions of Race in Education: Racial Minority and White Teachers," *Canadian Journal of Education* 22, 1 (1997): 71.
48 Lawrence Hill, *Women of Vision: The Story of the Canadian Negro Women's Association* (Toronto: Umbrella Press, 1996), 22.
49 Marcia Wharton-Zaretsky, "Foremothers of Black Women's Community Organizing in Toronto," *Atlantis* 24, 2 (2000): 68.
50 Wharton-Zaretsky, "Foremothers of Black Women's Community Organizing in Toronto," 69.
51 Enid Rubin, interview with author (audio recording), Toronto, ON, August 5, 2011.
52 See Cuthbert Brant, Black, Bourne, and Fahrni, *Canadian Women: A History*, 532–45; and Roberta Hamilton, *Gendering the Vertical Mosaic: Feminist Perspectives on Canadian Society*, 2nd ed. (Toronto: Pearson Prentice Hall, 2005), 94–114.
53 Calliste and Dei, *Anti-racist Feminism: Critical Race and Gender Studies*, 21.
54 Patricia Hill Collins, "Learning from Outsider Within: The Sociologist Significance of Black Feminist Thought," *Social Problems* 33, 6 (1986): 14–32.
55 Vijay Agnew, *Resisting Discrimination: Women from Asia, Africa, and the Caribbean and the Women's Movement in Canada* (Toronto: University of Toronto Press, 1996), 76.
56 Dian Million, "Felt Theory: An Indigenous Feminist Approach to Affect and History," *Wicazo Sa Review*, 24, 2 (2009): 58.
57 Ahmed, *Cultural Politics of Emotion*, 30.
58 Sarita Srivastava, "Tears, Fears and Careers: Anti-racism and Emotion in Social Movement Organizations," *Canadian Journal of Sociology* 31, 1, (2006): 66.
59 Gould, *Moving Politics: Emotion and ACT UP's Fight*, 40.
60 Lockette, interview.
61 Gould, *Moving Politics: Emotion and ACT UP's Fight*, 41.
62 In 1996, a court decision led to the merger of the FWTAO and the Ontario Public School Teachers' Federation, which represented male teachers. In 1998, the newly formed Elementary Teachers' Federation of Ontario was created to represent male and female teachers in Ontario. Spagnuolo and Glassford, "Feminism in Transition: The Margaret Tomen Membership Case," 56.
63 Lockette, interview with author.
64 Cecily Tremaine, interview with author, May 9, 2011.
65 Coulter, "'Looking after Ourselves,'" 72.
66 Coulter, "'Looking after Ourselves,'" 82.
67 Hill, *Women of Vision*.

11

"Briser le mur du silence" Emotions, Gender, and the 1981 Women Journalists' Conference in Quebec

JOSETTE BRUN, LAURIE LAPLANCHE, AND SOPHIE DOUCET

> October 23, 1981 ... We were excited, nervous, even anxious. This conference, which we'd been talking about endlessly since January, which we'd prepared to the best of our abilities – so, this conference was starting. From the first minutes on Friday evening, we were swamped, overwhelmed, amazed. But where had all these hundreds and hundreds of women, waiting patiently in front of the registration office, come from? And then, it was a huge whirlwind. "The event" took place. "The event" was over.[1]

This reflection by Raymonde Provencher, president of the Fédération professionnelle des journalistes du Québec (FPJQ), bespeaks the emotion-filled climate that ruled at a notable moment in the history of women journalists in Quebec: the conference called Les femmes et l'information, which took place during the federation's annual congress in Montreal, October 23–25, 1981.[2] Its objective was to "briser le mur du silence" (break the wall of silence) surrounding sexual discrimination in the profession and the marginalization of women in journalistic content.[3] After a series of speeches, testimonials, and workshops, the conference ended with a plenary session aimed at formulating recommendations for improving the situation of women journalists and the media coverage of current events affecting women.[4]

The conference was an unprecedented event in the history of women journalists in Quebec. Since they had begun to enter the profession and women's media were created (two interrelated phenomena facilitated by the transition to newspapers and the creation of specialized magazines at the turn of the twentieth century), women had been discriminated against in the trade, which was dominated by men.[5] Although women journalists formed associations and protested against their working conditions, notably during their union struggles, their actions have not been widely documented by historians and cannot be compared to the major strikes undertaken by female workers, teachers, and nurses in Quebec in the 1930s, 1940s, and 1960s.[6] Nevertheless, workplaces for journalists, including those at Société Radio-Canada, were affected by feminist demands catalyzed by Royal Commission on the Status of Women (also known as the Bird Commission) established in 1967.[7] These contestations also reflected the second-wave feminist movement in the United States, one of whose main preoccupations in the early 1970s was fair representation of women in the media.[8] In 1977, a group of women journalists in Milan held a conference called Donna e informazione (Woman and information) to denounce sexual discrimination; that same year, in Montreal, two women members of the FPJQ produced a report proposing a series of measures intended to establish a fair balance between the sexes in the profession.[9] It was four years later, in October 1981, that the women's committee of the FPJQ held the conference that we write about in this chapter. Les femmes et l'information was attended by "a record audience of eight hundred people," most of them women journalists, feminist activists, and female news consumers.[10]

In this chapter, we bring to light the emotions mobilized by the women's committee of the FPJQ in its report on the conference, *Thérèse, Janette, Hélène et les autres ou ... la face cachée de l'information*, published in 1982.[11] Our goal is to observe how these emotions contributed to the contestation of gendered dynamics in the wake of the second-wave feminist mobilizations in North America over the two preceding decades.[12] Using the concept of gender as a tool for feminist analysis, we analyze the social process of construction and reassessment of the "hierarchical binary categorization of the sexes" and the values associated with femininity and masculinity, usually in favour of the latter.[13] Our approach follows that used by social psychology researchers on gender and emotions, who attempt to understand how beliefs about emotions – the language of, and social conventions around, them – "inscribe and reinscribe gender boundaries."[14] In this chapter, therefore, we consider emotions not only as perceptions or descriptions of a lived experience, but also as discourses and actions that contribute – or not – to gendered dynamics in different ways. Notwithstanding the neurological bases of emotions, we approach them from a historical perspective, as the consensus emerging from historiography shows that they "are shaped, repressed, expressed differently from place to place and era to era" – that is, they are anchored in culture.[15] We draw two main observations from our corpus. First, the 1981 conference represented a privileged moment of exchange among women, which we see as related to the consciousness-raising movement popular among feminists at the time and to the notion of "emotional refuge."[16] Second, the conference exposed a painful entangling of women's identities as journalists and as feminists, illustrating the coexistence of, and tensions among, different "emotional communities" in a given culture.[17] These observations enable us to regard emotion as a site of historically situated power struggles around the meaning to impart to femininity and masculinity.[18]

Defying Gender

In its report on the conference, the women's committee of the FPJQ emphasized the organizers' decision to solicit testimonials from women journalists "to break through the anxiety that each thinks she is alone in feeling."[19] Indeed, although men were not banned from the conference, their presence was not explicitly sought, and they did not attend in large numbers.[20] This process was similar to the approach taken at the time by the feminist movement, whose objective was to make women aware of their specific condition: "Strongly influenced by the 'consciousness raising' groups in the late 1960s, the feminist intervention advocated an approach based on sharing personal and collective experiences in order to alleviate feelings of guilt, collectivize problems, and develop a political awareness likely to bring out new solidarities."[21] Consciousness-raising, which originated in the United States, has also been documented in Quebec.[22] It is associated with the radical feminist current behind the women's liberation movement, whose powerful slogan, "The personal is political," expressed the porous nature of the boundaries between the public and private spheres. In fact, it was during a consciousness-raising meeting – at which emotions regarding the oppression of women served as catalysts for political action – that the New York Radical Feminists and Media Women planned to occupy the offices of the *Ladies' Home Journal* in 1970, to denounce the professional inequalities and stereotypes rampant at the successful women's magazine.[23]

In the part of the report that we focus on in our analysis, emotion similarly served as a motivating force for describing this important moment of sharing that led to raising awareness of a common condition, steeped in injustice, among the women journalists present, followed by the denunciation of those inequalities and thus to the subversion of gendered relations. Some had not necessarily realized that they were discriminated against as women journalists before they were invited to speak at the congress. Journalist Thérèse Parisien was one of them:

> When Gisèle asked me to come and talk about my experience, she asked me how things were going for me in the profession. I answered, "It's going very well, there isn't really any problem." And then the bugs came out, things that were inside me, and I want to tell you about them today so I can exorcise them. This exorcism seems quite painful, though; it's hard to talk about the difficult things you've experienced.[24]

It was painful, too, for their colleagues to listen to these testimonials, as the report stated:

> All the women who attended this morning's session will remember it forever as a moment of intense and shared communication. Everyone's throat was tight, their hands moist; some wept as they heard their sisters, their friends, implacably engage in this agonizing game of truth-telling. The stories of ruined careers, wasted talents, accumulated dissatisfactions, repressed creativity, and fruitless struggles all too often were nothing to rejoice over. [This exercise consequently] revived a rage in the hearts [of the women journalists present] that moved mountains or [led to] sad contemplation of the gaping chasm of their powerlessness. But becoming aware of the extent of one's ghetto means starting to extricate oneself, to look for the exit, or to invent it.[25]

This, in fact, is the ultimate goal of consciousness-raising: to take women from self-discovery to collective awareness, from self-realization to social change.[26]

The report also mobilized emotion to describe the difficulties involved in the very process of becoming aware: "When we asked women journalists to come and speak publicly, to talk about themselves and what they've gone through, to tell us what they've personally experienced in this profession and not give a technical presentation, they were scared; they were all scared," remembered the conference organizer, journalist Gisèle Tremblay.[27] But that did not matter: a number of journalists, she continued, "stepped up to the challenge to talk, to explain, to criticize, to judge, to make their ideas count ... Most of them were not able to perfectly control the trembling voice, breathlessness, and nervousness that always accompany confessions, admissions, painful memories."[28] The report thus recognized the courage of the women who, in the space made for exchanges on the margins of the FPJQ's dominant structures, reflected on discrimination against women in the profession and in journalistic information. In the field of history of emotions, the notion of emotional refuge defines places where a group can escape the constraints of the dominant affective standards – in this case, gendered professional norms.[29] According to the testimonials gathered in the report, the injustices attached to these norms were related to a lack of acceptance of women's bodies, of the experience of motherhood, and of journalistic sectors and practices connoted as feminine, creating feelings of devaluation, frustration, marginalization, and alienation.

Feeling Devalued

In her testimonial, Lizette Gervais, who worked as a radio announcer at Radio-Canada before co-hosting *Femme d'aujourd'hui* for its first season, in 1965–66, deplored the lack of recognition of women's skills in the field, which created a sense of insecurity among women journalists. Despite her strong interest in public affairs, she explained, she was never allowed to cover that field, even though she had salaried and volunteer work experience in union activism, health, and human rights, including rights of women, children, detainees, and immigrants: "I told myself that whole time (twenty years), I had a thorough knowledge of public affairs issues, but the way things are in my profession I can't work on those subjects ... I ended up doubting my skill, devaluing myself, and finally feeling very, very, very insecure."[30] Such lack of recognition was even more flagrant for Thérèse Parisien, a journalist at a regional weekly, who was regularly called on to fill in for her boss during his vacations. Although she believed that she was a competent replacement, Parisien described the day when her boss, suffering from a serious illness, summoned her to his bedside and asked her to find a man to replace him. She said that she left, devastated, with the scrap of paper on which he had scribbled the name of a male journalist. "I was so shocked, so hurt inside, I was crying. I said to myself, 'I've worked at the paper for three years, and the boss is away often, and suddenly it takes a man.' I was disappointed. I never called him, he never came, and the newspaper kept getting published."[31]

The illusion that women had the same opportunities as men in the profession was shattered by the striking testimonial of Armande Saint-Jean, a well-known journalist in the prestigious public affairs department at Radio-Canada and the former president of the FPJQ (1977–78). During the Saturday morning session devoted to testimonials, Saint-Jean denounced the smokescreen thrown up by the integration of some women journalists into spheres that were strongholds of male journalistic power:

> I learned to like competition. I even became what was jokingly called "one of the guys." I had a good job, a high salary, a good reputation, and I liked that. I was very happy with it. Later, I realized I was living proof that there wasn't supposed to be discrimination against women in the news, because I was there. I was a token woman in the strictest sense of the word, and I absolutely applied the motto of all token women: "When you want to, you can."[32]

The report clearly revealed that women were suffering from lack of recognition of their journalism skills and exclusion from positions of power – especially those who were mothers, who experienced a deep sense of guilt.

A Sense of Guilt

It is notable that for many women who went to the conference, individual solutions allowing for the advancement of women in journalism were insufficient due not only to the valorization of norms associated with masculinity but also to the devaluation of norms associated with femininity. As the report showed, women journalists who became mothers were "punished" because they were guilty of infringing on professional standards, once again illustrating how difficult it was for women's bodies to be accepted in the profession.[33] A number of testimonials denounced this phenomenon by mobilizing emotion. Saint-Jean lifted the veil on the professional denigration that women suffered when they committed the journalistic "female sin" of "making a baby." "I think what hurt me most of all was the contrast between what I had experienced before, when I was given a hand and adored, and the treatment I received [once I became a mother]," she recounted. She described the consequences of her abrupt "fall from grace": she was asked to resign, on the pretext of a unilateral breach of contract, which left her without an income during the seven months that she was bedridden for medical reasons related to her pregnancy; the promised rehiring was made to a hierarchically inferior position with no prestige – and a lower salary.[34] This discriminatory, guilt-inducing process would require a "gender performance" from female journalists – a practice, repeated daily, the function of which was to make their reality as mothers invisible as they grappled with a combination of professional and domestic tasks (housework generally being a woman's responsibility).[35] This gives a good illustration of the political dimensions of women's experience in the private sphere. Many women journalists, including Gervais, described playing the role of superwoman for this purpose:

> For television, it was a bit more difficult because you had to arrive and look relaxed, have your makeup on, etc., after having solved the problems of school for the children, problems of food for the day, after having had a long discussion with one who wasn't feeling well, etc. ... If I talked about the profession or about me on a program ... someone always asked me, And so, how do you reconcile your professional work and your private life? And so I'd say, But it all takes care of itself, don't you know, in the end, you know, you just have to set priorities, and then blah, blah, blah ... It's not true that it all takes care of itself, it's done with I don't know how many acrobatics to try to please everyone.[36]

To conceal their reality as mothers, some journalists forced themselves to perform certain professional rituals connoting masculinity.[37] For instance, in her testimonial, freelance journalist Carmel Dumas disclosed that she felt propelled by a sense of professional guilt following her return from maternity leave and undertook to join her male colleagues for the regular after-work bar crawl. "So, I went back on the job market, which meant I acted as if I didn't have children. I went back and, I have to say, I went to the bars (to be a female freelance journalist, you had to go to bars), and slowly people forgot I had children."[38] The guilt was therefore doubled for women who were navigating between two apparently irreconcilable worlds. Hélène Lévesque, a political journalist in the press gallery in Quebec City, which she called a "boys' club," talked about

> the damned constant sense of guilt, which means that if you have to cover the budget speech and your kid caught the measles that morning, you couldn't say, I won't be there, because they can't replace you on short notice.

> You're the one who knows the issues, so your presence is essential. You go, always telling yourself, I'm a bad mother. So, you feel guilty and you're in an environment where they're expecting you to make mistakes. There are also the reactions from your own circle about this job that's so untraditional. They don't understand why you care about it so much. My little boy ... said to me, "You're not a real mother." "Why aren't I a real mother?" He answered, "A real mother isn't a journalist."[39]

Emotion as Critique of Journalistic Objectivity

The report also highlighted the devaluing of journalistic sectors and practices connoted as feminine, symptomatic of the exclusion of women from generalist news. At the turn of the twentieth century, information journalism, closely linked to the upheavals in North American society caused by growing industrialization, urbanization, and proletarianization, gave rise to a gendered diversification and separation of news content and to a focus on local events. This new journalism also set certain rules for the profession over the century; one of these was objectivity, according to which reporters are detached from the news that they produce, as news is related to facts rather than opinions or, even less, emotions.[40] The report offered a sustained critique of objective news, with its disembodied, dehumanized facts, that was imposed in a profession connoted by masculinity in the twentieth century, modelling female ghettos in journalism and muzzling news concerning women by marginalizing the journalists who covered it. The socio-professional opposition between objectivity, on the one hand, and emotion and subjectivity, on the other hand, was strongly challenged, as were the masculine and feminine connotations, respectively, that were associated with them in a hierarchical relationship. That is the point made in the report's introduction, written by Tremblay:

> According to the sexual division of roles that is still in force in our society, women, even when they work outside the home, remain devoted in a way to affective tasks, whereas men devote themselves to production activities and the responsibilities of power, in which they are forced to repress their emotions ... If objectivity in the news is often understood as the suppression of all emotion, it is in large part because men, who still collectively dominate the profession, have very naturally interpreted the notion of objectivity in the sense of repression of emotions, seen as a "masculine" value. Even for them, this is a contradiction, because to understand what's

> going on and report it as a journalist, one must have both sensitivity and intelligence. Sensitivity is one of our antennae on the world. Imagine now what a contradiction it is for women: women journalists are asked to be sensitive, affectionate, full of sympathy and compassion morning, noon – if they return home – evening, and night; then, during the workday, they are asked to be completely emotionless to comply with this false notion of objectivity.[41]

Keynote speaker Lise Payette, former radio and television host at Radio-Canada and ex-minister of Status of Women in the Quebec government, had a similar point of view. She maintained that women journalists "must abandon the sacrosanct objectivity, this myth – yes, I say, this tenacious myth – kept alive by men to define the male slant of the news."[42]

Although marginal, some passages in the report revealed how difficult it would be to revalorize women and the practices associated with them without rearticulating gendered assignments. Payette, for example, adopted an essentialist point of view that seemed to attribute the perceived differences between the sexes to biology when she stated "that a woman journalist sees realities and events differently from a male journalist, and [she] must therefore report on these realities and events differently from her male colleague." She felt that their socialization as women journalists distanced them from this feminine nature "because our profession has led us into worlds composed mainly of men, and to practise our profession we have had to learn the ABCs of the game of men who practise the same profession."[43] These words, which positively connoted the presence of women and their practices in news, nevertheless presumed a shared sensitivity exclusive to women, thus reinforcing age-old social norms and prejudices.[44] A similar idea was conveyed, though more subtly, in an article in the report titled, "Comment faire un journal qui touche les gens," by the editor-in-chief of the *Miami News*, Gloria Brown-Anderson, who described "a different conception of journalism and a different way to make a newspaper."[45] Brown-Anderson considered it "very important that all journalists, especially women journalists, convey through their profession the interest that generations have paid to the family, in order to bring human beings closer together."[46] She seemed to conceive the socialization of women as an absolute and unfailing process that affected them all in the same way and that impelled them to become "more [interested] in readers" and want to "help them live better. It's a different way of thinking. I don't believe that it's exclusive to [women]. A few men in the profession share my conception, but it is more difficult for them to achieve it, whereas it's natural for me."[47] In fact, what might seem at first glance to arise from female sensitivity, free choice, or women's natural preference for "soft news" was related instead to gendered professional dynamics. In France in the late-twentieth century, for example, there were as many men beginning in the profession or working freelance – and therefore having a precarious status – as women writing about subjects connoted as feminine.[48] In any case, the idea that women had an inherently different way of doing journalism was not further defended in the report, whose editors were no doubt aware of the perverse effects of such a generalization on their recognition in a profession characterized by gendered assignments and the overvaluing of the masculine.[49]

Feeling Marginalized

The report supported this hypothesis by accentuating, through the reproduction of testimonials, the sense of being devalued and the frustration expressed by women journalists with regard to the discrediting of the spaces generally relegated to them in the media – those associated with female content.[50] The surprise expressed by feminist columnist, playwright, and television host Janette Bertrand with regard to the breach to this separation and hierarchy, which had been going on since the early twentieth century, was eloquent. "I'm so astonished to be here," said Bertrand, who, as the women's advice columnist at *Le Petit Journal* from 1958 to 1971, had addressed what were, at the time, highly taboo questions mainly affecting women such as incest and rape.[51] "I'm very impressed, and very hung up too, because it's the first time someone has considered me a journalist."[52] She voiced her exasperation with the marginalization of the so-called women's programs in which most women on radio and television worked, which were scheduled at less desirable times – and rarely in the evening during prime time.[53] As host of *Janette veut savoir*, a program on the Quebec Télé-Métropole network, Bertrand was continuing her journalistic work of raising awareness about issues affecting women and wanted "the time of [her] program to change, but it was still considered (even though there had been progress among men) a talk show about women's affairs," intended to be broadcast in the afternoon for an audience of homemakers.[54]

The feeling of marginalization was also mobilized in the report to describe the situation of women working in the feminine-connoted "arts and letters, education" sections of newsrooms or in general newsrooms, to which most women journalists were constantly assigned during the second half of the twentieth century. According to journalist Marie-Agnès Tellier, these journalists "sometimes don't feel like they're taken seriously ... Even if there's something big in a women's sector, it's really hard to get headlines. And because of this, some women feel doubly marginalized, especially given certain attitudes ... at the desk."[55] Marginalization took different forms, all of them equally devaluing for these women. In the early 1980s, women journalists were in the majority among contract and temporary workers, placing the journalists, some with children, in the situation of being in a constant struggle to earn a living. As Louiselle Lévesque, journalist in the Radio-Canada newsroom in Rimouski, put it,

> I don't think I'm a paranoid person, but I think that women stay in a temporary status longer than men. When I was hired, I was the only woman; one other woman, also temporary, was added. I've been temporary for two years. They say there's no discrimination in unionized workplaces. I don't agree. There's lots of discrimination; we don't have access to permanent status. The seven men in the newsroom are all permanent. It's just by chance, they say.[56]

Carmel Dumas, a freelance journalist, reporter, interviewer, researcher, host, and scriptwriter at the *Montreal Star*, Radio-Canada, and Radio-Québec, described how difficult the situation was:

> Working freelance is hell. You work all the time because, if you stop once because you're burned out, you say to yourself they won't hire you again. So, you take everything, you do sixteen jobs at once, you let yourself be – I don't like the word – "exploited" (even though it's true). And the fact remains that the psychological and financial insecurity is well recognized.[57]

The discrediting of things connoted feminine also affected news about the "status of women" and those who covered it, the report noted. Women journalists working in situations emblematic of information – prestigious newsrooms – expressed the feeling that they had to repress perspectives that would reveal the mechanics and the consequences of belittling women in different social sectors so that they would not impede their advancement in the profession that they loved. Hélène Lévesque described this gendered process:

> When you're the least bit career-oriented, you're very aware that "stories about ... women" won't make the headlines. And you know very well that if your news is rarely on the front page you'll have a low rating on the political

> journalism market. If you want to have a good career, you watch yourself. So, there comes a time when a sort of automatic self-censorship sets in, you know what has to be talked about and in what terms you have to talk about it. I experienced it, because at a given moment you get bored with being the professional nag or the professional feminist.[58]

Armande Saint-Jean described her career path, illustrating the process of marginalization that began in her professional life when she started to produce programs on issues affecting women:

> I made programs to try to find out what other women experienced, what other women thought, what other women wanted. And it was an extremely important period in my career. But in the end, at the same time, a strange thing was happening: the more I specialized in this marginal part of the news ... the more I advanced in it, the more my professional situation deteriorated. My prestige dropped. The recognition that I was gaining from my colleagues for the importance of my work fell to almost zero and my working conditions were extremely difficult.[59]

Covering feminist news remained difficult, even in the left-wing media familiar to French journalist Martine Storti, formerly a journalist at the newspaper *Libération,* where she had hoped "to produce a sort of articulation of the political and the professional, to create an activist journalism by wagering that, at a daily newspaper open to all innovations and every adventure, it would be possible to highlight the importance of the feminist movement – all the demands raised by women, all the critiques that they were making of patriarchal society."[60] Although she felt there was a slightly wider margin of manoeuvre at *Libération* than elsewhere, she said that she was quickly confronted with resistance by its majority-male editorial board, notably on the question of rape: "Articles that weren't published for 'lack of space,' articles delayed, and ultimately out of date, thrown in the wastepaper basket, articles that, to be published, had to be rewritten ... until the final confrontation." This, she said, was how "male journalists solved, through the feminist journalists that they had at hand, the problems that they might encounter with the women's movement as a whole."[61] Exhausted by this war of attrition, she founded a magazine, *Histoire d'Elles,* "in which one could say everything that had to be said concerning women and their view of the world," and later was a reporter at *F magazine,* a French commercial publication open to coverage of these issues.[62]

Emotional Communities in Tension

The report underscored the emergence of a sense of sisterhood among women journalists in the process of raising awareness and denouncing injustices against them. It also described how a feeling of ambivalence threaded its way through this emotional community like a grain of sand in the gears, uncovering a fracture regarding the identity of woman journalist and that of feminist journalist – irreconcilable in the eyes of the majority of professionals in the trade. This coexistence of different emotional communities in a given culture – in this case, one that was professional and gendered – constitutes one of the central notions in the field of history of emotions: "Rather than being a single set of rules that governed emotional life in a particular society, there were, at any given moment, multiple emotional communities... every day and in all societies, individuals moved through various environments, each of which has its own guidelines, standards, and expectations for emotional expression."[63]

Mobility between emotional communities at the conference was anything but fluid, according to the account in the report of what took place during the plenary session, at the end of the conference, at which women gathered to formulate proposals resulting from the joint workshops. "Are we at a conference of journalists or of feminists?" one journalist is said to have asked, outraged by the suggestion that joint committees of "women journalists/activist women, feminist groups, regional groups" be created to critique the news put out about women (oversight committees) and discuss women's information needs.[64] This widely shared rejection was crystallized in the notable position taken by *La Presse* journalist and columnist Lysiane Gagnon, who helped to squelch the feminist energy of the event: "Still, we women journalists shouldn't get carried away with unbridled enthusiasm and challenge the nature of our profession ... It would do a disservice to the news to transform ourselves into activists and take part in all the feminist debates."[65]

At the end of the report used for our analysis, the FPJQ gave voice to the point of view of the feminist magazine *La Vie en rose*. Journalist Françoise Guénette, who worked for the well-known publication, said that she was

> deeply troubled ... by the distrust [of these] women journalists who, by differentiating themselves from women's groups and their demands, by reiterating the pre-eminence of their professional criteria and the specificity of the profession, seem to me to be defending their privileges rather than the right of the public to news, journalistic credibility, and all these facile justifications for non-engagement ... Despite the fact that everyone listened to

> each other, the accuracy of the political analyses, the tons of emotions and of truth poured out, this convergence of women journalists and women consumers has not been made.[66]

Yet, Guénette continued, "frustrated feminist journalists or frustrated feminist activists, in the end it's two sides of the same coin."[67] Saint-Jean also felt that the cost of such an abdication was too high:

> The price that we pay [by ignoring these issues in our practices as women journalists] is to be cut off from ourselves. For a very long time, I was completely disconnected from my values, my needs, my interests, and my identity. I was on the way to becoming, and I had become, a different person in relation to myself, which is the very definition of alienation.[68]

This key notion of second-wave feminism describes the state from which the consciousness-raising approach sought to extract women. This hope – to bring women journalists out of alienation – which was stymied at the end of the process, seems to have been that of the women's committee of the FPJQ, given the point of view adopted in the report.

In the light of scholarly literature on gender and journalism, these two emotional communities, which clashed at the plenary session of Les femmes et l'information, in 1981, can be associated with two professional strategies. One was that of being "one of the boys," which describes the adaptation to dominant male norms in order to get around the stereotypes that disadvantaged women in the trade. The other was to be "one of the girls," which describes discourses and actions aiming to subvert discriminatory practices with regard to women. These two phenomena, which infused North American journalism, were also observed in Quebec journalism until the twenty-first century.[69] For example, among women foreign correspondents at the turn of the 2000s, some considered journalism a neutral practice despite the competitiveness and almost constant availability expected of them. These masculine-connoted norms were, however, criticized by others because of the systemic constraint that they represented for women journalists given the domestic responsibilities that they had, or that their bosses attributed to them.[70]

Conclusion

The conference of women journalists in 1981 gave the participants a rare opportunity, in Quebec, to share their perceptions of discrimination in their work environment. The report on the event, published by the women's committee of the FPJQ, *Thérèse, Janette, Hélène et les autres ou ... la face cachée de l'information,* showed the range of emotions mobilized by the attendees to express their sense of marginalization and their perception of the injustices that they were suffering (frustration, sense of guilt, fear of speaking up, and so on) as they practised a profession dominated by men. The report also exposed the difficulty of devising concrete solutions that would improve women's professional conditions, revealing the tensions associated with their identity-related positioning as journalists, women, and feminists. It may also have testified to the loss of the subversive dimension of the consciousness-raising approach that likely accompanied its democratization following its popularization during the 1970s, as liberal and radical currents converged: "Instead of building a core base of followers who shared in the goals of revolution, CR [consciousness-raising]'s newer groups never got past the female-bonding stages to engage in political activism."[71]

Although the conference did not give rise to regular annual meetings devoted to the working conditions of women journalists, the testimonials of these women and their comprehension of professional issues formed the basis of a new theory on the media.[72] For instance, in her essay *Le Silence des médias,* published in 1987 in the wake of the conference, Quebec journalist Colette Beauchamp noted that the norm of objectivity was still a "convenient myth" that delegitimized associations with femininity, including the emotionality embodied in journalism by human interest news or by the manifesting of empathy with sources.[73] In 1992, attendees at the regional Femmedia conference applauded the progress that had been made but underlined the persistence of the injustices that had been exposed at the 1981 congress, observations reiterated in 2002 by Saint-Jean in her book on the ethics of news in Quebec.[74] In Saint-Jean's view, women had nonetheless influenced journalism practices, notably by introducing into their workplaces "a mentality more inclined to cooperation than confrontation, as well as a valorization of emotion and involvement"; this essentialist conception had not coloured Saint-Jean's words published in the conference report.[75] In contemporary journalism, in a context of hyper-competition, recourse to emotion and empathetic treatment of sources are still perceived as damaging to the news, thus continuing to devalue the work of many women who remain assigned mainly to "soft news" or to social and human interest subjects.[76]

Finally, although women journalists in rural regions described the difficulties they encountered, as well as the almost total silence regarding feminist issues in the regional media even if most participants supported the idea of holding seminars on women and news in the regions, the absence of testimonials by racialized journalists raises questions about the inclusive nature of the conference as an emotional refuge. Indeed, the report demonstrated that the privilege of the right to speak seems to have belonged exclusively to white, middle-class women journalists, sweeping the question of sexual diversity and the specific situation of women with disabilities under the rug. The consciousness-raising approach, which "stressed a belief in the similarity of women's experience under sexist oppression that transcended racial, class, ethnic, educational, and virtually any other differences between them individually," likely contributed to this state of affairs.[77] As Funké Aladejebi shows in her chapter in this book on the hierarchy of issues and emotions in favour of white women in the Ontario Teachers' Federation, the obstacles that racialized women faced to have their voices heard in Canadian feminist groups in the 1970s was reproduced in the context of feminist critiques of the media in Quebec at the time. In her description of the pitfalls encountered by Haitian women journalists working in community radio in Montreal during that period, Marlène Rateau presents the Quebec-majority feminist movement as a source of inspiration, without alluding to the specific relationship that she and her Black colleagues maintained with white women journalists in Quebec. She notes, however, that like the Black teachers interviewed by Aladejebi, Haitian women journalists in Quebec rarely received an attentive ear from the men in their community.[78]

The intersectional dimension of the gendered dynamics at work in the feminist consciousness-raising process of women journalists and the denunciation of their conditions could be explored further through an analysis of complementary sources on how the conference was received, notably on the program *Femme d'aujourd'hui*, which aired a one-hour special on the subject on Radio-Canada television, on October 27, 1981, and in the mainstream media.[79] However, interviews with racialized and minorized women who worked in journalism in Quebec during the 1960s and 1970s would be the best and most obvious way to access points of view and experiences that were not addressed in the FPJQ women's committee report.

Notes

This chapter was translated from the original version of our French text into English by Käthe Roth, the funding for which was provided by the Simon Fraser University Publications Fund. We would like to thank the editing and evaluation team of this book for their openness and their wise advice. This chapter was written with pleasure, in part at the welcoming Caffè Mille Gusti in Montreal and in the presence, at the very end, of a tiny Éléonore!

1 Fédération professionnelle des journalistes du Québec, *Thérèse, Janette, Hélène et les autres ou ... la face cachée de l'information, Bilan du colloque "Les femmes et l'information,"* 1981–1982 (Montreal: la Fédération, 1982), 3 (hereafter, *Bilan*). All quotations from this document are our translations.

2 Françoise Guénette, "L'envers du silence," *La Vie en rose*, Septembre–Novembre, 1981, 18.

3 The conference was organized in the wake of the Fédération professionnelle des journalistes du Québec's 1980 congress, at which only men (politicians, trade unionists, and journalists) were invited to speak on the theme, "Qui nous dit quoi dire?" (Who will tell us what to say?). Guénette, "L'envers du silence," 18.

4 "Un colloque sur les femmes et l'information," advertisement, *La Vie en rose*, Septembre–Novembre, 1981, 9.

5 Line Gosselin, *Les journalistes québécoises, 1880–1930* (Montreal: Regroupement des chercheurs-chercheures en histoire des travailleurs et travailleuses du Québec, 1995).

6 The Canadian Women's Press Club, a bilingual association founded in Montreal in 1904, admitted men in 1971. The Cercle des femmes journalistes, founded in 1951, was dissolved in 1993. On women's role in the union struggle, see Florence Le Cam, *Le journalisme imaginé. Histoire d'un projet professionnel au Québec* (Montreal: Leméac, 2009). On strikes by women workers, teachers, and nurses, see Denyse Baillargeon, *Brève histoire des femmes au Québec* (Montreal: Boréal, 2012), 129; Andrée Dufour and Micheline Dumont, *Brève histoire des institutrices au Québec de la Nouvelle-France à nos jours* (Montreal: Boréal, 2004), 139; and Collectif Clio, *L'histoire des femmes au Québec depuis quatre siècles*, 2nd ed. (Montreal: Le Jour, 1992), 314–15.

7 Florence Bird, *Report of the Royal Commission on the Status of Women in Canada* (Ottawa: Information Canada, 1970). The following studies analyze the interrelations between the media and the commission: Laurie Laplanche, "Pour vous, mesdames ... et messieurs. Production des émissions féminines à la Société Radio-Canada à Montréal (1952–1982). Promotion, conception des publics et culture organisationnelle genrées" (PhD diss., Université Laval, 2016); Barbara M. Freeman, *Beyond Bylines: Media Workers and Women's Rights in Canada* (Waterloo, ON: Wilfrid Laurier University Press, 2011); and Freeman, *The Satellite Sex: The Media and Women's Issues in English Canada, 1966–1971* (Waterloo, ON: Wilfrid Laurier University Press, 2001).

8 A prominent group in the movement was the National Organization for Women, founded in 1966 by Betty Friedan. Herself a former journalist for women's magazines, Friedan criticized the discourses conveyed in these publications, which advocated for the "homemaker" model widespread after the Second World War. Her book published in 1963 is recognized for having helped to instigate the second wave of feminism in the West. See Betty Friedan, *The Feminine Mystique* (New York: W.W. Norton, 1963).

9 On the Milan conference, see Groupe Femmes et Information de Milan, "Information masculine et information femme," in *Écrire Contre. Expériences, réflexions et analyses des femmes journalistes*, trans. Marie Pavan (Paris: Des femmes, 1977), 49–52. In parallel, the same year, Lysiane Gagnon and Armande Saint-Jean,

journalists at the Montreal daily *La Presse* and at Radio-Canada respectively, submitted a report to the FPJQ. Gagnon and Saint-Jean denounced the minority status of women in journalism, their concentration in "human interest" subjects, the absence of women in management positions, the lack of maternity leave, and the superficial nature of media coverage of women's issues. Fédération professionnelle des journalistes du Québec, *La situation des femmes dans l'information* (Montreal: Congrès d'avril, 1977).

10 Armande Saint-Jean, *Éthique de l'information. Fondements et pratiques au Québec depuis 1960* (Montreal: Presses de l'Université de Montréal, 2002), 231. Photographs published in the conference report show that a few men also attended.

11 *Bilan*. Our analyses are based on the first part of the conference report published by the FPJQ one year after the event. The report contains a preface and background information; the text of the opening speech; the proceedings of the conference; an interview; testimonials by women journalists and members of activist groups; and a news report published following the conference.

12 Baillargeon, *Brève histoire*.

13 Laure Bereni et al., *Introduction aux études sur le genre. 2e édition revue et augmentée* (Paris/Brussels: De Boeck Université, 2012), 10 (our translation); "bicatégorisation hiéarchisée des sexes."

14 Stephanie A. Shields, *Speaking from the Heart: Gender and the Social Meaning of Emotion* (Cambridge: Cambridge University Press, 2002), 170.

15 Susan J. Matt, "Current Emotion Research in History: Or, Doing History from the Inside Out," *Emotion Review* 3, 1 (2011): 118. See also Sophie Doucet, "'Toujours je sens mon âme se balancer entre les joies et les peines': Le paysage émotionnel de Marie-Louise Globensky (1849–1919) observé à travers ses écrits personnels" (PhD diss., Université du Québec à Montréal, 2019).

16 William M. Reddy defines the concept of emotional refuge as "a relationship, ritual, or organization (whether informal or formal) that provides safe release from prevailing emotional norms and allows relaxation of emotional efforts, with or without an ideological justification, which may shore up or threaten the existing emotional regime." William M. Reddy, *The Navigation of Feeling: A Framework for the History of Emotions* (Cambridge: Cambridge University Press, 2001), 129.

17 Emotional communities are social groups within which certain norms and codes prevail with regard to the perception and expression of emotions. Each individual is a member of several emotional communities, which may be superimposed, juxtaposed, and evolving. See Barbara H. Rosenwein, "Worrying about Emotions in History," *American Historical Review* 107, 3 (2002): 842; and Rosenwein, *Emotional Communities in the Early Middle Ages* (Ithaca, NY: Cornell University Press, 2006).

18 Joan W. Scott, *De l'utilité du genre*, trans. Claude Servan-Schreiber (Paris: Éditions Fayard, 2012).

19 *Bilan*, 13.

20 Guénette, "L'envers du silence," 20.

21 Linda Denis, *L'intervention féministe conscientisante, Bilan des pratiques contre la violence faite aux femmes au Québec. Des solidarités féministes du local au Mondial* (Montreal: Relais-femmes, 2003), 5 (our translation).

22 Collectif Clio, *L'histoire des femmes au Québec depuis quatre siècles*, 475.

23 Debra Michals, "From 'Consciousness Expansion' to 'Consciousness Raising': Feminism and the Countercultural Politics of the Self," in *Imagine Nation: American Countercultures in the 1960s and '70s*, ed. Peter Braunstein and Michael William Doyle (New York: Routledge, 2002), 41–68.

24 Thérèse Parisien, quoted in *Bilan*, 16.

25 *Bilan*, 13.

26 See Michals, "From 'Consciousness Expansion' to 'Consciousness Raising,'" 44.

27 Gisèle Tremblay, quoted in *Bilan*, 5.

28 Tremblay, quoted in *Bilan*, 13.

29 Reddy, *Navigation of Feeling*, 129.

30 Lizette Gervais, quoted in *Bilan*, 15.

31 Parisien, quoted in *Bilan*, 17.

32 Armande Saint-Jean, quoted in *Bilan*, 29.

33 Socially, motherhood is usually valued. See Marc Préjean, *Sexes et pouvoir. La construction sociale des corps et des émotions* (Montreal: Presses de l'Université de Montréal, 1994).

34 Saint-Jean, quoted in *Bilan*, 30.

35 On gender performance, see Judith Butler, *Gender Trouble: Feminism and the Subversion of Identity* (New York/London: Routledge, 1990), 163–80. On women and housework, see Camille Robert, *Toutes les femmes sont d'abord ménagères. Histoire d'un combat féministe pour la reconnaissance du travail ménager. Québec 1968–1985* (Montreal: Somme toute, 2017).

36 Gervais, quoted in *Bilan*, 14.

37 Monica Löfgren-Nilsson speaks of the context of male homo-sociability at work in "Le genre en pensée et en actes: le cas des informations télévisées suédoises," in *Le journalisme au féminin. Assignations, inventions, stratégies*, ed. Béatrice Damian-Gaillard, Cégolène Frisque, et Eugénie Saitta (Rennes: Presses universitaires de Rennes, 2010), 139–43.

38 Carmel Dumas, quoted in *Bilan*, 25. The necessary "decoupling of the man/masculine and woman/feminine pairing" in gender analysis was obvious here. Marlène Coulomb-Gully, "Inoculer le genre. Le Genre et les SHS: une méthodologie traversière," *Revue française des sciences de l'information et de la communication* 4 (2014): 4.

39 Hélène Lévesque, quoted in *Bilan*, 20–21. See also Jocelyn Saint-Pierre, *La Tribune de la presse à Québec depuis 1960* (Quebec City: Septentrion, 2016).

40 See Jean de Bonville, *La presse québécoise de 1884 à 1914. Genèse d'un média de masse* (Quebec City: Presses de l'Université Laval, 1988); Marc-François Bernier, *Éthique et déontologie du journalisme*, 3rd ed. (Quebec City: Presses de l'Université Laval, 2014), 293–300.

41 Tremblay, quoted in *Bilan*, 5. Tremblay also evokes the memory of the great reporter, foreign correspondent, and public affairs journalist Judith Jasmin, "the most venerated of women journalists in Quebec," who "knew how to return to the facts the share of emotions that belong to them." Tremblay, quoted in *Bilan*, 5. See also Colette Beauchamp, *Judith Jasmin: de feu et de flamme* (Montreal: Boréal, 1992).

42 Lise Payette, quoted in *Bilan*, 10.
43 Payette, quoted in *Bilan*, 7.
44 Préjean, *Sexes et pouvoir*.
45 Gloria Brown-Anderson, "Comment faire un journal qui touche les gens," in *Bilan*, 41–42.
46 Brown-Anderson, "Comment faire un journal qui touche les gens," 42.
47 Brown-Anderson, "Comment faire un journal qui touche les gens," 42. Theoreticians of gender insist that "gender socialization is ... not a mechanical and inevitable process" and that there are frequent transgressions, illustrating the possible gaps between the social norm and social diversities. Bereni et al., *Introduction aux études sur le genre*, 131 (our translation).
48 Éric Neveu, "Le genre du journalisme. Des ambivalences de la féminisation d'une profession," *Politix* 13, 51 (2000): 204.
49 Anne-Sophie Gobeil has shown that many Quebec women journalists who worked as foreign correspondents during the 1970s felt uneasy with the idea that women and men might do journalism differently. See Gobeil's "Les pratiques professionnelles genrées: Le cas des journalistes québécoises correspondantes à l'étranger," *Recherches féministes* 29, 2 (2016): 245–63.
50 See Marilou Tanguay, "La page féminine du *Devoir*, un 'espace public alternatif'? Une étude de cas des mécanismes d'exclusion et de contrôle du 'féminin' et du 'féminisme' dans le quotidien (1965–1975)," *Revue d'histoire de l'Amérique française* 72, 3 (2019): 29–59. These pages were created with the goal of strengthening newspapers' finances by drawing female readers with "feminine" content focusing on domestic work, body care, and women's emotional life, exposing them at the same time to ads for domestic products. See Josette Brun, "Présentation," in *Interrelations femmes-médias dans l'Amérique française*, ed. Josette Brun (Quebec City: Presses de l'Université Laval, 2009), 1–9; de Bonville, *La presse québécoise*, 228; Josette Brun and Laurie Laplanche, "Rendre le privé politique à la télévision de Radio-Canada: *Femme d'aujourd'hui* et le féminisme," in *La télévision de Radio-Canada et l'évolution de la conscience politique au Québec*, ed. Denis Monière and Florian Sauvageau (Quebec City: Presses de l'Université Laval, 2012), 57–71.
51 Janette Bertrand, quoted in *Bilan*, 27. See Johanne Sénéchal, "Fréquentations et mariage, les représentations de jeunes Québécoises à travers l'étude d'un courrier du cœur (1958–1968)" (master's thesis, Université Laval, 2006), 10–41.
52 Janette Bertrand, quoted in *Bilan*, 27.
53 Janette Bertrand, in *Bilan*, 28. For an analysis of the marginalization of women's programs at Radio-Canada, see Laplanche, "Pour vous, mesdames."
54 Bertrand, quoted in *Bilan*, 28.
55 Marie-Agnès Tellier, quoted in *Bilan*, 24.
56 Louiselle Lévesque, quoted in *Bilan*, 18.
57 Carmel Dumas, quoted in *Bilan*, 25.
58 Hélène Lévesque, quoted in *Bilan*, 21.
59 Armande Saint-Jean, quoted in *Bilan*, 30.
60 Martine Storti, quoted in *Bilan*, 11.
61 Storti, quoted in *Bilan*, 12.

62 Storti, quoted in *Bilan*, 11–12. At the time the report was published, however, she was no longer a major reporter at *F Magazine*.
63 Matt, "Current Emotion Research in History," 119.
64 *Bilan*, 44.
65 Lysiane Gagnon, quoted in *Bilan*, 46, 46n3.
66 Françoise Guénette, quoted in *Bilan*, 46.
67 Guénette, quoted in *Bilan*, 40.
68 Saint-Jean, quoted in *Bilan*, 31.
69 See Liesbet van Zoonen, "One of the Girls?," in *News, Gender, and Power*, ed. Cynthia Carter, Gill Branston, and Stuart Allan (London/New York: Routledge, 1998), 33–46; Margareta Melin-Higgins, "Coping with Journalism: Gendered Newsroom Culture," in *Gender and Newsroom Cultures: Identities at Work*, ed. Marijan De Bruin and Karen Ross (Cresskill, NJ: Hampton Press, 2004), 197–222.
70 Gobeil, "Les pratiques professionnelles genrées," 245–63.
71 Michals, "From 'Consciousness Expansion' to 'Consciousness Raising,'" 59–60.
72 Michals, "From 'Consciousness Expansion' to 'Consciousness Raising,'" 56.
73 Colette Beauchamp, *Le silence des médias. Les femmes, les hommes et l'information* (Montreal: Remue-ménage, 1987), 148, 150–51. See also Yasmine Berthou and Josette Brun, "Le Silence des médias ... 20 ans après. Entrevue réalisée avec Colette Beauchamp," in *Interrelations femmes-médias dans l'Amérique française*, ed. Josette Brun (Quebec City: Presses de l'Université Laval, 2009), 161–76.
74 *Rapport Colloque Femmedia 92. Alice au pays des médias ou si réalité m'était comptée* (Sherbrooke, QC: Centre des femmes de l'Estrie, 1993); Saint-Jean, *Éthique de l'information*.
75 Saint-Jean, *Éthique de l'information*, 233 (our translation).
76 Deborah Chambers, Linda Steiner, and Carole Fleming, *Women and Journalism* (London/New York: Routledge, 2004), 231–32.
77 Michals, "From 'Consciousness Expansion' to 'Consciousness Raising,'" 57.
78 See Marlène Rateau, "Pawòl Fanm: Des femmes haïtiennes de Montréal au micro de Radio Centre-Ville," in *Interrelations femmes-médias dans l'Amérique française*, ed. Josette Brun (Quebec City: Presses de l'Université Laval, 2009), 177–86.
79 The host raised the question of the absence of testimonials by women from "ethnic communities." On the subject of *Femme d'aujourd'hui* and intersectional questions, see Adèle Clapperton-Richard and Catherine Laplante, "Pluralité et altérisation des voix féminines à *Femme d'aujourd'hui*: Les femmes blanches des régions et les femmes des Premières Nations," in *De l'exclusion à la solidarité. Regards intersectionnels sur les médias*, ed. Josette Brun (Montreal: Remue-ménage, 2020), 147–77.

12

Anger, Melancholia, and Hope

The Feminist Politics of Emotion and the Centre for Women and Trans People at Wilfrid Laurier University

MATTHEW FESNAK

One morning in September 1989, students arriving for breakfast at the dining hall at Wilfrid Laurier University, a small Ontario university located in Waterloo, Ontario, encountered the following scene: walls plastered with posters displaying women's underwear, some sprayed with ketchup to represent blood, others with accompanying captions such as "Do you take VISA?" One poster featured hand-drawn female genitalia overwritten with an obscenity. The display, the work of first-year male residence students, was part of an annual initiation-rite panty raid on the women's dormitory. When several graduate social work students and faculty members began tearing down the posters at lunchtime, they faced taunts of "Nazi" and "lesbian radical bitch" and the offer by one undergraduate "to show them 'what a real man is good for.'" In the weeks after the incident, the president of the university, John Weir, stated that some individuals "rightly took offence" but refused to immediately denounce the practice, refraining from comment pending a university investigation.[1]

Drawing ire from feminist women on campus, the panty raid scandal led, a year later, to the creation of the university's first Women's Centre. Prior to that point, the university not only had no women's centre but also had "no courses in women's studies, no sexual assault centre, [and] no status-of-women committee."[2] Feminists thus found themselves dispersed across campus, working through informal channels. The creation of the Women's Centre offered a space where students could disseminate feminist values and promote a feminist consciousness on campus. Still, in subsequent years, the centre often found itself short of funding and had to change its location multiple times.[3] Moreover, with a high turnover among the students running the space, there were disagreements and discontinuity in the governing philosophies of the coordinators and the political actions taken by the centre. This was particularly true when the Women's Centre changed its name in 2010 to the Centre for Women and Trans People. However, what has been consistent through this period of change is a commitment to creating a safe student-run space for people who have been affected by gendered violence to work through the emotional complexities of diverse experiences, societal narratives, and political pressure, and a commitment to leveraging those emotions to challenge the university community on gendered issues.

To date, historians and feminist scholars have been less interested in tracing the evolution of feminist campus activism in the 1980s and early 1990s than in earlier periods. Yet this activism occurred at an important moment in the history of feminist organizing. During the 1980s, women's studies programs and campus women's centres consolidated across the country. The University of Calgary has an informal women's centre that has opened, closed, and opened again at various times since the early 1970s, with its current iteration opening in 2013. The University of Guelph opened a women's centre in 1982, the University of Toronto in 1986, and York University in 1996.[4] These centres formed part of the larger movement of second-wave feminist institution-building, which produced women's bookstores, shelters, and rape crisis centres across the country. On university campuses, both women's studies programs and women's centres were built in response to the lack of inclusion of women in academic programming and to the unequal treatment of women on campus.[5] The campus-based activism I discuss in this chapter is, therefore, partially situated within the history of second-wave institution-building and feminist consciousness-raising. The history of the centre, however, also reflects the emergence of third-wave feminism in the 1990s, which was characterized by the leadership of younger, university-age women who were pursuing grassroots protests and drawing on ideas from feminist and queer theory, which pushed the boundaries regarding definitions of gender and sexual identity.[6] Their activism would extend and, at times, reshape the aims and purpose of the centre.

This chapter begins by briefly examining three moments in the history of the Centre for Women and Trans People: its origins, its name change in 2010 to include "Trans" in the title, and recent organizing against campus sexual assault. My aim here is not to provide a full history of the centre but rather to provide context for a discussion of two issues. First, I use these moments to think about the emotional work that centres do. Drawing on British-American philosopher Alison Jaggar's concept of "outlaw emotions" and intersectional theorist Sara Ahmed's characterization of the "feminist killjoy," I argue that the work of campus feminists in the centre relies on contemporary consciousness-raising: the collective labour of producing and enacting a desire to challenge gender normativity and imagine a more inclusive future. Feminist organizing for social change on the university campus was (and is) enacted through the emotional work of harnessing anger and frustration as well as hope for change.[7] Using insights from the work of psychoanalysts Sigmund Freud and Julia Kristeva, I also argue that hope for, and acting towards, a better future is often driven by melancholia, or a sense of loss for what the present is not.[8] Second, I briefly examine the problem of institutionalizing feminist activism that originates from this "emotion work." One challenge of feminist work on campus is how to work towards gender equality and inclusion without falling into the traps of faux or symbolic inclusivity created by what Ahmed and others refer to as "diversity" or "inclusion" work.[9] Too often, in finding a place on campus, women's centres have become co-opted into the administrative aims of universities without an incorporation of the centre's values or priorities.

Consequently, the capacity for such spaces on campus to effect change often does not take the form of radical direct action but of modern iterations of consciousness-raising. This chapter, then, uses psychoanalysis and affect theory to explore the emotional work that women's centres do. In the process, it illuminates the continuing influence of second-wave feminist approaches and methods of organizing well into the twenty-first century, as well as the ideological challenges to binary feminist definitions of gender.

From Panty Raid Protest to the Politics of Sexual Violence Policy

The 1989 panty raid at Wilfrid Laurier had a long antecedent in activities on the North American university campus, as did student initiations more generally. As part of the process of integrating new students into campus culture, senior students developed rites and rituals to increase camaraderie and cohesion. In creating initiations through which all students would pass, they developed campus traditions that would become part of the informal university identity. Marked in the late-nineteenth century by roughhousing and full-out physical battles between men in various years, initiations came under greater administrative oversight both with the entrance of women into universities and with administrators' attempts to secure greater control over student culture. Still, universities generally turned a blind eye to activities that did not raise public ire. Panty raids, for example, became a tolerated form of campus initiation in the 1950s.[10]

The activities at Wilfrid Laurier University (WLU), then, were clearly part of a broader pattern, and the first major moment of campus feminist activism related to the Women's Centre. A 1989 article in WLU's student newspaper, *The Cord*, described panty raiding as "a controlled activity in which male residents 'raid' a floor of women late at night and take underwear, negligees, bras, and other undergarments, then display them on posters in the Dining Hall the following morning."[11] Not to be left out, female students also engaged in these activities, providing men with underwear – often bought new for the very purpose of the raid – as well as engaging in a retaliatory raid the following evening. Though women's activities came under less scrutiny during the 1989 public outcry, female residents, too, put up posters, many of which were obscene, with at least one sporting the term "fag" written under a pair of pinned-up underwear.[12] In both cases, such displays involved misogynistic and homophobic text or images defiling the underwear in some way. In general, however, the images and text in these posters emphasized violent heterosexual gender binaries that defined masculinity as aggressive and penetrating, while "abjecting" femininity and queer sexuality. Associating the female and queer body with dirt, bodily fluids, and blood was meant to create a sense of "horror" and to underline the hierarchical difference between the normative, heterosexual male body and the "abjected" non-normative female body.[13] Like the feminists channelling their anger by protesting beauty pageants in Patrizia Gentile's chapter, "Tears and Tiaras," university women channelled their anger in an attempt to change the sexist reductionism that was typified by the panty raids and underwear displays.

The public protest against the 1989 raid, and the university's response to it, were shaped by a series of events across Canada that targeted female university students more generally. In the early fall of that year, male residence students at Queen's University mocked a campaign against sexual violence by displaying offensive signs such as "No Means More Beer." In December, a twenty-five-year-old man murdered fourteen female engineering students at École Polytechnique in Montreal, claiming that feminists were unfairly gaining advantages over men.[14] The violence directed at female university students intensified feminist protest in the 1989–90 school year. Some students and faculty at WLU protested the raids by marching, complaining to the administration, holding discussions, and creating an ad hoc group, the Gender Relations Committee.[15] As the committee members learned more about the initiation ritual, they became more appalled, discovering that the university sanctioned this activity.[16] Until September 1989, it had been acceptable to university administrators to introduce students to university life by having male students act in predatory ways towards female students, their bodies, and their personal space.

The panty raid scandal brought unwelcome attention and negative nationwide press coverage to Wilfrid Laurier. The university feared that the media coverage – which saw the university labelled "Dogpatch U" by a leading newspaper columnist – made WLU seem simple-minded and unsophisticated. Initially, university administrators, such as the president, John Weir, and the vice-president of student affairs, Jim Wilgar, acknowledged the anger expressed by those opposed to the raids but "insisted that the university was acting responsibly." They tried to distance the university from both the tradition of the panty raids and from the feminist protesters by claiming they were "managing" the raids and by reproaching protesters for "not going through proper channels."[17] On October 27, 1989, approximately two months after that year's panty raid event, and with ongoing and disparaging media coverage, WLU announced that panty raids were banned from campus.[18] "After being backed into a corner by nationwide media coverage," *The Cord* reported, "WLU President John Weir banned the tradition of residence panty raids," and "Dean Nichols arranged for an excellent presentation on acquaintance rape during frosh week. Unfortunately, only half a dozen people attended."[19] Banning panty raids on campus was certainly a step forward for feminist activists, but the half-hearted efforts to change attitudes towards women's bodies had little impact on the daily lives of students and instead drew attention away from the national scandal.

In the aftermath, a more permanent solution was sought. In August 1990, Wilfrid Laurier published a news release titled "WLU Makes Progress on Program to Promote Healthy Gender Relations." It highlighted the opening of a women's centre and the allocation of $10,000 for the space. According to the university, such initiatives were based on recommendations from a committee appointed by President Weir.[20] Women's Centre documents, on the other hand, suggest the centre had been proposed by an independent "group of women" who had continued to organize after the outrage of the panty raids.[21] *The Cord* reported that "the centre will be a resource and referral centre open to all to discuss and learn about women's issues."[22] This space would give feminist activists on campus a means of legitimizing the work they were doing. They could now use the Women's Centre as a

The Cord, September 13, 1990. (Wilfrid Laurier University Student Publications.)

location from which to produce a different narrative about gender identities and gendered relations on campus.

The second major moment in the history of the centre occurred in 2010, when the Women's Centre changed its name to the Centre for Women and Trans People in an attempt to expand the category of woman to include trans, gender queer, multigender, and agender people. This name change should be understood within the context of debates over the inclusion and exclusion of trans and non-binary-identifying people within feminism.[23] Women's centres were initially born from second-wave movements that emphasized a shared gender identity and experience based on the subordination of women's bodies. The name change was a response to a larger shift in feminist and queer theory away from understanding gender through the construction of binary categories.[24] Becoming a trans inclusive space meant more than just a name change, as volunteers deliberated on a way forward and the resource literature within the space required substantial revision. As Susan Stryker, Paisley Currah, and Lisa Jean Moore note, "Trans inclusion moves past traditions of feminism by challenging binary gender categories and systems and by using a self-reflexive anti-oppression framework."[25]

In 2010, the Centre for Women and Trans People produced a volunteer manual acknowledging that "the feminist movement has a history of excluding trans people, a history that we don't want to be a part of."[26] It reimagined its space as one that addressed multiple forms of oppression including race, imperialism, sexuality, and disability:

> In the spirit of constant growth and development, the Centre for Women and Trans People recognizes that it has historically participated in a tradition of feminism that primarily served the needs of white, heterosexual, cisgender, non-intersex, able-bodied women, and hereby commits to broadening our perspective through anti-oppressive training, allyship, actively seeking marginalized perspectives, and acting as a venue of all disenfranchised voices to be heard. This is an ongoing process, and we welcome suggestions, advice, and critiques.[27]

The centre now emphasized the affirmation and acceptance of diverse genders and gendered performances and encouraged students to be open-minded to the experiences and identities of others. By including trans people, the centre aimed not to "identify, consolidate, or stabilize a category or class of people, things or phenomena that could be denominated 'trans,' as if certain concrete somethings could be characterized as 'crossers,' while everything else could be characterized by boundedness and fixity,"[28] but to unlearn the assumed stability and fixity of naturalized categories. As a result, the Centre for Women and Trans People now provided resources and support to enable students to challenge, imagine, and reshape the definitions of woman, trans, and other gender categories to reflect a wider range of gender identities and experiences. The volunteers at the centre were motivated to become trans inclusive not only in order to challenge grand feminist narratives, but also in order to counter specific negative experiences that students had on campus. This activism fit into the work that the centre took on regarding gendered and sexual aspects of consent, assault, and discrimination.

In 2016, a third major moment in the history of campus feminist activism took place as the centre stood at the forefront of a major social and on-campus shift surrounding the discussion of sexual assault. Second-wave feminists across North America drew attention to the politics of sexual assault and gender-based violence beginning in the 1970s. By the early 1980s, Canadian feminist activists had successfully lobbied the Canadian government to modernize the Criminal Code and create a new term, that of sexual assault, which replaced earlier definitions of rape. The new term acknowledged for the first time that sexual assault could occur within marriage and that it could be perpetrated against boys and men.[29] But changes to legal definitions of sexual violence did not end violence against women. In the past several years, universities in both Canada and the United States have been pushed to take the issue of campus sexual assault more seriously. Critics have argued that unclear reporting guidelines, confusing disciplinary policies, inadequate education about consent, and underfunded support services have made it difficult for survivors of sexual assault. Universities across Canada have been pushed to develop stand-alone policies on sexual assault and harassment and to commit significant financial resources for support services and consent education. In 2016, for example, the provincial governments of Ontario and British Columbia introduced legislation mandating that all universities devise and implement such policies by 2017, and Ontario has introduced legislation to ensure that questions about sexual history or possible drug use are not taken into consideration with students alleging an instance of sexual assault or harassment.[30]

WLU had begun working on a sexual harassment policy as early as 1987, yet female students were still protesting sexual assault and harassment issues in 2016.[31] In 2016, students were able to successfully draw on the previous work of the centre, as well as on contemporary critiques of university sexual violence policies, to write an open letter to the university administration and student leaders about gendered violence.[32] The letter criticized university messaging on sexual violence that situated sexual assault as "avoidable" through individual responsibility and changes in behaviour. In 2015, for example, the university had warned students to "be aware of how much you drink and stay in control," to only "go out with groups of friends – never alone,"[33] to avoid walking alone on campus, and to avoid "listening to music through headphones" or "talking on cellphones" because both might "detract from your awareness of surroundings or the ability to spot suspicious activity."[34] Writing about similar issues in the American context, political theorist Wendy Brown argues that the university's discourse of personal responsibility acts as a form of victim blaming in which sexual assault is tolerated as an unfortunate individual occurrence rather than as a structural issue of gender and sexual inequality.[35] At Wilfrid Laurier, the open letter sparked a dialogue within the university community. One of the architects of the letter acknowledged its impact: "They're talking. It's not just students and faculty anymore, but also administration and community members, especially alumni."[36]

Around the same time that this letter circulated, Wilfrid Laurier researchers, including professor Ginette Lafrenière, initiated The Change Project, which surveyed students and found that 40 percent of student respondents reported experiences of gendered violence, with 13.4 percent saying they were victims of sexual assault.[37] Following this initiative, WLU created partnerships with local sexual assault support centres to reevaluate its efforts; formed a task force with students, faculty, and staff; hired a sexual violence support advocate; and created a new web resource focusing on gendered and sexual violence.[38] On the new website, created in 2016, the university's position has been substantially revised, stating, "If you have been drinking or taking drugs and have experienced sexual violence it is not your fault." The website details and defines various forms of assault and harassment, along with consent and rape culture.[39] WLU has also produced a new Gendered and Sexual Violence Policy and Procedures manual, which provides a comprehensive list of guidelines, definitions, and accountability measures that now reflects this new position.[40]

In the case of sexual assault, as with the panty raid scandal, feminist organizers provided a counter-narrative, one which stood in opposition to the approach of university administrators and eventually brought about considerable change. There was no women's centre in 1989 or 1990, when protesters were reproaching the university for panty raids and other issues on campus. While it is likely that feminists would have organized and protested against sexual assault on campus without the advent of the Centre for Women and Trans People in the mid-2010s, the centre has been able to support those activists by reaching a much wider audience and educating swaths of the university population through sustained initiatives.

The Emotional Work of Feminist Activism

In addition to advocating for equal rights and a safe educational space, Wilfrid Laurier's Centre for Women and Trans People also "envisions a time when the identities of all women and trans people are affirmed within the university culture."[41] To bring about this shift, organizations like the centre attempt to disrupt the acceptance and reproduction of misogyny, transphobia, and heteronormativity. This work draws on feminist traditions of consciousness-raising, which emerged from second-wave feminist activism as an attempt to apply feminist theories to everyday situations and to help women understand their individual circumstances in the context of structural inequality. Indeed, a former centre volunteer emphasized the important role of the centre in influencing their ideas about feminism:

> The centre was central in the development of my feminist thought and perspective, as it helped in acknowledging the importance of considering sex work as real work, consent, feminist resistance and the inclusion of trans individuals ... As a feminist space of activism, the space embodied the importance of fighting experiences and forms of oppression within the Wilfrid Laurier University campus, while also inviting members to engage in street-based activism such as Take Back the Night. Overall, my experience with the centre reinforced the importance of second wave feminist thought and practices through reinforcing individual rights to reproductive justice.[42]

The Centre was conceived as a space for people to "discuss and learn about women's issues,"[43] and grew to become a resource that could provide students with the opportunity to develop their identity and activism as feminists.

Consciousness-raising functioned "as a bridge between the women's movement and different areas of professionalization in which women were active, including the academy and professional therapy."[44] Feminist consciousness-raising focuses on sharing personal knowledge and experiences of social structures in order to expand understanding of the effects of naturalized gendered identities. A feminist consciousness ostensibly allows for the acceptance and affirmation of performances outside of the normative understandings of gendered selfhood, validating disillusionment with the way that things are expected to be and allowing women to understand and take action against oppressive politics. Taking a philosophical approach to "the personal is political," feminist consciousness-raising reconsiders the way that personal consciousness is developed through interactions with the medical system, media, educational institutions, and familial structures, and personal consciousness fights against the oppressive aspects of this consciousness.

Part of the job of consciousness-raising involves the practice of "feeling." Current feminist theorists suggest that emotion and feeling can do the work of changing the way we think about gender and also of shaping the way activists pursue social change. Alison Jaggar proposes the concept of "outlaw emotions" as "conventionally inexplicable emotions" that "may lead us to make subversive observations that challenge the status quo."[45] On the contrary, commonly held emotional attachments to gender norms allow those norms to remain in place. These positive attachments also come with opinions about non-normative performances that regulate what behaviour or emotional expression is accepted and what is not. The development of outlaw emotions is thus necessary for outlawed gender performances to be considered acceptable. Just as aberrant gender performances are regulated, so too are outlaw emotions. Feminists who challenge patriarchal gender norms and institutional responses to exclusion will frequently be perceived or labelled as "crazy" or irrational.[46] Individuals who do not want to listen to feminist criticisms see these emotions as examples of feminists being difficult, overly sensitive, or unable to let things go. In an act of reclamation, Sara Ahmed names the woman who persistently refuses to "let go" of criticism and anger as the "feminist killjoy."[47] She thus redirects our attention to the importance of emotions in spurring action.

We can see the process of emotional attachment to – and disruption of – gender norms at WLU in 1989. After feminists criticized the panty raids, one reporter noted that students involved in the incident responded in anger, deriding "reporters who exposed the situation at Laurier and the people who felt offended by the incident."[48] The normative position on campus, articulated by many administrators and students, was to explain the ritual as a tradition only meant in good fun, and nothing to get upset about. One student stated, "No one takes these things seriously." A residence don who helped lead the raid called it "a good community builder" and justified it based on mutual consent: "The girls agree and the guys agree."[49]

Protesters felt otherwise. Confronted with the poster of ketchup-splattered underwear, Martha Laurence, a professor in the School of Social Work, told a reporter, "My guts literally lurched ... I felt assaulted."[50] One female graduate of a different Canadian university reacted vociferously, commenting on campus culture more generally:

> I have been exposed to snow sculptures of male genitalia outside the women's residence, panty raids, sexist posters, rudely displayed pictures of female genitalia and a publication that for years supported a degradation of women. As always, university administrations will acknowledge these actions as "first-year" fun ... How can we expect women's issues to be heard, accepted or endorsed, if our future is these students[?] ... [A]ll sides – men, women and the administration – have demonstrated backward and insulting actions.[51]

When female students and faculty expressed discomfort and anger with the panty raids, they were expressing outlaw emotions and attempting to change public discourse about women on campus. Rather than being immediately supported by the university community, they were derided, in current terms, as killjoys, sucking the fun out of harmless orientation events. Much like the 1970 protest of the Miss Canadian University pageant, described by Gentile in this collection, protests against the panty raids reveal the existence of an underlying attachment to, and desire for, oppressive traditions.

While consciousness-raising is most commonly associated with second-wave activism, feminist theorist Judith Butler's work on gender performativity demonstrates how current feminist consciousness-raising can integrate scholarly work that challenges the construction of selfhood through naturalized gender roles. Butler argues that the "gendered self" does not exist "prior to its acts," and that gendered acts not only constitute "the identity of the actor," but also constitute "that identity as a compelling illusion, an object of *belief*."[52] In a later work, Butler shifts her focus from analyzing gender as a performance to analyzing the ways that affective attachment to disciplinary power is produced.[53] Butler finds that gender is entrenched through the interpolation of bodies into binary identities that support patriarchal, transphobic, and racist authorities. The choices that we make in producing our performances of gender are dictated by our psychological attachments to ideas of gender. Binary gender is a way to organize around people's conscious and unconscious desires to hold an identity that is affirmed and recognized by others. Even though gender may be an illusion, binaries are deeply ingrained in most people's psychic constitution, making consciousness-raising crucial in order to change the ideas that people hold as natural or good. Asserting that we are all gendered in numerous ways, Butler hopes to raise feminist consciousness in ways that will allow for more diverse performances of gender.

For gender to be acted out or developed in an unexpected way, there must be a desire to challenge normative behaviour or an ambivalent, rather than positive, attachment to gendered normativity. Moving away from rights-based identity politics, attentiveness to emotion can help us see this desire in motion. Emotions have been thought of as a hindrance to the development of rational ideas and opinions, and this ideology has marginalized people who get emotional about the impact of misogyny, racism, transphobia, and more. However, negative emotional responses are crucial to changing the status quo and expanding the types of gender performances that are regularly affirmed.

If emotions such as anger can lead to immediate action, long-term activities are sustained through hope. How does this process occur? Some answers may be found in the concept of melancholia. Feminist groups and organizations create spaces that counter the silencing of feminist outlaw emotions, where people are encouraged to discuss issues and emotions of anger, sadness, or irritation. But women's centres and the activism that emerges from them are also about loss. Sigmund Freud described the correlated reasons that cause both mourning and melancholia and argued that they are reactions to the "loss of a loved person, or to the loss of some abstraction which has taken the place of one, such as one's country, liberty, an ideal, and so on. In some people the same influences produce melancholia instead of mourning and we consequently suspect them of a pathological disposition."[54] While Freud is seemingly thinking of melancholia and mourning as a reaction to a tragic past occurrence, the work of Julia Kristeva points to the way in which melancholia can develop from the loss of some abstraction,[55] thus shaping the work of feminist activists. When the lost object is a hoped-for ideal, such as a general acceptance and understanding of more fluid, multifaceted identities, or a campus in which all students are respected and able to live without fear of assault or harassment, the constant reification of violent, patriarchal gender can bring about feelings of attachment to the lost object. Freud sees this attachment to loss as potentially leading to inaction and lethargy and pejoratively characterizes melancholia as "a profoundly painful dejection, cessation of interest in the outside world, loss of the capacity to love, inhibition of all activity, and a lowering of the self-regarding feelings."[56] However, a melancholic disposition can be meaningful when understood as a political stance against specific kinds of oppression that permeate everyday life and persist over generations.

Activists often frame their work as a fight, a battle, or a process. Losing the battle or the momentum of a movement can be incredibly disheartening. While WLU began developing a sexual harassment policy in the late 1980s, female students found themselves still working on the issue nearly two decades later.[57] Attempting to effect change over such a long period of time is an incredibly daunting task. Safe spaces like the Centre for Women and Trans People at WLU are important for feminism because they allow for melancholic attachments to ideas and ideals of change to be sustained and for emotional reactions to experiences of sexism and transphobia to be discussed and valued. Melancholia, in the sense of holding on to a loss, becomes a political act that itself can be turned into commitment, action, and gradual change. Alternative desired futures do not develop quickly, and a certain amount of sadness over the loss of what could be in the present is necessary in order for systemic change to occur. The centre itself could not set university policies, but it could (and can) help students hold on to their emotional responses to traumatic, degrading, or paternalistic events in order to work towards change. The relative permanency of the place allows the long-standing work of feminist change to carry on over lengthy periods of time.

We can see this process of consciousness-raising and "holding on to loss" at play in the way the centre changed its name and attempted to destabilize the centrality of a male/female binary. The "transing" of the Women's Centre at WLU has expanded the range and diversity of gendered activism on campus.[58] The centre argues that "sexism and cissexism are really closely connected forms of oppression, and it doesn't really make sense to talk about and address them as though they are completely separate systems. Both systems of thought argue that 'male' and 'female' are rigid, non-overlapping, mutually exclusive, 'opposite' categories."[59] When binary gender is understood as part of the problem, resistance expands to include ways that binary gender as a universalized construct is inadequate. Instead of writing only about the experiences of cisgendered women, the inclusion of trans issues in the centre's activism expands the capacity for equality. Spaces like the Centre for Women and Trans People proliferate the possible ways that students can perform gender. Because so many people feel attached to normative gender performances, alternative performances that counter the hegemonic norm are often met with anger, confusion, and efforts to reinforce normative behaviour. Understood in Butler's terms, feminist spaces provide a place for resistive and "failed" gender performances to go on without policing, and the activism of the space is effective when it focuses on affirming radical ways of thinking or being that are normally disavowed and targeted for violence and harassment. Gender is a social force and like race, heterosexuality, and citizenship it has been naturalized to bodies in a way that entrenches hierarchies. The contemporary feminism of the centre builds on the traditional feminist mantra of "the personal is political" but pushes further to challenge the ways that biopolitical power is buried in the processes of gendered identity formation.

Feminist Institutional Spaces

Certainly, campus spaces like the centre perform an important role. As a public space, the centre fosters discussion, dialogue, and social change, provides important material resources for safe sex, and nurtures opportunities to engage with feminist ideas. Feminist campus spaces may at times act as safe spaces and affirmations of positive feeling, but they do so with a specific political aim: to dismantle patriarchal, homophobic, racist, and transphobic understandings of gendered selfhood and the attachments that people have to them.

Clearly, the physical space of the Centre for Women and Trans People is something that independent activists were not able to offer students without university support. But the centre exists within a university framework in which such organizing can be co-opted into token moves toward diversity or inclusion and which acts to contain feminist anger and emotion rather than to address deeper structural inequalities. With a university-sanctioned space in which to organize, activist feminist students now must resist being integrated into the system they often oppose. The centre's history shows how feminist activism in the institutional campus framework produces a particular kind of emotional frustration – what scholar Sara Ahmed refers to as bodies coming up against institutional "brick walls."[60]

Both Ahmed's *On Being Included* and Robyn Wiegman's *Object Lessons* demonstrate that diversity and inclusion projects in higher education institutions often act as token representations of diversity and equity and share the limitations of liberal feminism, which aims for women's visibility and inclusion into already existing structures and systems.[61] At WLU, the centre acts as evidence of the university's commitment to diversity and simultaneous failure to provide faculty and students with the financial support, time, or institutional power needed to allow for a diversity of people and ideas to flourish in the university. For example, the ongoing reluctance of the university to develop a clear and comprehensive policy and well-funded support system regarding sexual assault demonstrates this ongoing tension. The existence of organizations like the centre allows universities to "prove" to prospective students and donors how diverse and equitable the school is and to aid in expanding the number of students that universities can pass through their systems. Miranda Joseph, a gender studies scholar, argues that "like pluralism, diversity performs a kind of assimilation – an assimilation to corporate culture of production and consumption."[62] The Centre for Women and Trans People makes the university look more progressive than it is without making fundamental changes to the way that the rest of the university operates.

The history of the Women's Centre demonstrates the tensions that exist between feminist organizations and university administrations. Women's centres were not always welcome spaces for university administrations, and the Women's Centre at WLU initially had an antagonistic relationship with university managers, struggled to find a permanent place to operate, and was shifted between different buildings on the outskirts of campus.[63] At the same time, the university used the establishment of the centre as proof of its commitment to women's issues at a time when it was under intense pressure to respond to the protests.

These tensions persisted into the 2010s. The centre was shuffled around and, as of 2020, was moved to a central location and joined other campus groups (the Association of Black Students and the Rainbow Centre) to form the Diversity and Equity Office. It now boasts large bright rooms, a flat-screen TV, couches, a computer, and many resources paid for with university funding. Instead of the centre representing something that disrupts the norms of the university, the work of the centre is welcomed and encouraged by administrators seeking evidence of a commitment to diversity and inclusivity as a liberal institution. Feminist spaces like the centre also may have been allowed to proliferate across university campuses because they function as safe spaces intended to provide a feeling of positivity, support, and affirmation.[64]

The decision to open a university-supported campus women's centre in 1990, in the fallout of the panty raid scandal and in the context of campus-based gendered violence, was not a coincidence. Concerned about negative national attention but also about managing ongoing feminist protest, the university supported the creation of a feminist space that was contained within the administrative structure of the university.[65] The Women's Centre was a space where students could organize yet still be integrated within the university. It was also a space that the university could use to advertise its commitment to inclusion and tolerance. A 1990 editorial for *The Cord* argued that this move was made "to appease the trigger happy media pounding on the university's door since the panty raid incident."[66] Whether or not the motives of the university were altruistic, the space certainly gave feminist activists on campus a means of legitimizing the work they were doing. They could now use the Women's Centre as a location from which to produce a different narrative about gender identities and gendered relations on campus. Still, that very institutionalization risks dampening more radical strands within feminist campus activism.

Conclusion

While some of the issues addressed in this chapter are unique to Wilfrid Laurier University's history, androcentrism, misogyny, and cultures of sexual assault and harassment overall are common to most universities, despite inconsistent reporting.[67] Over its twenty-five years of existence, the Centre for Women and Trans People at WLU has adapted with the times, starting at the end of the second wave, through the contentiously defined third, fourth, and (maybe) fifth waves of feminism. The landscape at Canadian universities has also changed. Admission to university programs in North America has increased as has the number of women attending university, with 20 percent more women enrolled in all Canadian undergraduate, master's, and doctorate programs since the 1980s.[68] Yet government funding for higher education remains precarious, tuition has increased, and universities are susceptible to the impact of funding cuts like the ones carried out by Premier Mike Harris in Ontario in the 1990s.[69] Activist centres and related academic programs worry they might be the targets of cuts if they voice opposition to the administration. In addition, feminism has had to respond to the rise of the alt-right, including to figures such as University of Toronto professor Jordan Peterson (who rejects trans inclusive language), and to Trumpism on social media. While the attitudes and opinions expressed by populist politicians and public figures are not exactly new, the way they are influencing politics at universities remains relevant. Opponents of places like the Centre for Women and Trans People claim, in the name of free speech, to have the freedom to insult, harass, and sue those that challenge them or their standing.[70]

The second-wave feminism that inspired activists at Wilfrid Laurier to take a stand against panty raids thirty years ago has thus led to positive changes at WLU. But that movement has rightly been challenged and, in many ways, surpassed by more diverse and inclusive campaigns that reflect a continued need for a feminist presence on campus. As academia and broader society have changed, so too has the centre. The centre allows students to be melancholic, to share with others in order to acknowledge their experiences, or have the space to form their activism. The centre provides a meaningful way for students to engage with the baggage and experiences of specific forms of harassment, assault, and discrimination, not allowing the status quo to persist without acknowledgement. With decades of history of violence against female, trans, and gender-queer students, a defeatist attitude has set in for those in positions of power. Like so many forms of institutional violence, there is a malaise of silence towards these issues.[71]

In 2021, social media platforms such as Twitter and TikTok have become spaces where students share their experiences and draw attention to widespread issues that might otherwise go unaddressed.[72] Thus, a place like the Centre for Women and Trans People at WLU may not be necessary for raising awareness in the 2020s; however, the continued violence and mistreatment of female students shows the importance of a feminist institution for coordinated activism, comradery, and educational campaigns about consent.

The activities of the Centre for Women and Trans People have affected (and benefited) many people over its years of existence not because undergraduates are easily influenced, but because the ideas and politics of the space resonate with so many, and because it has grown and changed in accordance with criticisms of the second wave. The name "Women's Centre" was important when the organization began in order to combat the sexism and misogyny reflected in the panty raids, and the name "Centre for Women and Trans People" continues to be important in the 2020s because of the harassment and hatred transgender students face on campus.[73]

Notes

1 Michele Landsberg, "University 'Sanctions' Student Panty Raids," *Toronto Star*, October 25, 1989.

2 Editorial, "Black Eye for Laurier," *Toronto Star*, October 26, 1989, A32.

3 The Women's Centre initially opened in a space on the outskirts of campus ("Herstory," accessed 2016, https://students.wlu.ca/student-life/diversity-and-equity/

womens-centres.html). In the 2000s, it was located within the Maureen Forrester Recital Hall and then moved to a central building with other related services as part of the diversity and equity office, in 2011.

4 "Women's Resource Centre," University of Calgary, accessed June 14, 2021, https://www.ucalgary.ca/student-services/womens-centre/home; "Welcome: The Centre for Women and Trans People," University of Toronto, accessed June 14, 2021, http://womenscentre.sa.utoronto.ca/; "The Centre for Women and Trans People at York," York University, accessed June 14, 2021, https://web.archive.org/web/20160430164223/http://cwtpyork.ca/; "Guelph Resource Centre for Gender Empowerment and Diversity," University of Guelph, accessed June 14, 2021, https://gryphlife.uoguelph.ca/organization/grcged.

5 See Wendy Robbins et al., eds., *Minds of Our Own: Inventing Feminist Scholarship and Women's Studies in Canada and Quebec 1966–76* (Waterloo, ON: Wilfrid Laurier University Press, 2008); Nancy Janovicek, *No Place to Go: Local Histories of the Battered Women's Shelter Movement* (Vancouver: UBC Press, 2007); and Robyn Wiegman, *Object Lessons* (Durham, NC: Duke University Press, 2012), 6.

6 On third-wave feminism, see Allyson Mitchell and Lara Karaian, "Third-Wave Feminisms," in *Feminist Issues: Race, Class, and Sexuality*, 4th ed., ed Nancy Mandell (Toronto: Pearson), 58–79; Leslie Heywood and Jennifer Drake, eds, *Third Wave Agenda: Being Feminist, Doing Feminism* (Minneapolis: University of Minnesota Press, 1997); Rory Dicker and Alison Piepmeier, eds., *Catching a Wave: Reclaiming Feminism for the 21st Century* (Lebanon, NH: University Press of New England, 2003).

7 Alison Jaggar, "Love and Knowledge: Emotions in Feminist Epistemology," in *The Feminist Philosophy Reader*, ed. Alison Bailey and Chris Cuomo (New York: McGraw Hill, 2008), 687–705; Sara Ahmed, *On Being Included: Racism and Diversity in Institutional Life* (Durham, NC: Duke University Press, 2012).

8 Sigmund Freud, "Mourning and Melancholia," in *The Standard Edition of the Complete Psychological Works of Sigmund Freud*, trans. James Strachey et al. (London: Hogarth, 1953); Julia Kristeva, *Black Sun: Depression and Melancholia* (New York: Columbia University Press, 1989).

9 Ahmed, *On Being Included*.

10 See Keith Walden, "Hazes, Hustles, Scraps, and Stunts: Initiations at the University of Toronto, 1880–1925," in *Youth, University and Canadian Society: Essays in the Social History of Higher Education*, ed. Paul Axelrod and John G. Reid (Montreal/Kingston: McGill-Queen's University Press, 1989), 94–121; and Beth Bailey, "From Panty Raids to Revolution: Youth and Authority, 1950–1970," in *Generations of Youth: Youth Cultures and History in Twentieth-Century America*, ed. Joe Austin and Michael Nevin Willard (New York: New York University Press, 1998), 187–204.

11 Chris Starkey, "Panty Raid Furor Rages," *The Cord*, October 5, 1989, 3, http://scholars.wlu.ca/cgi/viewcontent.cgi?article=1767&context=thecord.

12 Landsberg, "University 'Sanctions' Student Panty Raids."

13 Julia Kristeva, *Powers of Horror: An Essay on Abjection* (New York: Columbia University Press, 1982).

14 Penelope Hutchison, "No Now Really Does Mean No," *Queen's Alumni Review* 3 (2018), https://www.queensu.ca/gazette/alumnireview/stories/no-now-really-does-mean-no. On the Montreal massacre, see Theresa O'Donovan, *Rage and Resistance: A Theological Reflection on the Montreal Massacre* (Waterloo, ON: Wilfrid Laurier University Press, 2007).

15 Tracey Tyler and Matt Maychak, "Students Defend Panty Raids as 'Harmless Rituals,'" *Toronto Star*, October 26, 1989, A8; Tracey Tyler, "Panty Raid Report Urges Mixed Dorms at Wilfrid Laurier," *Toronto Star*, January 31, 1990.

16 Indeed, *The Cord* reported that "Andrea Thyret, Head Resident at Clara Conrad was surprised at the uproar over the incident, considering the fact that Director of Housing Mike Belaner, Security Chief John Baal, head residents, dons and residents themselves were informed ahead of time about the raids." Starkey, "Panty Raid Furor Rages," 3. See also WLU Women's Centre, *Women's Centre Herstory* (Waterloo, ON: Women's Centre, 1994).

17 Landsberg, "University 'Sanctions' Student Panty Raids."

18 News from Wilfrid Laurier University, "President of Wilfrid Laurier University Bans Panty Raids," news release 075-1989, October 27, 1989, http://images.ourontario.ca/Partners/WLU/0023425371T.PDF.

19 Gail Cockburn, "Take Back the Night," *The Cord*, September 13, 1990, 10–11, http://scholars.wlu.ca/cgi/viewcontent.cgi?article=1787&context=thecord. See also Frances Kelly, "Panty Raids Banned at Wilfrid Laurier," *Toronto Star*, October 29, 1989, A1.

20 News from Wilfrid Laurier University, "WLU Makes Progress on Program to Promote Healthy Gender Relations," press release no. 034-1990, August 24, 1990, http://images.ourontario.ca/Partners/WLU/0023437561T.PDF.

21 While the group is not identified, the Women's Centre documents note that those women went on to hold public meetings about opening a women's centre and later worked with a university committee in the summer of 1990. See WLU Women's Centre, *Women's Centre Herstory*.

22 Cockburn "Take Back the Night."

23 Kat Callahan, "I Don't Care about MichFest's Trans Exclusion, You Shouldn't Either," *Jezebel*, August 14 2014, https://roygbiv.jezebel.com/i-dont-care-about-michfests-trans-exclusion-you-should-1621468728; Susanne Sreedhar and Michal Hand, "The Ethics of Exclusion: Gender Politics at the Michigan Womyn's Music Festival," in *Trans/Forming Feminisms*, ed. Krista Scott Dixon (Toronto: Sumach Press, 2006), 161–70. To understand the roots of this debate, see the work of anti-transgender writer Janice Raymond and the many responses to her work. Janice Raymond, *The Transsexual Empire* (Boston, MA: Beacon Press, 1979); Sandy Stone, "The Empire Strikes Back: A Post-transexual Manifesto," in *Transgender Studies Reader*, ed. Susan Stryker and Stephen Whittle (New York: Routledge, 2006), 221–35. There is a plethora of current trans inclusive feminist theory. See, for example, Cressida Hayes, "Feminist Solidarity after Queer Theory: The Case of Transgender," *Signs: Journal of Women in Culture and Society* 28, 4 (2003): 1093–120; and Jean Bobby Noble, *Sons of the Movement: FtMs Risking Incoherence on a Post-Queer Cultural Landscape* (Toronto: Canadian Scholars Press, 2006). See also current issues of the *Transgender*

Studies Quarterly. On challenges to the category "woman," see Denise Riley, *"Am I That Name?" Feminism and the Category of "Women" in History* (New York: Macmillan Press, 1988).

24 Susan Stryker, Paisley Currah, and Lisa Jean Moore define "'transing' as a practice that takes place within, as well as across or between, gendered spaces. It is a practice that assembles gender into contingent structures of association with other attributes of bodily being, and allows for their reassembly." See Susan Stryker, Paisley Currah, and Lisa Jean Moore, "Introduction: Trans-, Trans, or Transgender," *Women's Studies Quarterly* 36, 3–4 (2008): 13.

25 Stryker, Currah, and Moore, "Trans-, Trans, or Transgender," 14.

26 Centre for Women and Trans People, *Volunteer Training Manual 2010–2011* (Waterloo, ON: Centre for Women and Trans People, 2010), 16.

27 Centre for Women and Trans People, *Volunteer Training Manual*, 8.

28 Centre for Women and Trans People, *Volunteer Training Manual*, 11.

29 For information on the history of changes to sexual assault laws in Canada, see Constance Backhouse, *Carnal Crimes: Sexual Assault Law in Canada, 1900–1975* (Toronto: Irwin Law, 2008); and Kwong-leung Tang, "Rape Law Reform in Canada: The Success and Limits of Legislation," *International Journal of Offender Therapy and Comparative Criminology* 42, 3 (1998): 258–70.

30 Zane Schwartz, "Canadian Universities Are Failing Students on Sexual Assault," *Macleans*, March 1, 2018; Ministry of Advanced Education, *Preventing and Responding to Sexual Violence and Misconduct at British Columbia Post-Secondary Institutions: A Guide for Developing Policies and Actions*, n.d., https://www2.gov.bc.ca/assets/gov/education/post-secondary-education/institution-resources-administration/5233_sexual_violence_and_misconduct_policy_guidelines_web.pdf; and Ontario Government, "Ontario Strengthens Sexual Violence and Harassment Policies at Postsecondary Institutions," news release, January 27, 2021, https://news.ontario.ca/en/release/60131/ontario-strengthens-sexual-violence-and-harassment-policies-at-postsecondary-institutions.

31 Tony Burke, "Between the Wheels," editorial, *The Cord*, October 12, 1990.

32 Justin Smirlies, "Laurier Students Send an Open Letter to Administration on Gendered Violence," *The Cord*, January 8, 2014. For best practices in sexual violence policies, see Cecilia Benoit, Leah Shumka, Rachel Phillips, Mary Clare Kennedy, and Lynne Belle-Isle, "Issue Brief: Sexual Violence against Women in Canada," Status of Women Canada, December 2015, https://www.swc-cfc.gc.ca/svawc-vcsfc/index-en.html#section_5_1.

33 "Sexual Assault and Drugs," MyLaurier, accessed May 25, 2015, http://waterloo.mylaurier.ca/content/documents/fileItemController/sexual%20assault%20and%20drugs.pdf.

34 "Safety Notice: Police Issue Alert about Sexual Assaults in Waterloo," Wilfrid Laurier University, accessed June 17, 2016, http://www.wlu.ca/news_detail.php?grp_id=1150&nws_id=11901.

35 Wendy Brown, *Regulating Aversion: Tolerance in the Age of Identity and Empire* (Princeton, NJ: Princeton University Press, 2006), 24.

36 Smirlies, "Laurier Students Send an Open Letter."

37 Jay Harrison and Ginette Lafrenière, "University Campuses Ending Gendered Violence: Final Report and Recommendations," *The Change Project* (Waterloo: Sexual Assault Support Centre of Waterloo Region, 2015), 24, accessed 2016, http://www.sascwr.org/files/www/change_project/The_Change_Project_Laurier_Final_Report_01_09.pdf.

38 "Laurier Formalizes Partnerships with Sexual Assault Centres to Enhance Support on Its Campuses," Wilfrid Laurier University, September 8, 2016, accessed November 2016, https://www.wlu.ca/news/news-releases/2016/sept/laurier-formalizes-partnerships-with-sexual-assault-centres-to-enhance-support-on-its-campuses.html.

39 Wilfrid Laurier University, "Addressing Gendered Violence at Laurier," accessed November 2016, https://students.wlu.ca/wellness-and-recreation/gendered-violence-prevention-and-support/addressing-gendered-violence.html.

40 "The Prevention of Sexual Violence: Policy and Procedures," Wilfrid Laurier University, revised June 2, 2020, https://www.wlu.ca/about/governance/assets/resources/12.4-gendered-and-sexual-violence-policy-and-procedures.html.

41 Centre for Women and Trans People, *Volunteer Training Manual*, 8.

42 E.P., interview with author (email correspondence), June 5, 2019.

43 Cockburn "Take Back the Night."

44 N. Ruck, "Liberating Minds: Consciousness-Raising as a Bridge between Feminism and Psychology in 1970s Canada," *History of Psychology*, 18, 3 (2015): 297–311. See also Debra Michals, "From 'Consciousness Expansion' to 'Consciousness Raising': Feminism and the Countercultural Politics of the Self," in *Imagine Nation: The American Counterculture of the 1960s and '70s*, ed. Peter Braunstein and Michael William Doyle (New York: Routledge, 2001), 41–64; Alice Echols, *Daring to Be Bad: Radical Feminism in America, 1967–1975* (Minneapolis: University of Minnesota Press, 1989).

45 Jaggar, "Love and Knowledge," 698.

46 I use the term here in a colloquial sense but am referring to the history of seeing women and their opinions as hysterical, paranoid, etcetera.

47 Sara Ahmed, *The Promise of Happiness* (Durham, NC: Duke University Press, 2010), 59–60; see also Sara Ahmed, *Living a Feminist Life* (Durham, NC: Duke University Press, 2017).

48 Cockburn "Take Back the Night," 11.

49 Tyler and Maychak, "Students Defend Panty Raids as 'Harmless Rituals,'" A8.

50 Martha Laurence, quoted in Tyler and Maychak, "Students Defend Panty Raids as 'Harmless Rituals,'" A8.

51 Annette Borger, "Panty Raids Demonstrate Lack of Class," *Toronto Star*, November 2, 1989, A28.

52 Judith Butler, "Performative Acts and Gender Constitution: An Essay in Phenomenology and Feminist Theory," in *The Feminist Philosophy Reader*, ed. Alison Bailey and Chris Cuomo (New York: McGraw Hill, 2008), 98 (emphasis in original).

53 Judith Butler, *The Psychic Life of Power: Theories in Subjection* (Stanford, CA: Stanford University Press, 1997).

54 Sigmund Freud, "Mourning and Melancholia," in *The Standard Edition of the Complete Psychological Works of Sigmund Freud*, trans. James Strachey et al. (London: Hogarth, 1953), 245.

55 For a detailed analysis of feminism and melancholia, see Kristeva, *Black Sun*.
56 Freud, "Mourning and Melancholia," 244.
57 See Smirlies, "Laurier Students Send an Open Letter," and Burke, "Between the Wheels."
58 Stryker, Currah, and Moore, "Trans-, Trans, or Transgender," 13.
59 Centre for Women and Trans People, *Volunteer Training Manual*, 16.
60 Ahmed, *Living a Feminist Life*, 140.
61 Ahmed, *On Being Included*; and Weigman, *Object Lessons*. See also Anonymous, "Sugar-Free Kool Aid," *Eukariot 1: Firm Statements (Soon to Be Proven Wrong)*, accessed July 2, 2018, https://www.eukariot.com/kool-aid.html. For the Canadian context, see Frances Henry et al., *The Equity Myth: Racialization and Indigeneity at Canadian Universities* (Vancouver: UBC Press, 2017).
62 Miranda Joseph, *Against the Romance of Community* (Minneapolis: University of Minnesota, 2002).
63 WLU Women's Centre, *Women's Centre Herstory*.
64 For example, the Toronto District School Board has a Safe and Positive Spaces initiative, which provides space at primary and secondary schools where "staff and students can feel comfortable to discuss sensitive issues openly such as: positive sexual health, healthy relationships, sexual orientation, identity and expression, gender identity and expression." "Safe and Positive Spaces," Toronto District School Board, accessed August 18, 2014, www.tdsb.on.ca/HighSchool/YourSchoolDay/SafeandPositiveSpaces.aspx.
65 The funding for the Women's Centre and other initiatives to promote healthy gender relations were all officially announced in a news release on August 24, 1990, days before the first orientation week since the ban of panty raids. See News from Wilfrid Laurier University, "WLU Makes Progress on Program to Promote Healthy Gender Relations," press release no. 034-1990, August 24, 1990, http://images.ourontario.ca/Partners/WLU/0023437561T.PDF.
66 Burke, "Between the Wheels."
67 Timothy Sawa and Lori Ward, "Sex Assault Reporting on Canadian Campuses Worryingly Low, Say Experts," *CBC News*, last updated February 9, 2015, https://www.cbc.ca/news/canada/sex-assault-reports-on-canadian-campuses-too-low-say-experts-1.2948321?cmp=rss%20.
68 Association of Universities and Colleges of Canada, *Trends in Higher Education*, vol. 1, *Enrolment* (Ottawa: AUCC, 2011), https://www.univcan.ca/wp-content/uploads/2015/11/trends-vol1-enrolment-june-2011.pdf.
69 Léo Charbonneau, "The Death of Canada's Education Advantage," Margin Notes, *University Affairs/Affaires universitaires*, October 16, 2009, https://www.universityaffairs.ca/opinion/margin-notes/the-death-of-canadas-education-advantage/.
70 Sarah Berman, "Lindsay Shepard Is Suing Laurier for $3.6 Million over Jordan Peterson Video Controversy," *Vice*, June 13, 2018, https://www.vice.com/en_ca/article/zm88yw/jordan-peterson-video-controversy-lands-laurier-dollar36-million-lawsuit.
71 Hannah Martin (@hannahmartinn), "Can we just talk about the fact that 30 girls at western university were drugged this weekend, and two sexually assaulted and it is no where to be found on the news (I legitimately found out through comment

section of a tik tok)," Twitter, September 12, 2021, 6:20 a.m., https://twitter.com/hannahmartinn/status/1437043480275169281?s=19.

72 See, for example, Kat (@katrinaxdj), "I'm a 4th year Western student and 3 time orientation leader. This entire O-Week was horrific. I helped lead a predominantly female team. There were multiple instances where myself or other sophs were screamed at, pushed, and touched inappropriately by men. 1/10." Twitter, September 15, 2021, 3:48 p.m., https://twitter.com/katrinaxdj/status/1438273529506668545?s=19; and Kate Dubinski, "Police Taking Western University Sexual Violence Rumours 'Seriously' as They Try to Separate Fact from Fiction," *CBC News,* September 14, 2021, https://www.cbc.ca/news/canada/london/police-probing-western-university-sexual-violence-allegations-work-to-separate-fact-from-social-media-fiction-1.6175607.

73 Ryan Flanagan, "WLU Trans Students Facing Hate On-Campus and Online: Advocate," *CTV Kitchener,* November 22, 2017, https://kitchener.ctvnews.ca/wlu-trans-students-facing-hate-on-campus-and-online-advocate-1.3689827.

Contributors

Funké Aladejebi is an assistant professor in the Department of History at the University of Toronto. Her book, *Schooling the System: A History of Black Women Teachers*, explores the importance of Black Canadian women in sustaining their communities and preserving a distinct Black identity within restrictive gender and racial barriers. She has also published articles in *Ontario History* and *Education Matters*. Her research interests are in oral history, the history of education in Canada, Black feminist thought, and transnationalism. Her current research projects can be found at www.funkealadejebi.com.

Taylor Antoniazzi recently completed her MA in history at the University of Victoria. Her thesis focused on the history of Everywomans Books, Victoria's feminist bookstore.

Marin Beck holds a PhD in political studies from Queen's University in Kingston, Ontario, Canada. She is a SSHRC Joseph-Armand Bombardier Doctoral Scholar (2016–19) and recipient of the Jean Royce (2016) and R.S. McLaughlin (2015) fellowships. Her research explored the interplay of neoliberal practices and gender within immigrant settlement service organizations in Canada. She is currently serving as a policy analyst in Winnipeg, Manitoba, on issues related to gender, race, and Indigenous self-governance and health transformation.

Josette Brun is a full professor in the Département d'information et de communication at Université Laval. She is the editor of *De l'exclusion à la solidarité. Regards intersectionnels sur les médias*; and *Interrelations femmes-médias dans l'Amérique française.* She is also the author of *Vie et mort du couple en Nouvelle-France.* Her research focuses on the history of women's media and women journalists in Quebec, including the television program *Femme d'aujourd'hui* (Radio-Canada, 1965–82), and on intersectionality in/and the media.

Kevin Brushett is an associate professor of history at the Royal Military College of Canada, where he teaches Canadian and American history, including the foreign relations of both nations. His research focuses on the intersection between community development programs and the Canadian state in the latter half of the twentieth century. He has published widely on the Company of Young Canadians, as well as on the relations between Canadian NGOs and the Canadian International Development Agency.

Lara Campbell is a professor of gender, sexuality, and women's studies at Simon Fraser University, where she teaches North American gender and women's history, social movement history, and feminist theory. She has published widely on the anti–Vietnam War movement in Canada, the history of the 1960s, and the history of the Great Depression. She is the author of *Respectable Citizens: Gender, Family, and Unemployment in Ontario's Great Depression*; and the coauthor (with Willeen Keough) of *Gender History: Canadian Perspectives.* Her most recent book is *A Great Revolutionary Wave: Women and the Vote in British Columbia,* which received the Basil Stuart-Stubbs Prize for Outstanding Scholarly Book on British Columbia.

Michael Dawson is a professor of history at St. Thomas University. His publications include *Selling Out or Buying In? Debating Consumerism in Vancouver and Victoria, 1945–1985* and *Selling British Columbia: Tourism and Consumer Culture, 1890–1970,* as well as the edited collections *Symbols of Canada; Worth Fighting For: Canada's Tradition of War Resistance from 1812 to the War on Terror;* and *Contesting Clio's Craft: New Directions and Debates in Canadian History.*

Sophie Doucet recently completed a postdoctoral fellowship in the History Department at Concordia University. She specializes in the history of women, family, and emotions. Her current research focuses on the history of brothers and sisters, and the subject of her PhD dissertation was the emotional landscape of Marie-Louise Globensky (1849–1919), a member of the Catholic bourgeoisie. In her master's thesis, she explored the ideology of women's journalism pioneer Joséphine Marchand-Dandurand (1861–1925).

Matthew Fesnak aspires to do things that are creative, significant, and insightful, including through academic pursuits and librarianship. He completed graduate and undergraduate degrees at Wilfrid Laurier University and wrote his contribution to this volume thinking about the utilitarian outcomes of a university education outside of the classroom.

Patrizia Gentile is an associate professor in the Human Rights and Social Justice Program and the Institute of Women's and Gender Studies at Carleton University. She coauthored *The Canadian War on Queers: National Security as Sexual Regulation* with Gary Kinsman. She is also coeditor of *Contesting Bodies and Nation in Canadian History*; and *We Still Demand! Redefining Resistance in Sex and Gender Struggles*. Her most recent book is *Queen of the Maple Leaf: Beauty Contests and Settler Femininity*.

Catherine Gidney is an adjunct research professor in the Department of History at St. Thomas University. Her recent publications include *Captive Audience: How Corporations Invaded Our Schools*; *Tending the Student Body: Youth, Health, and the Modern University*; and the edited collection *Symbols of Canada*, as well as articles and book chapters on the histories of youth, health, education, religion, gender, and food in twentieth-century Canada.

Laurie Laplanche is associate director of Institut EDI² (Équité, Diversité, Inclusion, Intersectionnalité) at Université Laval. She holds a PhD in public communication from the Département d'information et de communication at Université Laval. Her dissertation is titled "Pour vous, mesdames ... et messieurs. Production des émissions féminines à la Société Radio-Canada à Montréal (1952–1982). Promotion, conception des publics et culture organisationnelle genrées." She completed her postdoctoral research in the history department at the Université du Québec à Montréal, where she explored the historical processes of construction of gendered professional identities. Her research interests include power dynamics in organizational cultures and practices, and constructions of culturally feminized spaces in the media.

Margaret Little is a professor in gender studies and political studies at Queen's University and has been involved in anti-poverty activism for over thirty years. She is the author of the award-winning "*No Car, No Radio, No*

Liquor Permit": The Moral Regulation of Single Mothers in Ontario, 1920–1997; and *If I Had a Hammer: Retraining That Really Works.*

Lynne Marks is a professor in the History Department at University of Victoria. She is the author of *Revivals and Roller Rinks: Religion, Leisure, and Identity in Late-Nineteenth-Century Small-Town Ontario* and *Infidels and the Damn Churches: Irreligion and Religion in Settler British Columbia*, as well as a range of articles and book chapters on topics related to the history of religion, irreligion, ethnicity, social welfare, gender, class, and feminism in Canada.

Eryk Martin is a faculty member of the Department of History at Kwantlen Polytechnic University. His current research project explores the connections between anarchism in Canada and a global array of social movements in the context of the 1970s and 1980s.

Emma McKenna is a SSHRC Postdoctoral Fellow at the University of Ottawa and an Honorary Killam Postdoctoral Fellow at the University of Alberta, where she researches intersectional critical feminist history. Her work can be found in *Sexualities; On_Culture; Hypatia: A Journal of Feminist Philosophy; Women: A Cultural Review; Atlantis: Critical Studies in Gender, Culture, and Social Justice*; *Review of Education, Pedagogy, and Cultural Studies;* and *Journal of Gender Studies.* Emma is also involved in grassroots sex-worker rights activism in Ontario.

Liz Millward is a professor of women's and gender studies at the University of Manitoba. She is the author of *Making a Scene: Lesbians and Community across Canada, 1964–84* and *Women in British Imperial Airspace, 1922–1937* and is a coauthor of *Killing Off the Lesbians: A Symbolic Annihilation on Film and Television.*

Sarah A. Nickel is a Tk'emlupsemc associate professor of history at the University of Alberta. Her areas of research include comparative Indigenous histories, twentieth-century Indigenous politics, gender, Indigenous feminisms, and community-engaged research. Her first book, *Assembling Unity: Indigenous Politics, Gender, and the Union of BC Indian Chiefs*, won the Canadian Historical Association's award for the best book in Indigenous history, and she is the coeditor of *In Good Relation: Gender, History, and*

Kinship in Indigenous Feminisms. Sarah's next project explores Indigenous women's political work in the twentieth-century West.

Emma Paszat is a postdoctoral fellow in the Department of Political Science, University of Toronto Mississauga. Emma's research interests include politicized homophobias, LGBTQ politics, and decolonizing transnational LGBTQ activism.

Cheryl Krasnick Warsh, FRSC, is a professor of history at Vancouver Island University and coeditor of the journal *Gender and History*. She is the author of *Prescribed Norms: Women and Health in Canada and the United States since 1800*; *Moments of Unreason: The Practice of Canadian Psychiatry and the Homewood Retreat, 1883–1923*; and the upcoming *Frances Oldham Kelsey, and the Battle against Thalidomide*. Her edited and coedited collections include *Consuming Modernity: Gendered Behaviour and Consumerism before the Baby Boom*; *Gender, Health, and Popular Culture: Historical Perspectives*; *Children's Health Issues in Historical Perspective*; and the upcoming *Pleasure and Panic: New Essays on the History of Alcohol and Drugs*.

Whitney Wood is Canada Research Chair in the Historical Dimensions of Women's Health in the Department of History at Vancouver Island University. She earned her PhD from Wilfrid Laurier University in 2016, and she completed postdoctoral fellowships at Birkbeck, University of London, and at the University of Calgary. Her research interests include the history of women's bodies, reproduction, and pain in nineteenth-and twentieth-century Canada, and her work has appeared in the *Canadian Bulletin of Medical History*, *Social History of Medicine*, and *Medical Humanities*, in addition to a number of edited collections.

Index

Note: "(f)" after a page number indicates a figure.

Printed and bound in Canada by Friesens

Set in Warnock Pro and Futura by Apex CoVantage, LLC
Copy editor: Robyn So
Proofreader: Alison Strobel
Indexer: Emily LeGrand
Cover designer: George Kirkpatrick
Cover image: "Two women marching with arms wrapped around each other in the street during the 1978 Toronto International Women's Day (IWD) rally, Ontario," photograph CA 0N0034 10-001-S3-I205, Canadian Women's Movement Archives, University of Ottawa Library.